Marion Cunningham's Good Eating

THE BREAKFAST BOOK
THE SUPPER BOOK

Illustrations by Donnie Cameron

WINGS BOOKS®
NEW YORK

The Breakfast Book, Copyright © 1987 by Marion Cunningham
Illustrations copyright © 1987 by Donnie Cameron

The Supper Book, Copyright © 1992 by Marion Cunningham
Illustrations copyright © 1992 by Donnie Cameron

Grateful acknowledgment is made to Harcourt Brace Jovanovich, Inc., for permission to reprint an excerpt from the poem "Food and Drink" in *Long Feud* by Louis Untermeyer. Copyright 1932 by Harcourt Brace Jovanovich, Inc. Copyright renewed 1960 by Louis Untermeyer. Reprinted by permission of the publisher.

This 1999 edition is published by Wings Books®, an imprint of Random House Value Publishing, Inc., 201 East 50th Street, New York, NY 10022, by arrangement with Alfred A. Knopf, Inc., a division of Random House, Inc.

Wings Books® and colophon are registered trademarks of Random House Value Publishing, Inc.

Printed in the United States of America

Random House
New York • Toronto • London • Sydney • Auckland
http://www.randomhouse.com/

Library of Congress Cataloging-in-Publication Data
Cunningham, Marion.
[Breakfast book]
Marion Cunningham's good eating / illustrations by Donnie Cameron.
p.   cm.
First work originally published: The breakfast book. New York : Knopf, 1987; second work originally published: The supper book. New York : Knopf, 1992.
Contents: The breakfast book — The supper book.
Includes index.
ISBN 0-517-20402-9
1. Breakfasts.   2. Suppers.   I. Cunningham, Marion. Breakfast book.
II. Cunningham, Marion.   Supper book.   III. Cunningham, Marion. Supper book.   IV. Title.   V. Title: Good eating.
TX733.C83 1999
641.5—dc21   98-28799
CIP

8 7 6 5 4 3 2 1

THE BREAKFAST BOOK

Acknowledgments

My lasting appreciation to the following friends who gave their time and talent so generously to *The Breakfast Book*:

E. M. Ginger   Jim Dodge
Fritz Streiff   Abby Mandel
Helen Gustafson   Elaine Sherman
Loni Kuhn   Jacquie Lee
Sharon Kramis   Clark Wolfe

A special word: I thank John Hudspeth for his great taste and help and for bringing the breakfast dream alive through Bridge Creek Restaurant.

This book is dedicated to my husband, Robert,

and children, Catherine and Mark.

Contents

Introduction

As my interest in breakfast intensified over the last few years, I became more and more inspired to write this book. I have found that there are almost no books on the subject—no tempting recipes and nothing to encourage people to cook breakfast. There are lots of brunch books, but brunch, with its undefined ingredients and preparations, is entirely different from breakfast—it could be any meal. Brunch is almost always a partylike affair, served with wine and liquor, and with an assortment of unrelated dishes. Breakfast, on the other hand, involves no alcohol and usually consists of grains, dairy products, fruits, and maybe eggs or a little meat or fish.

I often ask people what they think of breakfast, and most reply instantly that it is their favorite meal. When pressed to tell what they eat for breakfast, their answers become rather vague. I've decided that they love the *idea* of breakfast, but they need some good guidance and recipes actually to get them to cook it. Breakfast has remained pure amid all the food trends with their stylish dishes and chic ingredients. The honest simplicity of breakfast is so captivating. The most delicious breakfasts usually derive from the humblest of ingredients (money alone does not buy good food).

The deeper reason that breakfast inspires me is that we have become so busy maintaining our lives in the working world that we often find ourselves sharing the same house with strangers. The meaning of "home" has disappeared. Surveys report that families no longer sit down together for the evening meal. Eating is a lonely experience for many, and we can be lonely without even knowing it sometimes. Standing up by a microwave oven, or refrigerator, or in front of the TV, automatically eating, leaves out a precious human element from our lives. Since when are business meetings, community gatherings, or basketball practice more important than talking with the people you care about and getting to know them better. If it is true that dinner is becoming a solitary, fast-feed-yourself experience, I'm hoping that breakfast, with its easy, wholesome honesty, will be an opportunity to be with and share oneself with friends and family. There is no greater inducement to conversation than sitting around a table and sharing a good meal. Gathering at the table for breakfast allows us to weave our lives with others—and that should be a daily pleasure.

More than ever, health has our attention these days. What we should and shouldn't eat, how to achieve good physical health, salt or no salt, sugar or no sugar... But we tend to overlook one of the healthiest parts of eating: that it is such a wonderful means of bringing people together. My sense of health is that getting a good start with breakfast makes it the most important meal of the day. After the night's abstinence, it is important to break fast and eat a nutritious meal. Lunch may be only a token meal, and dinner or supper a modest one, but before expending energy for the day, food is essential. As tired as the old adage "moderation in all things" may be, I'm of the mind that we should follow this edict, and not become too anxious about each and every bite. I believe we should eat a wide variety of foods, without eating too much of any of them.

THE BREAKFAST BOOK

Yeast Breads

Basic American White Bread
  Cinnamon Swirl Bread
Dairy Bread
Granola Breakfast Bread
Rusk or Zwieback
  Cream and Sugar Rusk
  Spiced Rusk
Raisin Cinnamon Wheat Bread
Dried Fruit Batter Bread
Sally Lunn
Oatmeal Orange Bread
  Orange Marmalade Bread
Orange Rye Bread
Mexican Bread
Chocolate Walnut Butter Bread
Crisp Whole Wheat Buns
Breakfast Baps
Glazed Cinnamon Rolls
Double-Proof Biscuits
Hot Cross Buns
Sticky Buns
Crumpets
English Muffins

Breakfast isn't breakfast without bread, and yeast breads possess a sturdiness and strength that quick breads just don't have. Quick breads can be delicious and lively with lots of variations of flavor and texture, but compared to yeast breads they seem like adolescents next to their parents. More than any other kind of cooking I know of, making yeast bread can give you an almost primitive sense that you can take care of yourself and survive. And yeast bread for breakfast is so sustaining and welcoming. Once you've made your first loaf, you're apt to be hooked.

When I started baking with yeast, I thought it was much more complicated to use than it really is. If you are plunging in and using yeast for the first time, I suggest you start out with the Crisp Whole Wheat Buns on page 18. This is a simple and almost foolproof recipe: you just stir it up and watch it rise. The kneadings, risings, and punchings-down called for in the other recipes are mostly means to obtain a smoother and more uniform texture.

You need to know only a few things about yeast. Too much heat will kill it (the liquid should not be more than 105°F), and cool temperatures slow it down. Once you have mixed up your dough, you can interrupt and retard the fermentation process at any point by covering and refrigerating your dough for up to 24 hours; this gives you a lot of leeway.

Cooking is one of the legacies we can leave to the future, and I would like to be remembered for my baking. We all know we're not immortal, but after I'm gone, I would like my son and daughter to be able to say, "Our mother made real yeast bread for breakfast."

Basic American White Bread

(two medium loaves)

Many people like white toast for breakfast. It seems exactly right with a bowl of oatmeal or cold cereal. And plain white toast often tastes better with jams than whole grain breads do. American white bread usually has a little fat, a little sugar, and some milk in the recipe. These ingredients give the loaves keeping qualities which help preserve flavor and moistness.

½ cup warm water	2 tablespoons butter, shortening,
2 packages dry yeast	or oil, room temperature
1 teaspoon sugar	2 teaspoons salt
2 cups warm water	5 cups all-purpose flour,
½ cup nonfat dry milk	approximately

Put the ½ cup warm water in a large mixing bowl; sprinkle in the yeast and sugar, stir, and let dissolve for 5 minutes.

Add the 2 cups warm water, nonfat dry milk, butter, salt, and 2 cups of the flour to the yeast mixture. Using an electric mixer or a large spoon, beat the dough until it is smooth. Add only enough additional flour to make a manageable dough. At this point, knead with your hands on a lightly floured board for about 2 minutes, or use a dough hook in your electric mixer for about 15 seconds. Let the dough rest for 10 minutes. Resume kneading until the dough is smooth and elastic.

Put the dough in a greased bowl and cover with plastic wrap, and let it rise until double in bulk. Punch down and divide the dough in half.

Shape the dough and place in two greased $8\frac{1}{2} \times 4\frac{1}{2} \times 3$-inch loaf pans. Loosely cover and let rise to the top of the pans.

Preheat the oven to 350°F. Bake for about 40 minutes, or until the loaves have shrunk away from the sides of the pans a trifle. Remove and cool on racks.

Cinnamon Swirl Bread After the dough has been punched down, divide the dough in half and pat each half into a piece that is about 8 inches square. Combine $\frac{1}{2}$ cup sugar in a small bowl with 5 teaspoons cinnamon. Sprinkle the sugar mixture over each square of dough. Roll each piece of the dough into a tube shape and place in a greased loaf pan. Bake as directed above.

Dairy Bread

(two plump round loaves)

Milk and cottage cheese give this bread a pure dairy taste. The texture is rather springy, but soft. The addition of $\frac{1}{4}$ teaspoon of ground ginger follows an interesting old notion that ginger or cumin added in very tiny amounts to the dissolving yeast helps the yeast to do its work more effectively.

$\frac{1}{2}$ cup warm water
2 packages dry yeast
$\frac{1}{4}$ teaspoon ground ginger
1 teaspoon plus 2 tablespoons
   sugar
$1\frac{1}{2}$ cups milk, warmed

1 cup cottage cheese
2 tablespoons butter, room
   temperature
$1\frac{1}{2}$ teaspoons salt
6 cups all-purpose flour,
   approximately

Put the warm water, yeast, ginger, and 1 teaspoon sugar in a large mixing bowl. Stir and let the mixture dissolve for 5 minutes.

Add the milk, cottage cheese, butter, the remaining 2 tablespoons sugar, salt, and 3 cups flour. Beat the mixture until it is smooth. Add only enough additional flour to make the dough manageable. Turn the dough onto a floured board or use the dough hook on an electric mixer to knead. Knead with your hands for 2 minutes or for 15 seconds with the dough hook. Let the dough rest for 10 minutes. Resume kneading until the dough is smooth and elastic.

Place the dough in a greased bowl and cover with plastic wrap. Let the dough double in bulk (this dough will rise faster than most, in about 1 hour). Punch down and divide the dough in half. Form two round loaves and place them on a greased baking sheet; or grease two 9- × 5- × 3-inch loaf pans and place the dough in these. Cover loosely and let rise for 45 minutes to 1 hour. Sprinkle a little flour on top and cut two slits or a cross on the top of each loaf.

Place in a preheated 375°F oven and bake for 40 to 50 minutes, or until the bread is golden on top. Cool on racks.

Granola Breakfast Bread

(two medium loaves)

This is my favorite bread. I eat a toasted slice almost every single morning for breakfast.

½ cup warm water
2 packages dry yeast
2 cups warm water
½ cup nonfat dry milk
2 tablespoons butter
1½ teaspoons salt

1 cup cornmeal
2 cups whole wheat bread flour
3 cups all-purpose flour,
    approximately
2 cups Granola (see page 90)

Put the ½ cup warm water in a mixing bowl; sprinkle the yeast over, stir, and let stand to dissolve for 5 minutes. Add the 2 cups warm water, nonfat dry milk, and butter, and stir to blend. Beat in the salt, cornmeal, and whole wheat bread flour and mix until smooth. Add 2 cups all-purpose flour and beat until well mixed. Beat in as much more flour as is needed to make a manageable dough. Add the granola.

Turn the dough onto a floured board (or use a dough hook on the electric mixer) and knead for a minute. Let the dough rest 10 minutes. Resume kneading until the dough is elastic, about 5 more minutes. Put the dough into a greased bowl and turn to coat all sides. Cover and let rise to double its bulk. Punch the dough down and divide in half. Put the dough into two greased $8\frac{1}{2} \times 4\frac{1}{2} \times 3$-inch loaf pans. Let rise to the tops of the pans. Bake in a preheated 350°F oven for 45 minutes, or until lightly browned and done. Cool on racks.

Rusk or Zwieback

(two medium loaves)

Rusk or zwieback is a light yeast bread that has been sliced and slowly rebaked until golden and crisp throughout (zwieback is old German for "twice baked"). A rusk used to be considered the ideal toast for an infant or invalid, digestible and nourishing, but more important, rusk or zwieback is very satisfying for breakfast, with fruit or hot cereal.

$\frac{1}{2}$ cup warm water	$1\frac{1}{2}$ teaspoons salt
2 packages dry yeast	$1\frac{1}{2}$ tablespoons sugar
$1\frac{1}{2}$ cups milk, warmed	$4\frac{1}{2}$ cups all-purpose flour,
2 tablespoons butter	approximately

Put the warm water in a large mixing bowl, sprinkle the yeast over, and let stand to dissolve for 5 minutes.

Add the warm milk and butter to the yeast mixture and stir in the salt, sugar, and 2 cups flour. Stir briskly to mix well. Add only enough additional flour to make the dough manageable. Knead, using either an electric mixer with a dough hook or your hands, until the dough is smooth and elastic.

Divide the dough in half and shape each half into a roll 9 inches long and 2½ inches wide. Place each roll on a greased baking sheet. Cover loosely with plastic wrap and allow to double in bulk.

Preheat the oven to 375°F. Bake for 40 to 45 minutes, or until the tops are brown. Remove from the oven and cool on racks.

At this point you may freeze one loaf and slice the other. Each loaf will provide about 14 slices of rusk. Slice the bread about ½ inch thick and place the slices, flat side down, on a baking sheet. Bake in a preheated 250°F oven for about 1 hour, or until the slices are light brown and completely dry and crisp throughout.

Cream and Sugar Rusk Mix ¼ cup cream with 6 tablespoons sugar and brush the tops of the slices of rusk halfway through the second baking.

Spiced Rusk Add ¼ teaspoon cinnamon or nutmeg to the cream and sugar and brush on the rusk as directed above.

What Hymns are sung, what praises said
For home made miracles of Bread?
LOUIS UNTERMEYER, "Food and Drink" (1932)

Raisin Cinnamon Wheat Bread

(two medium loaves or one round loaf)

Toast made with Raisin Cinnamon Wheat Bread always seems a little special. This recipe calls for 2 cups of raisins. This is important. If it's supposed to be a raisin bread, be generous with the raisins!

½ cup warm water
2 packages dry yeast
1 teaspoon granulated sugar
2 cups warm water
½ cup nonfat dry milk
6 tablespoons brown sugar
1 tablespoon cinnamon
1½ teaspoons salt

2 tablespoons butter
2½ cups whole wheat flour
2 cups raisins (use 1 cup golden raisins and 1 cup dark raisins, if you have both)
3 cups all-purpose flour, approximately

Put the ½ cup warm water in a mixing bowl and stir in the yeast and granulated sugar. Let stand to dissolve for 5 minutes.

Add the 2 cups water, nonfat dry milk, brown sugar, cinnamon, salt, butter, and whole wheat flour to the yeast mixture. Beat briskly until the batter is smooth. Add the raisins. Add only enough all-purpose flour to make a manageable dough. If kneading by hand, turn onto a floured board and knead for 2 minutes; if you are using an electric mixer with a dough hook, knead for 15 seconds. Let the dough rest for 10 minutes. Resume kneading until the dough is smooth and elastic.

Put the dough in a greased bowl and cover with plastic wrap. Let the dough double in bulk. Punch the dough down. If you are making two loaves, divide the dough in half, shape into two loaves, and place in two greased 8½ × 4½ × 3-inch loaf pans. If you are making one loaf, roll it into a smooth ball, place on a greased baking sheet, and, using a sharp knife, cut two slashes across the top. Let the dough rise, loosely covered, for 45 minutes.

Put the loaves (or loaf) in a preheated 375°F oven. Bake for about 45 minutes, or until done; the round loaf will take 10 minutes longer. Remove from the oven and turn onto a rack to cool.

Dried Fruit Batter Bread

(one large loaf or two small loaves)

Even though it is made with yeast, Dried Fruit Batter Bread is fast to make and quite delicious. If you get about an hour's headstart, you can make it fresh for breakfast because this recipe is so simple. Batter breads tend to get stale more quickly than kneaded yeast breads, but if you freeze the unused bread immediately, the freshness will be preserved.

$1/2$ cup warm water
1 package dry yeast
1 teaspoon plus $1/3$ cup sugar
1 cup warm water
4 tablespoons ($1/2$ stick) butter,
   room temperature

$1 1/2$ teaspoons salt
1 egg
3 cups all-purpose flour
$1 1/2$ cups chopped dried fruit
   (prunes, apricots, figs,
   or a mixture)

Put the $1/2$ cup warm water, yeast, and 1 teaspoon sugar in a large mixing bowl. Stir to blend and let stand for 5 minutes to dissolve the yeast.

Add the 1 cup warm water, butter, $1/3$ cup sugar, salt, egg, and 1 cup flour. Beat the mixture vigorously until smooth. Add the remaining 2 cups flour and beat again until smooth. Add the dried fruit.

Pour the batter into a greased $9 \times 5 \times 3$-inch pan or two $5 \times 3 \times 3$-inch pans, loosely cover with plastic wrap, and let stand until doubled in bulk or until risen to the top of the pan.

Preheat the oven to 375°F. Bake the bread for 35 minutes if you are baking two small loaves; or 45 minutes if baking one large loaf. Remove from the oven, turn out of the pan, and cool on a rack.

Sally Lunn

(one medium loaf, or ten buns, or one 10-inch tube loaf)

Ever so simple, and faintly sweet with a tender crumb, Sally Lunn breads will round out any breakfast menu. The ease with which you can make these light, yellow breads makes them a fine breakfast basic. And they are versatile — they can be served with sweetened whipped cream and sliced berries or fruit. Sally Lunn toast is also very good.

$\frac{1}{2}$ cup warm water
2 packages dry yeast
1 teaspoon plus $\frac{1}{4}$ cup sugar
$\frac{1}{2}$ cup heavy cream, warmed

$\frac{1}{2}$ cup (1 stick) butter, melted
4 eggs, room temperature
1 teaspoon salt
$3\frac{3}{4}$ cups all-purpose flour

Put the warm water in a large mixing bowl. Sprinkle the yeast and 1 teaspoon of sugar over, stir, and let stand to dissolve for 5 minutes.

Add the cream, butter, and eggs. Beat briskly until the mixture is well blended. Add the salt, remaining $\frac{1}{4}$ cup sugar, and 2 cups flour. Beat vigorously until the batterlike dough is smooth. Add the remaining flour and beat again until smooth. You can easily do this by hand, or with an electric mixer. Leave the dough in the mixing bowl but gather it into a ball off the sides of the bowl, cover the bowl with plastic wrap, and let the dough double in bulk. This will take about 2 hours.

Generously butter the pan or pans (I often make small buns, using muffin tins). Lightly flour your hands (the dough is a little sticky and "stretchy"). Then for buns, tear off pieces and fill the tins about two-thirds full; or place the dough in a loaf or tube pan. Cover and again let double in bulk: the dough should rise to the top of the tins or pans.

Preheat the oven to 350°F. Bake the buns for about 25 minutes. A loaf will take about 40 minutes, and a large tube bread about 50 minutes. Let cool 5 minutes in the pan, then turn out onto a rack to cool.

Oatmeal Orange Bread

(two medium loaves)

Freshly chopped orange and oatmeal make a very nice match. Try the variation recipe below for Orange Marmalade Oatmeal Bread: the additional step of spreading marmalade over the almost-baked loaves gives the bread a little extra sparkle.

$\frac{1}{2}$ cup warm water
1 teaspoon plus 2 tablespoons
   sugar
2 packages dry yeast
$1\frac{1}{4}$ cups milk, warmed
2 tablespoons butter, room
   temperature
$1\frac{1}{2}$ teaspoons salt

2 cups cooked oatmeal
5 cups all-purpose flour,
   approximately
1 orange, quartered, seeded,
   and ground in a food processor
   or coarsely chopped (to make
   1 cup)

Put the $\frac{1}{2}$ cup warm water and 1 teaspoon sugar in a large mixing bowl; add the yeast, stir, and let stand to dissolve for 5 minutes.

Add the milk, butter, salt, remaining 2 tablespoons sugar, oatmeal, and 2 cups flour to the yeast mixture. Stir briskly until well mixed. Add only enough additional flour to make a manageable dough. Add the ground orange. Knead the dough for 1 minute by hand, or if you are using an electric mixer with a dough hook, for 15 seconds. Let the dough rest for 10 minutes. Resume kneading until the dough is smooth and elastic.

Put the dough in a greased bowl, cover with plastic wrap, and let double in bulk. Punch the dough down and divide in half. Put each half in a greased $8\frac{1}{2} \times 4\frac{1}{2} \times 3$-inch loaf pan and allow to rise to the tops of the pans.

Bake in a preheated 375°F oven for about 45 minutes, or until done. Remove from the oven and turn onto racks to cool.

Orange Marmalade Bread Quarter, seed, and grind (in a food processor) or coarsely chop enough orange to make 1 cup. Cook with 1 cup sugar until the sugar melts and the marmalade looks shiny (about 5 minutes). Cool and spread half of the marmalade on top of each loaf 10 minutes before the bread is done.

Orange Rye Bread

(one medium loaf and ten rolls)

Rye and orange go together like ham and eggs. This makes good toast that is even better with orange marmalade.

2 packages dry yeast
1/2 cup warm water
1 teaspoon plus 1 tablespoon
  sugar
2 cups rye flour
1 tablespoon caraway seeds
2 tablespoons finely chopped or
  grated orange zest

1 teaspoon salt
1 cup milk, warmed
2 tablespoons shortening
1 egg
1 1/2 cups all-purpose flour,
  approximately

Sprinkle the yeast over the warm water in a large mixing bowl, stir in 1 teaspoon sugar, and let stand to dissolve for 5 minutes.

Add the rye flour, caraway seeds, orange zest, and salt; then add the milk, remaining tablespoon sugar, shortening, and egg, beating well to mix. Slowly add only enough all-purpose flour to make a manageable dough. Knead the dough by hand on a floured board for about 6 to 8 minutes, or with an electric mixer that has a dough hook. Rye flour never gets smooth and elastic the way wheat flour does, so don't worry about the dough remaining a little tacky—it is the nature of rye flour.

Place the dough in a greased bowl and cover with plastic wrap. Let double in bulk. Punch down and divide the dough in half. Place one half in a greased $8\frac{1}{2} \times 4\frac{1}{2} \times 3$-inch loaf pan. Divide the remaining half into 10 equal pieces and roll each one into a ball. Place balls an inch apart on a greased baking sheet. Loosely cover the loaf and rolls with plastic wrap and let rise about 1 hour.

Preheat the oven to 375°F. Bake the loaf for about 45 minutes and the rolls 25 to 30 minutes.

Mexican Bread

(two large loaves)

This is a wonderful bread full of the clear, snappy flavors of pepper and cheese with a slightly coarse texture from the cornmeal. Make breakfast sandwiches with this bread, spread with cheese and fresh cilantro and grilled. Serve the sandwich with cold melon and hot Mexican Chocolate (see page 292).

$\frac{1}{2}$ cup warm water
2 packages dry yeast
1 cup yellow cornmeal
2 teaspoons salt
1 tablespoon sugar
$\frac{1}{2}$ teaspoon baking soda
2 eggs
1 cup buttermilk

$\frac{1}{2}$ cup vegetable oil
1 cup creamed corn
5 cups all-purpose flour, approximately
$1\frac{1}{2}$ cups grated sharp Cheddar cheese
$\frac{1}{4}$ cup chopped mild green chilis (fresh or canned)

Put the warm water in a large mixing bowl and stir in the yeast. Let stand to dissolve for 5 minutes.

Add the cornmeal, salt, sugar, and baking soda and beat until well mixed. Add the eggs, buttermilk, oil, corn, and 2 cups flour. Beat vigorously until well blended. Add the cheese and chilis and more flour to make the dough manageable. Knead until the cheese and chilis are well distributed. Let the dough rest 10 minutes. Resume kneading until the dough becomes smooth and elastic. Put the dough into a greased bowl. Cover the bowl with plastic wrap and let stand until the dough doubles in bulk.

Punch down the dough. Divide the dough in half and form into two loaves. Place in two greased $9 \times 5 \times 3$-inch loaf pans, cover lightly, and let rise to the tops of the pans. Bake in a preheated 350°F oven for 50 to 60 minutes. Remove from pans and cool on racks.

Chocolate Walnut Butter Bread

(two medium loaves)

Save this recipe for a very special breakfast. When you eat this buttery, tender-crumbed bread you encounter a wonderful array of rich, surprising tastes. Chocolate Walnut Butter Bread also makes extraordinary French toast—just be sure to dip the sliced bread into the egg only briefly so that the slices don't get soaked through.

½ cup warm water
1 package dry yeast
3½ cups all-purpose flour
1 tablespoon sugar
1¼ teaspoons salt
4 eggs, room temperature
12 tablespoons (1½ sticks) butter, softened

1 cup chopped (into large pieces) walnuts
6 ounces (6 squares) semisweet chocolate, broken or chopped into large pieces

Put the water in a large mixing bowl and sprinkle in the yeast. Stir and allow to stand for 5 minutes to dissolve.

Add the flour, sugar, salt, and eggs to the yeast mixture and beat vigorously until well blended. Beat in the butter in tablespoon-size pieces until it is all incorporated and the batter is smooth. Cover the bowl with plastic wrap and let the batter rise to double its bulk.

Stir the batter down and add the walnuts and chocolate pieces. Spoon the batter into two greased $8\frac{1}{2} \times 4\frac{1}{2} \times 3$-inch loaf pans (the pans should be half full so the loaves will have nicely rounded tops when they finish baking). Bake in a preheated 350°F oven for about 45 minutes. Remove from the oven and allow to rest for 5 minutes, then turn loaves out onto racks.

Crisp Whole Wheat Buns

(one dozen buns)

No kneading is necessary for these crisp-crusted whole wheat buns. Split in half, toasted, and buttered, they are outstandingly good.

$\frac{1}{2}$ cup warm water	1 tablespoon sugar
2 packages dry yeast	2 cups whole wheat flour
1 cup warm water	$1\frac{1}{2}$ cups all-purpose flour
1 teaspoon salt	3 tablespoons yellow cornmeal

Put $\frac{1}{2}$ cup warm water in a large mixing bowl and stir in the yeast. Let stand to dissolve 5 minutes.

Add the remaining cup warm water, salt, sugar, and 2 cups whole wheat flour. Using a mixing spoon, beat the dough vigorously for a minute or two. Add the all-purpose flour and beat until smooth. Cover the bowl with plastic wrap and let the dough rise until double in bulk (this happens quickly, in about 45 minutes). The dough will be rather sticky, so lightly flour your hands. Punch the dough down, then pull off about $\frac{1}{3}$ cup dough at a time and shape into a ball.

Preheat the oven to 400°F. Sprinkle the yellow cornmeal over a baking sheet. Place the buns 1 inch apart on the baking sheet. Let the buns rest and rise slightly for 15 minutes. Sprinkle or spray cold water lightly over the buns (a plant mister is ideal), and place in the oven. After 15 minutes of baking, sprinkle or mist the tops of the buns once again with cold water (the water makes the crust crisper). Bake 10 minutes more, or until the buns are lightly browned on top. Remove and serve warm.

Breakfast Baps

(sixteen baps)

This is the Scot's breakfast roll. Crisp-crusted, soft-centered, and well buttered, a friendlier roll you'll never meet.

1 teaspoon sugar	1/2 cup lard or shortening
1/3 cup warm water	(try to use lard—it lends a
3 packages dry yeast	good "barny" taste)
4 cups all-purpose flour	1/2 cup milk, warmed
1 1/2 teaspoons salt	1/2 cup warm water

Dissolve 1 teaspoon sugar in a bowl with 1/3 cup warm water, sprinkle the yeast over, and stir. Let stand to dissolve for 5 minutes.

In another bowl mix the flour and salt and rub in the lard. Add the yeast mixture, then the milk and 1/2 cup water, and stir to mix. You want a soft dough. Use your hands to mix—it's easier. Cover the dough and let it rise for about an hour, or until double in bulk.

Turn the dough out onto a floured board and knead until smooth. Cut the dough into 16 pieces and form each piece into a small ball. Place the balls on a greased baking sheet. Allow to rise for 30 minutes.

Preheat the oven to 400°F. Bake the baps 20 to 25 minutes, or until golden brown. Serve hot.

Glazed Cinnamon Rolls

(two dozen round rolls)

These rolls are light but rich, with ample butter and modestly spiced —
the amount of cinnamon is not overpowering. The shiny glaze finishes
them in a pretty manner.

$1/4$ cup warm water
1 package dry yeast
1 teaspoon plus $1/4$ cup sugar
4 cups all-purpose flour
1 teaspoon salt
$1/2$ pound (2 sticks) butter, chilled
3 egg yolks
1 cup milk

Filling
$1/4$ cup ($1/2$ stick) butter, melted
6 tablespoons sugar
1 teaspoon cinnamon

Glaze
$1 1/2$ cups confectioners' sugar
2 tablespoons butter, room
    temperature
1 tablespoon water (a trifle more
    may be needed to make a
    manageable glaze)

Put the warm water in a small bowl and sprinkle the yeast over. Add 1
teaspoon sugar, stir, and let dissolve for 5 minutes.

In a large mixing bowl, stir together the flour, $1/4$ cup sugar, and salt
with a fork to mix them well. Cut the butter into pieces the size of
small grapes and add to the flour mixture. Using either your hands or
a pastry blender, rub or cut the butter into the flour mixture until it is
distributed and there are coarse little lumps of butter throughout. Stir
in the yeast mixture, the egg yolks, and milk. Beat until blended.
Cover with plastic wrap and chill in the refrigerator at least 6 hours
(this dough can be refrigerated for 12 to 14 hours).

Divide the dough in half. On a lightly floured board, roll out half
the dough into a rectangle about 10 by 12 inches. Spread 2 table-

spoons of the melted butter over the rectangle. Mix the remaining 6 tablespoons sugar and the 1 teaspoon cinnamon together in a small bowl. Sprinkle half the sugar mixture evenly over the rectangle. Starting with the wide side, roll up the rectangle like a jelly roll. Divide the roll into 12 pieces by first cutting the roll into 4 equal portions, then cutting each portion into 3. Put the rolls cut side down in a greased muffin tin. Repeat these steps with the other half of the dough. Cover loosely and let rise for 1 hour.

Bake in a preheated 400°F oven for 20 to 25 minutes. Remove the rolls and put them on a rack set over a piece of waxed paper.

To make the glaze, sift the confectioners' sugar into a small bowl, then beat in the butter and water until smooth. Spoon a little of the glaze over each roll while still hot.

Double-Proof Biscuits

(about four dozen biscuits)

Because leavening agents in the nineteenth century were often unreliable, cooks would often use more than one in the same recipe for insurance—which is undoubtedly how this recipe developed. Today, when yeast and baking powder are all sure-proof, combining them isn't necessary but it does make for a particularly ethereal biscuit. Appropriately, the old-fashioned name for these is angel biscuits.

1 package dry yeast	3 tablespoons sugar
½ cup warm water	¾ cup shortening
5 cups all-purpose flour	1 teaspoon baking soda
4 teaspoons baking powder	2 cups buttermilk
2 teaspoons salt	

Sprinkle the yeast over the water in a small bowl, stir, and let stand 5 minutes to dissolve.

In a large mixing bowl combine the flour, baking powder, salt, and sugar, and stir with a fork to mix. Add the shortening and cut into the flour mixture, either using your fingertips or a pastry cutter, until the mixture looks irregular and crumbly.

Add the baking soda to the buttermilk. Stir the buttermilk into the flour mixture. Add the yeast mixture. Mix well. Cover and refrigerate for about 8 hours.

Turn the dough onto a lightly floured board. Knead a dozen times. Roll dough out to about 1/2-inch thickness. Cut out the biscuits with a 2-inch cutter and place them 1 inch apart on greased baking pans. Cover and let rise for 1 hour.

Bake in a preheated 400°F oven for about 15 minutes, or until lightly browned. Serve hot.

Hot Cross Buns

(three dozen buns)

Hot Cross Buns symbolize the Easter season and are eaten on Good Friday (and other times, too). They are also the harbinger of spring for some of us. This recipe makes a mildly spiced bun with a scattering of currants and raisins.

1/2 cup warm water
2 packages dry yeast
1 teaspoon plus 1/2 cup sugar
1 cup warm water
1/2 cup nonfat dry milk
1/2 cup (1 stick) butter, melted
1/2 teaspoon salt
3 eggs, lightly beaten
6 cups all-purpose flour,
   approximately

3/4 teaspoon cinnamon
3/4 teaspoon allspice
1 cup raisins
1/2 cup currants

Glaze
1 cup confectioners' sugar
1 tablespoon hot water

Put the 1/2 cup warm water in a large mixing bowl and stir in the yeast and 1 teaspoon sugar. Let stand to dissolve for 5 minutes.

Add 1 cup warm water, dry milk, melted butter, the remaining $\frac{1}{2}$ cup sugar, salt, and eggs. Beat briskly to blend well. Stir in 3 cups flour, cinnamon, and allspice and beat thoroughly. Add the raisins and currants. Beat in only enough additional flour to make a manageable dough.

Turn the dough onto a floured board and knead for 1 minute. Let the dough rest for 10 minutes. Resume kneading until the dough is smooth and elastic. Put the dough in a greased bowl, turn to coat the dough on all sides, cover with plastic wrap, and let double in bulk.

Punch the dough down and turn out onto a lightly floured board. Roll out the dough, or pat and stretch it, to a $\frac{1}{2}$-inch thickness. Cut out the buns with a $2\frac{1}{2}$-inch circular cutter. Grease two baking sheets. Make the buns by forming each dough round into a smooth ball, smoothing the underside of the ball and pinching and tucking away any loose ends. Place the buns 1 inch apart on the sheets. Let them rise for 1 hour.

Preheat the oven to 375°F. Bake for approximately 20 minutes, or until the buns are golden on top. Remove and cool slightly on racks.

To glaze the buns, combine the confectioners' sugar and water (this glaze should be medium thick), adding a trifle more water if too thick. Using either a pastry bag fitted with a $\frac{1}{16}$-inch tube, or a toothpick, apply the glaze in the shape of a cross on the top of each bun.

Sticky Buns

(two dozen buns)

Cinnamon and other spices have no place in these sticky buns—they have the seductive flavor of caramel and pure, sweet butter and the crunch of nuts.

$\frac{1}{2}$ cup warm water
2 packages dry yeast
2 cups milk, warmed
$\frac{1}{2}$ cup vegetable shortening
6 tablespoons sugar
2 teaspoons salt
2 eggs, room temperature
6$\frac{1}{2}$ cups all-purpose flour,
  approximately

Caramel Glaze
$\frac{1}{2}$ pound (2 sticks) butter
3 cups brown sugar
$\frac{1}{2}$ cup light corn syrup
3 cups broken pecan or walnut
  pieces

Put the water in a small bowl and sprinkle the yeast over. Stir and let stand for 5 minutes to dissolve.

Put the warm milk, shortening, sugar, salt, and eggs in a large mixing bowl and beat until well blended. Add the yeast and 4 cups flour. Mix vigorously. Add only enough flour to make a soft, manageable dough. Sprinkle a board with flour and turn the dough out onto it. Knead for 1 minute. Let the dough rest for 10 minutes. Resume kneading until the dough is smooth and elastic. Put the dough in a greased bowl, cover with plastic wrap, and let rise until double in bulk.

Make the caramel glaze. Put the butter, brown sugar, and corn syrup in a heavy-bottomed saucepan. Put the pan over medium heat and stir often until the butter is melted, the sugar is dissolved, and the mixture is well blended. Remove from the heat and pour 1 cup of the glaze into a small bowl. Set aside. Spread the remaining 2 cups glaze over the bottoms of three 8-inch cake pans. Sprinkle 1 cup pecans or walnuts over the glaze in each of the pans.

Punch the dough down and divide into thirds; while you work with one part, cover the remaining pieces of dough. Roll the first third of dough into a rectangle about 8 by 12 inches. Spread $\frac{1}{3}$ cup of the caramel glaze that has been set aside over the rectangle. Loosely roll the rectangle from the wide side, making a long tube. Cut into eight pieces, each $1\frac{1}{2}$ inches thick. Place the rounds, flat side down, in one of the cake pans. Cover the pan loosely with plastic wrap. Repeat with each remaining third of the dough. Let the shaped dough rise for about 35 to 45 minutes, or until the dough looks a little puffy.

Preheat the oven to 375°F. Bake for 35 to 45 minutes, or until a straw comes out clean when inserted into the center bun—there should be no dough clinging to the straw. Invert the cake pans over racks with waxed paper underneath to catch dripping glaze. Serve warm.

CRUMPETS AND ENGLISH MUFFINS

One could spend weeks searching through food history books trying to define the exact differences between muffins and crumpets. Both English muffins and crumpets are made with yeast and baked in rings on a griddle, but they are somewhat different. I think of crumpets as being made from a batter that has a little baking soda dissolved in warm water added to it just before griddling. Baking soda helps create the honeycombed surface that characterizes the crumpet. Also, crumpets are baked on one side only and are thinner than English muffins.

English muffins are made of a soft yeast dough that is mixed, allowed to rise, turned onto a floured board, and just barely kneaded. They are shaped, left to rest on cornmeal for a bit, and then both sides are baked on the griddle.

Both English muffins and crumpets are easier and much quicker to make than other kinds of yeast breads—no kneading is necessary and only brief rising. It is important to know that crumpets and English muffins are not ready to eat until they are toasted.

If rings used for griddling crumpets and muffins are difficult to find, you can use 6½-ounce tin cans (the kind tuna fish comes in) with the tops and bottoms cut out.

Breakfast is a forecast of the whole day:
Spoil that and all is spoiled.

LEIGH HUNT

Crumpets

(one dozen round crumpets)

Good crumpets are holey and spongy and are best eaten doused with butter and spread with honey or jam.

1 package dry yeast	2 cups all-purpose flour
¼ cup warm water	1 teaspoon salt
1 teaspoon sugar	½ teaspoon baking soda
1½ cups milk, warmed	¼ cup warm water

Sprinkle the yeast over the warm water in a mixing bowl. Add the sugar, stir, and let the yeast dissolve for 5 minutes. Add the milk, flour, and salt. Beat until smooth. Cover the bowl with plastic wrap and let stand for 1 hour (if you want to make the batter the night before, cover and refrigerate overnight). Stir down, dissolve the baking soda in $1/4$ cup warm water, and stir into the batter. Cover and let rest for 30 minutes.

Heat a griddle and grease some 3-inch rings (you can use $6 1/2$-ounce tuna-type cans with tops and bottoms cut out). When the griddle is medium hot, grease it and place the rings on it. Spoon about 3 tablespoons batter into each ring, just enough to cover the bottom. Lower the heat and cook slowly on the griddle for about 8 minutes, or until the tops of the crumpets have lost their shine and are dull and holey. Remove the rings and set aside the crumpets. When you've finished the batch, toast the crumpets, butter them generously, and serve.

English Muffins

(sixteen muffins)

Proof again that everything is best when baked at home. Crusty and pleasantly tough on the outside, tender and lavishly buttered on the inside, these should be on your agenda weekly.

$1/2$ cup warm water	$3 1/2$ cups all-purpose flour
1 package dry yeast	3 tablespoons vegetable oil or
$1 1/2$ teaspoons salt	melted shortening
1 tablespoon sugar	$1/2$ cup cornmeal
1 cup milk, warmed	

Pour the water into a large mixing bowl, sprinkle the yeast over, and stir. Let stand for 5 minutes to dissolve. Stir in the salt, sugar, warm milk, 2 cups flour, and the oil. Stir briskly with a spoon for a minute to mix well. Add the remaining flour and stir to blend smoothly. This dough will be very soft. Cover and let the dough double in bulk (it will take about an hour).

Flour a board and your hands. Put the dough on the board, and add a little flour if it is too sticky to manage. Knead the dough three or four times. Pat and push the dough out so it is about $1/4$ inch thick. Using a 3-inch ring (or a $6\frac{1}{2}$-ounce tuna can with top and bottom cut out) as a cutter, cut the dough out and place the muffins 1 inch apart on a baking sheet that has been sprinkled with the cornmeal. When the muffins are all cut, cover them lightly with a towel and let them rest for 30 minutes. Heat a griddle until medium hot and film it with grease. Grease the inside of the rings and place on the griddle. Put the muffins in the rings and cook for 10 minutes on one side and 5 minutes on the other. Before serving, split the muffins in half with a fork and toast them. Butter generously and serve warm.

Toasts, French Toast, and Breakfast Sandwiches

Melba Toast
Pulled Bread
Milk Toast
  Stove Top
  Oven
Cinnamon Toast
Toasts
  Sausage Applesauce
  Apple and Cheese
  Ham
  Banana
  Tomato
  Mushroom
  Creamed Mushroom
  Smoked Salmon
Welsh Rabbit with Beer
Tomato Rabbit
French Toast
  Spiced
  Lemon or Orange
  Maple Syrup
  Fruit Syrup
  Buttermilk
J.B.'s French Toast
Breakfast Sandwiches
  Fig and Ham on Rye Bread
  Sausage and Melted Cheese
  Walnut Butter
  Date and Breakfast Cheese
  Strawberry
  Ham and Farm Cheese Butter-Fried
  Mexican Breakfast

For some of us, a complete breakfast can be toast all by itself. Toasting brings out bread's good qualities—when toasted, bread has a deep grainy flavor and an irresistible fragrance. There is nothing like the smell of bacon frying and bread toasting to hurry one to the breakfast table.

I think toast is best when it is evenly golden. If you ever take the time to toast bread under the broiler, you will agree that it's lots better than toast made in an electric toaster. Keep your butter spreadable so you can butter your toast right to the edges and have butter in every bite.

Melba Toast

Melba Toast was invented at the Ritz in Paris at the turn of the century for a dieting diva—the same Nellie Melba who gave her name to the peaches. Tea and Melba Toast make a harmonious duet.

You will need a frozen loaf of unsliced white bread (commercial or homemade) or Cinnamon Swirl Bread (see page 7). Homemade grain breads are too dense to slice thin enough for Melba Toast. Slice the frozen bread into 1/8-inch-thick slices and remove the crusts. Spread the slices on a baking sheet in a single layer and put into a preheated

225°F oven for 45 minutes, checking after 30 minutes. The bread should be lightly golden and very crisp and the edges of the slices will have curled up. Melba toast keeps indefinitely in an airtight container.

Pulled Bread

Either you're a crunchy person or you're not. If you like crunch, pulled bread is for you. To make it, you slowly toast a loaf of crustless bread that has been shredded apart into pieces just the right size for munching along with a piece of cheese or a spoonful of jam. This was a popular kind of dry toast in the eighteenth and nineteenth centuries, especially in hotel restaurants.

Preheat the oven to 250°F. Cut the crust from a loaf of unsliced bread (feed the crusts to the birds). Pull irregular-size pieces about 2 or 3 inches long from the loaf until it is all broken up. Spread the pieces on a baking sheet. Bake for about 1 hour, until the bread is dry, crisp, and golden. Remove from the oven, pile in a napkin-lined basket or dish, and serve. Pulled bread will keep almost indefinitely stored in an airtight container.

Milk Toast

Why in the world did we ever abandon milk toast? Although it sounds deceptively bland and dull, it isn't; and as the Victorians discovered, it can revive the peaked or sad. Nourishing and soul-satisfying, milk toast will banish the blues.

STOVE TOP For each serving of the simplest of milk toasts, first lightly toast 2 slices of bread. Place the slices in a bowl. Pour 1½ cups milk into a saucepan, bring just to a boil, remove from the heat, and stir in $1\frac{1}{2}$ tablespoons butter. If you like, add a tablespoon of sugar and a pinch of ground nutmeg. Pour the milk into the bowl over the bread. Cover, and let stand for 5 minutes—don't stir or you will spoil the texture. Serve hot.

OVEN To make baked milk toast for two, preheat the oven to 350°F and butter a shallow baking dish that will hold four slices of bread in a single layer. Butter four slices of bread (preferably homemade and cut $\frac{3}{4}$ inch thick). Place the slices in one layer in the baking dish. Pour $1\frac{1}{3}$ cups of milk over the bread and cover the baking dish (with foil if it has no lid). Bake for 30 minutes. Sometimes a light sprinkle of granulated sugar is just right on milk toast. Serve hot.

Cinnamon Toast

Though Cinnamon Toast comes and goes in one's life, it is always welcome as an old friend. For 2 slices of toast, first mix together in a small bowl 4 teaspoons sugar and $\frac{1}{8}$ teaspoon cinnamon. Sprinkle 2 teaspoons of the cinnamon sugar over each buttered slice of lightly, freshly toasted bread. Place the toast under the broiler for about 1 minute (watch closely), or until the sugar has melted. Serve warm.

TOASTS

Old American cookbooks often have a chapter called The Toast Family or Divers Kinds of Toast with recipes for little garnished toasts as breakfast or lunch dishes. These modest-size meals on toast make a nice change from toast and sweet jam, and offer a little more nourishment and variety. Another nice thing about them is that they are practical and manageable if you get the notion to carry them back to bed.

Sausage Applesauce Toast

Lightly toast 2 slices rye bread and butter them right to the edges. Crumble about 1/4 cup cooked sausage (if you want to try making your own sausage—and it's well worth the effort—follow the recipe for Breakfast Sausage on page 197) over each slice of toast and cover with 1/4 cup applesauce. Put under the broiler for about 1 minute (watch carefully) or in a hot oven until the toast is very hot. Serve immediately.

Apple and Cheese Toast

For 2 pieces of toast, peel, core, and slice up an apple. Melt 2 tablespoons butter in a small skillet and add the apple slices. Cook over low heat for 3 or 4 minutes, or until the apple is tender. Set the apple aside. Sprinkle 1/3 cup grated Cheddar cheese over each of 2 buttered slices of fresh, lightly toasted bread. Place them under the broiler.

Keep an eye on them, and broil just until the cheese has melted. Arrange the apple slices over the melted cheese and serve warm.

Ham Toast

For 2 toasts, mix $2/3$ cup cooked, ground ham, 3 tablespoons heavy cream, and $1/8$ teaspoon nutmeg together in a small bowl. Butter 2 slices of fresh, lightly toasted bread and spread half the mixture over each one. Place the toasts in a hot oven or under the broiler until well heated. Serve hot.

Banana Toast

For 2 pieces of toast, peel a banana and cut in half, then slice each half lengthwise into 3 pieces. Melt 2 tablespoons butter in a small skillet over low heat. Put the banana slices in the skillet and cook over low heat for about 1 minute on each side. Butter 2 slices fresh whole wheat toast and put 3 slices of banana on each one. Stir together 1 teaspoon sugar and a pinch of nutmeg and sprinkle this over the banana slices. Serve warm.

Tomato Toast

For 2 pieces of toast, chop up enough fresh tomato to make about 1 cup and have ready 6 tablespoons fresh bread crumbs. Melt $1\frac{1}{2}$ tablespoons butter in a skillet and stir in the bread crumbs. Lightly brown them over medium heat, stirring constantly. Remove the bread crumbs from the pan, mix in ¼ teaspoon finely chopped fresh sage, and set aside. Add 1½ tablespoons more butter to the skillet and stir in the tomato. Add salt and pepper to taste and cook for 1 minute, stirring constantly. Remove from the heat, spread the tomato mixture over 2 slices buttered toast, and sprinkle the bread crumbs and sage over the top. Serve warm.

Mushroom Toast

For 2 pieces of toast, prepare about 2½ cups sliced mushrooms. Melt 4 tablespoons (½ stick) butter in a skillet over low heat. Stir in the mushrooms and continue to cook over low heat until the mushrooms soften a little. Salt lightly and pepper amply. Stir 2 teaspoons fresh lemon juice into the mushrooms, and spread them over 2 slices of fresh, light toast buttered right to the edges. Serve hot.

Creamed Mushroom Toast

For 2 slices of toast, you will need ½ pound medium-size mushrooms. Wipe them clean, remove the stems (save and add to an omelet), and slice the caps in half. Melt 3 tablespoons butter in a large skillet and add the mushrooms. Cook, stirring constantly, over medium heat only until they have darkened slightly. Add salt and pepper to taste. Then add ½ cup heavy cream and, if you like, 1 tablespoon dry sherry. Stir only until the mixture is well blended and hot. Spoon the creamed mushrooms over 2 slices of freshly toasted and buttered white bread. Garnish with flat-leaf Italian parsley.

Smoked Salmon Toast

On each slice of buttered rye toast, spread 1/4 cup softened cream cheese. Sprinkle 1/2 teaspoon fresh or dried dill and a few drops of lemon juice over the cheese. Cover each piece of toast with a thin slice of smoked salmon and serve cold. Very compatible with a halved hard-boiled egg on the plate.

BREAKFAST IN BED

One of the most blissful escapes is breakfast in bed with something good to read. Breakfast in bed is cozy, quiet, and private. I instantly forget that it was I who fixed the tray. The simplest food tastes special. Since food that spills or sloshes can ruin the mood, this is the moment when toasts should be considered. A thermos of hot coffee or tea is ideal.

As one is softly propped up in bed the world falls away, and breakfast becomes what some poet called "a parenthesis in time."

M.C.

Welsh Rabbit with Beer

(four servings)

Welsh Rabbit is certainly a warm and comforting dish, the kind that clears the head and quiets the stomach.

2 tablespoons butter	Salt to taste
2 tablespoons flour	2 cups grated sharp Cheddar
1 cup beer or ale	cheese
1 teaspoon Worcestershire sauce	6 slices whole wheat or rye bread,
1 teaspoon dry mustard	toasted and buttered

Melt the butter in a skillet and add the flour, stirring constantly. Cook over medium-low heat until well blended, about 2 minutes. Slowly add the beer, stirring constantly, until thickened and smooth. Add the Worcestershire sauce, dry mustard, and salt and stir until smooth and blended. Add the cheese and cook, stirring until smooth and thick. Taste and correct seasonings.

Put 1½ slices of buttered toast on each plate. Spoon the Welsh Rabbit over the toast and serve hot.

Tomato Rabbit

(six servings)

½ cup finely chopped tomato	Cayenne pepper to taste
⅛ teaspoon baking soda	2 tablespoons butter
2 cups grated extra sharp	2 tablespoons flour
Cheddar cheese	1 cup light cream
2 eggs, slightly beaten	Salt to taste
1 teaspoon dry mustard	6 slices toast, buttered

In a mixing bowl, stir together the tomatoes with the baking soda, cheese, eggs, mustard, and cayenne pepper. Melt the butter in a saucepan. Stir in the flour and cook for 2 to 3 minutes, stirring. Slowly pour in the cream and cook, stirring, until the mixture thickens. Add the tomato mixture to the sauce and cook over gentle heat, stirring constantly, until the cheese melts—do not boil. Taste and add salt if needed. Spoon over the toast and serve hot.

French Toast

(four servings)

French toast is so good that you forget how economical it is. The French don't call this French toast. They call it *pain perdu* or "lost bread," because it is a way to use up leftover bread you would otherwise lose—the only bread you've got on the baker's day off. French toast is actually better if the bread is a little old or sliced and dried out overnight.

3 eggs
3/4 cup milk, light cream, or
  heavy cream
Salt to taste

6 slices bread (preferably a
  dense homemade type;
  typically white, but try rye or
  whole wheat, too)
4 tablespoons (1/2 stick) butter

Stir the eggs, milk, and salt briskly in a bowl with a fork until well blended. Strain the mixture through a sieve into a shallow bowl in which you can easily dip a slice of bread. Dip both sides of each slice of bread in the batter and place the slices on a piece of waxed paper.

Melt 2 tablespoons of the butter in a skillet big enough to hold 3 slices at once. Fry the bread over medium heat until very lightly browned, turning once. Keep the cooked slices warm in a 250°F oven while frying the other three in the remaining 2 tablespoons of butter. Serve warm sprinkled with confectioners' sugar.

Spiced French Toast   Add ½ teaspoon cinnamon or nutmeg to the batter.

Lemon or Orange French Toast   Add 2 teaspoons grated lemon or orange zest to the batter.

Maple Syrup French Toast   Instead of ¾ cup milk, use ½ cup milk and ¼ cup maple syrup in the batter.

Fruit Syrup French Toast   Reduce the milk in the batter to ½ cup, and add ¼ cup of any fruit syrup.

Buttermilk French Toast   Substitute buttermilk for sweet milk in the batter.

J.B.'s French Toast

(four servings)

This is my favorite French toast recipe. James Beard once told me that they used to serve this in the dining cars on the Santa Fe Railroad. The crumbled-up cornflakes give every bite a crisp crunch that is mighty good.

3 eggs	2 cups cornflakes
½ cup milk	4 tablespoons (½ stick) butter
½ teaspoon nutmeg	6 slices dense white bread
¼ teaspoon salt	6 tablespoons sugar

Stir the eggs, milk, nutmeg, and salt together in a bowl until well blended. Strain the mixture through a sieve into a shallow bowl in which you can dip the bread easily (a soup bowl works well).

Crumble the cornflakes slightly (to make each flake about half its original size) and spread them on a piece of waxed paper.

Dip (don't soak) both sides of each slice of bread into the milk batter. Then press each slice of bread on both sides into the cornflakes to coat the bread well.

Melt 2 tablespoons butter in a 12-inch skillet over medium heat and fry 3 slices of the bread until golden on each side. When done, sprinkle about 1 tablespoon sugar on top of each slice and keep warm in a 250°F oven while you fry the other 3 slices in the remaining 2 table-spoons butter. Serve hot.

BREAKFAST SANDWICHES

Children of all ages love sandwiches, so why not have them for breakfast. Here are some sandwiches that use breakfast ingredients.

Fig and Ham on Rye Bread

For 2 sandwiches, butter 2 slices of bread to the edges. Trim the blossom end and stem from 5 ripe green figs (the Adriatic variety is delicious) and slice each one into 3 slices. Divide the slices of fig between 2 unbuttered slices of bread. Place a very thin slice of ham over each and cover with the buttered bread. Gently press down on each sandwich. Cut in half and serve.

Sausage and Melted Cheese Sandwiches

For 4 open-face sandwiches, slice ¼ pound cooked sausage links lengthwise and place in a single layer over 4 slices whole wheat bread. Sprinkle 1½ cups grated Cheddar cheese over the sausage. Put the sandwiches under the broiler (watch carefully) and broil until the cheese melts and bubbles.

Walnut Butter Sandwiches

For 2 sandwiches, mix 4 tablespoons room-temperature butter, ⅔ cup ground walnuts, and ⅓ cup golden raisins together in a small bowl, briskly stirring until the mixture has blended. Trim the crusts from 4 slices white bread. Spread the mixture over 2 slices and cover with the other 2 slices. Cut the sandwiches in half and serve with melon.

Date and Breakfast Cheese Sandwiches

For 2 sandwiches, stir together ⅔ cup chopped, pitted dates and ⅓ cup Breakfast Cheese (see page 286) or soft cream cheese until blended. Spread equal amounts on 2 slices of raisin bread and cover with another 2 slices. Cut the sandwiches in half and serve with a few walnut halves on the side.

Strawberry Sandwiches

To make 4 delicious summer Sunday breakfast sandwiches, first wash and hull 4 cups (about 2 baskets) fresh strawberries. Slice half of them, mash the other half, and add sugar to taste to both batches. Combine the sliced and mashed berries, reserving enough slices to garnish the tops of the sandwiches. Whip 1 cup heavy cream and sweeten with 3 tablespoons confectioners' sugar. On each plate, put a slice of good fresh white bread trimmed of its crust (feed the crusts to the birds). Spread the strawberries evenly over each slice, cover with another slice, and spread the whipped cream neatly over the top and sides. Garnish each sandwich with a few strawberry slices and serve at once. (You may prepare the fruit, cream, and bread in advance, and assemble the sandwiches just before serving.) This is not a pick-up sandwich— eat with a knife and fork.

Mexican Breakfast Sandwich

Spread a slice of Mexican Bread (see page 16) with Breakfast Cheese (see page 286) and cover with a layer of fresh cilantro leaves. Top with another slice of Mexican Bread. Melt 2 tablespoons butter over medium-low heat in a skillet, put the sandwich in the pan, and cook, pressing down on the sandwich several times with a spatula. Turn the sandwich over when the bottom is golden, add a little more butter to the skillet if necessary, and cook until golden. Serve with fresh spears of pineapple.

Ham and Farm Cheese
Butter-Fried Sandwiches

(two sandwiches)

Here nourishing breakfast ingredients are brought together in a simple form that appeals especially to children.

4 slices fresh whole wheat or
    white bread
About 3 ounces soft cream cheese
    (many markets carry fresh cream
    cheese, which is much better
    than the foil-wrapped variety)

4 thin slices ham
4 tablespoons ($\frac{1}{2}$ stick) butter

Lay the 4 slices of bread on a surface and spread each slice on one side with a rounded tablespoon of cream cheese. Place 2 ham slices on top of 2 of the slices and cover with the remaining slices of bread.

Melt the butter over medium-low heat. Place the sandwiches in the pan and fry gently until the bottom is golden, pressing down on each sandwich occasionally with a spatula—this will help to melt the cheese. Turn and fry the other side. Serve warm.

Quick Breads

Cream Biscuits
Oatmeal Biscuits
Buttermilk Barley Biscuits
White Cornbread with Fresh Sage
Custard-Filled Cornbread
Scones
    Brown, Dried Fruit Cream,
    Oatmeal Raisin
Bannocks
    Cheese
Raw Apple Muffins
Bran Muffins
Banana Bran Muffins
Boston Brown Bread Muffins
Chewy Brown Sugar Muffins
Peerless Cornbread Muffins
Cranberry Orange Muffins
Fig Muffins
Bridge Creek Fresh Ginger Muffins
Lemon Yogurt Muffins
Last Word in Nutmeg Muffins
Irish Oatmeal Muffins
Orange Walnut Muffins
Persimmon Muffins
Cinnamon Butter Puffs
Sunday Loaf
Blueberry Cranberry Bread
Date Nut Bread
    Fig Nut, Prune
Dried Fruit Bread
Christmas Bread
Oatmeal Popovers

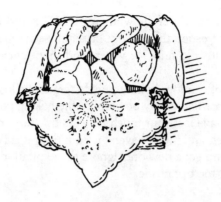

Breakfast quick breads, warm from the oven, puffy and delicious, will gladden the heart. As Marion Harland, once a leading American cook, wrote in 1903, the appearance of hot quick breads on the breakfast board "is a means of breakfast grace not to be underrated by the wise housewife."

Breads leavened with baking powder or baking soda are called quick breads because they are much faster to prepare than breads made with yeast. In our short history, American cooks have invented a marvelous and unique bounty of quick breads. In this chapter you'll find some reinterpretations of traditional favorites, but most are strikingly different recipes with new flavors that you will encounter nowhere else.

It is the easiest thing in the world to have muffins or slices of a quick bread loaf for breakfast. You don't need an electric anything to make them, and the dry ingredients and wet ingredients can be prepared (separately) the night before. In the morning all you will need to do is mix them together, and your biscuits, muffins, or bread can be baking while you're in the shower.

The ideal texture for most quick breads is usually described as pebbly—coarser and more crumbly than the fine, even texture of cake, but still tender. To achieve this, do not overbeat: just mix the wet and dry ingredients together until no floury streaks are showing.

Muffins served hot, straight from the oven, are perfection. Quick breads baked in loaves should rest a while before slicing, but they are nice served warm. Carefully wrap any leftovers and freeze; they keep well. You can freshen thawed-out or slightly stale muffins by dipping them rapidly in cold milk (or water) and then reheating them in the oven.

One word of caution: baking powder gradually loses its strength. If your muffins are flat, it may be because the baking powder is stale, not because you have lost your touch. Always buy the smallest-size can of baking powder, and if you haven't used it up, get rid of it after four or five months and get a new one. Ignore the expiration date on the can: it is always far too optimistic.

Cream Biscuits

(one dozen biscuits)

These biscuits are superior, and no student ever failed to make good ones in James Beard's cooking classes. They are better than most baking powder biscuits, and they are so ridiculously simple, you don't have to be awake to make them. They should be in your permanent recipe file.

2 cups all-purpose flour
1 teaspoon salt
1 tablespoon baking powder
2 teaspoons sugar

1 to 1½ cups heavy cream
⅓ cup (5⅓ tablespoons) butter, melted

Preheat the oven to 425°F. Use an ungreased baking sheet.

Combine the flour, salt, baking powder, and sugar in a mixing bowl. Stir the dry ingredients with a fork to blend and lighten. Slowly add 1 cup of the cream to the mixture, stirring constantly. Gather the dough together; when it holds together and feels tender, it is ready to knead. If the dough seems shaggy and pieces are dry and falling away, then slowly add enough additional cream to make the dough hold together.

Place the dough on a lightly floured board and knead for 1 minute. Pat the dough into a square that is about 1/2 inch thick. Cut into 12 squares and dip each into the melted butter so all sides are coated. Place the biscuits 2 inches apart on the baking sheet. Bake for about 15 minutes, or until the biscuits are lightly browned. Serve hot.

Oatmeal Biscuits

(one dozen biscuits)

These biscuits are not too rich — just oats and buttermilk to give a plain, made-on-the-farm taste.

1/2 cup rolled oats	1/2 teaspoon baking soda
13/4 cups all-purpose flour	4 tablespoons (1/2 stick) butter,
1/2 teaspoon salt	chilled
1 teaspoon baking powder	3/4 cup buttermilk

Preheat the oven to 425°F. Grease a baking sheet.

Combine the oats, flour, salt, baking powder, and baking soda in a mixing bowl. Stir and toss to mix and blend all the dry ingredients.

Cut the cold butter into pieces and add to the flour mixture. Using your fingers or a pastry cutter, cut or rub the butter into the flour until the mixture is in coarse, irregular bits. Add the buttermilk and stir the mixture with a fork until the rough mass somewhat holds together.

Gather the dough up and place on a lightly floured board. Knead about 10 times, pushing some of the pieces into the ball (this is a rather dry dough). Pat or roll into a 1/2-inch thickness. Cut into 2-inch rounds and place 1 inch apart on the baking sheet.

Bake 12 to 15 minutes, or until lightly browned. Serve hot.

Buttermilk Barley Biscuits

(thirty biscuits)

These rather flat biscuits (they will be only $\frac{3}{8}$ inch high) are very tasty spread with cream cheese and jam. The barley lends a homey taste. Eat them warm and freeze whatever is left over.

1 $\frac{1}{4}$ cups barley flour (available in health food stores)	$\frac{1}{2}$ teaspoon baking soda
1 $\frac{1}{4}$ cups all-purpose flour	1 teaspoon salt
2 teaspoons sugar	1 cup buttermilk
1 $\frac{1}{2}$ teaspoons baking powder	$\frac{1}{4}$ cup ($\frac{1}{2}$ stick) butter, melted

Preheat the oven to 425°F. Grease a baking sheet.

Put the flours, sugar, baking powder, baking soda, and salt in a mixing bowl. Stir with a fork to mix well. Stir in the buttermilk and beat briskly until mixed and smooth. Add the melted butter and blend well.

Dust a board with flour and turn the dough onto the board. Pat the dough into a piece about $\frac{1}{4}$ inch thick. Use a 2- or 2$\frac{1}{2}$-inch cutter to cut out the biscuits. Prick each biscuit 2 or 3 times on top with the tines of a fork. Place the biscuits a little apart (although these won't spread during baking) on the baking sheet. Bake for 10 to 15 minutes, or until lightly golden. Serve warm.

White Cornbread with Fresh Sage

(one 8-inch square cornbread)

Cornbread has an affinity for sage. Bits of crisp bacon incorporated into the batter can also produce delicious results.

1/4 cup water
1 tablespoon finely chopped
    fresh sage (or, if not available,
    2 teaspoons crumbled
    dried sage)
1 cup all-purpose flour
1 cup white cornmeal
1/2 teaspoon baking soda

1 1/2 teaspoons baking powder
1/2 teaspoon salt
3/4 cup buttermilk
1 egg
1/4 cup (4 tablespoons) vegetable
    shortening, melted
Optional: 1/3 cup crumbled crisp,
    pan-fried bacon

Preheat the oven to 425°F. Grease the square pan.

In a small saucepan, bring 1/4 cup water to a boil, remove from the heat, and stir in the sage. Set aside while you mix the dry ingredients to let the sage infuse the water with flavor.

Combine the flour, cornmeal, baking soda, baking powder, and salt in a mixing bowl. Stir with a fork to mix well. In a small separate bowl, combine the buttermilk, egg, shortening, and the sage and sage-flavored water. Add to the dry mixture with the bacon, if you are using it, and stir only to blend barely.

Spread evenly in the greased pan. Bake about 20 minutes, or until a straw comes out clean when inserted into the center. Remove from the oven and serve hot with butter.

Custard-Filled Cornbread

(eight servings)

This recipe is magic. When the cornbread is done, a creamy, barely set custard will have formed inside, and everyone will try to figure out how you got it there. Jane Salfass Freimann rediscovered this recipe, which was popular in the thirties; for instance, it appeared in Marjorie Kinnan Rawlings' *Cross Creek Country* in a much sweeter version.

2 eggs	1 cup all-purpose flour
3 tablespoons butter, melted	¾ cup yellow cornmeal
3 tablespoons sugar	1 teaspoon baking powder
½ teaspoon salt	½ teaspoon baking soda
2 cups milk	1 cup heavy cream
1½ tablespoons white vinegar	

Preheat the oven to 350°F. Butter an 8-inch-square baking dish or pan that is about 2 inches deep. Put the buttered dish or pan in the oven and let it get hot while you mix the batter.

Put the eggs in a mixing bowl and add the melted butter. Beat until the mixture is well blended. Add the sugar, salt, milk, and vinegar and beat well. Sift into a bowl or stir together in a bowl the flour, cornmeal, baking powder, and baking soda and add to the egg mixture. Mix just until the batter is smooth and no lumps appear.

Pour the batter into the heated dish, then pour the cream into the center of the batter — *don't stir*. Bake for 1 hour, or until lightly browned. Serve warm.

Breakfast Table Civility and Deportment

1. Clean up before you come to the breakfast table: wash your face and comb your hair.
2. You don't have to get dressed.
3. Clean fingernails, please.
4. Reading the newspaper at the table is permissable, but a pleasant word or salutation must be spoken to all present.
5. Sit up straight and try to be cheerful.
6. Talk to one another politely; talk and listen in turn.
7. Because everyone is defenseless at breakfast, there should be no contentiousness or crossness.
8. Don't ever mention food dislikes or criticize the food.
9. Don't lick your fingers or stuff your mouth with food.
10. Don't play with your food.
11. Don't talk with your mouth full.
12. Butter your bread one part at a time; don't put your uneaten pieces back in the bread basket.
13. And don't answer questions in a saucy manner.
14. Remember, guests always receive the choicest portions.

M.C.

SCONES

Scones have always been served with afternoon tea, but now they are in vogue on the breakfast table. The ones in this book are all oven-baked scones (there are also drop scones, made like pancakes from a thin batter, and griddle scones, made like oven scones but baked on a griddle). I like scones to be crisp and brown on the top and rather dense on the inside, with a nudge of richness from the butter in them or on them. Scones are delicious when served warm, split and buttered and spread with jam.

Brown Scones

(about one dozen scones)

1½ cups all-purpose flour
½ cup bran
2 teaspoons baking powder
½ teaspoon salt
3 tablespoons sugar
4 tablespoons (½ stick) butter, chilled

1 egg
½ cup milk

Glaze
2 tablespoons milk
2 tablespoons dark brown sugar

Preheat the oven to 450°F. Use an ungreased baking sheet.

Combine the flour, bran, baking powder, salt, and sugar in a bowl and mix well. Cut the butter into bits and add to the flour mixture. Rub the butter into the flour, using your fingertips or a pastry blender, until the mixture resembles coarse bread crumbs. In another bowl, beat the egg lightly, add the milk, and mix until well blended. Stir the milk mixture into the flour mixture, and stir only until just blended.

Lightly dust a board with flour and turn the dough onto the board. Knead about 12 times. Pat into a circle about $1/2$ inch thick. Make the glaze by blending the milk and brown sugar until smooth. Brush this over the dough and cut the dough into 12 wedges. Place the wedges on a baking sheet so that there is a $1/2$-inch space between them.

Bake for 10 to 12 minutes, or until the tops are golden. Serve hot.

Dried Fruit Cream Scones

(one dozen scones)

2 cups all-purpose flour	$1/4$ cup golden raisins
1 tablespoon baking powder	$1 1/4$ cups heavy cream
$1/2$ teaspoon salt	
$1/4$ cup sugar	*Glaze*
$1/2$ cup chopped dried fruit	3 tablespoons butter, melted
(apricots, prunes, or figs)	2 tablespoons sugar

Preheat the oven to 425°F. Use an ungreased baking sheet.

Combine the flour, baking powder, salt, and sugar in a bowl, stirring with a fork to mix well. Add the dried fruit and raisins. Still using a fork, stir in the cream and mix until the dough holds together in a rough mass (the dough will be quite sticky).

Lightly flour a board and transfer the dough to it. Knead the dough 8 or 9 times. Pat into a circle about 10 inches round. For the glaze, spread the butter over the top and side of the circle of dough and sprinkle the sugar on top. Cut the circle into 12 wedges and place each piece on the baking sheet, allowing about an inch between pieces.

Bake for about 15 minutes, or until golden brown.

Oatmeal Raisin Scones

(eighteen scones)

These are super with Caramel Oatmeal Topping (see page 280). Before you cut the dough into wedges, sprinkle $\frac{1}{2}$ cup topping evenly over it, and press firmly into the dough.

4 cups all-purpose flour	$\frac{1}{2}$ pound (2 sticks) butter, chilled
$\frac{1}{3}$ cup sugar	3 cups rolled oats
$1\frac{3}{4}$ teaspoons baking powder	1 cup raisins
1 teaspoon baking soda	2 cups buttermilk
1 teaspoon salt	

Preheat the oven to 375°F.

Mix together the flour, sugar, baking powder, baking soda, and salt in a large bowl. Cut the cold butter into small pieces and add to the flour mixture. Use either your fingers or a pastry cutter to rub or cut the butter into the flour mixture until it resembles coarse crumbs. Add the oats and raisins, tossing or stirring with a fork to distribute evenly. Add the buttermilk and stir with a fork until you can gather the dough into a rough ball.

Sprinkle a board with flour and put the dough on it. Knead 6 or 7 times. Divide the dough into 3 equal parts. Pat each part into a circle about $\frac{1}{2}$ inch thick. Cut each circle into 10 wedges. Put the wedges on ungreased baking sheets $\frac{1}{2}$ inch apart. Bake for about 25 minutes, or until the scones are lightly brown. Serve warm.

Bannocks

(eight bannocks)

Bannocks originated in Scotland and northern England centuries ago. Also known as oatcakes, they were made with either barley or oats and cooked on a griddle. Bannocks are the quickest of quick breads, and with little nubbins of oats throughout, they have an appealing taste.

1 cup rolled oats	4 tablespoons ($\frac{1}{2}$ stick) butter,
1 cup oat flour	chilled
(available in health food stores)	$\frac{1}{2}$ cup water
$\frac{1}{4}$ teaspoon salt	

Preheat the oven to 400°F. Grease a baking sheet.

Put the oats, flour, and salt in a mixing bowl and stir with a fork to blend. Cut the cold butter into small pieces and add to the flour mixture. Rub the butter and flour together until coarse bits form. Stir in the water and mix. Gather the rough dough together and place on a board that has been lightly dusted with oat flour. Knead the dough about 6 times. Divide the dough in half and pat each half into a circle about $\frac{1}{4}$ inch thick. Cut each circle into 4 wedges. Place the wedges on the greased baking sheet $\frac{1}{2}$ inch apart. Bake about 20 minutes, or until lightly colored.

Cheese Bannocks Add 1 cup grated Cheddar cheese to the mixture after rubbing in the butter. Proceed as directed above.

Raw Apple Muffins

(sixteen muffins)

These muffins are different because they are not light and airy; instead, they are dense with fruit and raisins and nuts. You'll find them particularly moist and full of spicy good flavor.

4 cups diced apple	2 teaspoons baking soda
(peeled or unpeeled)	2 teaspoons cinnamon
1 cup sugar	1 teaspoon salt
2 eggs, beaten lightly	1 cup raisins
1/2 cup oil (corn oil is very good)	1 cup broken walnuts
2 teaspoons vanilla extract	(leave in large pieces)
2 cups all-purpose flour	

Preheat the oven to 325°F. Grease 16 muffin tins.

Put 3 mixing bowls on the counter. Mix the apples and sugar in one bowl and set aside. Put the eggs, oil, and vanilla in the second bowl and stir to blend well. In the third bowl, put the flour, baking soda, cinnamon, and salt, and stir the mixture with a fork until blended.

Stir the egg mixture into the apples and sugar, and mix thoroughly. Sprinkle the flour mixture over the apple mixture and mix well. (I use my hands because this is a stiff batter.) Sprinkle the raisins and walnuts over the batter and mix until they are evenly distributed. Spoon into the muffin tins.

Bake for about 25 minutes, or until a straw comes out clean when inserted into the center of a muffin. Serve warm.

Bran Muffins

(eighteen muffins)

This is a perfect recipe for a child to make: just measure, stir, and spoon into muffin tins. These bran muffins are moist and lightly sweetened, with a nice balance of flavor—quite a good contrast to some of the sticky, cloyingly sweet bran muffins that are supposed to be good for you.

2½ cups bran	⅔ cup buttermilk
1⅓ cups whole wheat flour	⅓ cup vegetable oil
2½ teaspoons baking soda	⅓ cup dark molasses
½ teaspoon salt	¼ cup honey
2 eggs	1 cup raisins

Preheat the oven to 425°F. Grease the muffin tins.

Put the bran, flour, baking soda, and salt in a bowl and stir to blend. Add the eggs, buttermilk, oil, molasses, and honey to the bran mixture and beat until blended. Stir in the raisins.

Fill the muffin tins two-thirds full. Bake for about 12 to 15 minutes, or until the muffins have shrunk from the sides of the pan. Serve warm.

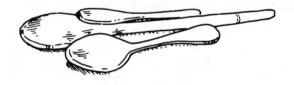

Banana Bran Muffins

(two dozen muffins)

These are head and shoulders above the dense, serious, prescription-type bran muffins that are eaten because they are good for you; and the cake flour makes them particularly light. They are moist, tender, and nicely flavored with banana.

12 tablespoons (1½ sticks) butter,
   room temperature
⅔ cup sugar
4 medium-size *ripe* bananas
   (to make 2½ to 3 cups purée)
3 eggs
2 cups cake flour

1½ cups bran
¾ teaspoon salt
1½ teaspoons baking soda
Optional: 1 cup chopped walnuts;
   1 tablespoon grated orange zest;
   ¾ cup granola

Preheat the oven to 375°F. Grease the muffin pans.

Put the butter in a mixing bowl and beat until creamy. Add the sugar and blend well. Stir in the banana purée and eggs, and beat until the batter is light and smooth.

Sift the flour, bran, salt, and baking soda together (I sift onto a sheet of waxed paper), then add the flour mixture to the batter and mix well. Add any or all of the optional ingredients at this point. Spoon the batter into muffin pans, almost filling them. Bake 15 to 20 minutes. Serve warm.

Serve with fruit or a tangy yogurt, like lemon.

Boston Brown Bread Muffins

(one dozen muffins)

Boston Brown Bread Muffins have all the virtues of classic steamed brown bread but are much quicker to make.

$1/2$ cup rye flour	$1/3$ cup molasses
$1/2$ cup yellow cornmeal	$1/3$ cup firmly packed dark brown
$1/2$ cup whole wheat flour	sugar
$3/4$ teaspoon salt	$1/3$ cup vegetable oil
$11/2$ teaspoons baking soda	1 cup buttermilk
1 egg	1 cup golden raisins

Preheat the oven to 400°F. Grease the muffin tins.

Mix together with a fork the rye flour, cornmeal, whole wheat flour, salt, and baking soda in a large bowl until blended. In a small bowl combine the egg, molasses, brown sugar, oil, and buttermilk. Stir or beat to blend well. Stir the egg mixture into the flour mixture and mix well. Add the raisins and stir to mix.

Fill the muffin tins about one-half to two-thirds full. Bake for 15 minutes, or until a straw comes out clean when inserted into the center of a muffin. Don't overbake! Serve hot.

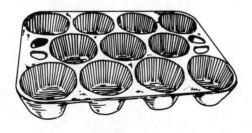

Chewy Brown Sugar Muffins

(eighteen muffins)

There is nothing flimsy about these muffins—the distinct tastes of brown sugar and oats come through, with a hint of maple. Eat them with crisp bacon, or maybe even an egg.

1 cup heavy cream	¾ teaspoon salt
1 cup pancake syrup*	2 teaspoons baking powder
2 eggs	1 teaspoon baking soda
¾ cup whole wheat flour	1½ cups rolled oats
¾ cup all-purpose flour	Optional: 1 cup broken walnut
½ cup firmly packed dark brown	pieces
sugar	

*Do not substitute all maple syrup. If you wish to, you may use ½ cup maple syrup and ½ cup dark corn syrup in place of the pancake syrup.

Preheat the oven to 350°F. Grease the muffin tins.

In a large mixing bowl, combine the cream, syrup, eggs, flours, sugar, salt, baking powder, baking soda, and oats and beat with a whisk (this is so easy that you don't need an electric anything to make these). If adding the walnuts, stir them in now.

Fill the muffin tins three-quarters full. Bake about 20 minutes, or until a straw comes out clean when inserted into the center.

Peerless Cornbread Muffins

(one dozen muffins)

Tender-textured yellow muffins—the only bread I know that isn't improved by being buttered. Do I need to remind you that honey is pleasing with cornbread?

1 egg, room temperature
½ cup (1 stick) butter, melted
¼ cup vegetable oil
1 cup milk, warmed
1 cup cake flour

⅔ cup yellow cornmeal
1 tablespoon baking powder
½ teaspoon salt
1 tablespoon sugar

Preheat the oven to 400°F. Grease the muffin tins.

Beat or whisk the egg, melted butter, and oil in a mixing bowl until well blended. Stir in the warm milk. Combine the cake flour, cornmeal, baking powder, salt, and sugar in another bowl and stir with a fork until well mixed. Add the dry ingredients to the egg mixture and stir until blended. This is a light, medium-thick batter.

Spoon the batter into the muffin tins so each cup is three-quarters full. Bake for 15 to 20 minutes, or until the edges of the muffins are slightly golden and a straw comes out clean when inserted into the center. Remove from tins and cool a little on racks, or simply serve in a basket, hot from the oven.

Cranberry Orange Muffins

(about three dozen tiny muffins)

These small, moist, bite-size muffins are best served slightly warm, so if you make them ahead, reheat them on a baking sheet in a hot oven for a few minutes before serving and then toss again in cinnamon sugar. At Thanksgiving time, you might want to buy a few extra bags of cranberries and store them in the freezer, so you can make cranberry muffins all year long. These should be made in small cupcake pans—those with a top diameter of $1\frac{3}{4}$ inches.

$1\frac{1}{2}$ cups all-purpose flour
1 teaspoon baking soda
$\frac{1}{2}$ teaspoon baking powder
$\frac{1}{4}$ teaspoon salt
$\frac{1}{4}$ cup sugar
1 egg
$\frac{1}{2}$ cup buttermilk
$\frac{1}{3}$ cup ($5\frac{1}{3}$ tablespoons) butter, melted

$\frac{1}{4}$ cup orange marmalade
$\frac{1}{2}$ cup finely chopped fresh cranberries

Cinnamon Sugar
$\frac{2}{3}$ cup sugar
2 teaspoons cinnamon

Preheat the oven to 375°F. Butter small cupcake pans ($1\frac{3}{4}$ inch top diameter, and about $\frac{3}{4}$ inch deep). If you don't have enough muffin tins, bake the muffins in relays, like cookies.

In a small mixing bowl, stir and toss together the flour, baking soda, baking powder, and salt. In another, larger bowl, place the sugar, egg, buttermilk, melted butter, marmalade, and cranberries, and beat until completely blended. Add the combined dry ingredients and beat just until blended.

Spoon the batter into the prepared muffin tins, filling each cup almost to the top. Bake for 12 to 15 minutes, or until a toothpick or straw inserted into the center of a muffin comes out clean.

While the muffins bake, stir the sugar and cinnamon together in a pie plate or shallow dish. As soon as the muffins are done, immediately remove them from the pans and roll them gently, 4 or 5 at a time, in the sugar mixture. Transfer them to a rack until ready to serve. Once muffins are completely cool, wrap airtight and freeze any you won't use immediately.

Fig Muffins

(eighteen muffins)

Figs are often overlooked in baking, but they are high on the list of fruits that are good for you.

$1/4$ cup vegetable shortening
$1/3$ cup sugar
1 egg, lightly beaten
$1/2$ cup milk
2 cups coarsely chopped fresh figs
   (either Mission or Adriatic);
   or $1 1/2$ cups coarsely chopped
   dried Calimyrna figs

1 cup all-purpose flour
$1/2$ cup whole wheat flour
$1/2$ teaspoon salt
2 teaspoons baking powder

Preheat the oven to 375°F. Grease the muffin tins.

Combine the shortening and sugar and mix until smooth and blended. Add the egg and milk and beat well. Add the figs and mix thoroughly.

Put the flours, salt, and baking powder in a bowl and stir with a fork just enough to mix. Add to the fig mixture and stir only until no floury streaks show—don't overmix.

Spoon the batter into the muffin tins, filling two-thirds full. Bake about 20 minutes, or until a straw comes out clean when inserted into the center of a muffin. Remove muffins from tins to cool.

Bridge Creek Fresh Ginger Muffins

(sixteen muffins)

These muffins have an abundance of fresh ginger and lemon zest. Every time I make them I am overcome by how good they are.

A 2-ounce piece unpeeled
   gingerroot
$3/4$ cup plus 3 tablespoons sugar
2 tablespoons lemon zest (from 2
   lemons), with some white pith
8 tablespoons (1 stick) butter,
   room temperature

2 eggs
1 cup buttermilk
2 cups all-purpose flour
$1/2$ teaspoon salt
$3/4$ teaspoon baking soda

Preheat the oven to 375°F. Grease the muffin tins.

Cut the *unpeeled* ginger into large chunks. If you have a food processor, process the ginger until it is in tiny pieces; or hand chop into fine pieces. (You should have $1/4$ cup. It is better to have too much ginger than too little.) Put the ginger and $1/4$ cup sugar in a small skillet or pan and cook over medium heat until the sugar has melted and the mixture is hot. Don't walk away from the pan — this cooking takes only a couple of minutes. Remove from the stove and let the ginger mixture cool.

Put the lemon zest and 3 tablespoons sugar in the food processor and process until the lemon peel is in small bits; or chop the lemon zest and pith by hand and then add the sugar. Add the lemon mixture to the ginger mixture. Stir and set aside.

Put the butter in a mixing bowl and beat a second or two, add the remaining $1/2$ cup sugar, and beat until smooth. Add the eggs and beat well. Add the buttermilk and mix until blended. Add the flour, salt, and baking soda. Beat until smooth. Add the ginger-lemon mixture and mix well.

Spoon the batter into the muffin tins so that each cup is three-quarters full. Bake 15 to 20 minutes. Serve warm.

Lemon Yogurt Muffins

(about one dozen muffins)

These yellow muffins with brown pebbly tops are fine-textured and not too sweet. They go especially well with hot tea. Lemon syrup drizzled over after baking makes them extra moist.

2 cups all-purpose flour	$1/4$ cup ($1/2$ stick) butter, melted
1 teaspoon baking powder	1 tablespoon grated lemon zest
1 teaspoon baking soda	
$1/4$ teaspoon salt	*Lemon Syrup*
$1/4$ cup sugar	$1/3$ cup lemon juice
2 tablespoons honey	$1/3$ cup sugar
2 eggs	3 tablespoons water
$1 1/4$ cups plain yogurt	

Preheat the oven to 375°F and butter the muffin tins.

In a small mixing bowl, stir and toss together the flour, baking powder, baking soda, and salt. In another, larger bowl, combine the sugar, honey, eggs, yogurt, melted butter, and lemon zest and beat until thoroughly mixed. Add the combined dry ingredients and beat just until blended.

Spoon the batter into the prepared muffin tins, filling each cup about two-thirds full. These should bake for about 15 minutes, or until the tops are delicately browned and a toothpick or straw inserted into the center of a muffin comes out clean.

While the muffins bake, prepare the syrup. Combine the lemon juice, sugar, and water in a small saucepan. Bring to a boil, boil for 1 minute, then set aside.

When the muffins are done, remove the pan from the oven and

gently poke the top of each muffin two or three times with a fork. Drizzle about 2 teaspoons of the syrup over each hot muffin, letting it run over the top and around the edge. Let cool in the pans for a few minutes, then remove and serve warm.

Last Word in Nutmeg Muffins

(one dozen muffins)

Fragrant, creamy-crumbed nutmeg muffins, the best of their kind, but you must grate one and a half whole little nutmegs to make these perfect creations. Although whole nutmegs feel like rocks, they are rather soft and easy to grate. The flavor of freshly grated nutmeg is incomparable. These muffins taste good with fruit, or butter, or all by themselves.

2 cups all-purpose flour	1 egg
¾ cup sugar	¾ cup heavy cream
1 tablespoon baking powder	¾ cup milk
1½ whole nutmegs, grated	5 tablespoons butter, melted
½ teaspoon salt	

Preheat the oven to 400°F. Grease the muffin tins.

Stir together with a fork the flour, sugar, baking powder, nutmeg, and salt in a medium-size bowl, thoroughly combining the ingredients. Beat the egg well in a small bowl, then stir in the cream, milk, and butter and blend well. Add the cream mixture to the flour mixture and stir only until there are no streaks of flour. Don't overmix.

Spoon batter two-thirds full into each muffin cup. Bake for about 20 minutes, or until the rounded tops are lightly golden. Remove muffins from the pan, and serve warm. Or cool on a rack and store or freeze for later use; warm before serving.

Irish Oatmeal Muffins

(two dozen muffins)

The Irish often cook their oatmeal all night long for a rich and creamy effect. These muffins take on that same flavor from overnight soaking in buttermilk. Try spreading a little Whipped Maple Syrup (see page 281) on them.

2 cups buttermilk	$1\frac{2}{3}$ cups whole wheat flour
1 cup rolled oats	1 teaspoon baking soda
2 eggs	1 teaspoon salt
$\frac{3}{4}$ cup dark brown sugar	2 tablespoons vegetable oil

Combine the buttermilk and the oats at least 6 hours (preferably overnight) before mixing and baking the muffins. Stir well, cover, and let rest in the refrigerator.

Preheat the oven to 400°F. Grease the muffin tins.

Put the eggs in a mixing bowl and beat just until yolk and white are blended. Add the sugar and beat until smooth and well blended. Add the buttermilk-oatmeal mixture. Add the flour, baking soda, salt, and oil. Beat until the batter is well mixed.

Fill the muffin tins three-quarters full of batter. They usually bake about 20 minutes, but start testing for doneness after 15 minutes. Either remove the muffins from the tins and cool on racks or serve hot from the pan.

Orange Walnut Muffins

(sixteen muffins)

It is amazing how the flavor of two oranges can so completely permeate sixteen muffins that they taste of the essence of orange. Chopping the zest and the flesh of the orange is done in a flash with the food processor, although it is also easy to do this little bit of chopping by hand.

2 large oranges	2 cups all-purpose flour
(not too many seeds)	2 teaspoons baking powder
2 eggs	$\frac{1}{2}$ teaspoon baking soda
$\frac{1}{2}$ cup sugar	$\frac{1}{2}$ teaspoon salt
$\frac{1}{2}$ cup (1 stick) butter, melted	$\frac{1}{2}$ cup chopped walnuts

Preheat the oven to 400°F. Grease the muffin tins.

Using a small paring knife or grater, remove the zest from the orange (the zest is the colored skin without the bitter white pith beneath). Trim off the pith and the white membrane and discard, leaving just the orange flesh. Chop the oranges fine along with the zest (by hand or in a food processor); you should have about 1 cup. Set aside into a small bowl.

Put the eggs in a large bowl and lightly whisk to blend. Add the sugar and butter and stir well. Combine the flour, baking powder, baking soda, and salt in another bowl and stir to blend. Then add the orange and the flour mixture to the egg mixture and stir until blended. Stir in the walnuts.

Fill the muffin tins one-half to two-thirds full. Bake for about 15 minutes, or until a straw comes out clean when inserted into the center of a muffin. Serve hot.

Persimmon Muffins

(eighteen muffins)

This recipe is adapted from my favorite steamed persimmon pudding, which is the only cakelike recipe I know using persimmons that works. Persimmons have a short season, but peeled and puréed they freeze well.

1 cup puréed persimmons	1/2 teaspoon salt
1 teaspoon baking soda	1 teaspoon cinnamon
12 tablespoons (1 1/2 sticks) butter, room temperature	1 teaspoon vanilla extract
	2 teaspoons lemon juice
1 1/4 cups sugar	Optional: 2 tablespoons bourbon
2 eggs	1 cup walnut pieces
1 1/3 cups all-purpose flour	3/4 cup currants

Preheat the oven to 325°F. Grease the muffin tins.

Put the puréed persimmons into a small bowl and stir in the baking soda. Set aside.

Put the butter in a mixing bowl and beat, slowly adding the sugar, until the mixture is creamy and smooth. Add the eggs and beat well. Add the flour, salt, and cinnamon along with the persimmon mixture and beat until well blended. Add the vanilla, lemon juice, and optional bourbon. Stir in the walnuts and currants.

Fill each muffin cup three-quarters full. Bake for 45 minutes, or until a straw comes out clean when inserted into the center of a muffin. Remove from the muffin pans and let cool on racks or serve warm.

Cinnamon Butter Puffs

(about one dozen puffs)

Recipes for puffs—really just muffins rolled in spiced sugar (with cinnamon, mace, etc.)—were popular at the beginning of this century. Although not necessarily puffier than most muffins, they give the illusion of cake doughnuts.

$\frac{1}{3}$ cup shortening
$\frac{1}{2}$ cup sugar (less if desired)
1 egg
$1\frac{1}{2}$ cups all-purpose flour
$1\frac{1}{2}$ teaspoons baking powder
$\frac{1}{2}$ teaspoon salt
$\frac{1}{4}$ teaspoon nutmeg
$\frac{1}{2}$ cup milk

Topping
$\frac{1}{2}$ cup (1 stick) butter, melted
$\frac{1}{2}$ cup sugar combined with
   1 teaspoon cinnamon

Preheat the oven to 350°F. Grease the muffin tins.

Put the shortening, sugar, and egg in a mixing bowl. Beat well. Mix together the flour, baking powder, salt, and nutmeg and add to the first mixture. Pour in the milk and beat until blended and smooth.

Fill the muffin tins about two-thirds full. Bake about 20 minutes, or until lightly golden.

For the topping, have the melted butter ready in a bowl that is just large enough to hold one puff. Have a shallow bowl ready nearby with the combined sugar and cinnamon. As soon as the puffs are done, remove them from the pan and dip them one by one into the melted butter, and then roll in the cinnamon-sugar mixture.

Sunday Loaf

(one large loaf)

This shiny-topped bread is alive with lots of berry flavor. Slice and freeze any leftover loaf and reheat by the slice in your toaster.

3 cups all-purpose flour
1/2 cup sugar
4 teaspoons baking powder
1 teaspoon salt
8 tablespoons (1 stick) butter, chilled
2 eggs
1/2 cup raspberry or strawberry jam or preserves (not jelly)
3/4 cup milk

Glaze
2 tablespoons butter
2 tablespoons sugar
2 tablespoons raspberry or strawberry jam

Preheat the oven to 350°F. Grease a 9 × 5 × 3-inch loaf pan.

Combine the flour, sugar, baking powder, and salt in a large mixing bowl. Stir with a fork to mix all the dry ingredients well. Cut the butter into small pieces and drop into the flour mixture. Using your fingers or a pastry cutter, rub or cut the cold butter into the flour until the mixture resembles coarse bread crumbs.

Beat the eggs well in a small bowl, add the jam and milk, and whisk until the mixture is blended smooth. Stir the jam mixture into the flour mixture and stir only until no flour streaks show — the mixture will be lumpy.

Spoon into the loaf pan and bake for about 1 hour and 15 minutes, or until a straw inserted into the center comes out clean. Allow the loaf to remain in the pan for 15 to 20 minutes before turning it onto a rack.

Meanwhile, make the glaze by combining the butter, sugar, and jam in a pan. Stir and bring to a simmer; continue stirring until dissolved and blended. Strain and then spoon the glaze over the loaf after it has cooled on the rack.

Blueberry Cranberry Bread

(one large loaf)

Blueberries and cranberries bring out the best in each other. This bread is nicest when you serve it warm.

1 cup fresh cranberries	1 cup buttermilk
¾ cup granulated sugar	3 cups all-purpose flour
1 cup brown sugar	1 teaspoon baking soda
8 tablespoons (1 stick) butter,	1 teaspoon baking powder
room temperature	1 teaspoon salt
2 eggs	1 cup blueberries

Preheat the oven to 375°F. Grease a 9 × 5 × 3-inch loaf pan.

Put the cranberries and granulated sugar in a small skillet and cook over medium heat, stirring often, until the sugar has dissolved. Remove from heat and set aside to cool.

Put the cup of brown sugar and the butter in a mixing bowl and beat until blended. Add the eggs and beat well. Stir in the buttermilk.

Put the flour, baking soda, baking powder, and salt in a bowl and stir with a fork until well mixed. Add to the butter mixture and beat only until blended. Stir in the cranberry mixture and the blueberries. Spoon the batter into the loaf pan.

Bake for about 1 hour and 10 minutes, or until a straw comes out clean when inserted into the center. Remove from the oven and turn onto a rack to cool a little.

Date Nut Bread

(one medium loaf)

I have one finicky eater in my house, and when he tasted this bread and said it was good I knew I had a winner. Bake it and see.

1 cup pitted and chopped dates	¾ cup boiling water
1 cup coarsely chopped walnuts	2 eggs
1½ teaspoons baking soda	¾ cup sugar
½ teaspoon salt	½ cup whole wheat flour
3 tablespoons vegetable shortening	1 cup all-purpose flour

Preheat the oven to 350°F. Grease an 8½ × 4½ × 3-inch loaf pan.

Put the dates, walnuts, baking soda, salt, and shortening in a bowl. Pour the boiling water over and stir. Let the mixture stand for 15 minutes.

Using a fork, beat the eggs and sugar together in a bowl. Add the flours and stir (this will be too stiff to mix well). Add the date mixture and mix briskly until the batter is well blended. Spoon into the loaf pan and bake for about 1 hour, or until a straw comes out clean when inserted into the center. Remove and cool on a rack.

Fig Nut Bread   Substitute 1 cup chopped figs for the dates. Proceed as directed above.

Prune Bread   Omit the dates and walnuts. Substitute 1½ cups pitted, chopped prunes. Proceed as directed above.

Dried Fruit Bread

(two medium loaves)

This is a fine holiday bread when a small tasty breakfast is in order. Dried Fruit Bread with a good homemade eggnog is a simple and complete breakfast. My family is fond of this recipe because there is no spice to hide the good natural flavor of the fruits. You may use any dried fruit or fruits you choose; we favor figs, apricots, and raisins.

1 cup dried Calimyrna figs	1 egg
1 cup dried apricots	1 teaspoon grated lemon zest
1 cup golden raisins	2 cups all-purpose flour
1½ cups water	2 teaspoons baking powder
1 cup pitted dates	1 teaspoon baking soda
¼ cup shortening	1 teaspoon salt
¾ cup sugar	

Preheat the oven to 350°F. Grease two 8½ × 4½ × 3-inch loaf pans.

Put the figs, apricots, and raisins in a small saucepan and add the water. Partially cover the pan with a lid and simmer for 5 minutes. Drain, reserving ⅔ cup liquid. Cool. Chop the figs, apricots, raisins, and dates.

Put the shortening in a bowl and add the sugar, egg, and lemon zest. Beat until smooth and creamy. Put the flour, baking powder, baking soda, and salt in a bowl and stir with a fork until well mixed. Add all the fruit to the flour mixture, stir in the reserved fruit liquid, and mix until all is blended. Spoon the batter into the loaf pans. Let the pans stand for 15 minutes. Put into the oven and bake for about 45 minutes, or until a straw comes out clean when inserted into the center.

Christmas Bread

(two medium loaves or two dozen muffins)

The citrus zest and fresh spiciness—in combination with an abundance of raisins and currants that have been soaked in almond liqueur—evoke all the tastes of Christmas. I predict that this splendid but easy recipe will become a tradition in your Christmas festivities.

1 cup raisins	2 eggs
$\frac{1}{2}$ cup currants	$\frac{1}{2}$ cup vegetable oil
Grated rind with a little white pith of 1 orange	$2\frac{1}{2}$ cups all-purpose flour
	$\frac{1}{2}$ teaspoon salt
Grated rind with a little white pith of 1 lemon (orange and lemon zest combined should make about $\frac{1}{2}$ cup)	1 teaspoon baking soda
	1 tablespoon baking powder
	1 cup brown sugar
	$\frac{1}{4}$ teaspoon ground cloves
$\frac{1}{4}$ cup almond liqueur (or brandy, rum, or bourbon)	1 teaspoon nutmeg (freshly grated, if possible)
$\frac{1}{3}$ cup granulated sugar	1 cup milk

Preheat the oven to 325°F. Grease two $8\frac{1}{2} \times 4\frac{1}{2} \times 3$-inch loaf pans or muffin tins.

Put the raisins, currants, and grated orange and lemon rind in a small bowl. Pour the liqueur over and add the granulated sugar. Toss the mixture and let macerate for 30 minutes or longer.

Put the eggs and oil in a mixing bowl and whisk until smooth and creamy. Add the flour, salt, baking soda, baking powder, brown sugar, cloves, nutmeg, and milk. Stir vigorously until the mixture is well blended. Stir in the raisins, currants, and orange and lemon rind along with any of the liquid at the bottom of their bowl. Mix well.

Spoon the batter into the loaf pans or muffin tins. Bake the loaves for 1 hour and 15 minutes, or until a wooden skewer comes out clean when inserted into the center. Let the loaves rest 10 minutes in the pans, turn onto racks, and cool before slicing. The bread is best when it is cooled and then rewarmed before serving. If making muffins, bake for about 25 minutes, or until a straw inserted into the center of one comes out clean. The muffins may be turned out onto racks immediately and served hot.

Oatmeal Popovers

(ten popovers)

Popovers are a type of quick bread that rises on egg power alone. The foolproof trick for making high and mighty popovers is to start them in a cold oven. I use some ground oatmeal in this recipe to give the popovers additional texture, and I like to put a rounded teaspoon of tart orange marmalade in the bottom of the custard cups or muffin tins—the combination of oatmeal and orange marmalade is very good.

2 eggs
1 cup milk
1 tablespoon butter, melted
$\frac{1}{3}$ cup rolled oats, coarsely
   ground in a food processor
   or blender

$\frac{3}{4}$ cup all-purpose flour
$\frac{1}{2}$ teaspoon salt
Optional: $\frac{1}{2}$ cup tart orange
   marmalade

Butter the custard cups or muffin tins. Put a rounded teaspoon of marmalade in the bottom of each cup.

Mix the eggs, milk, butter, oatmeal, flour, and salt just until well blended. Half fill the prepared pans with the batter and set them in a cold oven. Turn the heat to 450°F and bake for 15 minutes, then reduce the heat to 350° and bake another 10 to 15 minutes, or just until golden and round. Remove from the pans and serve piping hot.

Cereals

Hot Cereals
  Wheat
  Rice
  Corn
    Bacon Scrapple
    Pumpkin Mush
    Good Grits
  Brown Barley
  Oats and Oatmeal
    Rolled Oats
    Steel-Cut Oats
Cold Cereals
  Granola
  Unsweetened Granola
  Four-Grain Toasted Cereal with
  Bananas and Pecans
  Original Bircher Muesli
  Muesli Ballymaloe

Never think of cereals as being humble—they can be as delicious as caviar, and as healthy as sunshine.

The dried seeds of grassy plants have fed and strengthened us for centuries. Because we don't have beaks like birds and can't chew like horses, man has inventively shaped these grains into many forms: we've milled them, cracked them, puffed them, cooked them and steamed them, and rolled them flat.

HOT CEREALS

All grains can be made into hot cereals. If you're ambling through a health food store, you have an opportunity to have an adventure with some grains you may not have tried—or even heard of—like sorghum, millet, barley, buckwheat, or triticale. There are three basic ways to eat them: raw, with water or milk; slightly cooked by pouring boiling water over them and letting them sit a minute; or as porridge, cooked slowly in simmering water. Read the packaging for cooking instructions—some grains are precooked and need little additional cooking, others, like whole wheat berries, take hours.

There are plenty of ways to prepare and serve hot cereals: you can cook different cereals together for variety; you can serve them with butter, with maple syrup or brown sugar, with applesauce stirred in, with fresh fruit, with raisins and other dried fruits, with nuts, with granola . . .

It seems that most of the world has forgotten that leftover cooked mush — for example, hominy grits or cornmeal mush — is one step away from a delicious fried dish. When the mush is cool, it is put into a buttered loaf pan, covered, and chilled until firm. When ready to fry, the loaf of mush is removed from its pan and cut into ½-inch-thick slices which are fried in hot butter or bacon fat on each side until golden around the edges. Fried mush is good as is, with maple syrup or honey on top, or with eggs and sausage — a fine example of a simple food rising to heights when properly seasoned and cooked.

Wheat

Hulled wheat kernels are called wheat berries and make delicious cereal, but they do take up to three hours to cook. Farina, or cream of wheat, is a ground meal made from refined wheat, and usually enriched or fortified. It is especially good with a little granola stirred in for crunch and flavor. Bulgur is precooked, cracked wheat; it takes only about 15 minutes to cook and makes a nutty-tasting earthy breakfast cereal. It is even better when it is toasted first in the oven to bring out its flavor.

Rice

You might want to try eating rice porridge for breakfast, as they do in China. Try making it with brown rice — it's better for you. Cream of rice is a precooked hot cereal made from granulated white rice, and is usually fortified.

Corn

Both white and yellow cornmeal is available and the two taste identical: choose whichever color you like better—you can make mush with either kind. You can keep cornmeal from lumping by wetting it with cold water before you add it to boiling water.

Dried corn treated with lye to remove the hull and germ is called hominy. It is eaten for breakfast ground up into a coarse meal, called hominy grits, which cooks up into a soothing and satisfying mush. Grits are good with maple syrup or brown sugar, butter, and raisins; or you can jazz them up by serving them with Salsa Verde (see page 284).

Bacon Scrapple

(four servings)

This scrapple will convert scrapple loathers into scrapple addicts. Yellow cornmeal is cooked with a bay leaf and a little bacon fat until it is thick and creamy. Bits of crisp-cooked bacon are added, then the mixture is packed into a loaf pan and chilled overnight. At breakfast time, the loaf is sliced and the slices are fried in a little bacon fat until brown and crisp around the edges. Serve alone with maple syrup or with well-peppered eggs.

½ pound sliced bacon
⅔ cup yellow cornmeal
1 cup cold water
3 cups boiling water

1¼ teaspoons salt
½ teaspoon coarsely ground
   pepper
1 bay leaf, crumbled

Fry the bacon until crisp, pat dry of excess fat on paper towels, and chop into small pieces. Reserve the bacon fat.

Stir the cornmeal into the cold water (always stir cornmeal into cold liquid before adding it to boiling liquid—this keeps the cornmeal from lumping). In a heavy-bottomed saucepan, to the 3 cups boiling water add the salt, pepper, and bay leaf. Stir in the cornmeal and 4 tablespoons bacon fat, lower the heat to medium, and cook, stirring often (as the mixture thickens, be careful not to get too close because the cornmeal will sputter). Cook for about 20 minutes, or until the mixture is no longer runny and thick enough to plop off the spoon.

Remove from the heat and stir in the bacon bits. Oil a medium-size loaf pan and spoon the scrapple into the pan. Let cool, cover, and refrigerate at least 4 hours before pan frying. The mixture must set and become firm.

Cut the loaf into ½-inch slices. Heat a skillet over medium heat with some of the bacon fat, and fry each slice until it is brown and crisp around the edges. Serve hot.

Pumpkin Mush

(three cups)

This Pumpkin Mush, adapted from a recipe by Eliza Leslie in her 1852 cookbook, *New Receipts for Cooking*, is, as she says, "an excellent and wholesome breakfast dish." It combines pumpkin purée, yellow cornmeal, and milk and has a slight ginger flavor. Served hot, with a pat of butter and a spoonful of brown sugar, this is *good*.

2 cups milk	⅓ cup cold water
1 cup puréed pumpkin	¼ teaspoon salt
⅔ cup yellow cornmeal	1 teaspoon ground ginger

Put the milk and pumpkin in a heavy-bottomed saucepan with a lid. Heat, stirring to blend, over medium-low heat.

Put the cornmeal in a small bowl and stir in the cold water (always wet cornmeal with cold water before adding to a hot liquid—this prevents it from getting lumpy). Stir the cornmeal mixture into the milk and pumpkin, and add the salt and ginger. Cook until thickened, stirring every minute or two to keep the mush from burning. (Like all mush, when the mass gets hot it begins to sputter and spurt, so keep the pan partially covered when cooking and remove the pan from the heat to stir to protect yourself from burns.) The mush will be done cooking in only 3 or 4 minutes. Remove from the heat and spoon into bowls. Serve hot. Or serve as fried pumpkin mush, referring to the basic recipe for fried mush on page 82.

Good Grits

(two cups cooked grits)

Many of us Northerners have been awakened late in life to the down-home deliciousness of a bowl of piping hot grits with brown sugar and milk. Grits also make a breakfast pie that is just right for a summer morning.

For variety, try adding ½ cup Grape-Nuts or granola to the cooked grits, or adding 2 tablespoons of yellow cornmeal while cooking.

2 cups water   Optional: butter
Salt to taste
½ cup grits
  (quick-cooking variety)

Bring the water to a boil and add salt. Slowly stir in the grits, and stir for a few seconds more. Turn the heat to medium-low and cover the pan. Cook, stirring once or twice, for 5 minutes. Remove from the heat and stir in a pat of butter, if desired. Serve hot.

Brown Barley

(three cups)

Cooked whole kernel barley has a chewy texture and the compelling taste of field, sun, and rain. The marvels of this grain have escaped me all these years because I always have cooked pearl barley, which is pallid in comparison. Serve yourself a hot bowl of barley with a dot of butter, a sprinkle of brown sugar, and a dash of cream. Make enough to keep and reheat for several days.

3 cups water
Salt to taste
1 cup whole grain barley

Bring the water to a boil and add salt. Stir in the barley, turn the heat to low, and cover the pot. Cook over low heat for about 1 hour to 1 hour and 15 minutes, stirring occasionally and checking for doneness. It should be tender but chewy. Serve hot.

Oats and Oatmeal

In Scotland, where oats are the staple grain, inventive cooks over the centuries have come up with an amazing array of oat dishes. There is porridge, brose (porridge cooked with butter), sowans (fermented oat husks), meal-and-ale (oatmeal cooked up with ale, molasses, and whiskey), hodgils (a kind of oatmeal dumpling), crowdie (raw oatmeal with buttermilk or fresh spring water), to name a few.

Oats make perhaps the best hot cereal because they have more protein than most grains and a high fat content. Porridge made with oatmeal is extremely filling.

Gruel is one oatmeal dish that sounds pitiful and frugal to us, but it was an old-fashioned curative that was supposed to do all kinds of wonderful things for a person. I think it behooves us all to cook up a little gruel once and see how it makes us feel. It is made by pouring 1 cup of cold water over 2 tablespoons of oatmeal. Let stand for 20 minutes, then strain, forcing all the liquid out of the meal and into a pan. Put the pan on the stove and bring to a simmer, adding a bit of butter, honey, or sugar. Sometimes a pinch of nutmeg or a little wine is added.

Rolled Oats

(two servings)

In this country, almost all the oats we eat are rolled oats—steam-treated oats rolled into flakes. You will find regular and quick-cooking kinds in the supermarket. The only difference between the two is the thickness of the oat flake—regular rolled oats are thicker flakes than the quick oats. I prefer the regular kind for its coarser texture.

Try toasting oatmeal before cooking it: spread the oatmeal out on a baking sheet and toast the flakes until they are dark golden. Cook them in the usual way. Toasting the oats gives them a tasty, nutty flavor.

1½ cups boiling water
½ teaspoon salt
⅔ cup rolled oats

Stir the oats into the boiling salted water. If you want creamy oatmeal, cook for about 7 minutes, stirring often. Remove from the heat, cover the pot, and let stand for 5 more minutes.

If you want coarser oatmeal, stir the oatmeal into the boiling water and cook for just 2 minutes, stirring often. Remove from the heat and cover the pot. Let stand for 2 more minutes.

Serve oatmeal with milk or buttermilk, butter, and maple syrup, molasses, or brown sugar. For a nice contrast, sprinkle uncooked oats over cooked oatmeal.

Steel-Cut Oats

(two servings)

Steel-cut oats are oats that have been through a machine that cuts the whole oat kernels into cream-colored tiny bits. Steel-cut oats (sometimes labeled Scotch or Irish oatmeal) are chewy and capture more of the good oat taste than rolled oats. They take longer to cook, but if you are an oat lover, *please* try these.

2½ cups water
¼ teaspoon salt
1 cup steel-cut oats

Mix the water, salt, and oats together in the top of a double boiler. Cook, covered, over simmering water, stirring occasionally, for 1 hour. Remove from the heat and serve.

A delicious way of cooking steel-cut oat porridge is to combine water, salt, and oats and put overnight in a Crock-Pot or in a covered pot in a 225°F oven. In the morning remove the cover. Do not stir, or the oatmeal will lose some of its delicate, translucent creaminess. Carefully spoon the servings into bowls.

Another way of cooking oats is to shake 1 cup of oats into 3 cups of boiling water without stirring, boil for 5 minutes, and remove from the heat. Let the oats sit all night, covered, in a double boiler or in another larger pan in very hot water. In the morning heat the water in the bottom of the double boiler or larger pot, and let the oatmeal get hot for about 15 minutes. (You won't recognize rolled oats cooked in this way. They become jellylike rather than pasty, and their flavor is more distinctly oaty.)

Steel-cut oats cooked overnight with brown sugar stirred in in the morning, and with yogurt flavored with lemon zest (see page 285) spooned over, make a fine meal.

When serving oatmeal, the Scots insist on providing a bowl of cold rich milk or cream on the side; the porridge eater is supposed to take a spoonful of hot cereal and cool it off in the cold milk before guiding it to his mouth. Serving hot milk over hot cereal is unpardonable in Scotland.

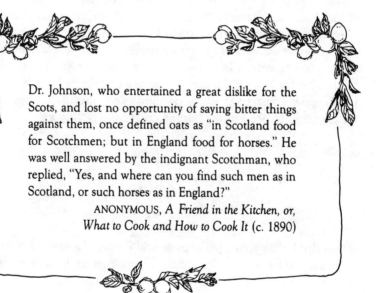

Dr. Johnson, who entertained a great dislike for the Scots, and lost no opportunity of saying bitter things against them, once defined oats as "in Scotland food for Scotchmen; but in England food for horses." He was well answered by the indignant Scotchman, who replied, "Yes, and where can you find such men as in Scotland, or such horses as in England?"

ANONYMOUS, *A Friend in the Kitchen, or,*
What to Cook and How to Cook It (c. 1890)

COLD CEREALS

Completely cooked, ready-to-eat cold cereals are the invention of a band of nineteenth-century health food enthusiasts centered in a sanatorium in Battle Creek, Michigan. They shredded, baked, rolled, and puffed various grains, and started the breakfast cereal industry that is still going strong today.

The best cold cereals, and the best healthy buys, are the plain old basics invented long ago: shredded wheat, Grape-Nuts, Cheerios—and any other whole grain cereals with a short list of ingredients on the box and little or no added sugar and salt. I have never been crazy about cold cereals for breakfast, but for people who love air and crunch they are hard to beat. Just buy them plain and basic and sweeten them yourself—it's economical *and* healthy. I like to eat shredded wheat sometimes—I toast it up in the oven for a few minutes and serve it warm with a little butter. Cornflakes are good toasted, too. Cornflakes are also good crumbled up as a coating for French toast (see J.B.'s French Toast, page 40), in puddings and custards, and as a lining for pie shells to prevent the bottom crust from getting soggy.

Granola

(about five cups)

If you think that your own granola will be just the same as what you can buy, you have to try this recipe. The gain in fresh flavor is tremendous and the cost is about a third of store-bought granola.

4 cups mixed flakes
   (oats, rye, barley, wheat, rice)
Salt to taste
1 teaspoon nutmeg

$\frac{1}{2}$ cup honey
$\frac{1}{2}$ cup (1 stick) butter, melted
1 cup roughly chopped walnuts

Put the flakes in a large bowl and sprinkle with a little salt and the nutmeg. In a small bowl, stir the honey into the butter and blend well. Pour the honey syrup over the flakes and toss until they are well coated.

Spread the mixture on foil in a single layer on a baking sheet. Bake in a preheated 300°F oven for about 20 to 30 minutes, or until the flakes begin to look golden, turning the cereal every 10 minutes with a spoon or a spatula. Be careful not to overbake. The flakes will seem a little sticky when done, but they will crisp as they cool. Stir in the walnuts after baking. Store the granola in plastic bags or an airtight container. Use within a month or store in the freezer.

Unsweetened Granola

(about five cups)

Unsweetened granola has its place. I find that it is more versatile than the sweetened kind. I use it all the time in yeast breads and muffins, and over fruit.

4 cups flakes (oats, rye, barley, wheat, and rice—either all of one kind or mixed)	½ cup safflower oil
	Optional: 1 teaspoon nutmeg; 2 teaspoons grated orange zest
1¼ teaspoons salt	1 cup walnuts

Preheat the oven to 300°F.

Combine the flakes, salt, oil, nutmeg, and orange zest in a large bowl. Toss so that the ingredients are well mixed.

Spread the coated flakes on a baking sheet. Bake about 20 to 30 minutes, turning and stirring the flakes around every 10 minutes. Don't overbake—the cereal is done when it is golden all over. The flakes will seem slightly sticky when first removed from the oven, but they become crisp as they cool. Add the walnuts. Store tightly covered or in plastic bags.

Four-Grain Toasted Cereal with Bananas and Pecans

(about five cups)

This granola recipe is a specialty of Bridge Creek Restaurant, the popular Berkeley, California, breakfast establishment.

1 cup each of the following flakes: oats, rye, barley, wheat	1/2 cup safflower oil
1/3 cup sugar	Salt to taste
1 teaspoon nutmeg	1 cup broken pecans
	Sliced banana to taste

Preheat the oven to 300°F.

Toss the flakes together in a large bowl until they are mixed.

Stir together the sugar, nutmeg, oil, and salt in a small saucepan. Place over medium heat and stir until the sugar dissolves. Pour the sugar mixture over the flakes and toss until each flake is coated.

Spread the flakes in an even layer on a large baking sheet. Bake for about 20 to 30 minutes, turning the flakes every 10 minutes with a spoon or spatula. Be careful not to overbake; the cereal is done when it is slightly golden. The flakes may seem slightly sticky when they are first removed from the oven, but they become crisp as they cool. Mix in the pecans and serve with sliced banana. Store in an airtight container.

Original Bircher Muesli

(one serving)

Muesli is a Swiss word that means mush. Back in 1895, a Dr. Bircher-Benner invented this combination of fruit and cereal and demonstrated its nutritional value when he successfully treated children with rickets by feeding them Bircher muesli three times a day. It is delicious with fresh strawberries, raspberries, or loganberries in season; and any time of year you can add raisins and chopped hazelnuts and almonds.

1 heaping tablespoon rolled oats
3 tablespoons water
1 tablespoon cream
1 tablespoon honey

1 tablespoon lemon juice
1 small apple
1 tablespoon blackberries

Soak the oats and water in a small bowl overnight.

Just before serving, stir the cream, honey, and lemon juice into the oat mixture. Grate the unpeeled apple and quickly mix into the oats. Add the blackberries. Serve with brown sugar and cream.

Muesli Ballymaloe

(about eight cups)

This is a good recipe from the Allens at Ballymaloe Cooking School in County Cork, Ireland.

8 large shredded wheat biscuits,
   crumbled
2 cups rolled oats
$\frac{1}{2}$ cup bran
$\frac{3}{4}$ cup wheat germ

$\frac{1}{2}$ cup raisins
$\frac{1}{3}$ cup nuts
2 tablespoons lecithin
   (available in health food stores)
$\frac{1}{2}$ cup brown sugar

Put all the ingredients in a large bowl, toss, and mix. Store in an airtight jar.

Serve in the Swiss way, by soaking the muesli first in yogurt, milk, or cream, grating apples into it, and adding lots of berries or other fruit; or serve as you would any cold cereal, with milk.

Doughnuts and Fritters

Raised Doughnuts
    Jelly Doughnuts or Berlins
Doughnut Glaze
Baked Doughnuts
Buttermilk Breakfast Doughnuts
Dewey Buns
Fruit Fritters
Calas

Homemade doughnuts and fritters have their very own marvelous character, totally unlike anything you can buy out and about. If you've never known the glory of fresh homemade doughnuts and fritters, with their outside crispness and inside buttery rich crumb, get a deep-fat thermometer (the only special piece of equipment you need) and give it a try. Frying at home is a bit of a luxury because you really have to use fresh fat or oil every time: no matter how you try to clarify it, used fat tastes tired. But you shouldn't miss out on giving friends and family (and, most especially, yourself) the opportunity to taste hot, freshly fried doughnuts.

For those with an incurable fear of frying, this chapter has a recipe for wonderful oven-baked doughnuts; but frying is much simpler than you might think. You can fry doughnuts in quite a small amount of fat—a depth of an inch to an inch and a half is plenty in a skillet. You'll have to make one or two test doughnuts before you really get the hang of it—just to know whether you're cooking them too fast or too slowly.

Raised Doughnuts

(about thirty doughnuts)

This is a dough you'll be glad to meet. It is soft and easy to handle, and it turns out light, airy doughnuts.

$\frac{1}{3}$ cup milk, warmed	2 eggs
1 package dry yeast	4 cups all-purpose flour,
1 cup water	approximately
$\frac{1}{4}$ cup vegetable shortening	$1\frac{1}{2}$ teaspoons salt
$\frac{1}{2}$ cup sugar plus about 1 cup	$1\frac{1}{4}$ teaspoons mace
sugar for sprinkling	Vegetable oil for frying

Put the warm milk in a mixing bowl and add the yeast; stir and let dissolve for about 5 minutes.

Put the water in a small saucepan and bring to a boil. Add the shortening and $\frac{1}{2}$ cup sugar, stir until they have dissolved, and remove from the heat. When the water mixture has cooled to warm, add to the yeast mixture. Stir in the eggs and 2 cups flour. Beat well. Add 2 more cups flour and the salt and mace. Stir until well mixed. Add only enough more flour to make a manageable dough; it should be very soft. Turn onto a lightly floured board and knead until smooth and elastic. Place in a large greased bowl, cover, and let rise until double in bulk.

Punch down and put the dough on a lightly floured surface. Roll it out $\frac{1}{2}$ inch thick, and then cut out the doughnuts using a 2-inch cutter. Place the doughnuts on a piece of waxed paper or greased baking sheet about 1 inch apart. Let rise until light, about 1 hour.

Heat the oil to between 365°F and 375°F. Fry only about 3 doughnuts at a time—don't crowd the pan. Fry until golden on each side. Remove and pat free of excess oil on paper towels. Roll in the remaining 1 cup of sugar. Or let cool and coat with a sugar glaze.

Jelly Doughnuts or Berlins   Roll out the dough 1/4 inch thick. Cut out 2- or 2 1/2-inch rounds. On half of the rounds put about 1/2 teaspoon jelly. Beat 1 egg white just until it is slightly foamy. Brush the beaten egg white around the edges of all the rounds, cover each round with jelly on it with a plain round, and seal together, pinching the edges. Proceed to fry as directed on page 98. Dust with confectioners' sugar after patting dry of any excess oil.

Doughnut Glaze

(covers a dozen doughnuts)

Mix 2 cups confectioners' sugar with 1/3 cup hot water. Stir until smooth. Put the glaze in a shallow bowl. While the doughnuts are freshly made and hot, dunk all sides of each doughnut in the glaze. If the glaze thickens, thin out with a teaspoon or so of hot water.

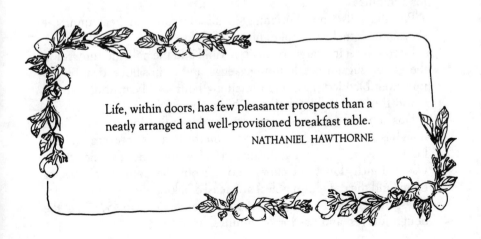

Life, within doors, has few pleasanter prospects than a neatly arranged and well-provisioned breakfast table.
NATHANIEL HAWTHORNE

Baked Doughnuts

(about two dozen doughnuts plus holes)

If you wish to avoid the deep-frying method, baked doughnuts are the ticket. Light and tender, brushed with butter and rolled in cinnamon sugar, from start to finish these take a little under two hours to make. They freeze well.

2 packages dry yeast
$1/3$ cup warm water (105°F)
$1 1/2$ cups milk
$1/3$ cup vegetable shortening
$1/4$ cup sugar
2 teaspoons salt
2 teaspoons nutmeg
  (freshly grated if possible)

2 eggs, lightly beaten
$4 1/2$ cups all-purpose flour,
  approximately
$1/2$ cup (1 stick) butter, melted
1 cup sugar mixed with
  1 teaspoon cinnamon

Sprinkle the yeast over the warm water in a small bowl and let dissolve for 5 minutes.

Put the milk and shortening in a saucepan and heat until the shortening is melted. Cool to lukewarm.

Put the yeast in a large mixing bowl and add the milk mixture, stir in the $1/4$ cup sugar, the salt, nutmeg, eggs, and 2 cups flour. Beat briskly until well blended. Add the remaining flour and beat until smooth. Cover the bowl and let double in bulk, about 1 hour.

Dust a board generously with flour and turn the dough onto it. This dough is soft and needs enough flour on the board to prevent sticking, but it is easy to handle. Pat the dough into a circle about $1/2$ inch thick. Use a 3-inch doughnut cutter and cut out the doughnuts, placing them (and the doughnut holes) on greased baking sheets, 1 inch apart. These don't spread much; they rise. Preheat the oven to 450°F. Let the doughnuts rest and rise for 20 minutes, uncovered.

Bake about 10 minutes, or a little longer, until they have a touch of golden brown. Remove from the oven. Have ready the melted butter and a brush. On a sheet of waxed paper spread the cinnamon sugar. Brush each doughnut and doughnut hole with butter and roll in the cinnamon sugar. Serve hot.

Buttermilk Breakfast Doughnuts

(about two dozen doughnuts)

These doughnuts are lightly spiced, round and fat, crisp on the outside and tender on the inside.

$\frac{1}{4}$ cup vegetable shortening
1 cup sugar plus sugar for
   sprinkling
2 eggs
$\frac{3}{4}$ cup buttermilk
$3\frac{1}{2}$ cups all-purpose flour
2 teaspoons baking powder

1 teaspoon baking soda
$\frac{1}{2}$ teaspoon cinnamon
$\frac{1}{2}$ teaspoon mace
$\frac{1}{2}$ teaspoon nutmeg
$1\frac{1}{2}$ teaspoons salt
Oil for frying

Put the shortening and 1 cup sugar in a large mixing bowl and beat to blend. Add the eggs and beat well. Add the buttermilk and blend.

Put the flour, baking powder, baking soda, cinnamon, mace, nutmeg, and salt in a mixing bowl and stir with a fork until all the ingredients are well mixed. Add the flour mixture all at once to the shortening mixture and beat just until mixed.

Lightly flour a board and turn out the dough. Roll out the dough $\frac{1}{2}$ inch thick. Cut the doughnuts out with a $2\frac{1}{2}$- to 3-inch doughnut cutter and place on a sheet of waxed paper. Reroll the scraps and cut out more doughnuts until you run out of dough.

Heat the oil to between 365°F and 375°F. Drop 3 or 4 doughnuts into the hot oil—don't crowd the pan. Fry each side about 2 minutes and turn over with a slotted spoon or wire skimmer. Remove and place on paper towels. Pat to remove any excess oil, and sprinkle sugar over the doughnuts.

Dewey Buns

(eighteen buns)

Dewey Buns are plump squares of light dough filled with vanilla cream. A Dewey Bun business could make someone rich.

1 cup milk, warmed	*Dewey Cream*
$1/3$ cup granulated sugar	1 egg white
1 teaspoon salt	$2\,1/2$ cups confectioners' sugar
$1/4$ cup vegetable oil	4 tablespoons ($1/2$ stick) butter,
3 cups all-purpose flour	room temperature
1 package dry yeast	1 tablespoon nonfat dry milk
$3/4$ teaspoon nutmeg	(this stabilizes the cream)
1 egg	1 tablespoon vanilla extract
Oil for frying	$1/4$ teaspoon salt
	$1/2$ cup heavy cream
	Confectioners' sugar for dusting

Mix the warm milk with the sugar, salt, and oil and stir to blend.

Stir together 2 cups flour, dry yeast, and nutmeg in a mixing bowl. Add the milk mixture and beat for about 3 minutes. Add the egg and remaining 1 cup flour and beat for 2 minutes. Cover and refrigerate for 4 to 8 hours, or overnight.

Lightly dust a board with flour and turn the dough onto it. Roll the dough into a rectangle about $1/4$ inch thick. Cut the dough into squares that are $2\,1/2$ by 3 inches. Heat oil to about 365°F. Fry the squares, a few at a time, until golden on both sides (it takes about 1 minute on each side). Put the buns on paper towels and pat free of excess oil.

Make the Dewey Cream by putting the egg white, confectioners' sugar, and butter in a mixing bowl. With an electric mixer, beat 3 minutes on high speed, until smooth. Stir the nonfat dry milk, vanilla, and salt into the cream and add to the sugar mixture. Beat until smooth and creamy.

To assemble and fill the buns, cut them in half lengthwise and, using a spoon, scoop out a small shallow pocket from the inside of one of the halves. The pocket should be large enough to hold 1½ tablespoons filling. Fill with Dewey Cream and thinly spread the cream out to the edges. Put the two halves together and gently press the bun edges so that the halves will bind. Sift confectioners' sugar over each side of the bun.

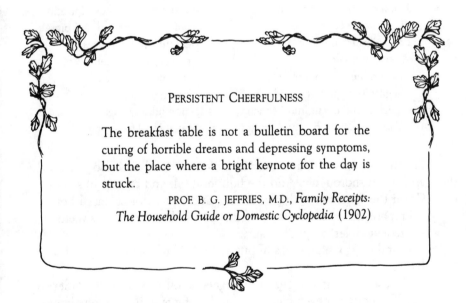

PERSISTENT CHEERFULNESS

The breakfast table is not a bulletin board for the curing of horrible dreams and depressing symptoms, but the place where a bright keynote for the day is struck.

PROF. B. G. JEFFRIES, M.D., *Family Receipts:*
The Household Guide or Domestic Cyclopedia (1902)

Fruit Fritters

(six servings)

Fruit Fritters are special. One doesn't make them often and they are not easily found in shops or restaurants, except in New Orleans, where they are called beignets. Fruit Fritters are pieces of fresh fruit dipped in fritter batter, fried to a golden crispness, and sprinkled with confectioners' sugar. Eaten hot, they are wonderful. Most fresh fruits make good fritters. Fruit Fritters are sometimes served with a little maple syrup.

1 egg, separated
3 tablespoons vegetable oil
¾ cup flat beer
1 cup all-purpose flour
½ teaspoon salt
Any combination of the follow-
    ing fruits: apples, ripe and firm,
    peeled, cored, cut into ¼-inch
    slices; bananas, ripe and firm,

peeled, cut into ½-inch slices;
    apricots or peaches, ripe and
    rather firm, peeled and pitted,
    cut into ½-inch slices;
    pineapple, rind removed,
    cut into ½-inch slices,
    2 inches long
Lemon juice or sugar
Vegetable oil for frying

Put the egg yolk, oil, and beer in a blender, food processor, or bowl and blend thoroughly. Add the flour and salt and beat until smooth. Cover the container with plastic wrap and let rest for at least 1 hour.

Prepare the fruit and taste. If the fruit lacks tartness or sweetness, sprinkle with lemon juice or sugar.

Beat the egg white until stiff but moist. Fold the white into the fritter batter.

Heat approximately 1½ cups vegetable oil in a 10-inch skillet to 370°F. Gently pat each piece of fruit dry of lemon juice or any liquid. Dip each piece of fruit in the batter to coat completely, and put it into the hot oil. If the batter becomes dark brown within a few seconds, remove the skillet from the heat and turn the heat down a little. Cook about 20 seconds, turn the fritter over with a slotted spoon, and cook another 20 seconds, until golden.

Pat the fritters dry of oil on paper toweling, and sprinkle with confectioners' sugar. Keep the fritters warm in a 250°F oven until you have fried enough to serve. You may have to fry a few fritters before they are satisfactory—that is, until you get the hang of it.

Calas

(approximately thirty-two 3-inch fritters)

Calas are a classic rice fritter from New Orleans. Generations ago in the French Quarter, the black Creole cala women would walk through the streets in the morning with large covered bowls on their heads filled with the hot fritters, calling out, "Belles calas!"

1½ cups water
½ cup long grain white rice
1 teaspoon salt, approximately
½ cup warm water (105°F)
2 packages dry yeast
3 eggs
⅓ cup sugar

Optional: 1 teaspoon grated
   lemon zest
1 teaspoon nutmeg
1½ cups all-purpose flour
Vegetable oil for frying
Confectioners' sugar for sprinkling

Bring the 1½ cups water to a boil. Stir in the rice and salt, lower the heat, cover the pot, and cook for about 25 minutes, longer than you usually cook rice, so the rice will be mushy. If there is any liquid left in the rice, drain well. Mash the rice with a fork.

Put the ½ cup warm water in a bowl, sprinkle the yeast over, stir, and let dissolve for 5 minutes. Add the yeast to the lukewarm rice, stir well, cover with plastic wrap, and let stand overnight.

Put the eggs in a bowl and beat well. Beat in the sugar, optional lemon zest, nutmeg, and 1 cup flour. Add the mixture to the rice mixture and beat well for 2 minutes. Add the remaining ½ cup flour and beat well. Taste and add more salt if needed. Cover the bowl and let rise for 30 minutes.

Into a large sauté pan pour vegetable oil to about $1\frac{1}{2}$ inches deep and heat to about 370°F. Drop the batter by heaping tablespoons into the hot oil. I find that you have to make 2 or 3 calas in order to adjust the temperature of the oil. At too high a temperature, they will overfry and get too brown on the outside while remaining raw in the center. Too low, and they will absorb too much oil without coloring. Fry a few at a time, without crowding the pan, for about 1 minute on each side, then turn over with a slotted spoon and fry until golden. Remove the calas to paper towels and pat free of excess oil. Sprinkle with confectioners' sugar and keep warm in a 200°F oven. Serve warm.

Griddling

Plain Pancakes
  Fresh Berry
  Fresh Fruit
  Dried Fruit
  Granola or Nut
Buttermilk Pancakes
  Rye Buttermilk
  Whole Wheat Buttermilk
  Yellow Cornmeal Buttermilk
Bridge Creek Heavenly Hots
Don Chappellet's Zeppelin Pancakes
Lemon Pancakes
Ginger Pancakes
Bridge Creek Spiced Quince Pancakes
Banana Oat Cakes
Bridge Creek Oatmeal Pancakes
Thin Yellow Cornmeal Pancakes
Cornmeal Rye Pancakes
Wheat Crumb Pancakes
Buckwheat Pancakes
Brown Rice Pancakes
Baked German Pancake (or Dutch Babies)
Apple Pancake
Sour Milk Pancakes or Waffles
Raised Waffles
Classic Waffles
  Waffles with Fresh Fruit and Berries
  Strawberry Whipped Cream Waffles
  Waffles with Chopped Nuts
  Cornmeal, Buckwheat, or Rye Flour Waffles
Whole Wheat Buttermilk Waffles
Whole Wheat Granola Waffles

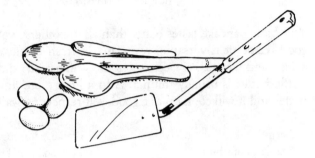

All of the recipes in the griddling family have similar batters, and they are cooked quickly on a very hot surface with very little fat. Time was, every kitchen had a griddle; nowadays most people don't have that extra piece of equipment. But a skillet or frying pan works fine, and a nonstick pan, like an old-fashioned soapstone griddle, requires no fat.

I wonder why pancakes and waffles aren't served at home more often. They certainly are never as good anywhere else, and they are quick and easy to make. Many of these recipes can be prepared the night before or can be assembled very quickly in the morning. Griddlecakes or waffles make a good, sustaining hot breakfast that hits the spot on a cold winter morning, and in the summertime they are great with fresh fruits and berries.

Waffle and pancake batters usually keep well for a couple of days in the refrigerator, but be sure to taste them before use. At refrigerator temperature, batters will thicken somewhat; to thin them out, add a tablespoon or more of milk. They should never be so thick that they aren't pourable and spreadable.

Plain Pancakes

(two dozen 4-inch pancakes)

This basic pancake tastes better than all the others I've tried. Like any good recipe, it is versatile: you can add fresh berries, fruit, granola, spices, and flavors. Pancake batter and waffle batter differ only in that waffle batter is usually thinner. Add a little more liquid to pancake batter and it will cook up as a good, self-respecting waffle.

2 eggs
5 tablespoons butter
1 cup milk
1¼ cups all-purpose flour

1 tablespoon sugar
4 teaspoons baking powder
¾ teaspoon salt

Beat the eggs in a mixing bowl until they are thoroughly blended. Put the butter and the milk in a small saucepan and warm over low heat until the butter has melted. Set aside and allow to cool a little—you don't want to add this mixture to the eggs while it is very hot or it will cook the eggs. Stir the butter mixture into the eggs and mix well. Put the flour, sugar, baking powder, and salt into a bowl and stir with a fork until well mixed.

Pour the egg mixture into the flour mixture and stir only until the dry ingredients are well moistened. Don't overmix.

Heat a griddle or skillet until a few drops of water dance on it, then lightly film with grease. Drop 2 or 3 tablespoons of batter for each pancake onto the griddle (a 12-inch griddle will hold 4 pancakes) and cook until bubbles break on the surface. Turn the pancake over and cook another 30 seconds, or until the bottom is lightly browned. Serve the pancakes hot.

Fresh Berry Pancakes Using 2 cups berries (raspberries, strawberries, blueberries, etc.), make sure they are trimmed, cleaned, cut into the desired size, and ready in a bowl by the griddle. Sprinkle 2 to 3 tablespoons of berries on the top of each pancake after the pancake has cooked to the point where the bubbles are breaking on the top, gently pressing the berries down a trifle with a spatula. Turn the pancake over and finish cooking for about 30 seconds, or until set.

Fresh Fruit Pancakes Use 2 cups of peeled and trimmed fresh fruit (banana, peach, apricot, or orange), cut into small pieces. Follow the directions for Fresh Berry Pancakes.

Dried Fruit Pancakes Use 2 cups of dried fruit (prunes, dates, raisins, pears, apricots, peaches). Put the dried fruit in a bowl and pour boiling water over. Allow to stand for 10 minutes, drain well, and then chop into small pieces. Follow the cooking directions for Fresh Berry Pancakes.

Granola Pancakes or Nut Pancakes Add 1 cup granola (see page 90 for homemade granola) or 1 cup chopped walnuts or pecans to the pancake batter and cook as directed in the basic recipe.

Buttermilk Pancakes

(fourteen 3-inch pancakes)

Among buttermilk pancakes, I don't think you can beat these. They are slightly sourish and light, easy to make, and the batter holds well for several days in the refrigerator.

1 cup buttermilk	¾ cup all-purpose flour
1 egg, room temperature	½ teaspoon salt
3 tablespoons butter, melted	1 teaspoon baking soda

Put the buttermilk, egg, and melted butter in a mixing bowl. Stir briskly until the mixture is smooth and blended.

Stir the flour, salt, and baking soda together in a small bowl so they are well blended. Stir into the buttermilk mixture only until the dry ingredients are moistened—leave the lumps.

Heat a skillet or griddle to medium hot. Grease lightly and spoon out about 3 tablespoons of batter per pancake. Spread the batter with the back of the spoon so it is thinned out a little. Cook until a few bubbles break on top. Turn the pancake over and cook briefly. Keep pancakes warm until enough are cooked to serve.

Rye Buttermilk Pancakes   Use ½ cup all-purpose flour and ¼ cup rye flour.

Whole Wheat Buttermilk Pancakes   Replace up to ½ cup all-purpose flour with an equivalent amount of whole wheat flour.

Yellow Cornmeal Buttermilk Pancakes   Substitute ¼ cup yellow cornmeal for ¼ cup of the flour in the recipe.

All through the year we ate pancakes and maple syrup for breakfast; from November to April these were made of buckwheat, large and rather thick, grayish white inside, and light, reddish brown outside. The rest of the year flour and corn-meal pancakes came to the breakfast table. Pancakes were fried on a long, heavy cast-iron griddle, which stretched across two lids of the kitchen stove. Flour and corn-meal pancakes were smaller in diameter and thinner and lighter in color than those made from buckwheat. One could eat a dozen of the summer brands, whereas a half-dozen of the heavy buckwheat cakes sufficed for a boy. As with the biscuit, we first covered the cakes with butter and then with maple syrup.... The cheery noise of bubbling pancake batter was as plainly heard as the singing teakettle every morning of the year in our house. I often lifted the cover of the batter crock to look at the bubbles, which reminded me of the eyes of animals.

U. P. HEDRICK, *The Land of the Crooked Tree*

Bridge Creek Heavenly Hots

(fifty to sixty dollar-size pancakes)

These are the lightest sour cream silver-dollar-size hotcakes I've ever had—they seem to hover over the plate. They are heavenly and certainly should be served hot.

4 eggs	¼ cup cake flour
½ teaspoon salt	2 cups sour cream
½ teaspoon baking soda	3 tablespoons sugar

Put the eggs in a mixing bowl and stir until well blended. Add the salt, baking soda, flour, sour cream, and sugar, and mix well. All of this can be done in a blender, if you prefer.

Heat a griddle or frying pan until it is good and hot, film with grease, and drop small spoonfuls of batter onto the griddle—just enough to spread to an approximately 2½-inch round. When a few bubbles appear on top of the pancakes, turn them over and cook briefly.

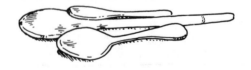

Don Chappellet's Zeppelin Pancakes

(about eighteen 6-inch pancakes)

Don Chappellet, owner of Pritchard Hill Vineyards, perfected this recipe while raising six children for whom he regularly made pancakes on Sunday mornings. I call them zeppelin pancakes because they are very light.

2 eggs, separated
1½ cups buttermilk
½ cup sour cream
¼ cup (½ stick) butter, melted

1 cup all-purpose flour
¾ teaspoon baking soda
½ teaspoon salt

Mix together the egg yolks, buttermilk, and sour cream in a large bowl until well blended. Add the butter and stir until just mixed. Add the flour, baking soda, and salt. Beat until smooth. Beat the egg whites until stiff but still moist. Gently stir the whites into the batter.

When your griddle or frying pan is moderately hot, film with grease and spoon on about ⅓ cup of batter per pancake (these can be made larger or smaller). Turn them over when little bubbles appear on top and cook briefly on the other side.

This batter keeps well in the refrigerator for several days; it will, however, lose a little of its airiness, so just stir in another beaten egg white before using.

Lemon Pancakes

(twelve 3-inch pancakes)

These pancakes make you sit up and take notice. Serve them with fresh raspberries or raspberry syrup and you will have a summer morning special.

3 eggs, separated	2 tablespoons sugar
1/4 cup all-purpose flour	1/4 teaspoon salt
3/4 cup cottage cheese	1 tablespoon grated lemon zest
1/4 cup (1/2 stick) butter, melted	

Separate the eggs and beat the egg whites until they hold stiff peaks. In another bowl, stir together the egg yolks, flour, cottage cheese, butter, sugar, salt, and lemon zest until well mixed. (I use the rotary egg beater I used for beating the egg whites.)

With a large spoon or a spatula, fold the egg whites into the yolk mixture. Gently stir until there are no yellow or white streaks.

Heat a skillet or griddle over medium heat. Grease lightly and spoon out about 3 large tablespoons of batter for each pancake. Cook slowly for about 1 1/2 minutes, then turn the pancake over and cook about 30 seconds. Keep the pancakes warm in a 250°F oven until ready to serve.

Ginger Pancakes

(about two dozen 3-inch pancakes)

There is no mistaking the ginger flavor in these unusual pancakes. Everyone will remember them and ask for them again. Ginger pancakes are at their best served with Green Mango Fool (see page 177).

$1\frac{1}{2}$ cups all-purpose flour
1 tablespoon ground ginger
$\frac{1}{2}$ teaspoon salt
1 teaspoon baking soda

3 tablespoons butter, melted
$1\frac{1}{4}$ cups buttermilk
1 egg, lightly beaten

Combine the flour, ginger, salt, and baking soda in a mixing bowl. Stir with a fork until the dry ingredients are well mixed. Add the melted butter, buttermilk, and egg all at once and stir only until the batter is completely moistened but still lumpy.

Heat a greased griddle or skillet over medium heat. Using a serving spoon, drop approximately $1\frac{1}{2}$ tablespoons batter onto the griddle— this batter is thick, so spread it a little with the back of the spoon after you have dropped each portion onto the griddle. Cook over medium heat, and turn the pancakes as soon as they hold together when you slide a spatula under them.

Keep the pancakes warm in a low oven until you have made enough to serve, or use the time-honored system of cooking pancakes for all present and doing yours last—in other words, serve as you go.

Bridge Creek Spiced Quince Pancakes

(about two dozen pancakes)

Raw quinces have a rather harsh and almost puckery taste. Stewing them in water and sugar removes that characteristic and brings out their spicy flavor. Enjoy these delectable pancakes for that short time in the autumn when quinces are available—everyone will wonder what the elusive flavor is.

Stewed quince purée
2 large quinces
1/2 cup water
1/4 cup sugar

Batter
1 cup milk
2 tablespoons butter, melted
1 egg
1 cup all-purpose flour
2 teaspoons baking powder
1/4 teaspoon ground ginger
1/4 teaspoon cinnamon
1/4 teaspoon salt

To prepare the quince purée, peel the quinces, remove the cores, then chop the quinces into rough pieces. Place in a saucepan with the water and sugar, cover, and simmer gently for 30 to 40 minutes, until the quinces are tender and the liquid has almost entirely evaporated. Purée in a food processor, or beat with an electric mixer (the mixture should not be perfectly smooth). Allow to cool.

Put the rough purée in a mixing bowl and beat in the milk, butter, and egg. In another bowl, toss together the flour, baking powder, ginger, cinnamon, and salt. Add to the quince mixture and beat until the batter is blended.

Heat a lightly greased skillet over moderate heat. Pour on about 2 tablespoons batter for each pancake, allowing room for them to spread.

Cook until bubbles form on the top and the edges begin to look dry, about 1 minute. If necessary, keep the pancakes warm in a 225°F oven until you have made enough to begin serving.

Banana Oat Cakes

(one dozen pancakes)

I serve these oat cakes with sage sausages, adding a few dates and shelled walnuts to the plate.

About 3 bananas
  (to make 1½ cups, mashed)
¼ teaspoon salt
1½ tablespoons sugar

2 teaspoons lemon juice
1 cup oat flour
  (available in health food stores)
2 tablespoons butter

Put the mashed banana, salt, sugar, and lemon juice in a bowl. Beat until smooth. Stir in the oat flour and blend until smooth.

Heat about 2 tablespoons of butter over low heat in a skillet. From a large spoon, drop about 2 or 3 tablespoons of batter onto the skillet for each pancake. Cook briefly, or until lightly golden on both sides. Serve hot.

Bridge Creek Oatmeal Pancakes

(about twelve 4-inch pancakes)

The buttermilk-soaked oatmeal in these pancakes gives them a nubby texture and an agreeable edge of sourness to their taste. Sometime try using steel-cut oats—they accentuate these qualities. Drizzle a little maple syrup over the top or serve with a helping of warm homemade Applesauce (see page 168) on the side.

2 cups buttermilk	$1/3$ cup whole wheat flour
$2/3$ cup oatmeal	1 teaspoon baking soda
1 egg	$1/2$ teaspoon salt
2 tablespoons brown sugar	2 tablespoons vegetable oil
$1/3$ cup all-purpose flour	

At least 6 hours before making the pancakes, mix the buttermilk and oats together in a bowl. Cover and refrigerate (overnight is fine).

Put the egg in a mixing bowl and beat well, then stir in the brown sugar and blend. Add the flours, baking soda, salt, oil, and the oatmeal-buttermilk mixture. Stir until thoroughly mixed.

Heat a griddle or skillet until it is good and hot, then film with grease. Drop the batter by tablespoons (about $2\frac{1}{2}$ per pancake) onto the griddle and cook until lightly browned on each side.

Thin Yellow Cornmeal Pancakes

(two dozen 3-inch pancakes)

These light and tasty pancakes become stellar when served with Salsa Verde (see page 284) spooned on top. If you are serving the cornmeal pancakes with Salsa Verde, eliminate the sugar in the recipe.

$\frac{1}{2}$ cup yellow cornmeal
$\frac{1}{2}$ cup boiling water
$\frac{1}{2}$ cup all-purpose flour
$\frac{1}{2}$ teaspoon salt
1 tablespoon sugar

1 tablespoon baking powder
1 egg, beaten
$\frac{1}{4}$ cup ($\frac{1}{2}$ stick) butter, melted
$\frac{1}{2}$ cup milk

Put the cornmeal in a mixing bowl and pour the boiling water over, stirring briskly until well blended. Add the flour, salt, sugar, baking powder, the well-beaten egg, the melted butter, and the milk. Beat the batter until it is thoroughly mixed.

Heat the griddle over medium-high heat (don't cook these pancakes over as high a heat as you would normally use). Film the griddle with grease when it is hot. Use 2 tablespoons batter for each pancake. Cook until bubbles break on top of the pancakes and turn them over. Cook another few minutes, or until the bottoms of the pancakes are lightly browned and set. Serve hot.

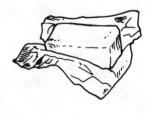

Cornmeal Rye Pancakes

(about a dozen 4-inch pancakes)

These pancakes have lots of taste and crunch — rye flour and cornmeal mixed with buttermilk do the trick. Maple syrup was invented for them.

1 cup yellow cornmeal	$\frac{1}{2}$ teaspoon baking soda
$\frac{1}{2}$ cup rye flour	3 tablespoons butter, melted
1 teaspoon salt	2 cups buttermilk

Mix the cornmeal, rye flour, salt, and baking soda together in a large mixing bowl. Stir in the butter and buttermilk, and mix until blended.

Heat a griddle to medium hot and film with grease. Spoon on about 2 tablespoons batter for each pancake. Cook until a few bubbles form on top, turn the pancakes over, and cook until the bottoms are lightly browned. Serve hot.

Wheat Crumb Pancakes

(about a dozen 5-inch pancakes)

Milk-soaked whole wheat bread crumbs make these pancakes light and wheaty-tasting — such a simple procedure for such a good pancake.

$1\frac{1}{2}$ cups fresh whole wheat bread crumbs (from about 2 slices bread)	2 eggs, lightly beaten
	$\frac{1}{2}$ cup all-purpose or whole wheat flour
$1\frac{1}{2}$ cups milk	$\frac{1}{2}$ teaspoon salt
2 tablespoons butter	2 teaspoons baking powder

Put the crumbs in a mixing bowl. Heat the milk and butter until the butter melts and the milk is hot. Pour over the crumbs and let soak for about 5 minutes.

Add the eggs, flour, salt, and baking powder to the crumb mixture and stir until blended.

Heat a griddle or frying pan and then film it with grease. Drop about 2 tablespoons batter on the hot griddle and cook until bubbles appear on the pancakes. Turn them over and allow to brown on the bottom. Keep the pancakes warm in a 225°F oven until enough are cooked to serve.

Buckwheat Pancakes

(about three dozen 3-inch pancakes)

In the wintertime, after the buckwheat crop was in, raised buckwheat pancakes replaced cornmeal and flour pancakes on the breakfast tables of frontier America. Buckwheat has a rustic, nutty flavor that tastes almost primitive to me. Plan ahead when you want to make Buckwheat Pancakes, because they are yeast leavened and take an hour or two to rise (or leave the batter overnight in the refrigerator). Serve with butter and maple syrup, or as they do in Russia (where buckwheat pancakes are called blinis), with caviar and sour cream.

½ cup warm water	¾ cup all-purpose flour
1 package dry yeast	2 eggs
½ teaspoon sugar	3 tablespoons butter, melted
1 cup milk, warmed	3 tablespoons sour cream
1½ teaspoons salt	1 tablespoon lemon juice
¾ cup buckwheat flour	

Put the warm water in a large mixing bowl and sprinkle the yeast and sugar over it. Stir and let stand 5 minutes to dissolve.

Add the milk, salt, and ¼ cup buckwheat flour and ¼ cup all-purpose flour. Stir briskly to blend. Cover with plastic wrap and let stand until the batter has doubled in bulk. It will be bubbly and very thin. The rising may take 1 to 2 hours, depending on how warm the room is.

Stir the batter and add the remaining $\frac{1}{2}$ cup buckwheat flour and $\frac{1}{2}$ cup all-purpose flour, eggs, butter, and sour cream. Stir until the batter is smooth. If time allows, let the batter rest again for an hour or so. At this point, you may refrigerate overnight.

Heat a griddle or skillet. Add the lemon juice to the batter and stir to blend. Ladle about 1 tablespoon batter to form a 3-inch pancake. Cook until small bubbles appear on top, turn the pancake over, and cook until the bottom is lightly browned. Serve warm.

Brown Rice Pancakes

(two dozen 3-inch pancakes)

These light, airy pancakes will please anyone who loves rice custards. If you use brown basmati rice, your pancakes will have a distinctive, delicious taste.

2 eggs, separated	3 tablespoons all-purpose flour
$\frac{1}{2}$ cup cooked brown rice	1 tablespoon butter, melted
$\frac{1}{2}$ cup milk	Optional: $\frac{1}{2}$ cup golden raisins
$\frac{1}{4}$ teaspoon salt	

Put the egg yolks in a mixing bowl and beat until light. Stir in the rice, milk, salt, flour, and melted butter. Beat until well mixed.

In another bowl, beat the egg whites until stiff but moist. Gently fold the whites into the yolk mixture. Gently stir in the optional raisins at this point.

Film a hot griddle or the bottom of a hot skillet with a little vegetable oil. Stir the batter and drop about 1 tablespoon of batter per pancake onto the griddle or into the skillet. Cook the pancakes over medium-high heat until golden on the bottom, and turn them over gently (these pancakes *are* slightly delicate, but easy to manage), then cook until the other side is golden. The rice in the batter settles to the bottom of the bowl, so be sure to stir the batter before making more pancakes.

Baked German Pancake (or Dutch Babies)

(one 12-inch Baked German Pancake or four 6-inch Dutch Babies)

This is not a griddled pancake at all, but an eggy batter baked in the oven, like Yorkshire pudding or popovers. A baked German pancake (small ones are called *Dutch* babies for some reason) is dramatic and captivating for children. You wouldn't believe what three eggs can do when beaten with milk and flour—this mixture billows up to unbelievable heights and turns golden. The pancake should be sprinkled with lemon juice and confectioners' sugar and served quickly while hot and high and mighty.

3 eggs, room temperature	2 tablespoons butter, melted
1/2 cup milk	2 tablespoons lemon juice
1/2 cup all-purpose flour	Confectioners' sugar
1/2 teaspoon salt	

Preheat the oven to 450°F. Butter one 12-inch skillet or four 6-inch small skillets (with ovenproof handles) or pans (you can use small pie pans or cake pans).

Break the eggs into a mixing bowl and beat until thoroughly mixed. Add the milk and blend well.

Sift the flour and salt onto a square of waxed paper. Lift the waxed paper up by two corners and let the flour slowly drift into the egg and milk, whisking steadily. Or slowly sift the flour and salt directly into the egg mixture, while whisking to blend and smooth. Add the melted butter and mix briskly so the batter is smooth.

Pour the batter into the pan or pans and bake for 15 minutes at 450°F. If you are baking small pancakes, they will be done after 15 minutes. If you are baking just one big pancake, reduce the heat to 350°F and bake another 10 minutes.

Sprinkle the lemon juice over the pancake (or pancakes) and dust the top(s) with confectioners' sugar. Serve at once.

Apple Pancake

(one puffy 10-inch pancake)

This combination of apples cooked in butter and a great big fluffy baked pancake is more exciting than an apple tart.

6 tablespoons ($3/4$ stick) butter
2 large apples, peeled, cored, and
   sliced (McIntoshes are good)
3 tablespoons lemon juice
$1/4$ teaspoon cinnamon
About 5 tablespoons
   confectioners' sugar (depending
   on the sweetness of the apples)

3 eggs, room temperature
$1/4$ teaspoon salt
$1/2$ cup all-purpose flour
$1/2$ cup milk

Preheat the oven to 425°F.

Melt the butter in a 10-inch skillet or shallow pan and take off heat. If the handle of the skillet is not ovenproof, wrap it with several layers of foil. Remove 2 tablespoons melted butter and set aside in a small bowl.

Put the apple slices in a large bowl with the lemon juice. Stir the cinnamon into the sugar and sprinkle the sugar mixture over the apple slices. Toss to mix. Put the skillet back on the burner and turn the heat to medium. Add the apples and cook, stirring often, for about 3 or 4 minutes, or until the apples are tender but still hold their shape.

In a separate bowl (or blender, or food processor) combine the eggs, salt, flour, milk, and the reserved 2 tablespoons melted butter. Beat until smooth. Spread the apples evenly over the bottom of the skillet and pour the batter on top. Bake for about 20 minutes, or until golden and puffy. Turn immediately onto a warm platter so the apples are on top. Dust with a little confectioners' sugar and serve at once.

The season of buckwheat cakes has arrived. With buckwheat cakes, country-made sausages, a delicate roll or two, and a cup of Mocha coffee, with cream, one can make a very comfortable breakfast. But the cakes must be light, nicely browned, and hot from the griddle; then eaten with plenty of fresh, golden-hued butter, — and, for those who are not particular about the flavor of their coffee, a spoonful or two of refined syrup may be added; and, for my part, I am sorely tempted, I confess, to use maple-syrup, — and you have a dish good enough for any one. The sausages, too, must be well cooked; if they incline to be a little crispy, reminding one just a trifle of the cracklings of roasted pig, it is not amiss. You should be cautious though, as to where you obtain your sausages; if you have ever so slight an acquaintance with the woman who makes them, it is well, provided you have confidence in her. Confidence in your sausage-maker is an excellent thing. One of the best ways for possessing this confidence is to have your sausages prepared in your own house, with materials furnished by yourself.

BARRY GRAY, *Out of Town, A Rural Episode* (1867)

Sour Milk Pancakes or Waffles

(about two dozen 3-inch pancakes or about ten waffles)

Both pancakes and waffles made with this batter are light and tender. Sour milk adds a slightly sour taste that is quite good with sweet maple syrup. Sour the milk by adding 1 tablespoon white vinegar to every cup of milk, then stir and let stand for 10 minutes.

2 eggs, separated
2 cups sour milk (see above)
2 cups all-purpose flour
1 tablespoon sugar

1 teaspoon salt
1½ teaspoons baking soda
½ cup (1 stick) butter, melted

Put the egg yolks in a mixing bowl and beat well. Stir in the sour milk. In another bowl, put the flour, sugar, salt, and baking soda and stir with a fork until well mixed. Add the flour mixture to the yolk mixture and beat until smooth. Stir in the melted butter and mix until well blended.

Beat the egg whites until stiff but still moist. Gently fold the whites into the batter.

Cook as pancakes on a lightly greased hot griddle or skillet, or as waffles in a hot waffle iron. (This is a thin batter, so you do not have to dilute it to use as a waffle batter.)

WAFFLES

It's so drab to just buy a frozen waffle and put it in the toaster, compared to the satisfaction you can get from lifting your own home-made waffles out of a steaming waffle iron. You can take your time and make yeast-risen waffles or you can make quick waffles with baking powder. Waffles are versatile—they are just as good with sausage as they are with fresh strawberries. A friend remembers the special treat of Sunday supper waffles: his mother would serve a waffle covered with liberally peppered creamed hominy, and a dessert waffle would follow with sliced sugared fruit on top.

One minor problem with cooking waffles is that waffle irons vary in size and shape so it's impossible to give specific instructions about the quantity of batter per waffle or the exact yield of these recipes. However, it generally takes ½ to ¾ cup batter to make one waffle.

Raised Waffles

(about eight waffles)

This recipe, from an early Fannie Farmer cookbook, is still the best waffle I know. The mixing is done the night before and all you have to do in the morning is add a couple of eggs and some baking soda. These waffles are very crisp on the outside and delicate on the inside.

½ cup warm water
1 package dry yeast
2 cups milk, warmed
½ cup (1 stick) butter, melted
1 teaspoon salt

1 teaspoon sugar
2 cups all-purpose flour
2 eggs
¼ teaspoon baking soda

Use a rather large mixing bowl—the batter will rise to double its original volume. Put the water in the mixing bowl and sprinkle in the yeast. Let stand to dissolve for 5 minutes.

Add the milk, butter, salt, sugar, and flour to the yeast mixture and beat until smooth and blended (I often use a hand-rotary beater to get rid of the lumps). Cover the bowl with plastic wrap and let stand overnight at room temperature.

Just before cooking the waffles, beat in the eggs, add the baking soda, and stir until well mixed. The batter will be very thin. Pour about $1/2$ to $3/4$ cup batter into a very hot waffle iron. Bake the waffles until they are golden and crisp.

This batter will keep well for several days in the refrigerator.

Classic Waffles

(about eight waffles)

These waffles are crisp, flavorful, and ideal for that spur-of-the-moment breakfast when you haven't had time to make yeast-risen waffles.

2 cups all-purpose flour
1 teaspoon salt
4 teaspoons baking powder
2 tablespoons sugar
2 eggs, room temperature

$1 1/2$ cups milk, warmed slightly
$1/3$ cup vegetable shortening, melted
$1/3$ cup ($2/3$ stick) butter, melted

Put the flour, salt, baking powder, and sugar in a mixing bowl and stir the mixture with a fork until blended.

In another bowl, beat the eggs well and stir in the milk. Combine with the flour mixture until mixed. Add the melted shortening and butter and beat until blended.

Pour about $1/2$ cup batter into a very hot waffle iron. (It takes from $1/2$ to $3/4$ cup of batter to make one waffle, depending on the size of your waffle iron.) Bake the waffles until they are golden and crisp. Serve hot.

Waffles with Fresh Fruit and Berries   Berries of all kinds, fresh sliced peaches, nectarines, apricots, and bananas are all delicious with waffles, but they should not be added to the batter or they can alter and spoil the waffle's texture. Fruits and berries are best served on top of hot, cooked waffles, or on the side of the plate.

Strawberry Whipped Cream Waffles These linger in the minds of many as a Sunday morning treat when the family gathered around the breakfast table. They are traditionally served with lightly sweetened whipped cream piled on top of the hot, cooked waffles. With a mound of strawberries on top, this is a glorious sight.

Waffles with Chopped Nuts It is best to add chopped nuts to waffles when they have nearly finished cooking. Sprinkle about 1/4 cup chopped nuts evenly over the top of the waffle about 30 seconds before it is done.

Cornmeal, Buckwheat, or Rye Flour Waffles Substitute 1/2 cup cornmeal, buckwheat flour, or rye flour for 1/2 cup of the all-purpose flour called for in the basic recipe.

Whole Wheat Buttermilk Waffles

(six to eight waffles)

These waffles are appealing because of their tart, wheaty taste. The perfect complement is warm honey—which becomes thin and pours like syrup when heated.

3/4 cup whole wheat flour	2 tablespoons sugar
3/4 cup all-purpose flour	3 eggs
2 teaspoons baking powder	1 1/2 cups buttermilk
3/4 teaspoon baking soda	3/4 cup (1 1/2 sticks) butter, melted
1/2 teaspoon salt	1/4 cup milk, if needed

Put the flours into a mixing bowl and add the baking powder, baking soda, salt, and sugar. Stir with a fork to blend.

In another mixing bowl, beat the eggs until well blended. Stir in the buttermilk and the melted butter (cooled off a little). Add the flour mixture and stir until well mixed—if the batter seems rather thick, add the $1/4$ cup milk to thin it. The batter should flow from the spoon, not plop.

Bake in a hot waffle iron until crisp and golden. Serve hot.

Whole Wheat Granola Waffles

(ten waffles)

Adding granola makes a chewy, tasty, and substantial waffle that soaks up lots of butter and syrup and is delicious served with sliced bananas or melon. Use your own homemade Granola (see page 90) in these waffles and the flavor will be worlds better.

$1 1/2$ cups granola
   (without raisins or dried fruit)
$1 3/4$ cups milk, plus a few
   tablespoons more if needed
$1/2$ cup (1 stick) butter, melted
2 eggs

$1 1/2$ cups whole wheat flour
1 tablespoon baking powder
$1/2$ teaspoon baking soda
$1/4$ teaspoon salt
Melted shortening or oil,
   if needed

Stir together the granola and milk in a medium-size mixing bowl and allow to stand for 10 to 15 minutes, until the granola has softened.

Beat the melted butter and eggs into the granola-milk mixture. In a separate bowl, stir together the flour, baking powder, baking soda, and salt. Add to the first mixture and beat just until the batter is blended.

Heat the waffle iron and brush lightly with melted shortening or oil, if necessary. Pour in just enough batter ($1/2$ to $3/4$ cup) to barely fill the grids. Close the iron and cook just until the steaming stops and the waffles are golden. If the batter becomes too thick while standing, stir in a tablespoon or two more milk.

Eggs

Soft-Boiled Egg
Coddled Egg
Hard-Boiled Eggs
Goldenrod Eggs
Scalloped Eggs
Scotch Eggs
Chinese Tea Eggs
Fried Eggs
Knothole Eggs
Poached Eggs
Butter-Crumbed Eggs
Huevos Verdes
Eggs Beatrice
Eggs Benedict
Shirred Eggs
   with Cheese, with Ham or Bacon, with Mixed Herbs
Shirred Lemon Eggs
Buttermilk Baked Egg
Scrambled Eggs
   with Ham; with Bacon;
   and Cheese; and Herbs; and Croutons
Crackered Eggs
Omelets
Filled Omelets
   Ham, Apple, Cheese, Bacon,
   Herb, Mushroom, Jelly, Bread and Butter,
   Smoked Salmon, Caviar, Bridge Creek
Puffy Omelets
   Mushroom, Mexican, Ham or Bacon,
   Cheese, Herb, Jelly or Jam
Frittata with Cheese and Crumbs
Featherbed Eggs
   Apple Ham, Fresh Fruit and Cream Cheese
Oatmeal Soufflé
   Oatmeal Bacon
Lemon Zephyrs

I grew up in the small rural foothill town of La Crescenta, California, in the twenties. I was an only child, and my mother was twenty-seven when I was born (which is like being forty-five today). As a result, she was an anxious mother, always sending away for government pamphlets for advice on how to feed me. One of the things the pamphlets said was that an egg and a glass of goat's milk were perfect whole foods for a growing child. So my father had to get a goat to join the chickens we already kept.

I still love eggs. And if I'm going to have one small thing for breakfast, I cook one egg until it's almost hard, shell it, and have it with lots of pepper on it. I can eat only one hard-boiled egg, but if I'm soft-boiling them I do it by twos, mash them up in a bowl, sprinkle salt over them and a little bit of pepper, and eat them with toast—and that suffices for hours. Where is it written in stone that we always have to be served two eggs cooked the same way? I sometimes serve one buttercrumbed poached egg with one softly scrambled egg. Eggs really do satisfy those nudging little eleven o'clock hunger pangs like no other breakfast food.

Today eggs are more widely available and cheaper than ever before. And the eggs from our big supermarkets have been stored carefully and are fresher than you probably think they are. Once you get your eggs home, you should put them in the refrigerator and keep them there—eggs can deteriorate as much in one day at room temperature as they would in a week in the refrigerator.

It is easy to cook eggs properly if you follow a couple of basic guidelines. With few exceptions, eggs should be cooked slowly, and over low heat, because both egg white and egg yolk coagulate at well below the temperature of boiling water. When cooking an egg in its shell, if you first pierce its large end with an egg-piercing gadget or pushpin, it will help keep the shell from cracking as it cooks. The recipes in this book call for size large eggs, unless otherwise specified.

Soft-Boiled Egg

For a perfect soft-boiled egg, first bring about 4 cups water (enough to cover an egg by at least an inch) to a simmer. Take an egg from the refrigerator, pierce its large end, and lower it with a large spoon into the simmering water. After 3 minutes, half the white will be set and half will be runny and clear. After 4 minutes, two thirds of the white will be set; the rest will be runny. After 5 minutes, the white will be completely set. The yolk will be warm and creamy at each stage. Remove from the water and serve.

Coddled Egg

To coddle an egg, first bring about 4 cups water to a simmer. Take an egg from the refrigerator, pierce its large end, and lower it with a spoon into the simmering water. Remove from the heat, cover the pan, and let it sit for 10 minutes. The white will be delicate and tender.

The breakfast egg was a Victorian institution (only a century old); whatever else there was for breakfast— kidneys, chops, bacon, or kedgeree, with tea or coffee, marmalade or honey— there was always a meek little cluster of boiled eggs, set modestly apart upon a chased silver stand, with their spoons beside them (like St. Ursula's virgins on shipboard).

Really nice homely families kept their little flotilla of breakfast eggs coddled in hot water under a china hen. Many of these hens were beautifully modelled. Our hen is of pure-white china with dull-gold beak, her crimson top-knot is studded with white raised dots, in toadstool pattern, her tail smoothly plumed, and her basket-nest most carefully moulded and touched with gold. She has a pure but friendly eye. There were handsome black hens (like plump matrons in black alpaca). Black hens usually had gold-lustre spots and white wattles. There were naturalistic brown hens on yellow baskets, and rather coarse red-and-white Staffordshire hens on green tub bases.

The bases in all cases held the eggs in hot water, which kept them from going hard and drying up. . . .

Smaller, larger, or less-punctual households had table egg-boilers and "did" their own eggs for themselves as they came down. . . .

"Breakfast trays" and "single gents" had egg-cosies—not today's church-bazaar fancies, but solid thick woollen coats. Cooks today crack the boiled egg on top "to let the steam out," but the old-fashioned idea was to keep the steam in—as a new-laid egg should be steamy and milky within.

According to superstition, empty egg-shells should always be broken up—lest witches make boats thereof.

DOROTHY HARTLEY, *Food in England*

Hard-Boiled Eggs

Take the desired number of eggs from the refrigerator, pierce the large end of each egg with an egg piercer or pushpin, and place them in a saucepan in a single layer. Add enough cold water to completely immerse the eggs to a depth of 1 inch. Bring the water to a boil, reduce the heat, and let simmer for 20 minutes. Remove and place in cold water.

To peel hard-boiled eggs, tap the egg gently all over and crack the shell. Loosen the shell at the larger end and peel it off under running water.

Goldenrod Eggs

(two or three servings)

Goldenrod Eggs are a traditional dish that I learned to make years ago in home economics class (the lesson taught us how to make a cream sauce and how to temper egg yolks). The yolks sieved over the whites are supposed to look like goldenrod. I was very taken with the dish, and once in a blue moon I make it again. It's nutritionally complete, and it's tasty.

4 hard-boiled eggs, shelled	Salt and pepper
2 tablespoons butter	1 raw egg yolk
2 tablespoons flour	2 tablespoons lemon juice
1¼ cups milk (whole or skim)	2 slices buttered toast

Separate the whites and the yolks of the hard-boiled eggs. Dice the whites and set aside. Reserve the yolks.

Put the butter into a small saucepan and melt over medium-low heat. Stir in the flour and cook, stirring constantly, until the butter and flour are well blended; then cook over low heat, stirring, at least 2 minutes more.

Slowly add the milk, stirring constantly, and cook for 5 minutes, stirring until the sauce has thickened. Add salt and pepper to taste. In a small bowl, combine the raw yolk and lemon juice. Stir several tablespoons of the hot sauce into the yolk mixture, then add the yolk mixture to the sauce. Cook another minute or two, until smooth and hot. Add the diced egg whites to the sauce.

Assemble by spooning the sauce over the toast. Using the fine-grating side of a grater or a sieve, rub a yolk or two over each portion. Serve immediately.

Scalloped Eggs

(four servings)

Served with crisp bacon and a baked apple on the side, this makes a good breakfast.

8 tablespoons (1 stick) butter
3 cups bread crumbs
8 hard-boiled eggs, sliced
Salt and pepper to taste

½ teaspoon freshly grated
  (or ground) nutmeg
1½ cups milk

Preheat the oven to 400°F. Butter a round, shallow baking dish; a 9- or 10-inch round glass pie plate would be ideal.

Melt the butter in a large skillet or sauté pan. Add the crumbs and cook over low heat, stirring often until the crumbs are golden and have absorbed the butter.

Spread half of the crumbs evenly over the bottom of the baking dish. Arrange the egg slices over the crumbs. Sprinkle with salt, pepper, and half the nutmeg. Pour the milk evenly over the egg slices and distribute the remaining crumbs evenly over the top. Lightly salt and pepper the top and dust with the rest of the nutmeg. Bake for about 25 minutes. Serve hot.

Scotch Eggs

(eight eggs)

Scotch Eggs are a classic English pub food: hard-boiled eggs encased in sausage, breaded, and deep fried. They are especially wonderful if you use your own sausage meat seasoned with fresh sage and lots of black pepper (see page 197). Buy the smallest eggs you can find—supermarket medium will do. Scotch Eggs are good hot or cold.

3 tablespoons flour	2 eggs, lightly beaten
1 pound sausage meat	8 medium hard-boiled eggs,
1½ cups bread crumbs	shelled
Salt and pepper	Vegetable oil for deep frying

You may do all the preparations the night before and keep the sausage-coated eggs covered in the refrigerator.

Put the flour on a piece of waxed paper or in a shallow dish. Divide the sausage meat into eight pieces. Season the bread crumbs with salt and pepper. Have the beaten eggs and the crumbs in separate shallow dishes.

Roll each hard-boiled egg in flour to coat all over. Flatten each piece of sausage meat in the palm of your hand. Place the egg in the center and press the meat all over the egg. Dip the egg into the beaten eggs and then into the crumbs, rolling the egg to cover all sides.

Use a sauté pan or deep fryer to cook the Scotch Eggs. If you use a sauté pan, fill it with oil 1 inch deep. Heat the oil to 360°F. Slip the coated eggs into the hot oil (don't crowd the pan) and fry until golden on all sides. This will take only a few minutes. Don't let them get dark brown; if the eggs seem to be getting too brown too quickly, take them out and lower the heat, or pull the pan a little off the burner to cool the oil down a bit. Remove and pat dry of oil on paper towels. Serve warm, or refrigerate until needed.

Chinese Tea Eggs

(eight eggs)

These eggs simmer in their shells for an hour and a half so that they become thoroughly infused with the flavors of tea and star anise, and the whites become beautifully marbled. Make Chinese Tea Eggs on those days when you want to try something a little adventurous.

8 hard-boiled eggs	2 tablespoons star anise (available
6 cups water	in Oriental grocery stores), or
3 tablespoons black tea leaves	1 tablespoon anise seeds
(or 4 tea bags)	4 teaspoons salt, approximately

Do not shell the eggs, just lightly tap each one all over to make a network of cracks.

Put the water, tea leaves, star anise, and salt in a saucepan and add the eggs. Bring the liquid to a simmer and cook for 1½ hours. Let the eggs cool in the liquid. They are good warm or cold.

Serve peeled and halved, dome side up, on a bed of hot steamed rice. Surround with wedges of tangerine, lemon, and lime. Squeeze the lemon and lime on the rice and eggs, and pass around a dish with more tangerine wedges.

Fried Eggs

Eggs should be fried with restraint. Fried too fast over high heat, their whites will be tough and rubbery.

Use a heavy, well-seasoned skillet or a nonstick frying pan, large enough so that the eggs aren't crowded. An 8-inch-diameter pan is perfect for two eggs. Heat the pan over medium-low heat. When the pan is hot, add 1 teaspoon butter for each egg and swirl the butter around to coat the bottom. When the butter is melted and starts to foam, carefully crack the eggs into the pan. The white will start to set immediately; make sure it isn't sticking by giving the pan a gentle shake. If necessary, free the egg by sliding a spatula under it. Fried without turning, or *sunny-side-up*, the egg will be done in 3 to 4 minutes; or cover the pan and the egg will be done in 2 to 3 minutes.

For eggs *over easy*, fried on both sides, turn gently with a spatula after 3 to 4 minutes and allow the other side to cook for just a few seconds. For eggs *over hard*, the yolks no longer runny, allow 1 full minute after turning.

For *butter-basted* eggs, use 1 additional tablespoon butter per egg. Proceed as you would for eggs sunny side up, but spoon the extra butter over the top of the eggs as they fry.

Knothole Eggs

(two servings)

A dish to delight a child, but you will smile and relish this, too.

2 slices sandwich bread	2 eggs
2 tablespoons butter	Salt and pepper to taste

Toast the bread lightly. With a circular cutter or a wine glass about 2 inches in diameter, cut a hole out of the center of each slice.

Melt the butter over medium-low heat in a large skillet and put the bread slices side by side in the pan. Crack an egg into each hole, letting the yolk fall into the center. Some of the white will run over the bread and down the side. Turn the heat to low and sprinkle with salt and pepper to taste. Cover the pan and cook gently for 2 or, at the most, 3 minutes, until the whites are barely set. Serve on warm plates.

Poached Eggs

The eggs to be poached will be getting a preliminary short boil. In a saucepan, boil enough water to completely cover the eggs. Gently lower the unshelled eggs into the saucepan. Count to 30 and remove the eggs. This preliminary cooking in the shell will harden the egg white a little so that the egg will hold its shape better as it poaches.

Bring to a simmer 4 cups water and 2 teaspoons cider vinegar in a 10-inch deep-frying pan or sauté pan. If you are poaching more than 4 eggs and need a larger pan, add 1 teaspoon vinegar for each additional 2 cups water. One by one, crack each egg on the edge of the frying pan, open up the shell just over the simmering water, and let the egg fall gently into the water. If the eggs are not totally submerged, spoon the simmering water over them as they poach. They will be ready after 1 to $1\frac{1}{2}$ minutes. Or remove the pan from the heat immediately after adding the eggs, cover, and the eggs will be poached after 4 to 5 minutes.

Remove the eggs with a skimmer or slotted spoon and let them drain on a towel. If you are not using the poached eggs right away, put them directly into a bowl of ice water and refrigerate. They will keep for 2 or 3 days. Reheat them in a bowl of very hot water for about 1 minute.

Butter-Crumbed Eggs

(eight eggs)

In this recipe, poached eggs are dipped first in raw egg, then in crumbs, and fried in butter. It may seem like a lot of trouble, but this recipe is easier than it sounds—and once you taste these eggs, you will agree that they are well worth the effort. There is something divine in this perfect combination of bread, butter, and egg.

8 poached eggs
2 raw eggs
8 tablespoons (1 stick) butter

2 cups fresh bread crumbs
Salt and pepper to taste

Trim any ragged edges from the poached eggs, and blot them dry.

In a shallow dish, beat the 2 raw eggs with a fork until well blended. Start melting the butter in a large skillet over medium-low heat while you crumb the poached eggs. Salt and pepper the bread crumbs in a shallow bowl.

Have a piece of waxed paper ready so you can place the crumbed eggs on it. I use a small spatula to move the eggs without breaking the tender yolks. Dip each egg into the beaten eggs, then gently coat the top and bottom with the bread crumb mixture. Place the eggs on the waxed paper.

When the butter has melted, slide the eggs one by one into the skillet and fry each side just until lightly golden and watch carefully to see that they don't brown too much. Place on a warm platter and serve.

Huevos Verdes

(four servings)

There is nothing like Salsa Verde, a fresh and lively green sauce, over eggs and tortillas to wake up a sleepy palate.

Salsa Verde (see page 284)
4 flour tortillas, about 8 inches
　in diameter
8 poached eggs, either freshly
　poached or reheated
　(see page 144)

2 cups grated Monterey Jack
　cheese
Fresh cilantro sprigs for garnish

Heat the Salsa Verde, but don't bring to a boil—you want to keep the sauce fresh-tasting. Over high heat on a griddle or in a dry skillet, cook the tortillas until their surfaces blister.

Place a tortilla on each plate and spoon 3 tablespoons of sauce in the center. Place 2 eggs on each sauced tortilla and sprinkle 1/2 cup cheese over each. Place the plates under the broiler for 1 minute (watch closely), until the cheese is just melted. Spoon a tablespoon or two of the sauce on top, add garnish, and serve.

Eggs Beatrice

(four servings)

Eggs Beatrice are a lighter and more delicate version of Eggs Benedict.

8 thin slices ham
8 slices thin-sliced white bread
   (dense, rather than airy bread)

8 poached eggs
1 1/4 cups Blender Hollandaise

Blender Hollandaise

(1 1/4 cups)

Hollandaise is more easily made in a blender than a food processor because the container is smaller and the ingredients blend more easily. Be sure to thin this sauce with a little hot water to the point where it flows readily from a spoon. Hollandaise that is too thick will coarsen the dish.

2 egg yolks
2 tablespoons boiling water,
   approximately
1 cup (2 sticks) butter, melted
   and hot

2 tablespoons lemon juice
Salt to taste

Put the yolks in a blender. Blend at low speed for a couple of seconds. Slowly add the boiling water, then very slowly add the hot, melted butter. Be patient at this point—you must pour the butter in the thinnest of streams, almost in fast drops. Add the lemon juice and salt. If the sauce is very thick, add a little more boiling water. Set aside while you are poaching the eggs—don't worry if your sauce is room temperature.

To assemble, put the ham in a small skillet, cover, and place over the lowest possible heat while you make the toast. Put a piece of lightly buttered toast on each warmed plate, cover with 2 slices of ham, then place 2 eggs on the ham. Spoon 3 to 4 tablespoons of hollandaise on top of each serving. Lightly butter and cut the remaining 4 slices of toast and bring to the table. Serve the rest of the hollandaise sauce in a small bowl.

Eggs Benedict Follow the recipe for Eggs Beatrice but use 8 thin slices of frizzled Canadian bacon instead of ham and substitute 4 English muffins for the bread. Split and toast the muffins and then put them in a low oven while you poach your eggs. Assemble as you would Eggs Beatrice.

Shirred Eggs

Whole eggs gently baked in buttered ramekins are known as shirred eggs. For each egg, melt 1 teaspoon butter in a ramekin in a 325°F oven. Break an egg into each ramekin, salt and pepper it, and bake for 12 minutes, or until the egg is just set. Serve immediately. You may pour 1 teaspoon melted butter or 2 teaspoons cream over the egg before putting it into the oven. Shirred eggs are a convenient dish to serve when you have invited a number of people over for breakfast; you might try cooking a number this way using buttered muffin tins instead of ramekins.

Shirred Eggs with Cheese Sprinkle 1 tablespoon grated cheese on top of each egg about 3 minutes before the egg has finished baking.

Shirred Eggs with Ham or Bacon Put 1 tablespoon chopped ham or crisp, crumbled bacon in the bottom of each ramekin before adding the egg.

Shirred Eggs with Mixed Herbs Put 1 teaspoon finely chopped fresh parsley and $1/2$ teaspoon each dried thyme and marjoram (or any mixture of herbs you like) in the bottom of each ramekin before adding the egg.

Shirred Lemon Eggs

(four eggs)

We think of something citrus as part of morning, and eggs have a special affinity for lemon. The lemon zest enhances the flavor of the eggs and it looks nice, too. Buttered, warm Melba Toast (see page 31) would be good with this dish.

$1/2$ cup heavy cream
$11/2$ teaspoons grated lemon zest
$1/3$ cup grated Gouda cheese
   (or any mild cheese)

4 eggs
Salt and pepper to taste
1 tablespoon finely minced
   parsley

Preheat the oven to 325°F. Liberally butter four ramekins—they should hold approximately $1/2$ cup each.

Pour 1 tablespoon cream into the bottom of each ramekin. Sprinkle about $1/4$ teaspoon lemon zest over the cream in each. Divide the cheese evenly among the four ramekins, sprinkling it on top of the cream. Gently drop an egg into each ramekin and add salt and pepper. Measure 1 tablespoon cream and spread it over each egg; scatter a little parsley over the tops. Bake for about 12 minutes, or just until the egg is slightly set. Serve immediately.

Buttermilk Baked Egg

(one egg)

You will be quite taken with what buttermilk does to an egg—it lends a creamy sharpness and yet has fewer calories than an equivalent amount of cream or cream sauce.

1 slice sandwich bread	Salt and pepper to taste
1 egg	¼ cup buttermilk

Preheat the oven to 350°F. Toast the bread lightly. Cut a hole in the center with a 1½-inch circular cutter. Butter an ovenproof dish. Put the toast in it and break open the egg over it so that the yolk falls in the hole in the center. Salt and pepper to taste. Spoon the buttermilk over the egg. Bake for 15 minutes.

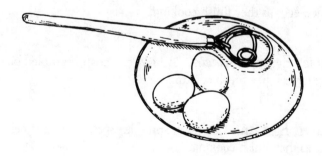

Scrambled Eggs

(two eggs)

2 tablespoons butter
1/4 cup water

2 eggs
Salt and pepper to taste

Heat a small frying pan (about 8 inches in diameter) over low heat and add 1 tablespoon butter. In a small saucepan, heat the water with the other tablespoon butter. Break the eggs into a bowl and beat them briskly with a fork for about 10 seconds, until the yolks and whites are mixed. When the butter in the frying pan has melted and has just started to foam, pour in the eggs. Stir them constantly but gently, keeping them moving so that the uncooked liquid egg runs under the curds of coagulating egg. After about 10 seconds, salt and pepper them. After 2 minutes, add 1 to 3 tablespoons hot water and butter and gently stir into the eggs as they finish cooking. Take the eggs off the heat just before they have reached the consistency you prefer; they will continue to cook for a few seconds. Dish up onto warm plates.

Scrambled Eggs with Ham Add 1/4 cup chopped ham to the scrambled eggs as they finish cooking.

Scrambled Eggs with Bacon Add 1/4 cup crisp, crumbled bacon to the eggs just as they finish cooking.

Scrambled Eggs and Cheese Sprinkle 1/4 cup grated cheese onto the eggs as they finish cooking.

Scrambled Eggs and Herbs To the beaten eggs, add 1 teaspoon chopped fresh parsley and 1 teaspoon of one or more of the following herbs: tarragon, chervil, chives, savory, borage (fresh or dried).

Scrambled Eggs and Croutons Fry 1/2 cup small bread cubes in 2 tablespoons butter until they are brown and crisp. Add to the eggs as they finish cooking.

Crackered Eggs

(four servings)

It is amazing that these ingredients result in such a moist, savory dish. Serve the wedges with syrup, or spread lightly with preserves, or have them plain with bacon or ham.

2 eggs	3 tablespoons butter
1 cup milk	Pepper to taste
20 saltines	

Whisk the eggs and milk together thoroughly. Crumble the crackers and stir them into the egg mixture. Let this sit for about 10 minutes.

Melt the butter in a 10-inch skillet over medium-low heat. Pour the mixture into the skillet, distributing the bits of cracker evenly over the bottom of the pan with a fork. Cook slowly for about 2 or 3 minutes, or until the bottom of the mixture is lightly browned. Using a large spatula, cut the round in two and turn over first one half and then the other. Allow to cook for another minute or two, until the other side has browned lightly. Sprinkle with pepper and cut into wedges.

Omelets

(one serving)

I make omelets in a rather casual way. You don't need a special omelet pan—just about any pan with a nonstick surface will work. (By the way, I find that the cast-iron pans you buy today don't temper well and the egg sticks.) The right size pan for a two- or three-egg omelet is one with a bottom diameter of 8 inches. If you have never made an omelet before, first read this recipe all the way through—the whole process takes only about a minute.

2 eggs
Salt and pepper to taste
2 teaspoons butter

Break the eggs into a small bowl, add salt and pepper, and whisk vigorously with a fork for about 10 seconds, just enough to thoroughly blend yolks and whites. Put an 8-inch nonstick skillet over high heat. When it is quite hot, add the butter and tilt the pan, swirling the butter in all directions to coat the bottom and sides. The butter should not get brown. When the foaming butter starts to subside, pour in the eggs. Let them set about 5 seconds. Using a spatula, pull the cooked egg from the edges of the pan toward the center, allowing the liquid egg to run under onto the hot pan. After about 20 seconds, while the eggs are still very moist and creamy, push the omelet toward one side of the pan, and then with a spatula fold half the omelet over the other half. Let the omelet cook for 5 seconds more to lightly brown the bottom, and then quickly tilt the pan upside down over a plate so the omelet falls out bottom side up. You can pat the omelet into shape with your hands and draw a piece of butter over the top to make it shiny.

Filled Omelets

If you fill your omelet, mind the proportion of filling to egg. The tender, softly cooked egg is spoiled by too much filling. For every 2-egg omelet, 4 tablespoons or 1/4 cup filling is just right, with few exceptions. Never add a very wet filling: the liquid dilutes the egg and makes it puddly. Any of the following variations is delicious:

Ham Omelet   Add 1/4 cup finely chopped ham to the beaten eggs.

Apple Omelet   Fill with 1/4 cup applesauce or cooked diced apples.

Cheese Omelet   Spread 1/4 cup grated cheese over the eggs just before folding.

Bacon Omelet   Add 1/4 cup crisp, crumbled bacon to the beaten eggs.

Herb Omelet   Mix 2 teaspoons finely chopped parsley with 1 teaspoon fresh sage, tarragon, thyme, or savory and add to the beaten eggs.

Mushroom Omelet   Sauté 1/2 cup raw sliced or chopped mushrooms in 2 tablespoons butter and add to the eggs just before folding.

Jelly Omelet   Put about 1/4 cup of your favorite jelly onto the eggs just before folding over.

Bread and Butter Omelet   Fry ½ cup small bread cubes in 2 tablespoons butter until lightly browned and crisp. Sprinkle the croutons onto the eggs just before folding over.

Smoked Salmon Omelet   Just before you fold over the omelet place 1 thin slice smoked salmon and 2 tablespoons cream cheese or farmer's cheese onto the eggs.

Caviar Omelet   Spoon 2 tablespoons salmon roe or caviar over the eggs before folding.

Bridge Creek Omelet   Put ⅓ cup grated Tillamook cheese and enough thick-sliced bacon that has been cooked crisp and cut into ½-inch pieces to make ⅓ cup onto the eggs before folding them over.

Puffy Omelets

(two servings)

I like these airy, foamy omelets—they look so grand and filling. The trick is not to cook them until they are too dry. Breakfast Baps (see page 19) and a puffy omelet make a good breakfast team.

3 eggs, separated
¼ teaspoon salt, or to taste
¼ teaspoon pepper

2 tablespoons butter
Filling (see following recipes)

Preheat the oven to 400°F. For a three-egg omelet, use a 10-inch skillet with sloping sides—they usually measure about 8 inches across the bottom. You may cook the omelet completely on top of the stove, but I prefer the oven finish because it is easier to keep the omelet moist.

Briskly beat the yolks a few seconds, until they are thoroughly blended. Sprinkle salt over the whites and beat them until they are stiff but moist. Fold the yolks and whites together until they are barely incorporated.

Put the butter into the skillet over high heat. When the butter begins to foam, pour the eggs into the skillet. Shake the pan a little, or gently spread the omelet with a spatula. Sprinkle the pepper over the eggs. Allow the omelet to cook for about 1 minute, or until the bottom is brown. Remove from the stove and put into the oven. Have the filling ready and the plates warm. Take a look at the omelet after a minute or so and press the top with your finger. It is done when it is spongy, but moist. It takes about 3 minutes to set.

Remove from the oven and quickly spread the filling across the center and fold the omelet in half with a spatula. If you aren't using any sauce to cover the omelet, spread a little butter over the top. Serve at once.

Mushroom Omelet

4 tablespoons (½ stick) butter
2 cups fresh mushrooms, wiped
   clean and sliced
Salt and pepper to taste

¼ cup finely chopped parsley
Optional: Goldenrod Eggs sauce
   (see page 138)

Melt the butter in a skillet, add the mushrooms, and stir over low heat just until they begin to soften and change color. Salt and pepper them and set aside; stir the parsley into the mushrooms just before you are ready to use them. Put half the mushrooms in the center of the omelet before folding. If you are using the optional sauce, stir the remaining mushrooms into it and spoon the sauce on top of the omelet just before serving. If no sauce is used, spoon the mushroom-parsley mixture over the top.

Mexican Omelet

1 cup grated Monterey Jack
   cheese

1 cup Salsa Verde (see page 284),
   warmed

Sprinkle the cheese and $\frac{1}{2}$ cup sauce in the center of the omelet before it is folded in half. Spoon the remaining $\frac{1}{2}$ cup sauce over the omelet before serving.

Ham or Bacon Omelet

1 cup finely chopped ham or
   crisp, crumbled bacon

Freshly ground black pepper
   to taste

Just before folding the omelet in half, spread the ham or bacon down the center. Grind lots of black pepper over it. Fold the omelet and grate a little more pepper on top before serving.

Cheese Omelet

1 cup grated Cheddar,
   Monterey Jack, or any favorite
   melting cheese

$\frac{1}{4}$ cup finely chopped parsley

Sprinkle the cheese down the center of the omelet just before folding in half. Sprinkle half the parsley on top of the cheese and the rest on top of the omelet after folding it.

Herb Omelet

1 tablespoon finely chopped fresh
    herbs; or half as much dried
    herbs (try an equal mixture
    of parsley, thyme, and sweet
    marjoram, or your favorite
    herb combination)

½ cup sour cream
2 tablespoons milk

Sprinkle 2 teaspoons of herbs down the center of the omelet and spoon over all but 2 tablespoons of the sour cream. Fold the omelet in half. Stir together the milk and remaining sour cream until smooth. Spoon over the top of the omelet and sprinkle the remaining herbs on top.

Jelly or Jam Omelet

Orange marmalade is delicious in omelets. When using orange marmalade, grate the zest of an orange into the omelet batter before cooking.

1 cup jelly or jam

Warm the jelly or jam in a small pan, stirring constantly until it is melted. Spoon ¾ cup in the center of the omelet before folding in half and spoon the rest on top before serving.

Frittata with Cheese and Crumbs

(five servings)

A frittata is a useful dish for serving many. This frittata is not full of vegetables, like most versions, but suits my early-breakfast sensibilities: rumbled eggs (that's an old term meaning mixed eggs) with buttered crumbs and Cheddar cheese, and a hint of winter savory.

8 tablespoons (1 stick) butter	2 teaspoons finely chopped fresh
2 cups fresh, coarse bread crumbs	winter savory, or 1 teaspoon
10 eggs, gently beaten	crumbled dried winter savory
Salt and pepper to taste	1 cup grated Cheddar cheese

Preheat the oven to 350°F. Use a 10-inch ovenproof skillet or sauté pan.

Melt 4 tablespoons butter in the skillet over medium heat. Stir in the bread crumbs and cook, stirring often, until they have absorbed the butter and are golden. Remove from the heat and set the crumbs aside. Clean the skillet. In the clean skillet melt the remaining butter over low heat. Sprinkle half the crumbs over the bottom of the skillet. Pour the eggs on top, add salt and pepper sparingly, and then the winter savory. Cook without stirring for a minute or a trifle more (it is important not to overcook), until the bottom has just begun to set. You can tilt the skillet just a little to see. Put the skillet in the oven and bake for just 2 minutes. Sprinkle the cheese and the remaining 1 cup bread crumbs evenly over the top. Bake 1 more minute and remove from the oven. Loosen the edges and slide the frittata onto a large serving plate. This is good hot or cold. Cut into wedges to serve.

Featherbed Eggs

(four servings)

Featherbed Eggs are layers of bread and custard with the addition of cheese or fruit or a favorite something (as long as it isn't too moist or liquid). The joy of this dish is that it must be prepared the day before, or at least six hours before baking, so it is all ready well in advance of need.

6 slices bread, buttered
Salt and pepper to taste
1½ cups grated sharp Cheddar,
   Gouda, Provolone, Monterey
   Jack, or any other melting
   cheese

1½ cups milk
6 eggs, slightly beaten

Arrange the slices of bread in a single layer in a shallow, buttered baking dish. Sprinkle lightly with salt and pepper. Sprinkle the grated cheese evenly over the bread. Combine the milk and eggs, and stir until blended. Pour the milk mixture over the bread and cheese. Cover and refrigerate at least 6 hours, or overnight.

As the dish will be chilled when you are ready to bake it, start it in a cold 350°F oven. Bake for about 1 hour, or until the bread custard is puffy and lightly golden.

Apple Ham Featherbed   Omit the grated cheese and place thin slices of ham over the buttered bread. Pour the custard over. Spread ¼ cup applesauce over each slice of ham; this can be done just before baking, if you wish. Cover and refrigerate at least 6 hours. Bake as directed above.

Fresh Fruit and Cream Cheese Featherbed Omit the grated cheese and spread each slice of buttered bread with 3 tablespoons softened cream cheese. Pour the custard over, cover, and refrigerate at least 6 hours. Peel and slice any firm, ripe fruit (nectarines, pears, peaches, strawberries). Place a single layer of sliced fruit over the cream cheese. Sprinkle a little sugar over the fruit if it tastes too tart. Bake as directed on page 159.

Oatmeal Soufflé

(four servings)

This is a surprising and good way to eat oatmeal.

1 cup milk	$\frac{1}{2}$ teaspoon nutmeg
2 tablespoons butter	$\frac{1}{2}$ teaspoon cinnamon
$\frac{3}{4}$ cup quick-cooking oatmeal	3 eggs, separated
$\frac{1}{3}$ cup cream cheese (low-fat)	$\frac{1}{2}$ cup raisins
$\frac{1}{4}$ teaspoon salt	$\frac{1}{2}$ cup chopped walnuts
$\frac{1}{2}$ cup brown sugar	

Preheat the oven to 325°F. Butter and sugar a 1½-quart soufflé dish or casserole.

Put the milk and butter into a small saucepan and heat until barely boiling. Slowly add the oatmeal, stirring constantly. Cook the oatmeal until thick, stirring often. Remove from the heat and add the cream cheese, salt, sugar, nutmeg, and cinnamon. Stir briskly to blend and smooth the mixture. Beat the 3 yolks slightly and slowly add them to the oatmeal, stirring constantly. Stir in the raisins and walnuts.

Beat the egg whites until they are stiff but still moist. Using a rubber spatula, gently stir and fold the whites into the oatmeal mixture. Don't overfold; fold only until no large lumps of whites remain. Spoon the mixture into the soufflé dish. Bake for 35 to 40 minutes, or until the center still trembles a trifle but most of the soufflé is set. Serve immediately, with cream or warm milk. This soufflé is still tasty when cold and fallen.

Oatmeal Bacon Soufflé Omit the sugar when buttering the soufflé dish. In the recipe, leave out the nutmeg, cinnamon, raisins, and walnuts. Instead, add 1 cup crisp, crumbled bacon, 1¼ teaspoons prepared mustard, and Tabasco to taste.

Lemon Zephyrs

(four servings)

These small free-form soufflés are light as clouds and sweet as the west wind. Breathe carefully or else these fluffy zephyrs may blow right off your plate. Serve with a slice of buttered, toasted pound cake.

4 tablespoons (½ stick) butter	1 teaspoon flour
2 tablespoons milk	2 teaspoons grated lemon rind
7 tablespoons confectioners' sugar	1 cup fresh raspberries
6 egg whites	(or any fresh berries)
¼ teaspoon cream of tartar	Sugar to taste for berries
3 egg yolks	

Preheat the oven to 425°F. Use a shallow (about 2 inches deep) 14-inch oval baking dish; or use a rectangular dish that is an inch shorter. Have a 8- or 9-inch round paper plate at hand.

Combine the butter, milk, and 1 tablespoon confectioners' sugar in the baking dish. Heat the mixture until the butter has melted, stir, and set aside.

Beat the egg whites with the cream of tartar until foamy, then gradually add the remaining 6 tablespoons sugar, and beat until stiff but moist.

Beat the egg yolks thoroughly and add the flour and lemon rind to the yolk mixture. Gently fold the yolk mixture into the beaten whites.

Now you are going to shape the batter into four balls. Using the paper plate as a scoop, pile in a football shape one quarter of the soufflé mixture at the end of the baking dish. Scoop up three more equal portions and drop next to each other. There should be a row of four balls of approximately the same size in the baking dish.

Place the dish in the preheated oven and bake for 5 to 6 minutes, or until the peaks of the soufflés are slightly golden. Sprinkle the berries with sugar if they need some. Remove the soufflés from the oven and sprinkle the berries all over the zephyrs. Bring to the table and serve. Or serve on four individual dessert plates, with a little of the sauce from the bottom of the baking dish spooned over each serving.

Fruit Fixing

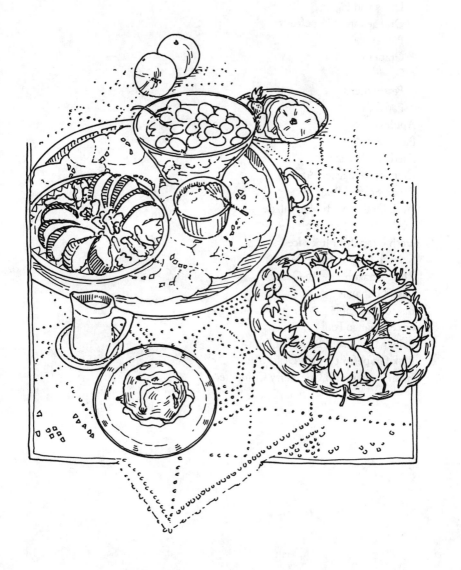

Simple Ways of Fixing Fruit
Inside-out Mango
Apples
Dates and Figs
Oranges and Grapefruit
Pineapple
Grapes
Berries
Persimmons
Papaya
Applesauce
Baked Apples
Fried Apple Rings
Cranberry Poached Apples
Baked Stuffed Pears
Fresh Orange with Marmalade
Fresh Lemon Juice Ice
Fresh Grapefruit Juice Ice
Fresh Orange Juice Ice
Rhubarb with English Custard
Baked Bananas
Baked Pineapple
Green Mango Fool
Ballymaloe Baked Breakfast Fruit
Pink Grapefruit Apple Dish
Fresh Orange and Cranberry Compote

One of the reasons I love this subject of breakfast has to do with its utter simplicity—what could be simpler than ripe, fresh fruit? I had a magazine assignment a few years ago that required me to come up with some recipes for tropical fruits—mango, papaya, pineapple, banana. I worked very hard for several weeks and when I got finished with every variation I could think of—and there were lots of them—the fact was that every one of those fruits was best when it was left alone.

When people see bowls of fruit, they think they're just for decoration and don't reach for the fruit. One thing that will encourage your friends or your family to think of fruit as ready to eat and not just something to look at is to put fruit knives and a fork in the bowl. Or put the fruit in bowls with lots of ice and water as another inviting way of saying, "This is something to eat." Keeping a pair of scissors nearby for grapes is a nice touch.

For the sake of demonstrating our desire to please, it is sometimes nice to carve, poach, bake, or ice fresh fruits and berries. The recipes in this chapter with these little extra preparations have not robbed nature of the perfect essence of the fruit.

Simple Ways of Fixing Fruit

Inside-out Mango   I love mangoes—they taste cloudlike, sort of like peaches and ginger. Hold the mango end-up on a board. Using a paring knife, cut as close as possible on either side of the long, flat pit (the mango pit is shaped like a cuttlebone). This will give two shallow halves of mango. Hold one half in the palm of your hand and with the knife cut a pattern like tic-tac-toe squares on the flesh without cutting through the skin. Push the skin-side center of the half upward, as if to turn inside out, so the cut squares protrude. The mango will look quite tailored this way and it will be much easier to eat. Eating a mango left on the pit is best done over the kitchen sink.

Apples   Serve apple slices with walnut halves. Apple slices may be held in salted water—1 tablespoon salt to 1 quart water. Rinse before serving and the salt disappears. This salted water keeps pears from discoloring, too.

Dates and Figs   Dates and figs are both luscious stuffed with Breakfast Cheese (see page 286) and eaten with walnuts on the side.

Oranges and Grapefruit   Removing sections is a nice gesture. Cut the skin away from the fruit. It is easy to hold the fruit upright on a board and cut away the skin in large strips from the blossom end to the stem end. Cut off any white pith. Cut each section of flesh away from the dividing membranes, so only clean citrus sections are collected.

Pineapple Cut off the large leafy top. Cut round slices about 1 inch thick and then cut the skin and eyes off each slice. Cut the center core out. Serve the clean slice with raspberry jam or a little coconut.

Grapes I love the Italian custom of serving bunches of grapes in a bowl of ice and water.

Berries Strawberries in a ring around some Breakfast Cheese (see page 286) make a lovely presentation. Or serve them with a wedge of lemon and bowls of different kinds of sugar. Strawberries and blueberries are wonderful mixed with finely chopped crystallized ginger, sprinkled with brown sugar, and served with sour cream.

Persimmons An old California recipe for persimmons is to freeze them, slice them, sprinkle them with brown sugar, and serve with yogurt. Sliced persimmons and grapefruit sections make a fine compote.

Papaya Papaya becomes a beguiling fruit with a few crunchy, peppery papaya seeds and a little lime juice sprinkled over it. Cut a papaya in half and seed it. Save 1 tablespoon of the seeds, rinse them, and sprinkle over the fruit. Squeeze the juice of half a lime over the top.

Applesauce

(three cups)

I take applesauce so much for granted that I almost left out this recipe. But I had to put it in because it's such a good companion to so many breakfast dishes.

4 large, firm green apples, peeled, cored, and cut into eighths ½ cup water	Sugar to taste 3 tablespoons lemon juice

Put the apples and water into a sauté pan. Turn heat to medium and cook, stirring often, until the apples become tender, about 5 or 6 minutes. Add sugar and lemon juice and stir to blend well. Cook another 1 or 2 minutes. Remove from heat and mash with a fork.

Baked Apples

(four servings)

To my mind, the humble, homey baked apple, done properly, is equal to, if not better than, the fanciest pastry.

4 firm, ripe apples
  (pippins or Granny Smiths)
⅓ cup sugar
½ cup water
	⅛ teaspoon salt
	Zest of 1 lemon, cut into large
	  strips

Peel the top third of the apples and core.

Put the sugar, water, salt, and lemon zest in a small pan, bring to a boil, stir, and remove from the heat.

Set the apples upright in a baking dish and pour the syrup over. Cover (use foil if there is no lid that fits) and bake in a preheated 350°F oven for 30 minutes, or until the apples are easily pierced with the tip of a knife. Spoon some of the syrup over the apples and sprinkle a little sugar over the top. You may put them under the broiler for 2 to 3 minutes to brown. Serve warm with cream.

Fried Apple Rings

(eight rings)

Has America forgotten how good apple rings taste, cooked golden with bacon or ham drippings, covered with a little sugar glaze, and served next to bacon or a bit of ham? Apple rings made in this way are also quite good put into a bowl of hot oatmeal, mashed slightly, and covered with milk or cream.

2 tablespoons bacon or ham fat, or butter
2 firm apples, cored, sliced into rings 1/4 to 1/2 inch thick (each apple should yield 4 rings)

1/3 cup sugar, or to taste

Put the fat into a large skillet that will hold 8 apple rings in a single layer. Heat the fat to medium hot, add the rings, and cook for 2 minutes. Sprinkle the sugar over the rings and turn over. Cook for another minute or two, or until the sugar has melted and the apple rings are golden on both sides. Serve hot.

Cranberry Poached Apples

(six small apples)

These apples are a pretty pink and have a slight tartness from the cranberry juice. The fig filling is a nice bonus. They can be prepared the night before.

6 small apples (preferably about the size of a peach)	3/4 cup figs, chopped fine
3 cups cranberry juice	2 tablespoons brown sugar
1/2 cup sugar	1/4 cup finely chopped walnuts
1 small lemon, cut into pieces, seeds removed, and ground	2 tablespoons lemon juice

Peel the apples and core three quarters of the way to the base. Put the cranberry juice, sugar, and ground lemon into a saucepan large enough to hold the apples in one layer. Bring to a boil, stir, and add the apples to the pan. Add enough water so the liquid comes halfway up the sides of the apples. Cover the pan and bring to a simmer. Uncover and spoon the poaching liquid all over the apples every few minutes, and turn them around gently in the liquid so they are coated often. Depending on the size of the apples, they should simmer 10 to 20 minutes to become tender. Be careful not to cook them to the point where they are falling apart. When the apples are tender, remove the pan from the heat and let them cool in the poaching liquid.

In a small bowl, mix the figs, brown sugar, walnuts, and lemon juice. When the apples are cool, stuff the cored cavities with the fig mixture. Put them in a bowl, taste the liquid, and stir in more sugar or lemon juice as needed. Pour 1 1/2 cups of the liquid over the apples and refrigerate until needed.

Baked Stuffed Pears

(four servings)

This recipe makes a lovely dish. The pears keep their natural good flavor, and the filling adds a special touch.

4 pears, ripe and firm	1 tablespoon lemon juice
1/4 cup raisins	1/4 cup water
3 tablespoons chopped walnuts	1/4 cup light corn syrup
2 1/2 tablespoons sugar	

Peel the pears, leaving the stems on. Core the pears on the blossom end (the bottom).

Combine the raisins, walnuts, sugar, and lemon juice in a small bowl, and mix well. Fill the cavity of each pear, dividing the filling equally. Place the pears upright in a deep baking dish, preferably with a cover. Mix together the water and corn syrup and pour into the baking dish. Cover the dish with its lid (or foil) and bake in a preheated 350°F oven for about 1 hour and 15 minutes, or until the pears are easily pierced with a fork. Serve warm or cold with some of the syrup spooned over each pear.

Fresh Orange with Marmalade

(four servings)

A perfect example of a simple dish that is absolutely terrific.

4 oranges, peeled and sectioned
½ cup orange marmalade
  (use less if very sweet)

Place the orange sections in a glass dish. Add the marmalade to the orange sections, refrigerate, and stir to blend after an hour or so. The juice of the oranges will have partially liquefied the marmalade. Refrigerate until *very* cold. I sometimes put this into the freezer for an hour or more before serving to get the mixture quite icy.

Fresh Lemon Juice Ice

(about five cups)

1½ cups sugar
4 cups boiling water

¾ cup freshly squeezed lemon juice
1 tablespoon grated lemon zest

Put the sugar in a bowl and pour the boiling water over. Stir until the sugar dissolves. Cool and add the lemon juice and zest. Freeze as directed for Fresh Grapefruit Juice Ice (following recipe).

Fresh Grapefruit Juice Ice

(about three cups)

This ice is wonderful with ham and hot biscuits. Somehow the icy and slushy grapefruit juice gives an extra sparkle to freshly squeezed juice. Good as a breakfast starter with Gingersnaps (see page 238).

¾ to 1 cup sugar (depending on tartness of grapefruit juice)
½ cup water

3 cups freshly squeezed grapefruit juice

Combine the sugar and water in a saucepan and boil until the sugar is dissolved, about 1 minute. Cool, and stir in the grapefruit juice. Pour into ice cube trays (the small cubed trays are ideal because you can turn out a small dish of cubes for each serving). Or pour the juice mixture into a bowl, cover, and freeze. Remember to soften the ice a trifle so you can serve it easily if you are not freezing it in the tiny cubed ice trays. Serve in little glasses or bowls.

Fresh Orange Juice Ice Substitute orange juice for grapefruit juice, reduce the amount of sugar to ⅓ cup or less, and proceed as directed above.

Rhubarb with English Custard

(four servings)

Mary Hamblit, of Portland, Oregon, served this to me long ago, and it is wonderful. Don't overcook the rhubarb.

1 pound rhubarb, ends trimmed
   and cut into $\frac{1}{2}$-inch pieces
   (about 4 cups)
About $1\frac{1}{3}$ cups water
$\frac{3}{4}$ cup sugar

A $\frac{1}{2}$-inch-thick slice fresh
   gingerroot
2 cups English Custard
   (see page 283)

Put the rhubarb into a sauté pan that has a lid. Add 1 cup water and cook, covered, over medium heat for 4 to 5 minutes, just until the rhubarb is barely tender (watch the cooking carefully so the rhubarb doesn't turn to mush). Carefully remove the rhubarb from the pan and set aside; discard the water. Put the sugar, $\frac{1}{3}$ cup water, and the gingerroot into the sauté pan and heat a minute or two, stirring constantly until the sugar dissolves. Add the rhubarb, stir gently so the rhubarb is covered with syrup, cook 1 minute, and remove from the heat. Let cool. Remove the gingerroot and serve with the English Custard poured over the rhubarb.

Baked Bananas

(six servings)

Why something this easy and good is seldom made is puzzling. Warm baked bananas taste even more like bananas than cold bananas, and somehow anything caramellike is absolute perfection with bananas.

⅓ cup (⅔ stick) butter, melted
3 tablespoons fresh lemon juice
6 firm, ripe bananas, peeled
⅓ cup brown sugar

1 teaspoon cinnamon or
   ground ginger
1 cup grated coconut

Preheat the oven to 375°F.

Spread the melted butter and lemon juice over the bottom of a shallow baking dish that will hold 6 bananas. Stir the butter and lemon juice together until blended. Put the bananas in the dish and turn them until they are well coated with the butter mixture. Put the sugar and cinnamon or ginger in a small bowl and stir with a fork to blend thoroughly. Sprinkle the sugar mixture evenly over the bananas.

Bake the bananas for 18 to 20 minutes, or until the butter bubbles a little. Turn them over once after 10 minutes of baking. Sprinkle the coconut over the bananas about 5 minutes before they finish cooking. Serve warm with a little cream or maple syrup.

Baked Pineapple

(10 servings)

Don't overlook pineapple as a breakfast food; it satisfies that craving for something fresh and tart. Baking a pineapple with a little brown sugar gives it a softer character and a subtle caramel taste.

1 fresh medium pineapple
½ cup brown sugar

Remove the rind and eyes from the pineapple. Cut the fruit into quarters lengthwise and remove the core from each wedge. Cut each quarter in half lengthwise. Sprinkle 1 tablespoon brown sugar over each slice. Place the slices on a baking sheet and bake for 30 minutes in a preheated 325°F oven. Serve warm.

Green Mango Fool

(about 2½ cups)

No fooling, this is a fabulous dish and an indispensable topping for Ginger Pancakes (see page 117).

2 green (unripe) mangoes
  (very firm and hard), peeled,
  cut from seed, and diced
⅓ cup sugar (or more if the
  fruit is very tart)

⅓ cup water
1 cup heavy cream
1½ tablespoons nonfat dry milk

Put the diced mangoes in a saucepan and add the sugar and water. Cook over medium heat, stirring often, for about 10 minutes, or until the fruit is soft. Taste and add more sugar if the fruit is too tart. Remove from heat and mash the mango with a fork until it is a coarse purée. If there is extra liquid, drain some away—this should have the texture of applesauce. Cool before adding to the cream.

Put the heavy cream and nonfat dry milk in a bowl and whip until the cream holds firm peaks. (Adding nonfat dry milk is a tip from Abby Mandel on how to stabilize whipped cream.) Gently stir the mango purée into the whipped cream. Spoon a little mound on top of each ginger pancake. If you don't use all the mango fool, freeze it—it makes delicious ice cream.

Ballymaloe Baked Breakfast Fruit

(eight servings)

This good fruit recipe was given to me by Darina Allen, a lovely young Irish woman who directs the Ballymaloe Cooking School in County Cork, Ireland, with her mother-in-law, Myrtle Allen.

1 cup dried prunes, pitted	$1/2$ cup water
1 cup dried apricots	Grated zest of $1/2$ lemon
$1/3$ cup raisins	2 tablespoons butter
3 bananas, sliced thick	1 cup orange juice
2 tablespoons honey	

Put the prunes and the apricots in a bowl and cover with hot water. Soak overnight.

Drain, and put the prunes, apricots, raisins, and bananas in a baking dish. Dissolve the honey in the water. Sprinkle the lemon zest over the fruit and then pour the honey syrup over. Dot with the butter.

Bake in a preheated 350°F oven for about 35 minutes. Add the orange juice and continue to bake long enough for the orange juice to get hot, about 5 more minutes. Serve warm. It is nice with light cream poured over.

To serve cold: Follow the preceding directions, but omit the bananas and orange juice. Reserve $3/4$ cup of the water that the fruit soaked in, add it to the honey, and pour it over the fruit. Put into a baking dish, omit the butter, and bake as directed. Cool and refrigerate. Just before serving, add a little fresh orange juice and some sliced bananas. This keeps for about 10 days in the refrigerator.

Pink Grapefruit Apple Dish

(six servings)

The combination of grapefruit and apple is surprisingly right. The tart grapefruit keeps the apple crisp and white, and the bit of fresh mint makes the dish sparkle. Gingersnaps (see page 238) should be served with this.

4 pink grapefruit
4 sweet, firm apples

1 teaspoon finely chopped
fresh mint

Peel the grapefruit and remove the sections from the white pith and membrane. Put the sections in a bowl. Peel and core the apples and slice into thin wedges. Add the apple immediately to the grapefruit and gently stir so the apple slices are coated with the acid grapefruit juice. If there is not enough liquid to cover, boil ½ cup water with ¼ cup sugar, cool a little, and add to the fruit. Chill, and add the fresh mint.

Fresh Orange and Cranberry Compote

(six servings)

Why limit the use of cranberries to a relish for Thanksgiving turkey when it can be eaten with corn muffins year round? And if you yearn for a sharp, tasty complement to a plateful of Bannocks (see page 57), nothing could be better than this compote.

1½ cups fresh cranberries
⅓ cup sugar
¼ cup water

4 juice oranges, peeled, sliced
into rounds, and seeded

Put the cranberries in a small skillet and sprinkle the sugar over them. Add the water and cook over low heat, stirring often. Cook until the sugar has dissolved and the cranberries have popped, about 3 or 4 minutes. Remove the skillet from the heat and add the orange slices. Gently stir, spooning the cranberry juice over the slices until well saturated. Serve warm or chilled.

Potatoes

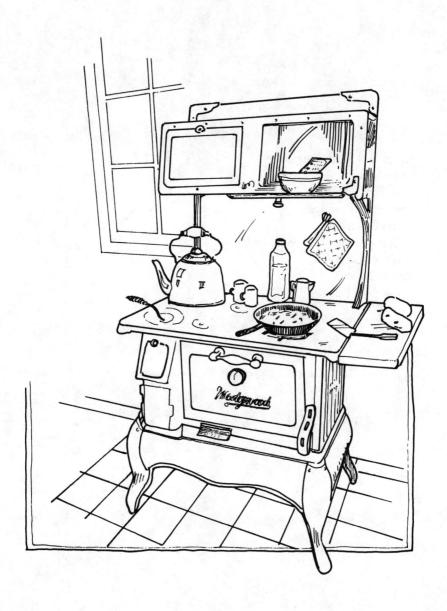

Rough and Ready Potatoes
Oven Fries
Hash Brown Potatoes
Raw Potato Pancakes
Potato Bacon Pie
    Cottage Cheese Potato Bacon Pie
Potato Apple Fry
Potato Custard
Creek Bank Potatoes

The potato is the strong, silent type, and because it is not assertive, it is the most popular breakfast vegetable. There is no food quite like the potato. We take them for granted, like an old friend, and seldom stop to think of their virtues: they are always available, cheap, nutritious, digestible. And like best friends, you can always count on them. Potatoes give substance to a meal and they have a wholesome gentle taste and down-to-earth goodness.

I happen to love potatoes and eggs; I could eat them every day of the week. Somehow they belong together, especially potatoes with eggs fried sunny-side-up (potatoes mop up that nice yolk better than toast).

Once in a blue moon, you may notice a greenish tinge on the surface of a potato. This indicates the presence of some natural poisons that form near the surface when the potato is about to sprout, so be sure to cut this all away.

Rough and Ready Potatoes

(two servings)

In under ten minutes you can have a batch of dark brown Rough and Ready Potatoes so delicious that you will want to make them every time you fry an egg.

1 large russet potato
1 tablespoon bacon fat or
    shortening

Salt and pepper to taste

Don't peel the potato but scrub it well; cut into cubes about $\frac{1}{2}$ inch square. Melt the fat in a skillet. When the fat is very hot, stand back and add the potatoes. Salt and pepper liberally. Let the potato cubes fry for about 4 minutes, turn them over with a spatula, and salt and pepper again. Cook the potatoes another 3 minutes, until they are dark and brown. Serve hot.

Oven Fries

(three servings)

Oven fries are like French fries: they are identically shaped, they taste delicious, but they aren't deep fried.

2 russet potatoes, peeled
$\frac{1}{4}$ cup vegetable oil

Salt and lots of pepper

Preheat the oven to 425°F.

Cut the potatoes into pieces $1/2$ inch wide and about $3\frac{1}{2}$ inches long. Pour the oil into a 10-inch pie pan or square pan. Put the pieces of potato in the pan and turn them over on all sides to completely coat with a film of oil. Salt and pepper liberally. Put the potatoes in the oven and set the timer for 15 minutes. When the timer goes off, turn the potatoes over and add salt and pepper. Set the timer again for 10 minutes, then pour off any liquid in the pan and turn the potatoes for the last time. Bake for another 15 minutes and they will be golden around the edges. Remove from the oven and serve hot.

Hash Brown Potatoes

(three servings)

Hash browns are an American native. Every diner, coffee shop, and truck stop in the country serves these crisp, browned potatoes with eggs. They give a fine balance and roughness to fried or scrambled eggs. Adding cream is optional; they will still be crisp, but slightly more moist inside.

3 tablespoons bacon fat, oil,
  or shortening
3 cups grated potatoes,
  raw or cooked

Salt and lots of pepper
Optional: $1/3$ cup heavy cream

Heat the fat in a large skillet. Spread the potatoes in a layer, pressing down with a spatula. Add salt and pepper to taste. Cook over medium heat for 6 or 7 minutes. With the edge of the spatula, cut the circle of potatoes down the middle. Turn each half over and, if using cream, pour it evenly over the potatoes. Sprinkle again with salt and pepper. Cook another 6 or 7 minutes, or until the potatoes are crisp and brown on the bottom. Serve hot.

Raw Potato Pancakes

(eight 3½-inch pancakes)

Potato pancakes are crisp and brown on the outside, and the inside has the nice, slightly biting flavor of fresh potato. Served two or three per person with hot homemade Applesauce (see page 168) and a couple of thick slices of bacon with a little maple syrup over, these make a fine winter breakfast. Sour cream or cottage cheese beaten until smooth is also good on these pancakes. Potato pancakes can be made in quantity and frozen. To cook, heat a little fat in a hot griddle or skillet and quickly fry the pancakes on both sides.

2 medium-size russet potatoes, peeled and grated (to make 2 cups)*	Salt to taste
⅓ cup heavy cream	Lots of coarsely ground black pepper
4 tablespoons clarified butter; or vegetable shortening or bacon fat, melted; or vegetable oil	

*NOTE: If you wish to do this in advance, put the grated potatoes in cold salted water to cover for up to 2 hours. Drain and pat dry on paper towels before using.

Just before you are ready to fry the pancakes, put the grated potatoes in a bowl and stir in the cream. Heat the fat until sizzling hot in a large skillet. Have some paper towels at hand. Don't worry if the potatoes become slightly pink while you are waiting for the fat to heat.

When the skillet is ready, measure out about ¼ cup potato and drop into the skillet. Stand back a little, as the cream tends to spatter when it meets the hot fat. Press the mound of potato down with a spatula to flatten and shape into a round pancake. Sprinkle the top lightly with salt and liberally with pepper. Cook until the edges are golden brown. Turn over and cook the other side until crisp and brown. Pat each pancake on the paper towels to get rid of excess fat, and keep them hot on a plate in a 250°F oven — or better yet, serve immediately. If needed for future use, pat them dry of excess fat, wrap well, and freeze.

Potato Bacon Pie

(one 8-inch pie)

The next time you bake or boil potatoes, make extra so that you will have enough left over to make this pie. Potato Bacon Pie has a nice texture since the cooked potato is grated or mashed into bits rather than puréed or whipped. Serve a wedge of this pie with eggs. Potato Bacon Pie can be prepared in advance, kept refrigerated overnight, and baked in the morning.

4 cups cooked potato, grated or mashed into bits	Salt to taste
Lots of coarsely ground black pepper	$\frac{1}{2}$ cup milk
	12 slices bacon, fried, patted dry of fat, and crumbled

Preheat the oven to 350°F. Butter an 8-inch pie pan.

Put the potato, pepper, salt, milk, and bacon in a bowl, and mix well. Spread the potato mixture evenly into the pie pan. Bake for about 40 minutes, or until the top has become lightly browned.

Cottage Cheese Potato Bacon Pie Substitute $1\frac{1}{2}$ cups cottage cheese for $1\frac{1}{2}$ cups of the cooked potato. Proceed as directed above.

Potato Apple Fry

(six servings)

This combination looks appealing, and tastes good for breakfast. The apples should be as tart as possible—dousing with lemon juice helps. Sour cream served on the side brings out the best of the sharp new potato and tart apple tastes.

3 firm, tart apples (pippin or Granny Smith)	2 tablespoons vegetable oil
5 tablespoons fresh lemon juice	6 medium-size new red potatoes
4 tablespoons ($\frac{1}{2}$ stick) butter	Salt to taste
	Sour cream

Peel and core the apples, and slice them $\frac{1}{8}$ inch thick. Put the apple slices in a shallow bowl and sprinkle the lemon juice all over. Toss until the lemon juice penetrates each slice.

Put the butter and oil in a large skillet that has a lid. Leave over very low heat while preparing the potatoes. Don't peel the potatoes, just scrub and then slice them $\frac{1}{8}$ inch thick. Turn the heat up to medium high and spread the potato slices evenly over the skillet. Salt to taste. Cook the slices until lightly browned, then turn them over to lightly brown the other side.

Drain the apple slices of lemon juice and add to the potatoes in the skillet, tossing to mix. Cover and cook over high heat for a minute or two. Uncover, and cook another 2 minutes, turning once or twice. Serve hot with sour cream.

Potato Custard

(three servings)

This is a dish fit for the fussiest eater. Potatoes are sliced thin, lightly salted and generously peppered, covered with eggs and milk and bits of butter, and baked into a congenial custard. It is nice to add some crumbled cooked sausage, ham, or bacon, if you have some on hand.

4 tablespoons (½ stick) butter
   (plus 1 tablespoon for buttering
   the dish)
2 medium-size baking potatoes

Salt and pepper to taste
2 eggs
½ cup milk

Preheat the oven to 350°F. Lavishly butter a shallow 1-quart baking dish.

Peel the potatoes and slice very thin. Spread a layer of potatoes over the baking dish in a single layer, sprinkle with salt and liberally with pepper, and dot a tablespoon or two of butter over the potatoes. Repeat layering, salting and peppering, and buttering, until all the potatoes are used.

Beat the eggs and milk together until mixed. Pour over the potatoes. Bake for 30 to 40 minutes, or until the potatoes are just tender when pierced with a knife. Serve hot.

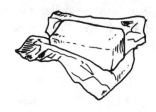

Creek Bank Potatoes

(four servings)

This recipe is for the kind of potatoes you would get on a fishing trip—cooked up at dawn in a skillet on a creek bank, and there waiting for you whether you caught anything or not. Just the thing you would want to eat on a cold morning when you are feeling lean.

4 russet potatoes
1 large onion
6 tablespoons (¾ stick) butter, melted

2 tablespoons vegetable oil
2 tablespoons bacon fat
Salt and lots of pepper

Don't peel the potatoes. Scrub and cut them into quarters lengthwise; then slice crosswise into ⅜-inch pieces. Rinse in cold water. Coarsely chop the onion. Mix the butter, vegetable oil, and bacon fat in a bowl. Add the potatoes and onion and toss with salt to taste and coarsely ground pepper. Throw the potatoes into the skillet over medium-high heat and shake to spread them evenly. Cover the skillet and cook over medium heat 40 minutes, shaking the pan occasionally.

Variation   If you're not on a creek bank, these potatoes are wonderful done in the oven. You will need a 10- or 11-inch ovenproof skillet; if yours has a handle that is not ovenproof, cover with several layers of foil. Put all the ingredients into the skillet, toss together, and put the skillet into a preheated 425°F oven. The potatoes will take approximately 20 minutes to bake.

Meat and Fish

Breakfast Steak
Creamed Chipped Beef with Mushrooms
Corned Beef Hash
Pork Tenderloin with Biscuits and Gravy
Breakfast Sausage
Ham and Bacon
   Ruffled Ham
   Ham Loaf
   Chipped Ham with Dried Apricots
Bacon
Fresh Fish
Trout Fried with Oatmeal
Fish Hash
Smoked and Salted Fish
Red Flannel Fish Hash
Kedgeree
Salt Cod Cakes
Salt Cod Potato Breakfast

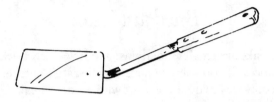

I hardly ever think of meat as the most important part of a breakfast menu, and never as the only dish. It should be considered more as an accompaniment to the main ingredients of breakfast—grains, dairy products, fruit, and sometimes eggs. I only serve meat in very, very small amounts, but that little bit can make everything else taste better.

To Mark Twain, and to many Americans a hundred years ago, breakfast meant "a mighty porterhouse steak an inch and a half thick, hot and sputtering from the griddle; dusted with fragrant pepper; enriched with little melting bits of butter...; the precious juices of the meat trickling out and joining the gravy, archipelagoed with mushrooms;... and a great cup of American homemade coffee... some smoking-hot biscuits, a plate of hot buckwheat cakes, with transparent syrup..." This *sounds* wonderful, but the small Breakfast Steak following is more appetizing to me. Big portions of ham, bacon, and sausage are all well and good for lumberjacks, but not for most everyday appetites. And after all, who wants to cook dinner for breakfast? And who can afford to?

Fresh fish, on the other hand, has a certain delicacy and lightness that occasionally seems right for breakfast. Simply broiled or pan fried, fish can be a refreshing high-protein alternative to high-fat meats like ham and bacon. Cured fish—salted, dried, or smoked—is practically a stranger to the American breakfast table. Try out the cured fish recipes in this chapter and you may become a convert.

Breakfast Steak

Breakfast steaks are small tenderloins, about ¼ inch thick, weighing about 3 ounces. If you want to have a well-seared outside and a raw inside, the only way to do it is to start with a frozen steak. Use a heavy skillet, and if you are not in a hurry, trim about 1 tablespoon of fat off the steak and let it slowly melt in the skillet over medium-low heat: I take the back of a spoon, and as the skillet heats up I press down on the fat until the skillet is lubricated. When the skillet is filmed with fat, turn the heat to high and let the skillet get super hot. Put the steak or steaks in the skillet, salt and pepper liberally, and pan fry for about 1 minute on each side.

Creamed Chipped Beef with Mushrooms

(four servings)

You might be disdainful of creamed dishes and I wouldn't blame you, having been served lots of pasty cream sauce over the years (and over the toast). But this dish, with a proper cream sauce, will change your mind. It is very nice over a crisp waffle or whole wheat toast.

2½ ounces sliced dried beef,
   rinsed under cold water
   if too salty
5 tablespoons butter
1½ cups cleaned and sliced fresh
   mushrooms

3 tablespoons flour
2½ cups milk
Salt and pepper to taste

Shred the beef into a bowl by tearing the slices into bits.

Melt 2 tablespoons butter in a skillet over medium heat. Add the mushrooms and cook for a minute, stirring, just until they change color a little. Remove the mushrooms with a slotted spoon to the bowl containing the beef.

Melt the remaining 3 tablespoons butter in the skillet over medium heat. Add the flour and cook, stirring constantly, for about 2 minutes. Still stirring, slowly add the milk. Add the salt and pepper. Stir and cook for at least 5 minutes, until the sauce has thickened. Stir in the beef and mushrooms, cook another 10 seconds, remove from the heat, and serve.

Corned Beef Hash

(four servings)

Patience is the essential ingredient for making good hash. Next, you will need lots of pepper and some salt. If you insist on using it, serve with warm chili sauce. This recipe makes a darn good hash.

4 cups cooked and finely diced corned beef	Lots of pepper
	Salt to taste
3 cups cooked and finely diced potatoes	3 tablespoons butter
	2 tablespoons oil
1 cup grated or finely chopped onion	1/2 cup heavy cream

Put the corned beef, potatoes, and onion in a large bowl. Sprinkle with pepper and salt. Toss and mix the ingredients well.

Heat the butter and oil in a large skillet that has a cover. Add the hash and spread over the bottom of the skillet. Press the hash down with a spatula. Pour the cream evenly over the hash. Cover and cook over medium-low heat for about 10 minutes—don't hurry this. Uncover and check the bottom of the hash to see how brown it is getting—it will take at least 10 minutes to get lightly browned if the heat is moderately low. Turn the heat to high and cook, uncovered, for 5 minutes more. Invert the hash onto a warm plate and serve.

Pork Tenderloin with Biscuits and Gravy

(four servings)

If you are going to be working hard physically, this farm breakfast will fortify you and keep your strength up the whole morning. Hot home-made Applesauce (see page 168) is a nice accompaniment.

Twelve ¾-inch-thick pork tender- loin pieces (about 2 inches in diameter)	*Gravy* ¼ cup bacon fat
½ cup all-purpose flour	¼ cup all-purpose flour
Salt and pepper to taste	Salt and pepper to taste
3 tablespoons bacon fat	2 cups half-and-half

Cream Biscuits (see page 48)

Trim any thick pieces of fat from the edges of the tenderloin, but leave a little. Blend together the flour, salt, and pepper on a piece of waxed paper. Dredge each round of pork in the seasoned flour. Shake to remove any excess flour and place on a piece of waxed paper.

Melt the 3 tablespoons bacon fat in a 10-inch skillet. When the fat is hot, place the pork pieces in a single layer in the skillet. Brown quickly on each side, lower the heat, and let the pork cook gently for about 5 minutes, or until cooked through. Remove the meat to a heated plate, and cover to keep warm while making the gravy.

To make the gravy, add the ¼ cup bacon fat to the fat left in the skillet that cooked the pork pieces. With a spatula, scrape up all the bits from the bottom of the pan to include in the gravy. Add the flour, salt, and pepper, and over medium heat stir slowly but constantly, cooking the roux until the flour is a nut-brown color. Slowly add the half-and-half, still stirring constantly, and cook over medium-low heat until the gravy is smooth and thickened.

Provide 3 tenderloin pieces for each serving, with biscuits on the side. Encourage everyone to split the biscuits and spoon gravy over them and the pork.

Breakfast Sausage

(sixteen 3-inch links or twelve patties)

The following recipe may be made into patties or into sausage links. If you choose to make the links (stuffing the sausage into casing) you will need three hands, so enlist the aid of some patient soul in the house. Sausage links make a juicier sausage when cooked than the patty, but I think both are splendid if some basic directions are followed. It is very important to have one-third fat to two-thirds pork. If you buy pork butt from a supermarket you will have ample fat. Ask the butcher to grind the pork butt or do it yourself. (It should be ground coarse or "chili-grind.") If the pork is too lean to supply the necessary proportion of one-third fat, ask to buy additional pork fat and have it coarsely ground in with the pork butt meat. If you are grinding your meat at home, have the meat well chilled so the fat doesn't soften and blend into the meat—chilling will help keep the fat more intact during the grinding and mixing.

2 pounds pork butt ($\frac{1}{3}$ fat to $\frac{2}{3}$ pork), ground coarse or "chili-grind," chilled
$1\frac{1}{2}$ teaspoons freshly ground pepper
$1\frac{1}{4}$ teaspoons salt

$1\frac{1}{2}$ tablespoons minced fresh sage, or $2\frac{1}{2}$ teaspoons crumbled dried sage
2 teaspoons minced fresh thyme, or 1 teaspoon crumbled dried thyme

Combine the ground pork, pepper, salt, sage, and thyme in a large mixing bowl. Thoroughly mix the ingredients, but do it as gently as possible so the mixture doesn't become "creamy." This will not be a problem if the meat is chilled.

Stuffing casing to make links Sausage casing may be either plastic or natural hog casing. The natural is much superior, so try using it. Many butcher shops carry hog casing—it comes in irregular lengths in small cartons and is packed in salt. It will keep for many months in the refrigerator if you keep it well packed in salt. Take about 5 feet of casing and soak it in water for about an hour before using. Rinse well to remove the excess salt.

Use a 12- or 16-inch pastry bag fitted with a $\frac{1}{2}$-inch tube. Open the end of the sausage casing and slip it up onto the tube fitting. Push all of the casing up onto the tube fitting so it is bunched up, leaving a tail about 2 inches long. Knot the little piece of casing tail. Fill the bag with sausage, leaving 3 inches of unfilled bag at the top so you can twist the bag and push the sausage through the tube opening. Here is the point where you will need an extra hand. Have someone firmly hold the bunched-up casing on the tube while you twist the top of the bag, then push the sausage through into the casing. As the sausage fills the casing to the length you want, give the casing a couple of turns, which will complete each link as it is filled. Proceed until you have used up all the sausage meat.

Just before frying the sausage, prick each link with the point of a sharp knife in several places so the fat can escape during cooking. Fry the sausage over medium-low heat, covered for 5 minutes; then cook uncovered, turning once or twice, to brown for about 5 minutes more.

Sausage Patties If the sausage is too sticky to handle, wet your hands with cold water. For each patty, use about $\frac{1}{2}$ cup sausage and pat into a round, flat disk. Cook over high heat for about 2 minutes on each side to brown, and then lower the heat and finish cooking for about another 2 minutes. Pat dry of excess fat on paper towels and serve hot.

Sausage Rolls This is a fine way to prepare sausage for lots of people. Preheat the oven to 400°F. Cut four strips of parchment paper 12 inches long and 5 inches wide. Butter each piece on one side. Divide the sausage mixture into 4 equal parts. Lightly flour your hands and roll and pat each piece into a 12-inch roll. Place each roll on a piece of buttered parchment and roll the parchment around it. Place each roll, loose side down, on a baking sheet. Bake the rolls for about 10 minutes. Unwrap and cut each roll into the desired size for serving.

HAM AND BACON

In the past, pork was salt-cured, dried, and sometimes smoked to preserve it. Our taste for cured ham and bacon has outlasted necessity, and most of the ham and bacon sold today is salted just for flavor. The curing process used to take a year or more. Today, bacon and ham are injected with brine and steam-smoked, all in less than a day.

Almost all supermarket hams are precooked and ready to eat. Many of them have the bone removed, and some are even presliced. All of these hams lack the complex character of hams cured the old-fashioned way. I think that a ham without its bone has lost its soul—it is bland and soft.

One of the best buys in cured pork is smoked picnic shoulder. (A ham is the hind leg of a pig; the picnic shoulder is the fore leg.) Smoked picnic shoulders are less expensive than ham, and they have a deep, smoky flavor—a world apart from canned hams.

It is still possible to buy country ham cured the same way hams have been cured for hundreds of years. Country hams will differ depending on the breed of pig, its age, and diet (the best Italian hams are supposed to be fed on chestnuts and cheese whey; some Southern pigs are still fed on peanuts). The curing process varies, too: the hams may be dry- or brine-cured and the cure may include sugar, maple sugar, molasses, pepper or other spices, and nitrite. And hams are smoked for different lengths of time, with different kinds of fuel—corncobs, apple, hickory, or sassafras, to name a few. Differences in climate, altitude, and the amount of time the ham is allowed to age will also alter the taste of a ham. Some hams are still aged for over a year. Here is a list of just a few mail-order sources of country hams. There are many more, and your taste will have to guide you to the ham you like best.

Col. Bill Newsom's Kentucky Country Hams
127 North Highland Avenue
Princeton, KY 42445
(502) 365-2482

Comstock Farms
Church Street
Barton, VT 05822
(802) 525-3444

Lawrence's Smoke House
R.R. 1, Box 28
Newfane, VT 05345
(802) 365-7751

Ozark Mountain Smokehouse
P.O. Box 37
Farmington, AR 72730
(800) 643-3437

Smithfield Ham and Products Company
P.O. Box 487
Smithfield, VA 23430
(804) 357-2121

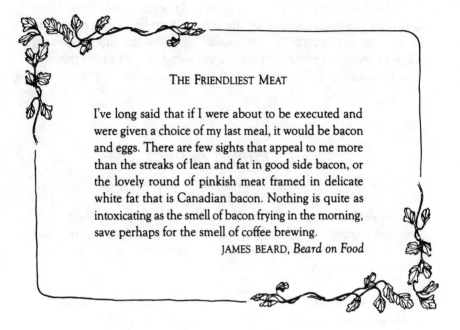

THE FRIENDLIEST MEAT

I've long said that if I were about to be executed and were given a choice of my last meal, it would be bacon and eggs. There are few sights that appeal to me more than the streaks of lean and fat in good side bacon, or the lovely round of pinkish meat framed in delicate white fat that is Canadian bacon. Nothing is quite as intoxicating as the smell of bacon frying in the morning, save perhaps for the smell of coffee brewing.

JAMES BEARD, *Beard on Food*

Ruffled Ham

This is an attractive and appetizing way to serve just a little bit of ham without feeling ungenerous. For some of us who are watching our weight, the flavor of even a little ham with eggs or whatever is satisfying. A couple of crinkled-up slices of paper-thin Ruffled Ham per serving will fill the bill. The ham can be "ruffling" while you cook eggs or something else to serve with it.

Buy a small piece of your favorite kind of ham and have it sliced paper-thin. Buying ham in a delicatessen, where slicing to order is the usual practice, can save you from looking for an accommodating butcher.

Preheat the oven to 350°F. For each serving, separate two slices of ham and, one at a time, crumple up the slices in your hand. Put them both in an ovenproof custard cup or a small bowl. Put the cup (or as many cups as there are servings) into the oven and allow to heat through, about 10 minutes. Turn each serving out onto a plate and serve.

Ham Loaf

(four servings)

This is extremely good, hot or cold: it sets nicely and it slices easily without crumbling. Of course, a good ham loaf depends on good ham—beware those watery canned ones. Serve with warm Raw Apple Muffins (see page 58).

3 cups ground ham
1½ pounds ground pork
½ teaspoon coarsely ground
  pepper
2 teaspoons finely chopped
  fresh thyme, or 1 teaspoon
  crumbled dried thyme

1 whole bay leaf, crumbled
1 cup fresh bread crumbs
  (preferably dark rye
  bread crumbs)
1 egg, lightly beaten
½ cup milk

Preheat the oven to 350°F. Butter a medium-size loaf pan.

Mix all ingredients together in a bowl, tossing until well combined. Lightly pack into the loaf pan. Bake for 40 to 50 minutes, or until the fat is bubbling around the edges. Remove and pour off any excess fat. Allow to set for 10 to 15 minutes in the pan before turning out. Serve hot or cold.

Chipped Ham with Dried Apricots

(four servings)

Tart and sour flavors have a traditional affinity for pork, ham, and sausages—think of sauerkraut. In this dish, the sour taste of dried apricots goes well with the smoky flavor of ham. Serve this hot, spooned over a crisp waffle, white toast, or rye toast.

1 cup dried apricots
2 cups boiling water
3 tablespoons butter
2 tablespoons flour
3 cups milk
1 teaspoon dry English mustard
   dissolved in 2 tablespoons
   water

Salt to taste (be careful—
   ham is quite salty)
1 cup shredded or coarsely
   chopped cooked ham

Put the dried apricots in a bowl and pour 2 cups boiling water over. Let stand for 15 minutes, until the apricots have softened. Cut them into small pieces and set aside.

Melt the butter in a skillet and stir in the flour. Cook over medium heat, stirring constantly, for 2 minutes. Continuing to stir, slowly add the milk. Add the mustard and salt, and cook the sauce for 5 minutes. Then add the apricots and ham and cook for another minute. Taste, correct seasoning, and serve.

Bacon

Bacon is cured pork belly. Bacon cut from a slab at a deli counter or by a reliable butcher may be better than packaged, presliced supermarket bacon. The taste of old-fashioned cured bacon is so much better that it will spoil you forever. Some of the smokehouses that supply country hams also sell bacon.

To pan-fry bacon, start it in a cold skillet and cook slowly, over medium-low heat, turning over at least once and pouring off excess fat. If you like your bacon slices quite flat, you can weight the bacon down in the skillet with the bottom of another, smaller pan.

To broil bacon, place the slices on the rack of a broiling pan or roasting pan with a little water in it. Put the pan about 4 inches from the broiling unit. Turn the slices once, midway through the 3- to 5-minute cooking time.

To bake bacon, place the slices on a rack in a pan and bake in a 400°F oven for 10 to 12 minutes.

Fresh Fish

Fresh fish cooked simply would be good for breakfast—try it lightly floured or cooked in cornmeal, pan fried or broiled, whole or filleted. A good rule of thumb for estimating cooking time, regardless of method or type of fish, is to figure 10 minutes of cooking time per inch of thickness (at the fish's thickest point). Remember that this 10-minute rule is a compromise—it overestimates the time needed to cook a thin piece of fish. The type of fish should be taken into account, too.

Very thin, very delicate fish fillets under $1/2$ inch thick are a snap to pan fry. Just cook in a little butter and oil for about 15 to 20 seconds, cover the pan, cook for 15 seconds more, take the lid off, and serve.

Trout Fried with Oatmeal

(four servings)

Rainbow trout is the kind of trout most commonly found in markets. It ranges in weight from 1 to 2 pounds and is 10 to 12 inches long. This delicate white fish is best when very little is done to it other than cooking briefly and serving with lemon. The oatmeal makes a good coating that is mild in taste but lends a nice texture.

$1/2$ cup milk	4 trout (leave the heads and tails
$2/3$ cup rolled oats	on, unless you are squeamish)
$1/4$ cup shortening, or a combina-	Salt and pepper to taste
tion of oil and butter	Lemon wedges

Pour the milk in a large deep plate and spread the oatmeal on a piece of waxed paper. If you want a finer-textured oatmeal than the flakes, whir the rolled oats in a food processor.

Put the shortening in a large skillet and heat it over high heat. Dip each trout in the milk and then in the oatmeal, coating each side completely. Put the trout in the hot shortening and turn the heat down to medium-high. Salt and pepper the trout and cook for 3 to 4 minutes; then turn the trout and cook for 3 to 4 minutes on the other side—don't overcook. Remove from the pan and serve with lemon wedges.

Fish Hash

(four servings)

The goodness of this simple hash depends on good fish and lots of freshly ground pepper.

3 tablespoons bacon fat	2 cups cooked, flaked fish
3 cups cooked potatoes, peeled and cut into small dice	Salt to taste
1 teaspoon freshly ground pepper	½ cup heavy cream

Melt the bacon fat in a large skillet over high heat. Spread the potatoes evenly over the skillet, sprinkle with the pepper, and reduce heat to medium to cook for 4 to 5 minutes. Spread the fish evenly over the potatoes, pressing down with a spatula, and salt lightly. Drizzle the cream evenly over the hash and let cook another 4 to 5 minutes. Lift the edge of the hash with a spatula and check to see that it is getting nicely browned on the bottom; turn the heat up a trifle if it isn't. Cook until good and brown, turn onto a warm platter, and serve.

Smoked and Salted Fish

When cod and similar fish are preserved by drying they are called stockfish; when preserved by partial drying after being salted they are known as salt cod. Salt cod requires soaking before it can be cooked to reconstitute its flesh and get rid of excessive saltiness.

Haddock is preserved by light salting and smoking. When split and smoked to a golden-yellow, it is called finnan haddie.

To freshen salt cod or salt mackerel, cover the fish with cold water and soak for 8 hours, changing the water at least once. Taste the fish; if it is still too salty, soak in another change of water for another hour or two, or cover with milk and simmer for 5 minutes or so.

To freshen finnan haddie, it is best to soak the fish in cold milk for an hour, drain, and then poach in milk. The milk sweetens the fish and tames its saltiness. The poaching milk can be thickened with flour, cooked, and made into a very tasty sauce.

Red Flannel Fish Hash

(four servings)

Red flannel hash always has beets in it. This dish is especially good with any salted fish—the beets lend a faint sweetness that balances the saltiness. Red Flannel Fish Hash is very tasty and looks inviting with its streaks of red and pink.

1 cup beets, cooked, peeled, and diced	½ teaspoon pepper
2 cups potatoes, cooked and diced	3 tablespoons butter
2 cups salted mackerel or cod, freshened (see above) and flaked	½ cup milk

Put the beets, potatoes, fish, and pepper together in a bowl, and toss to mix.

Melt the butter in a heavy skillet. Spread the hash evenly over the bottom of the skillet and drizzle the milk evenly over the hash. Cook over medium-low heat for about 10 minutes. Watch carefully and lift the edge of the hash with a spatula from time to time to make sure it isn't burning. Turn the hash over—it is easy to turn over one small section at a time. Continue to cook for another 5 minutes. Serve hot.

Kedgeree

(four servings)

Kedgeree is an English breakfast dish that originated in India. We made this dish many times in James Beard's cooking classes and it always met with great approval. The flavors and textures are wonderful: the faintly smoky finnan haddie and the mild spiciness of curry and nutmeg; the chewy basmati rice and the soft finnan haddie. We served this dish on a large platter with scrambled eggs in the center and the kedgeree in a ring around the eggs.

3 hard-boiled eggs, peeled and chopped fine
$1\frac{1}{2}$ cups freshened, boned, skinned, and flaked finnan haddie, or any cooked or smoked fish (see page 207)
3 cups cooked rice (try brown basmati rice)

$\frac{3}{4}$ cup heavy cream
1 teaspoon curry powder
$\frac{1}{2}$ teaspoon nutmeg
Generous grindings of black pepper
3 tablespoons lemon juice
Salt if needed

Put the eggs, fish, and rice in a large mixing bowl. Toss together lightly to mix. Put the cream in a small saucepan, add the curry powder and nutmeg, and heat, stirring until the spices are blended. Add the cream mixture, pepper, and lemon juice to the rice mixture, and gently toss. Taste for salt and add some if needed (the dish won't need any if the smoked fish is salty). Put the Kedgeree in a casserole and heat in a moderate (325°F) oven only until hot. Serve as described above.

Salt Cod Cakes

(six cakes)

It is a shame that salt cod seems to be fading away on our menus. It has a distinct character which absolutely shines in some dishes. These codfish cakes are a good example—serve them with plenty of lemon wedges and bacon, Crisp Whole Wheat Buns (see page 18), and slices of melon. Soak the salt cod in several changes of cold water for 12 hours. Drain, put in a saucepan, cover with cold water, and add a bay leaf and a little thyme. Bring the water to a bare simmer and let the cod poach for 10 minutes. Drain and proceed with the Salt Cod Cakes.

1 cup flaked salt cod	3 tablespoons milk
(prepared as directed above)	1/4 cup flour
1 1/2 cups mashed potatoes	1/4 cup yellow cornmeal
2 eggs, lightly beaten	3 tablespoons shortening
1 teaspoon pepper	

Mix the cod, potatoes, eggs, pepper, and milk if needed (add only if the mixture seems too dry to you) in a bowl. Using a large spoon, beat briskly until the mixture is well combined. Divide into 6 equal parts. On a piece of waxed paper combine the flour and cornmeal.

Heat the shortening in a large skillet over medium-high heat. Pat the cod cakes into 4-inch patties. Dredge with the flour and cornmeal. Cook the cakes until brown on each side. Serve hot.

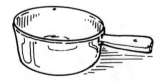

Salt Cod Potato Breakfast

(four servings)

This dish is easily made the night before and popped into the oven in the morning to be heated and served. Salt cod, potato, cream sauce, and crisp crumbs make a breakfast for champions.

4 tablespoons ($\frac{1}{2}$ stick) butter	1½ cups salt cod, freshened (see
3 tablespoons flour	page 207), poached, and flaked
3 cups milk	3 hard-boiled eggs, diced
¼ teaspoon pepper	Salt to taste
2 cups potatoes, cooked and cut	1 cup fresh bread crumbs
into small dice	

Butter a 3-quart casserole.

Melt the 4 tablespoons butter in a heavy-bottomed saucepan and stir in the flour. Cook over medium heat, stirring constantly, for 2 minutes. Slowly add the milk, still stirring, and continue to cook until the mixture thickens. Add the pepper and cook for 3 more minutes, stirring. Remove from the heat and add the potatoes, cod, and hard-boiled eggs. Taste and add salt if needed. Stir gently and spoon the mixture into the casserole. Sprinkle the crumbs evenly over the top. Put in a preheated 350°F oven and bake for 25 minutes; if the dish has been refrigerated, bake for 45 minutes, or until the sauce is bubbling a bit around the edges. Serve hot.

Custards and Puddings

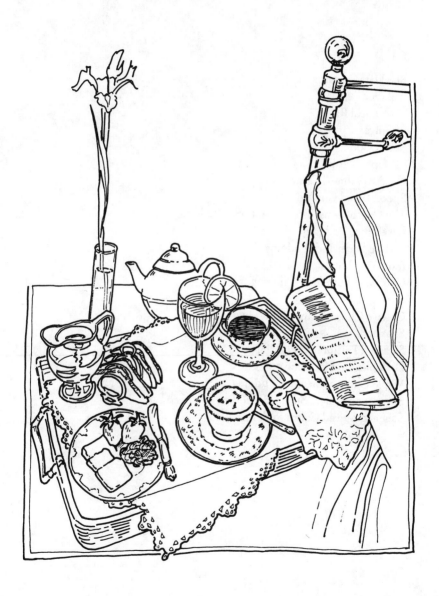

Breakfast Custards
  Basic
  Oatmeal Raisin
  Ginger
  Hot Cocoa
  Maple Syrup
Cheese Oatmeal Custard
Spoon Bread Custard
The Coach House Bread and Butter Pudding
Baked Rice Pudding
  Rose Water Rice Pudding
Indian Pudding
Cornmeal Buttermilk Pudding
Cornflake Pudding
Cottage Cheese Oatmeal Pudding
Sharlotka
Steamed Persimmon Pudding
Dark Steamed Pudding
Maple Oatmeal Steamed Pudding
Sherry and Ginger Steamed Pudding
Steamed Spiced Carrot Pudding

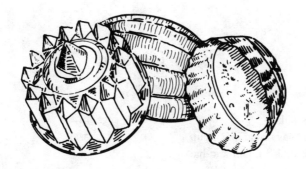

Custards and puddings are wholesome, soft and spoonable, and wonderfully moist—gentle food that won't ruffle your feathers in the morning. A breakfast custard or pudding is a complete breakfast in a bowl, and made from morning ingredients like dairy products, cereals, breads, and eggs. Though they cover a wide range of different flavors, they are essentially simple preparations: if you know how to make one, you can make them all.

Egg custards are quickly made and make great everyday breakfasts. Steamed puddings are sturdier and more cakelike—the perfect breakfast dish for Christmas, Thanksgiving, or Easter.

BREAKFAST CUSTARDS

For people who don't like eggs other ways, soft egg custards slide down deliciously and take no effort to enjoy. They always used to be considered good for the convalescing, and they do seem to be especially digestible and strengthening. Smooth, silky custards are wonderfully receptive to savory additions, and they are easy to make in quantity if you are having a large breakfast party.

Basic Custard

(four servings)

½ cup milk
½ cup heavy cream, or 1 cup
   milk, or 1 cup half-and-half

4 eggs
Salt to taste

Preheat the oven to 375°F. Butter 4 custard cups. Put a shallow baking dish, large enough to hold the custard cups, in the oven and fill it halfway with hot water.

Beat the milk, cream, eggs, and salt together in a bowl. Add the various ingredients for each kind of custard in the manner described in the recipes that follow. Place the filled cups in the water bath in the oven. Bake for 20 minutes, or until the custard is barely set. Remove from the oven. Run a knife around the edges and turn the custards out onto a serving plate; or serve in the cup.

Oatmeal Raisin Custard

½ cup quick oatmeal
3 tablespoons raisins, chopped
½ teaspoon nutmeg

Basic Custard (preceding recipe)
4 teaspoons brown sugar

Stir the oatmeal, chopped raisins, and nutmeg into the custard mixture, and sprinkle the brown sugar on top after filling the custard cups. Serve with bacon.

Ginger Custard

$\frac{1}{2}$ cup cream cheese
2 teaspoons grated fresh
  gingerroot

2 tablespoons marmalade
Basic Custard (see page 214)

Stir the cream cheese, ginger, and marmalade into the custard mixture until thoroughly blended before filling the cups. This stays rather creamy in the center, so bake about 25 minutes. Serve with oatmeal and toast.

Hot Cocoa Custard

2 tablespoons unsweetened cocoa
2 tablespoons sugar

$\frac{1}{4}$ cup very hot water
Basic Custard (see page 214)

Mix the cocoa and sugar together in a bowl, add the hot water, and stir to dissolve. Allow to cool a little, then add the ingredients for the basic custard recipe and pour into the custard cups.

Maple Syrup Custard

$\frac{1}{2}$ cup maple syrup
Basic Custard (see page 214)

Add the maple syrup to the basic custard recipe and stir to mix. This is one of the best custards I know.

Cheese Oatmeal Custard

(four servings)

This makes a good, wholesome, well-rounded breakfast. A dish of sliced banana and prunes is nice with it.

6 eggs
1½ cups milk (use skim milk
   if you wish)
⅔ cup quick oatmeal

⅔ cup grated Jack cheese
Salt
¾ cup shredded wheat
   (preferably bite-size)

Preheat the oven to 350°F. Butter a 1½-quart casserole.

Stir the eggs and milk together in a bowl. Add the oatmeal, cheese, and salt to taste. Pour into the casserole and strew the shredded wheat on top.

Bake for about 35 to 40 minutes, or until just set. Serve hot.

Spoon Bread Custard

(six servings)

Spoon Bread Custard is moister and lighter than most cornmeal recipes, and it has a little bite to it from the buttermilk. This is very good served with maple syrup.

1 cup yellow cornmeal
2 cups water
1 teaspoon salt

2 tablespoons butter
4 eggs, well beaten
1 cup buttermilk

Preheat the oven to 400°F. Butter a 1½-quart casserole.

Put the cornmeal in a bowl and stir in 1 cup cold water. Put the remaining 1 cup water in a saucepan with the salt and bring to a boil. Immediately stir in the wet cornmeal (wetting cornmeal first with cold water prevents lumping). Stirring constantly, cook for 1 minute. Remove from the heat and beat in the butter, eggs, and buttermilk, beating until smooth. Pour into the casserole and bake about 40 minutes, until a straw inserted into the center comes out clean. Serve hot.

The Coach House
Bread and Butter Pudding

(ten servings)

This is the best bread pudding ever. The recipe comes generously from Leon Lianides, owner of the legendary New York restaurant The Coach House. Don't overbake the pudding—remove it from the oven when the center still trembles slightly.

12 or 13 slices French bread, crusts removed (not sourdough)
8 tablespoons (1 stick) butter, room temperature
5 eggs
4 egg yolks
1 cup granulated sugar
1/8 teaspoon salt
4 cups milk
1 cup heavy cream
1 tablespoon vanilla extract
Confectioners' sugar for sprinkling

Preheat the oven to 375°F.

Butter one side of each slice of bread and set aside.

Put the eggs, yolks, granulated sugar, and salt in a large bowl and beat until thoroughly mixed.

Pour the milk and cream into a heavy-bottomed saucepan and heat until scalded (tiny bubbles will form around the edge of the pan). Remove from the heat and, whisking briskly, slowly add the egg mixture. Stir in the vanilla.

Have ready enough boiling water to come $2\frac{1}{2}$ inches up the sides of a pot large enough to hold a 2-quart baking dish. Layer the bread, buttered side up, in the baking dish. Strain the custard into the dish (the bread will float to the top). Put the pot of boiling water into the oven and then put the custard-filled dish into it.

Bake about 45 minutes, or until the custard is set except for a slight tremble in the center. Remove from the oven and sprinkle confectioners' sugar on top. It is delicious hot or cold, and just perfect with a little unsweetened heavy cream poured over.

Baked Rice Pudding

(six servings)

This old-fashioned, creamy rice pudding is soft and delicate. It will replace any of your new-fangled rice pudding recipes.

4 cups milk
$\frac{1}{2}$ teaspoon salt
$\frac{2}{3}$ cup sugar

4 tablespoons rice
Optional: $\frac{1}{2}$ teaspoon nutmeg

Preheat the oven to 300°F.

Put all the ingredients in a buttered baking dish and stir to blend. Bake for $3\frac{1}{2}$ hours, stirring 3 times in the first hour of baking so the rice doesn't settle.

Rose Water Rice Pudding　Follow the above recipe, omitting the nutmeg. Buy rose water (labeled Fluid Rose Soluble) at the pharmacy and dilute half and half with water. Put the mixture in a spray bottle, and just before serving the rice pudding, spray with rose water.

Indian Pudding

(six servings)

This old New England classic bakes basic breakfast ingredients together into a deep, hearty pudding. It is wonderful hot or cold.

4 cups cold milk	½ teaspoon cinnamon
½ cup yellow cornmeal	1 teaspoon salt
1 cup brown sugar	½ cup molasses
1½ teaspoons ground ginger	1 cup heavy cream
½ teaspoon nutmeg	

Preheat the oven to 275°F. Butter a 2-quart baking dish.

Stir together 1 cup cold milk and the cornmeal. In a heavy-bottomed saucepan, heat the remaining 3 cups milk to a bare simmer, stir in the cornmeal mixture, and stir briskly until smooth. Stirring constantly, cook about 4 or 5 minutes over medium heat, until the mush is well thickened. Remove from the heat and stir in the sugar, ginger, nutmeg, cinnamon, and salt. Mix well. Add the molasses and cream and blend well.

Pour the mixture into the baking dish and bake for 2 hours. Serve warm with a little heavy cream poured over.

Cornmeal Buttermilk Pudding

(four servings)

This light and spongy pudding is appetizingly tart with buttermilk and lemon zest—it is good with scrambled eggs or sausage.

2 eggs	1/2 teaspoon salt
1/2 cup yellow cornmeal	1 tablespoon grated lemon zest
2 cups buttermilk	

Preheat the oven to 350°F. Butter a 1 1/2-quart soufflé dish.

Put the eggs in a mixing bowl and whisk until well blended. Stir in the cornmeal, buttermilk, salt, and lemon zest.

Pour the mixture into the buttered dish. Bake for about 45 minutes, or until puffy and set. Serve hot.

Cornflake Pudding

(six servings)

This soft, gentle pudding is slightly crisp on top. It won't startle you first thing in the morning. This pudding can be made ahead and reheated.

4 cups milk	1 teaspoon ground ginger
2 eggs	3/4 teaspoon salt
2 tablespoons dark molasses	4 cups cornflakes
6 tablespoons sugar	

Preheat the oven to 350°F. Butter a 1½-quart soufflé dish or baking dish. Put a pan large enough to hold the baking dish in the oven and fill it with enough hot water to come halfway up the sides of the baking dish.

Put the milk, eggs, molasses, sugar, ginger, and salt in a bowl and stir briskly until all the ingredients are well mixed. Put the cornflakes in the bottom of the baking dish and pour the milk mixture over. Put the dish into the pan of hot water and bake for 45 to 50 minutes, or until the pudding is set. Serve warm.

Cottage Cheese Oatmeal Pudding

(four servings)

Cottage cheese and oatmeal have a natural affinity, and this recipe combines these two good breakfast ingredients in one dish.

2 cups cottage cheese	6 tablespoons sugar
2 cups cooked oatmeal	½ teaspoon nutmeg
2 eggs	Salt to taste
1 cup milk	

Preheat the oven to 325°F. Butter a 1½-quart baking or soufflé dish.

You can use a food processor or an electric mixer; or mix briskly by hand. Put the cottage cheese, oatmeal, eggs, milk, sugar, nutmeg, and salt in a processor or mixing bowl. Process or mix until the mixture is smooth. Spoon into the buttered dish and bake for about 40 minutes, or until the edges are golden and set. Serve hot or cold, with milk or cream.

Sharlotka

(about eight servings)

Sharlotka is a dark, moist, layered Polish pudding that combines several morning foods—bread, butter, jelly, and fruit: simple and inexpensive ingredients. Serve it with scrambled eggs and ham, bacon, or sausage.

A 1-pound loaf dark rye or
   pumpernickel bread
8 tablespoons (1 stick) butter
$\frac{1}{2}$ cup sugar
$\frac{1}{2}$ cup red wine or apple cider
2 tablespoons lemon juice
1 tablespoon grated lemon zest

1 tablespoon grated orange zest
2 teaspoons cinnamon
2 teaspoons vanilla extract
$\frac{1}{2}$ teaspoon salt
10 tart apples (about 4 pounds)
1 cup currant or raspberry jelly,
   melted

Tear the bread into $\frac{1}{2}$-inch pieces. Melt the butter in a large skillet, and when it is sizzling, toss in the bread. Fry the bread lightly for about 7 to 10 minutes over moderately high heat, stirring the bread and shaking the pan frequently to prevent scorching. Remove the pan from the heat and add the sugar, wine or cider, lemon juice, lemon zest, orange zest, cinnamon, vanilla, and salt. Stir until completely blended. Set aside while you prepare the apples.

Preheat the oven to 350°F. Butter a 2-quart baking dish.

Peel the apples, halve them, and remove the cores. Cut each half into 4 wedges. Steam the apple wedges on a rack over boiling water in a covered pan for 10 to 15 minutes, just until the apples are tender when pierced—don't overcook and let them become mushy.

Sprinkle about 1 cup bread mixture in the buttered baking dish. Spread an even layer of cooked apples over the top. Then spread on a generous cup bread mixture and top with the remaining apples. Drizzle the jelly over all, then top with the last of the bread mixture, which will not make a solid layer, but will have a dappled appearance.

Bake for 1 hour, until the top crumbs are crisp and the juices are bubbling. Serve warm, with milk poured over each serving if you wish.

Steamed Persimmon Pudding

(eight servings)

There are persimmon puddings and there are persimmon puddings. This ends the search—it is the best. The color is dark, the texture moist, and the flavor full and spicy. The pudding can be made ahead and reheated; it can even be frozen.

1 cup puréed persimmons (about 3 persimmons with skins removed)	1 tablespoon lemon juice
	2 tablespoons rum
	1 cup all-purpose flour
2 teaspoons baking soda	1 teaspoon cinnamon
8 tablespoons (1 stick) butter, room temperature	1/2 teaspoon salt
	1 cup broken walnuts or pecans
1 1/2 cups sugar	1 cup raisins
2 eggs	

Fill a kettle that is large enough to hold a 2-quart pudding mold with enough water to come halfway up the sides of the mold. Let the water come to a boil over medium heat while you are mixing the pudding batter. The mold must have a lid or be snugly covered with foil while steaming (a coffee can with a plastic lid works well). Also there must be a rack or Mason jar ring on the bottom under the mold in the kettle to allow the water to circulate freely while the pudding is steaming. Grease the mold.

Put the persimmon purée in a small bowl and stir in the baking soda. Set aside while mixing the other ingredients (the persimmon mixture will become quite stiff).

Cream the butter and sugar. Add the eggs, lemon juice, and rum, and beat well. Add the flour, cinnamon, and salt, and stir to blend. Add the persimmon mixture. Beat until well mixed. Stir in the nuts and raisins.

Spoon the batter into the mold, cover, and steam for 2 hours. Remove from the kettle, and let rest for 5 minutes. Turn onto a rack to cool, or cool just a little and serve warm. Serve with unsweetened whipped cream.

Dark Steamed Pudding

(eight servings)

This is a good old New England recipe. I love this kind of list of ingredients — all ever-ready straight off the pantry shelf. Together the coffee, spices, and molasses give this pudding a deep rich taste.

2 cups all-purpose flour	1/2 cup dark molasses
1/2 teaspoon ground cloves	1/2 cup coffee
1 teaspoon cinnamon	1 cup brown sugar
1 teaspoon nutmeg	2 eggs, room temperature
1/2 teaspoon baking soda	1 1/2 cups broken walnuts
1/2 teaspoon salt	
8 tablespoons (1 stick) butter, room temperature	

Put a kettle or Dutch oven on the stove and fill one-third full of water. Bring to a simmer. Grease a 2 1/2-quart pudding mold.

Put the flour, cloves, cinnamon, nutmeg, baking soda, and salt in a mixing bowl and stir to blend.

Put the butter, molasses, coffee, brown sugar, and eggs in a large mixing bowl. Beat until smooth. Add the flour mixture and blend well. Stir in the walnuts. Spoon the batter into the mold. Cover snugly. Place a rack or Mason jar ring under the mold on the bottom of the kettle so the pudding mold sits a little above the bottom of the kettle—the water must circulate on the bottom. Cover the kettle. Keep the water about halfway up the side of the mold. The water should be simmering. Steam for $1\frac{1}{2}$ hours. Check the pudding for doneness by inserting a wooden skewer into the center—it is done when it comes out clean. Remove from the kettle and let rest for 10 minutes, uncovered. Invert onto a rack and cool a little. This is to be served warm; it can be made ahead and reheated.

Maple Oatmeal Steamed Pudding

(four servings)

This is a nice change from the traditional steamed pudding: it doesn't have to steam for two hours, it only has four ingredients, and the maple-flavored oats give the pudding a unique, moist texture.

4 cups rolled oats	½ cup maple syrup
3 cups milk	1 teaspoon salt

Butter a $1\frac{1}{2}$-quart soufflé dish or mold. Fill a kettle or Dutch oven with water that will come halfway up the sides of the pudding container. Bring to a boil.

Put the oats, milk, maple syrup, and salt in the dish or mold and stir to mix well. Cover with a lid or a piece of foil, pinching the edges to seal.

Put the mold in the kettle on a rack or Mason jar ring so the mold is off the bottom of the kettle (the water must circulate freely). Put a lid on the kettle and turn the heat down so that the water simmers. Steam for 1 hour. For a firmer pudding, steam for 2 hours. Remove from the kettle, spoon from the mold, and serve hot.

Sherry and Ginger Steamed Pudding

(eight servings)

This pudding has a fine texture and lots of lively flavor. It is one of the best steamed puddings I know of and would be very appropriate for a late Thanksgiving or Christmas breakfast. To make it very special, serve with softly mounded whipped cream that has a little sherry added to it.

10 tablespoons (1 stick plus 2 tablespoons) butter	$\frac{1}{2}$ cup sweet or dry sherry (do not use cooking sherry)
1 cup sugar	$\frac{3}{4}$ cup coarsely chopped preserved ginger
2 eggs	
1$\frac{1}{2}$ cups all-purpose flour	$\frac{1}{2}$ cup ginger marmalade
1$\frac{1}{2}$ teaspoons baking powder	(use orange marmalade if
$\frac{1}{2}$ teaspoon salt	ginger is not available)

Butter a 2-quart covered pudding mold. Bring a pot of water to a boil—have enough water in the pot so the pudding mold will have water halfway up its sides while steaming.

Beat the butter and sugar in a medium-size bowl until smooth and blended. Add the eggs and beat well. Put the flour, baking powder, and salt in another bowl and stir with a fork until well mixed. Add the dry ingredients to the butter mixture and mix well again. Stir in the sherry and chopped ginger to blend thoroughly.

Spread the marmalade over the bottom of the mold and spoon in the batter. Cover. Put a trivet or Mason jar ring in the pot of water and place the pudding mold on it—the mold must have water circulating around the bottom. Cover the pot and steam for about 1 hour. The water should be kept at a gentle boil. During the steaming check the pot once or twice and replenish with boiling water when necessary.

The pudding is done when a straw inserted into the center comes out clean.

Remove the mold from the water. Allow the pudding to rest for 5 minutes in the mold before turning out onto a rack to cool. Wrap and freeze if the pudding is to be eaten later. To reheat, wrap the pudding in foil and place in a 350°F oven for 30 minutes.

Steamed Spiced Carrot Pudding

(eight servings)

This fine steamed pudding gracefully combines spices and molasses with the natural sweetness of carrots. Serve warm slices with Breakfast Cheese (see page 286) and sliced cantaloupe.

$1/2$ cup shortening	1 teaspoon cinnamon
$1/2$ cup sugar	1 teaspoon ground ginger
2 eggs	$1/2$ teaspoon ground cloves
1 cup dark molasses	$1/2$ teaspoon nutmeg
1 cup hot water	$1/2$ teaspoon allspice
$2 1/2$ cups all-purpose flour	$1 1/2$ cups grated carrots
$1 1/2$ teaspoons baking soda	1 cup raisins
$1/2$ teaspoon salt	

Fill a kettle that is large enough to hold a 2-quart mold with enough water to come halfway up the sides of the mold. Put the kettle over medium heat and let the water come to a boil while you are preparing the pudding batter. The mold must have a lid or be snugly covered with foil while steaming (a coffee can with a plastic lid will work). Put a rack or a Mason jar ring on the bottom of the kettle so that water can circulate under the mold while steaming. Grease the mold.

Put the shortening and sugar in a mixing bowl and beat until smooth. Add the eggs and mix well. Add the molasses and hot water and beat briskly. Stir in the flour, baking soda, salt, cinnamon, ginger, cloves, nutmeg, and allspice. Beat until well blended. Stir in the carrots and raisins.

Spoon the batter into the mold, cover, and let steam for $2\frac{1}{2}$ hours. Remove the mold from the kettle and let sit for 5 minutes. Turn onto a rack and let cool a little. Serve warm.

Cookies, Pies, and Cakes

Mother's Cookies
English Digestives
Cereal Cookies
Oatmeal Bran Breakfast Cookies
Orange Marmalade Cookies
Ginger Shortbread
Gingersnaps
Hard Ginger Cakes

Basic Pie Dough
Breakfast Apple Pie
Hominy Grits Pie
Apricot Shortbread Pie
Cranberry Raisin Pie
Shaker Stacked Pie
Mother's Pie
    Milk Pie

Whole Wheat Sponge Roll
Lemon Pound Cake
Granola Pound Cake
Raisin Almond Breakfast Cake
Indian Loaf Cake
Madeira Poppy Seed Cake
Fresh Ginger Cake
Soft Gingerbread
Great Coffee Cake
    Raisin and Spice
    Dried Fig and Almond
    Apple and Walnut
    Simple Vanilla
Fluffy Caramel Coffee Cake
Almond Coconut Coffee Cake
Apricot Prune Coffee Cake

These cookies, pies, and cakes are just good breakfast ingredients in another form, and they can make complete breakfasts along with fresh fruit or fruit juice, although we get so stuck in habit and tradition that we might not recognize these things right away as typical breakfast foods.

The cookie recipes are not too sweet. Cookies are made ahead as a matter of course, so they're on hand for an instant portable breakfast when you want to walk around in the morning and survey the day ahead. Cookies are perfect to take along with a thermos of coffee to the fireplace in cold weather, or out to the patio when it is warm out.

I guess that one reason we eat pie for breakfast is because it's there from last night's supper. I can think of nothing more appealing than several warm, plump pies laid out for the morning meal—there is something old-fashioned and homey about it. If you have a hard time arousing breakfast appetites, pies are a sure-fire way to get everyone to clean their plates.

The breakfast cakes in this chapter are meant to be sliced, toasted, and buttered, not frosted. With good cake the wholesomeness will shine through without the added frill of frosting. Breakfast cakes are wonderful, particularly if you are a sweet and not a savory breakfast person.

Mother's Cookies

(three dozen cookies)

I like to think that this is the cookie that all mothers would make if they knew about it. These cookies are crisp, and filled with irregular crunch and raisins.

1/2 cup shortening	1 teaspoon cinnamon
3/4 cup sugar	3/4 cup all-purpose flour
1 egg	1/2 cup rolled oats
1/2 teaspoon baking soda	1 cup cornflakes or Wheaties
1/2 teaspoon salt	3/4 cup golden raisins

Preheat the oven to 350°F. Don't grease the baking sheet(s).

Put the shortening, sugar, and egg in a mixing bowl. Beat until smooth. Add the baking soda, salt, cinnamon, and flour and beat until well blended. Add the oats, cornflakes or Wheaties, and raisins. This is going to be a stiff dough, but exert a little vigor and stir until the oats, flakes, and raisins are well distributed.

Drop rounded tablespoons of dough onto the baking sheet(s) about 1 inch apart. Bake for 15 to 17 minutes, or until lightly golden. Remove from the oven and let cool.

English Digestives

(six dozen biscuits)

These biscuits grow on you; in spite of yourself you will be reaching for one more. Wheat flour with bits of bran mixed in makes the best biscuit. These are mildly sweet and go well with a dish of fruit and coffee or tea.

1 cup all-purpose flour
1½ cups whole wheat flour
¼ cup bran
½ teaspoon baking powder
¼ teaspoon baking soda
½ teaspoon salt

8 tablespoons (1 stick) butter, chilled
¾ cup brown sugar
1 egg, well beaten
½ cup water

Preheat the oven to 375°F. Grease the baking sheets.

Put the flours, bran, baking powder, baking soda, and salt in a mixing bowl. Stir with a fork to mix well.

Cut the butter into small pieces and add to the flour mixture. Using either a pastry blender or your fingers, cut or rub the butter into the flour mixture until it is in coarse small bits. Add the sugar and, using a fork or your fingers, toss the mixture until the sugar is well distributed. Stir in the egg and water. Mix until you can gather the dough in a rough ball, and place on a floured surface. Knead about a dozen times. Divide into three equal pieces. Roll one piece out about ⅛ inch thick. Cut into 2½-inch rounds and place on a greased baking sheet. Prick each biscuit two or three times on top with the tines of a fork. Repeat with the other two pieces.

Bake about 20 minutes, or until the biscuits are lightly browned around the edges and on the bottom. Remove and cool. Store in an airtight container, or freeze.

Cereal Cookies

(thirty-two cookies)

These cookies are crisp and good, particularly with warm rice pudding. You may use either oatmeal or granola in the dough.

8 tablespoons (1 stick) butter, softened
$1/3$ cup brown sugar
$2/3$ cup granulated sugar
1 teaspoon vanilla extract
1 egg
$1 1/2$ cups all-purpose flour

$1/2$ teaspoon baking soda
$1/2$ teaspoon salt
1 cup rolled oats or unsweetened granola (see page 91 for homemade)
1 cup broken walnuts

Preheat the oven to 350°F. Grease two baking sheets.

Cream the butter and sugars until smooth. Add the vanilla and egg and beat well. Stir in the flour, baking soda, and salt. Mix vigorously. Add the cereal and walnuts. Blend well.

Lightly flour a board and turn the dough onto it. Roll out the dough about $1/8$ inch thick. Cut the cookies out with a 3-inch cookie cutter. Place the cookies slightly apart (they don't spread) on the baking sheets.

Bake for about 12 minutes, or until the cookies are lightly browned. Remove from the oven and cool on racks or on pieces of waxed paper.

Oatmeal Bran Breakfast Cookies

(three dozen cookies)

These chewy, crunchy cookies need no introduction.

¾ cup vegetable shortening	2½ cups rolled oats
1 cup brown sugar	1 cup all-purpose flour
⅓ cup granulated sugar	1 teaspoon salt
¼ cup strong coffee	½ teaspoon baking soda
1 egg	1½ cups All-Bran cereal

Preheat the oven to 350°F. Don't grease the baking sheet(s).

Put the shortening, sugars, coffee, and egg in a mixing bowl and beat until smooth and blended. Add the oats, flour, salt, and baking soda. Stir very well so the dough is well mixed.

Spread the All-Bran cereal out on a piece of waxed paper. This is a sticky dough, so wet your fingers with cold water before pinching off about 2 tablespoons of dough at a time and rolling it in the All-Bran. Don't worry if you can't get a heavy coating of cereal on each piece of dough; if just a little of the All-Bran sticks, it will give a nice texture to the cookies.

Place the dough pieces about 1½ inches apart on the baking sheet(s). Bake 12 to 15 minutes. Remove from the oven and cool on racks.

Orange Marmalade Cookies

(three dozen cookies)

This is an old-fashioned cookie that is rather thick and chewy with plenty of tasty orange marmalade in it. Orange Marmalade Cookies make splendid dunkers with coffee.

2 eggs
1½ cups sugar
1 teaspoon salt
⅓ cup shortening, melted and cooled
¾ cup orange marmalade

Grated zest of 1 lemon
3 tablespoons freshly squeezed lemon juice
3 cups all-purpose flour
2 teaspoons baking powder
1 cup broken walnuts

Preheat the oven to 375°F. Grease the baking sheet(s).

Put the eggs and sugar in a mixing bowl and beat until blended. Add the salt, shortening, orange marmalade, lemon zest, and lemon juice. Beat until the dough is thoroughly mixed. Add the flour and baking powder and beat well. This is a stiff dough. Add the walnuts, stirring well to distribute.

Drop the cookies by tablespoons onto the baking sheet(s) about 1 inch apart. Bake about 12 minutes, or until the edges of the cookies are golden. Remove from the oven and cool.

Ginger Shortbread

(two dozen wedges)

A crunchy, buttery cookie with a smooth texture and spicy overtones of ginger. The dough is pressed into pans like a plain shortbread, then cut into wedges while still warm and soft; it will crisp as it cools. Serve with fresh or poached fruit, or at the end of breakfast with coffee.

2 cups all-purpose flour	1 teaspoon baking soda
1 cup dark brown sugar	1/2 pound (2 sticks) butter,
2 tablespoons ground ginger	softened

Preheat the oven to 325°F, and get out two 8-inch round cake pans.

In a large bowl, stir and toss together the flour, brown sugar, ginger, and baking soda until thoroughly mixed. Cut the butter into half-tablespoon bits and drop them in. Blend the butter into the dry ingredients, using your fingertips or a pastry blender, as you would mix a pie dough, until the mixture is crumbly and you see no unblended pieces of butter.

Divide the dough in half and press each piece evenly into each of the cake pans. Prick all over with a fork at half-inch intervals. Bake for 40 to 45 minutes, until lightly browned around the edges—the center will stay low, and only the sides will rise slightly. Remove from the oven and let cool a minute or two, then cut each pan into 12 pie-shaped wedges. Lift from the pans and let cool completely on racks. Store in airtight containers.

Gingersnaps

(about forty cookies)

You will find these to be the best-tasting spicy, crisp gingersnaps there are. They are sweeter than most of the other breakfast cookies. Serve them at breakfast with sliced bananas and cream and you could start a trend. Try crumbling the gingersnaps over oatmeal or any other cooked cereal.

¾ cup vegetable shortening	2 cups all-purpose flour
1 cup sugar, plus extra to roll the cookies in	2 teaspoons baking soda
	½ teaspoon salt
1 egg	1 tablespoon ground ginger
¼ cup molasses	1 teaspoon cinnamon

Preheat the oven to 350°F and grease some cookie sheets.

Beat together the shortening and 1 cup sugar. Add the egg, beat until light and fluffy, and then add the molasses. In a separate bowl, stir and toss together the flour, baking soda, salt, ginger, and cinnamon. Add the dry ingredients to the first mixture, and beat until smooth and blended.

Gather up bits of the dough and roll them between the palms of your hands into 1-inch balls, then roll each ball in sugar. Place about 2 inches apart on the prepared cookie sheets and bake for 10 to 12 minutes, until the cookies have spread and the tops have cracked. Remove from the oven, take the gingersnaps off the baking sheet, and let cool on a rack.

Hard Ginger Cakes

(about forty-eight bars)

In the nineteenth century, hard ginger cakes were called ginger cookies and soft ginger cakes were known as gingerbread. This recipe makes a highly spiced ginger cookie.

2 cups all-purpose flour
1 cup firmly packed brown sugar
1 tablespoon ground ginger
1 teaspoon baking soda

½ teaspoon salt
8 tablespoons (1 stick) butter,
   room temperature

Preheat the oven to 325°F. Use an ungreased 7- or 8-inch square pan.

Put the flour, brown sugar, ginger, baking soda, and salt in a mixing bowl, and stir until well mixed. Add the butter and mix with a fork until well blended.

Press the mixture into the pan—it should be about ½ inch thick or a little thinner. Bake for 45 minutes to 1 hour. Remove and cut the cookies into finger-size bars, about ½ inch by 2 inches. Let cool in the pan. Remove from the pan, break up into bars, and store in an airtight container.

Basic Pie Dough

(for a 9-inch two-crust pie)

2¼ cups all-purpose flour   ¾ cup vegetable shortening
½ teaspoon salt   6 to 7 tablespoons cold water

Put the flour and salt in a mixing bowl and stir to blend, using a fork. Add the shortening, and, using your fingertips, a pastry blender, or two dinner knives, mix the fat and flour together (don't blend—the fat must remain in small pieces) until the mixture resembles coarse bread crumbs.

Add the water, a tablespoon or two at a time, gently stirring with a fork to distribute evenly. Add only enough water to allow the dough to be picked up and held together in a rough mass.

Sprinkle a board amply with flour and divide the dough into two pieces, one a little larger than the other. Roll the smaller piece out on the board into a circle 2 inches larger than the pie plate. Roll the dough up on the rolling pin and, starting on the far side of the pie plate, unroll the dough so that it is draped into the plate. Do not stretch the dough.

Add the filling, spreading it evenly. Roll the second piece of dough into a circle about 2½ inches larger than the pie plate. Again roll it upon the rolling pin and unroll over the filled shell, beginning from the far side of the pie plate. Turn the edges of the dough under and crimp neatly. Cut 2 or 3 heat vents on the top before baking.

Breakfast Apple Pie

(six servings)

A warm piece of apple pie, a small piece of Cheddar cheese, and a cup of hot coffee make a splendid breakfast. If they served this pie at truck stops, I'd become a truck driver.

1 cup cornflakes
One unbaked 8- or 9-inch pie
   shell (preceding recipe)
5 large, tart apples, peeled, cored,
   and cut into tenths
$\frac{1}{2}$ cup sugar
1 teaspoon cinnamon

Topping
$\frac{3}{4}$ cup all-purpose flour
$\frac{1}{2}$ cup sugar
7 tablespoons butter, chilled and
   cut into small pieces

Preheat the oven to 450°F.

Sprinkle the cornflakes evenly over the pie shell. Toss the apple slices, sugar, and cinnamon together in a large mixing bowl until all the apple slices are coated. Spread the apple mixture over the pie shell.

Make the topping. Put the flour, sugar, and butter in a bowl. Using a pastry blender or your fingers, work the butter into the flour until the mixture resembles irregular bread crumbs. Sprinkle the crumbs evenly over the apple slices.

Bake the pie for 10 minutes at 450°F, then reduce the heat to 350°F and continue to bake for about 35 minutes, or until the apples are tender and bubbling. Serve warm with a piece of Cheddar cheese on the side.

Hominy Grits Pie

(six servings)

Grits, believe it or not, make a creamy, delicate pie. I tried adding
$\frac{1}{2}$ cup raspberries to the filling and the flavor was fabulous.

3 eggs	One unbaked 8- or 9-inch pie
1 cup cooked grits	shell (see page 240)
$\frac{1}{2}$ cup light brown sugar	Optional: $\frac{1}{2}$ cup fresh berries
$\frac{1}{3}$ cup heavy cream	or sliced fruit

Preheat the oven to 400°F.

Put the eggs in a mixing bowl and beat until blended and smooth.
Stir in the grits, sugar, and cream and mix until blended. Pour the
mixture into the pie shell, and gently stir in the berries or fruit, if you
are using them.

Bake for about 40 minutes, or until the center is a trifle jiggly but
most of the filling is set. Cool for 5 minutes after removing from the
oven. Serve warm or cold.

Apricot Shortbread Pie

(eight servings)

The shortbread crust in this pie is crisp and butter-golden, and the apricot filling is tart, sweet, and boldly fresh. Apricot Shortbread Pie with a glass of milk makes a nice small breakfast.

8 tablespoons (1 stick) butter, room temperature
$1\frac{1}{3}$ cups all-purpose flour
1 cup granulated sugar, approximately
$1\frac{1}{2}$ cups pitted and coarsely chopped fresh apricots

$\frac{1}{4}$ cup water
1 egg, well beaten
$\frac{1}{4}$ teaspoon salt
$\frac{1}{2}$ teaspoon baking powder
Confectioners' sugar

Preheat the oven to 375°F.

Put the butter, 1 cup flour, and $\frac{1}{3}$ cup sugar in a mixing bowl and, using your hands or a large spoon, blend until the mixture is smooth. Pat the dough evenly over the bottom of a 9-inch pie pan. Bake about 25 minutes, or until the crust is lightly golden.

While the crust is baking, put the apricots and water into a skillet and turn the heat to high. When the fruit begins to bubble, turn the heat down to medium, stirring often so the fruit doesn't scorch. Cook until the fruit is thickened. Remove from the heat and let cool a little. Stir the egg into the apricots and blend well. Add up to $\frac{3}{4}$ cup sugar (depending on how sweet the apricots are), the remaining $\frac{1}{3}$ cup flour, the salt, and the baking powder. Beat until all the lumps are gone.

Spread the apricot mixture over the pie crust and bake about 25 minutes, or until the topping is puffy. Remove and shake confectioners' sugar over the top. Cut into 8 wedges and serve.

Cranberry Raisin Pie

(six to eight servings)

Cranberry Raisin Pie is a delicious combination of tart and sweet with a touch of orange, and is especially good when eaten warm. It is just the ticket for Christmas morning served with eggnog.

2 cups raisins	1/4 cup Grand Marnier
4 cups fresh cranberries	2 teaspoons grated orange zest
2 tablespoons all-purpose flour	Basic Pie Dough for a 2-crust pie
1 cup sugar	(see page 240)

Put the raisins in a bowl, add water to cover, and soak for at least 2 hours. Drain. Preheat the oven to 400°F.

Put the raisins and cranberries in a mixing bowl. In a small bowl, stir the flour into the sugar, mixing well, and sprinkle over the raisin-cranberry mixture. Add the Grand Marnier and orange zest. Toss all together until the fruit is thoroughly coated.

Line an 8- or 9-inch pie plate with pie dough and spread the filling evenly over. Cover the filling with pie dough, seal, and flute the edges.

Bake the pie for 15 minutes at 400°F, then reduce the heat to 350°F and bake for 45 minutes more, or until the juices bubble. Cool a bit before serving.

Shaker Stacked Pie

(twelve servings)

The Shakers have made a great contribution to American cooking with the simplicity, freshness, and good taste of their food. Stacked pie was born of the need for Shaker women to carry many pies to church suppers easily. Instead of trying to handle three or more separate pies, their clever solution was a many-layered pie. This version is not as deep and thick as the original, but it gives you the idea, and it is delicious for breakfast.

Pie Pastry	*Filling*
3 cups all-purpose flour	2 cups milk
1 teaspoon salt	$\frac{1}{2}$ cup sugar
1 cup vegetable shortening	6 tablespoons all-purpose flour
$\frac{3}{4}$ cup water, approximately	$\frac{1}{2}$ teaspoon salt
	8 egg yolks, slightly beaten
	4 teaspoons vanilla extract
	4 tablespoons ($\frac{1}{2}$ stick) butter

Preheat the oven to 425°F.

Mix together the flour and salt in a bowl. Add the shortening and, using your fingers or a pastry blender, mix the mass until it looks like irregular bread crumbs. While stirring with a fork, slowly add the water. You may need more or less water, but use enough to bring the dough together into a rough ball. Divide the dough into 4 balls—one should be about one-third larger than the others.

Dust a board with flour and roll the biggest ball into a circle large enough to line a 9- or 10-inch pie pan. Put the rolled pastry into the pie pan and flute the edges. Prick the bottom and sides all over with a fork, then line the pie pan with a heavy piece of foil to hold the pastry down. Bake for about 6 minutes, remove the foil, and bake for 5 minutes more.

Roll the other 3 balls into rounds the diameter of the pie pan (roll them thin). Place the 3 rounds on baking sheets and bake from 8 to 10 minutes, or until they are lightly colored. Remove the 3 pastries from the oven and gently place them on waxed paper to cool (don't worry if they break; you can put them back together when you are assembling the pie).

To make the filling, heat the milk until just before boiling (tiny bubbles will form around the edge of the pan). Meanwhile, stir together the sugar, flour, and salt in a mixing bowl until blended. Slowly add the hot milk, a little at a time, to the flour mixture, whisking or stirring briskly all the while. Return the milk-flour mixture back to the saucepan and cook, stirring, until it boils and becomes smooth and thick.

Put the slightly beaten egg yolks into a bowl; slowly spoon a few tablespoons of the thickened sauce into the yolks and blend. Pour the yolks into the sauce and cook, stirring constantly for another minute or so—allow the sauce to boil while you are doing this. Remove from the heat and put the filling into a bowl. Stir in the vanilla and butter. Either spread a film of butter over the top of the filling or cover with waxed paper so a crust won't form. Cool, then chill, until you are ready to assemble and serve the pie.

The pie is assembled with alternate layers of pastry and filling. First spread one quarter of the filling into the pastry shell, place the first round of pastry on top, and spread over it another quarter of the filling. Stack the second round of pastry on top, spread over that another layer of filling, place the third disk of pastry on top, and finish with the rest of the filling.

Mother's Pie

(six servings)

Mother's Pie and Milk Pie are surprisingly good, even though they are just ways to use leftover scraps of pie dough. Children have loved this for ages, and it would be a special treat to serve it for breakfast the day after a good report card.

Enough pie dough for an
   8- or 9-inch pie shell*
3 tablespoons flour

3 tablespoons sugar
$1/2$ teaspoon cinnamon
1 cup milk

*NOTE: If you have only a little leftover pie dough, roll out whatever scraps you have to about $1/8$ inch thick, crimp the edge, and reduce the other ingredients proportionately.

Preheat the oven to 400°F.

Roll out the pie dough scraps into one piece and place it in a pie tin. Stir the flour, sugar, and cinnamon together in a small bowl. Sprinkle over the pie dough. Pour the milk over and bake for about 35 minutes. Even if the milk still seems liquid, remove and let cool for 10 minutes—it will set and be perfect. Slice and eat warm.

Milk Pie   Proceed as above but use a mixture of $1/4$ cup sugar and $1/2$ teaspoon cinnamon and sprinkle it evenly over the pie dough. Pour $1/3$ cup milk on top and smooth over with your fingers or a spoon. Bake for 30 minutes, or until the crust is golden. Cool for 10 minutes. Serve warm.

Whole Wheat Sponge Roll

(about ten servings)

This simplest of recipes makes the lightest, best sponge roll I know. Fill it with Date Raisin Condiment (see page 277), or Lemon Curd (see page 274), or spread thinly with whipped cottage cheese and cover with soft sliced fresh fruit or berries. Roll this sponge wide side up so you can have a long roll that will provide about ten good portions. This roll can be baked the night before serving, rolled up in a tea towel, and left at room temperature until morning to fill and serve. If you wish to make this into a dessert roll, use all cake flour.

5 eggs	$1/2$ teaspoon baking powder
$1/2$ cup granulated sugar	$1/4$ teaspoon salt
$1/4$ cup whole wheat flour	1 teaspoon vanilla extract
$1/4$ cup cake flour	Confectioners' sugar for sprinkling

Preheat the oven to 350°F. Grease a $15\frac{1}{2}$- × $10\frac{1}{2}$- × 1-inch jelly-roll pan and line with waxed paper. Grease and lightly flour the waxed paper.

Put the eggs and sugar into a mixing bowl and beat for about 4 minutes (an electric mixer is almost a must for this recipe), until pale, fluffy, and light.

Mix the flours, baking powder, and salt in a bowl, stirring with a fork to blend well. Turn the mixer to the lowest speed and sprinkle the flour mixture and the vanilla over the egg mixture, mixing for just a few seconds. Remove the bowl from the mixer and, using a spatula, gently finish folding the flour into the egg mixture until no white streaks show.

Spread the batter evenly in the jelly-roll pan. Bake for about 12 minutes, or until the top of the cake is golden.

Spread a tea towel on the counter and sift a little confectioners' sugar evenly over the towel. Invert the cake onto the towel. Remove the waxed paper and roll the cake wide side up in the towel. Leave rolled up until you are ready to fill it. Unroll, spread the filling evenly over the roll, reroll, place on a serving plate, and sprinkle the top with confectioners' sugar. Slice and serve.

Lemon Pound Cake

(one large loaf)

The use of cake flour in this recipe gives this pound cake an extra-fine crumb and a delicate texture that suits its lemon flavor. But all-purpose flour will work well, too.

½ pound (2 sticks) butter, room temperature
1⅓ cups sugar
5 eggs, room temperature

2 cups cake flour
½ teaspoon salt
2 teaspoons grated lemon zest (the yellow outer rind of the lemon)

Preheat the oven to 325°F. Grease and flour a 9 × 5 × 3-inch loaf pan.

Put the butter in a large mixing bowl and beat until creamy. Slowly add the sugar, beating constantly, until the mixture is well blended. Add the eggs, one at a time, beating well after each addition. Add the flour and salt and beat until smooth and thoroughly blended. Add the lemon zest and beat another few seconds.

Pour the batter into the pan and smooth the top with a spatula. Bake for about an hour, or until a straw comes out clean when inserted into the center. Let cool in the pan 5 minutes before turning onto a rack to cool completely.

Granola Pound Cake

(one medium loaf)

This cake has only half the usual amount of sugar and, though mildly sweet, it is the combination of delicate crumb and good granola crunch that makes it special. Sliced, toasted, and buttered, it is wonderful.

½ pound (2 sticks) butter,
   room temperature
1 cup sugar
2 teaspoons vanilla extract
5 eggs, room temperature

1 cup all-purpose flour
1 cup cake flour
½ teaspoon salt
1¼ cups granola (see page 90
   for homemade granola)

Preheat the oven to 325°F. Butter an 8 × 5 × 3-inch loaf pan.

Combine the butter and sugar in a mixing bowl and beat until smooth. Add the vanilla and the eggs, one at a time, beating until very well mixed. Add the flours and salt and beat at least 2 minutes. Stir in the granola.

Spoon the batter into the loaf pan and bake for 45 to 55 minutes, or until a straw comes out clean when inserted into the center. Gently remove the cake from the pan and let cool on a rack.

Raisin Almond Breakfast Cake

(one round cake)

A complete breakfast in just one dish, this cake is made from milk, cream, eggs, wheat, raisins, and almonds. Serve warm with whipped cream, or with some heavy cream poured on top.

1 cup milk and 1 cup cream (or 2 cups milk)	2 eggs, lightly beaten
$\frac{1}{3}$ cup plus 2 tablespoons sugar	$\frac{1}{4}$ teaspoon almond extract
$\frac{1}{2}$ teaspoon salt	1 cup chopped almonds
$\frac{3}{4}$ cup Cream of Wheat (or Cream of Rice or Quick Grits)	1 cup golden raisins
	$\frac{1}{3}$ cup whole wheat bread crumbs

Preheat the oven to 350°F. Butter a baking dish, 7 inches in diameter and about 2 inches deep.

Put the milk, cream, $\frac{1}{3}$ cup sugar, and the salt in a heavy-bottomed saucepan. Bring to a boil and slowly stir in the Cream of Wheat. Stir constantly over medium heat until the mixture has thickened. Remove from the heat and blend a little of the hot milk mixture into the eggs, stirring constantly. Add the eggs to the milk mixture and beat until well blended. Stir in the almond extract, almonds, and raisins.

Mix the whole wheat bread crumbs with the remaining 2 tablespoons sugar in a small bowl. Sprinkle the crumbs generously over the bottom and sides of the buttered baking dish. Spoon in the mixture. Bake for 30 minutes. Remove and let rest for 5 minutes. Invert the cake onto a serving plate and serve hot in wedges with cream.

Indian Loaf Cake

(one medium loaf cake)

If you are a cornmeal fan you'll like this recipe for a mildly sweet cake with walnuts and raisins. Serve warm slices of this with applesauce.

1 cup yellow cornmeal	5 tablespoons butter
2 cups cold water	1 cup coarsely chopped walnuts
$\frac{1}{2}$ cup brown sugar	1 cup golden raisins
$\frac{1}{2}$ teaspoon salt	

Butter an $8\frac{1}{2} \times 4\frac{1}{2} \times 3$-inch loaf pan. Put the cornmeal in a bowl with 1 cup water, stir, and let stand while you put together the rest of the ingredients.

Put the remaining 1 cup water in a pan and add the brown sugar, salt, and butter. Turn the heat to medium and, stirring constantly, bring the sugar mixture to a boil. Cook for 1 minute. Stir in the cornmeal mixture. Stirring briskly and constantly, cook for about 5 minutes, or until the mixture is very stiff and comes away from the sides of the pan. Remove from the heat and add the walnuts and raisins.

Spread the stiff cornmeal into the loaf pan. Let cool, cover with plastic wrap, and refrigerate until needed. When ready to serve, slice and warm the slices before serving.

Madeira Poppy Seed Cake

(one 10-inch tube cake)

This cake is lighter than light, and quite perfect for that small second breakfast late in the morning. It can also be made into two 9- by 5- by 3-inch loaves with a little batter left over for a few cupcakes. Freezing is kind to this cake.

$2\frac{1}{3}$ cups cake flour	5 egg yolks
$1\frac{1}{3}$ cups sugar	$\frac{3}{4}$ cup Madeira wine
1 tablespoon baking powder	1 cup egg whites (6 or 7 whites)
1 teaspoon salt	$\frac{1}{2}$ teaspoon cream of tartar
$\frac{1}{2}$ cup vegetable oil	$\frac{1}{2}$ cup (2-ounce can) poppy seeds

Preheat the oven to 325°F. Don't grease the tube pan, but if you are using loaf pans and muffin tins, grease and lightly flour them.

Sift the flour, 1 cup sugar, baking powder, and salt together into a mixing bowl. Add the oil, yolks, and Madeira. Beat briskly until smooth.

Put the egg whites in an electric mixer bowl. Beat for a few seconds until the whites are frothy. Add the cream of tartar and continue to beat on high speed until the whites form soft peaks. Still beating on high speed, slowly add the remaining $\frac{1}{3}$ cup sugar. Beat until very stiff. Turn the mixer to the lowest speed and add the yolk mixture and the poppy seeds. Beat for just a few seconds until the batter looks blended. Remove from the mixer and use the spatula for a few folds to blend the batter completely.

Pour into the pan(s) and bake. A tube cake takes about 1 hour, loaves about 45 minutes, and cupcakes about 20 minutes. They are done when a straw inserted into the center comes out clean. Let the tube cake cool completely in its pan, turned upside down. Cool the loaves and cupcakes for 10 minutes in their pans, and remove to cool on racks.

Fresh Ginger Cake

(two 8-inch cakes)

This is a lovely, delicate cake. Frost with faintly sweetened whipped cream that has finely chopped crystallized ginger added. Slices of fresh mango around the bottom of the cake would be perfection.

$1/4$ cup fresh gingerroot, unpeeled,
   cut into large chunks
1 cup sugar
3 tablespoons lemon zest with a
   little white pith
8 tablespoons (1 stick) unsalted
   butter, room temperature

2 eggs
1 cup buttermilk
2 cups cake flour
$1/4$ teaspoon salt
$3/4$ teaspoon baking soda

Preheat the oven to 350°F. Butter the cake pans.

Put the ginger into a food processor and process until it is in small bits, or chop fine by hand. Put the ginger and $1/4$ cup sugar in a small skillet or saucepan and cook over medium heat, stirring constantly until the sugar has melted and the mixture is warm (this takes only a minute or two). Set aside. Put the lemon pieces in the processor and process until finely chopped — or chop fine by hand. Add the lemon to the cooled ginger mixture.

Put the butter into a mixing bowl and beat a second or two; slowly add the remaining sugar and beat until smooth. Add the eggs and beat well. Stir in the buttermilk. Add the flour, salt, and baking soda and beat until smooth. Add the ginger-lemon mixture and mix well.

Spoon the batter into the buttered cake pans. Bake for 25 minutes. Remove from the oven and cool in the pans for 5 minutes, then turn out onto racks until completely cooled.

Soft Gingerbread

(one 8-inch square gingerbread)

This fine-crumbed and finely spiced gingerbread is exceptionally good.

1 cup sugar
1 cup dark molasses
1 cup vegetable oil
3 eggs
¾ teaspoon salt
1 teaspoon ground cloves

1 teaspoon ground ginger
1 teaspoon cinnamon
2 cups all-purpose flour
2 teaspoons baking soda
1 cup boiling water

Preheat the oven to 350°F. Grease and lightly flour the baking pan.

Put the sugar, molasses, oil, and eggs in a mixing bowl and beat until smooth. In another bowl, combine the salt, cloves, ginger, cinnamon, flour, and baking soda and stir with a fork until well mixed. Stir into the first mixture. Add the boiling water and beat briskly until smooth. This is a thin batter. Pour into the pan and bake 40 to 45 minutes. Serve warm.

Great Coffee Cake

(one 10-inch tube cake)

This makes a moist, rich cake adaptable to many changes. Some very good variations to this splendid basic cake follow the recipe.

½ pound (2 sticks) butter, room temperature	2 teaspoons baking powder
1 cup sugar	1 teaspoon baking soda
3 eggs	1 teaspoon salt
2½ cups all-purpose flour	1 cup sour cream

Preheat the oven to 350°F. Grease and flour a 10-inch tube pan or Bundt pan.

Put the butter in a large mixing bowl and beat for several seconds. Add the sugar and beat until smooth. Add the eggs and beat for 2 minutes, or until light and creamy. Put the flour, baking powder, baking soda, and salt in a bowl and stir with a fork to blend well. Add the flour mixture to the butter mixture and beat until smooth. Add the sour cream and mix well.

Spoon the batter into the pan. Bake for about 50 minutes, or until a straw comes out clean when inserted into the center. Remove from the oven and let rest for 5 minutes in the pan. Invert onto a rack and cool a little bit before slicing. Serve warm.

Raisin and Spice Coffee Cake   Add 1 teaspoon mace and 1 teaspoon nutmeg when combining the dry ingredients. Stir ¾ cup raisins and ½ cup currants into the batter after adding the sour cream, and proceed with the basic recipe.

Dried Fig and Almond Coffee Cake   You will need 1½ cups of Calimyrna figs; if the figs are very dry, put them in a bowl, pour boiling water over them, and let stand for 15 minutes; then drain. Cut the figs into quarters. After adding the sour cream, add these along with 1½ cups unblanched, coarsely chopped almonds. Stir well, and proceed with the basic recipe.

Apple and Walnut Coffee Cake   Add 1½ cups coarsely chopped apple (peeled or unpeeled) and 1½ cups coarsely chopped walnuts to the batter after adding the sour cream, and stir to distribute well. Proceed with the basic recipe.

Simple Vanilla Coffee Cake   Follow the basic recipe, but add 5 teaspoons vanilla extract when adding the sour cream.

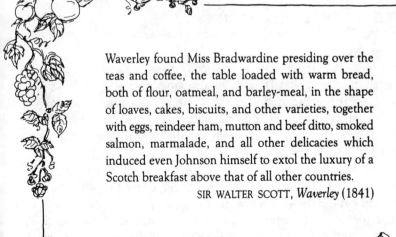

Waverley found Miss Bradwardine presiding over the teas and coffee, the table loaded with warm bread, both of flour, oatmeal, and barley-meal, in the shape of loaves, cakes, biscuits, and other varieties, together with eggs, reindeer ham, mutton and beef ditto, smoked salmon, marmalade, and all other delicacies which induced even Johnson himself to extol the luxury of a Scotch breakfast above that of all other countries.

SIR WALTER SCOTT, *Waverley* (1841)

Fluffy Caramel Coffee Cake

(one 10-inch square cake)

The texture of this cake is indeed fluffy and light; and the topping is sticky, crisp caramel. The batter can be mixed and put in its baking dish in the refrigerator the night before you need it. When you get up in the morning, put the baking dish in the cold oven and turn on the heat. And serve with butter, of course.

1 package dry yeast	*Caramel topping*
1/4 cup warm water	1 cup dark brown sugar
3/4 cup milk, approximately	1/2 cup sour cream
2 tablespoons vegetable shortening	1 teaspoon vanilla extract
1/4 cup sugar	
1/2 teaspoon salt	
1 egg, beaten	
2 cups all-purpose flour	

Sprinkle the yeast over the warm water and allow to rest 5 minutes until it dissolves.

Put the milk and shortening in a small pan and heat, stirring together until the shortening melts. Transfer to a mixing bowl and stir in the sugar and salt until blended. Let the mixture cool, then add the dissolved yeast. Add the egg and mix well. Stir in the flour and mix until the dough is smooth. The dough should be slightly sticky; if it isn't, add 2 or 3 more tablespoons milk.

Grease the baking dish or pan. Spread the dough out in the pan by dipping your fingers in cold water (so the dough doesn't stick to your hands), then pat the dough evenly into the pan.

For the topping, stir together the brown sugar, sour cream, and vanilla in a small bowl until well blended. Cover the dough and let rise for about $1\frac{1}{2}$ hours, or refrigerate overnight and bake in the morning.

Bake in a preheated 350°F oven for 15 minutes, then spread the topping over the cake. Bake an additional 20 minutes if the dough has risen at room temperature or bake an additional 30–35 minutes if the dough is chilled from resting overnight in the refrigerator.

Almond Coconut Coffee Cake

(three 8-inch twisted round cakes or three long twisted loaf cakes)

The lightly toasted almond and coconut in this rather flaky cake are very good. Long strips of unsweetened coconut, the best kind to use, can be found in natural food stores. The cake slices and toasts nicely and has a very fresh taste.

1 cup sliced or grated
   unsweetened coconut
1 cup sliced almonds
$\frac{1}{2}$ cup warm water
2 packages dry yeast
1 teaspoon plus $\frac{1}{2}$ cup sugar
4 cups all-purpose flour
1 teaspoon salt
8 tablespoons (1 stick) butter,
   chilled
3 egg yolks
1 cup light cream

Topping
$1\frac{1}{2}$ cups confectioners' sugar
2 tablespoons water,
   approximately
$\frac{1}{2}$ cup coconut
$\frac{1}{2}$ cup sliced almonds

Spread $1\frac{1}{2}$ cups coconut and $1\frac{1}{2}$ cups almonds (for both the bread and the topping) on a baking sheet in a single layer. Put in the oven and turn the heat to 350°F. It will take about 10 minutes to toast the coconut and almonds to a light golden color, but check on the toasting process every couple of minutes so you don't burn them. Set aside.

Put the warm water in a large mixing bowl, sprinkle in the yeast and 1 teaspoon sugar, stir, and let dissolve for 5 minutes.

Put the flour, salt, and remaining $\frac{1}{2}$ cup sugar in another bowl. Cut the cold butter into small pieces and add the flour mixture. Using your fingers or a pastry cutter, cut the butter into the flour mixture until it is in small bits.

Put the yolks and cream in a small bowl and beat until smooth and blended. Stir into the flour mixture. Add the yeast mixture and blend well. Add 1 cup each toasted coconut and almonds and mix to distribute.

Turn the dough onto a floured board (the dough will be slightly sticky), flour your hands, and divide the dough into 6 equal parts. Keeping your hands well floured, roll each piece into a rope 12 inches long. Twisting two ropes together at a time, make the coffee cakes either into long twisted loaves or into round twisted loaves. If you are making the round loaves, twist two ropes together, form a circle, pinch the ends together, and place the rounds on greased pie pans. Repeat with the remaining pieces of dough, to make three loaves altogether. If you are making long twisted loaves instead of rounds, bake them on greased baking sheets.

Let the cakes rise until double in bulk (this takes about 1½ hours). Bake in a preheated 350°F oven for about 35 minutes.

Stir together the confectioners' sugar and 2 tablespoons water to make the glaze. It should flow from the spoon; add a little more water if it doesn't. When you remove the cakes from the oven, spread the glaze over the cakes. Sprinkle the remaining ½ cup each toasted coconut and almonds over the frosting. Serve warm.

Apricot Prune Coffee Cake

(one 10-inch tube cake)

This is a large moist cake with brown sugar–walnut filling. It is always well liked and I've given away the recipe many times. Any dried fruit will do nicely in place of the apricots and prunes.

Brown Sugar Filling
1 cup brown sugar
1 teaspoon cinnamon
½ cup chopped walnuts

Cake Batter
1 cup finely chopped dried
   apricots
1 cup finely chopped pitted
   dried prunes
⅔ cup sugar
3 eggs
1 cup milk
½ cup (1 stick) butter, melted
2½ cups all-purpose flour
1 tablespoon baking powder
½ teaspoon salt

Preheat the oven to 350°F. Butter and flour a 10-inch tube pan or Bundt pan.

To make the filling, mix the brown sugar and cinnamon together in a small bowl, stirring with a fork until the cinnamon is well distributed. Stir in the walnuts and set aside.

Now make the cake batter. If the dried apricots and prunes are so dry that it is hard to chew them, put them in a bowl and pour boiling water over. Let stand for 10 minutes and drain, pressing out any excess water. Put the sugar, eggs, milk, and butter in a large mixing bowl and beat well. In another bowl, stir together the flour, baking powder, and salt to blend well. Stir the flour mixture into the sugar mixture, mixing until all ingredients are blended. Stir in the apricots and prunes.

Spread one third of the batter over the bottom of the prepared pan. Be sparing with the batter at this point. Spread half the brown sugar filling over the batter. Spread another third of the batter over the filling, then spread over the remaining brown sugar filling and top with the remaining batter.

Bake for 50 to 60 minutes, or until a straw comes out clean when inserted into the center. Remove from the oven and let cool for about 5 minutes in the pan. Carefully invert onto a rack to cool completely before slicing.

Condiments

Raw Fresh Fruit Jams
Peach Rose Jam
Rhubarb Ginger Jam
Strawberry Lump Preserves
Orange Marmalade
Orange Spread
Beet Marmalade
Lemon Jelly
   Orange Jelly
Lemonade Jelly with Orange Slices
Lemon Curd
Spicy Orange Slices
Lemon Pineapple Apple Relish
Date Raisin Condiment
Dried Apricot Orange Condiment
Papaya Pickle
Spice Walnuts
Caramel Oatmeal Topping
Maple Syrup Butter
Whipped Maple Syrup
Cinnamon Cream Syrup
English Custard
Salsa Verde
Homemade Yogurt
Breakfast Cheese

Here is a catch-all chapter for all the little side dishes that give an extra sprightliness to things we would otherwise eat plain. These small frills will give a little inspiration to a breakfast.

Some kind of fruit spread or jam always lends that extra dash to a piece of toast. Just as strawberry preserves seem to belong on white bread or biscuits, apple tastes wonderful on things like whole wheat and rye and pear jam belongs on things that are light and delicate. The idea of preserving fruit at home, however, has outlived its usefulness for most of us, partly because families are smaller and partly because so many things are available fresh. Moreover, people don't want to take the time for the all-day process of sterilizing jars, pressure cooking, and the rest. But you can easily have fresh jam by making it in small quantities—you'll need just a few pieces of fruit or a basket of berries.

I love the idea of raw fruit jams—there's nothing fresher and they are particularly appealing to those with a hectic routine. You can take something as small as one pear: peel it, add a little lemon juice and a little sugar, mash it in a bowl, and let it sit until the sugar dissolves. In just a little while, you will have made enough jam to tide you over a weekend of breakfasts.

Those of you who still take the time to make preserves the old-fashioned way will want to get a copy of *Fine Preserving*, by Catherine Plagemann, annotated by M. F. K. Fisher (Berkeley: Aris Books, 1986).

Raw Fresh Fruit Jams

(about two cups)

This is the very best, easiest, and most practical way to have splendid homemade jams on the table for each season. The fruit or berries must be properly ripe and mashable, and the texture of the jam should be coarse.

2 cups mashed fruit or berries
$\frac{1}{3}$ cup sugar (more or less, depending on sweetness desired)

Optional: lemon juice (if the fruit or berries are flat-tasting)

Put the fruit in a shallow dish, mash, and sprinkle the sugar and optional lemon juice over. Let the fruit sit until the sugar dissolves, about 30 minutes. Put in a pretty bowl and serve. Depending on the fruit used, the jam will keep anywhere from 3 days to 2 weeks, refrigerated.

Peach Rose Jam

(about two cups)

Rose water is available in pharmacies, labeled as Fluid Rose Soluble, at a reasonable price. Peach Rose Jam is heaven on wheat toast.

2 cups peeled, pitted, and coarsely mashed fresh peaches

Sugar to taste
3 or 4 drops rose water

Put the peaches and sugar in a skillet over low heat and stir the mixture for a minute, just long enough to melt and blend the fruit and sugar. Remove from the heat, cool, and carefully add the rose water to taste – the flavor should be a shy presence. The jam will keep about 3 days, refrigerated.

Rhubarb Ginger Jam

(four cups)

This jam has an arresting, different taste. It is splendid on rye or coarse wheat toast. The rhubarb flavor is not hindered by the piquant ginger.

About 2 pounds rhubarb, washed
   and cut into small pieces
   (to make 4 cups)
4 cups sugar (if tartness is desired,
   use only 3 cups)

¼ cup chopped unpeeled
   gingerroot

Put a layer of rhubarb in a shallow bowl, sprinkle with a layer of sugar, and continue layering until the last layer of rhubarb is covered with sugar. Cover the dish with plastic wrap and leave covered for 36 hours. Lots of juice will accumulate. Pour the juice into a saucepan. Tie the chopped ginger in a piece of muslin or cheesecloth. Put the ginger into the saucepan with the juice and boil for about 5 minutes. Add the rhubarb and simmer for about 15 minutes, or until the rhubarb begins to look translucent. Cool and transfer to sealed jars if storing for an indefinite time; or cover and refrigerate until needed. This will keep for a couple of weeks in the refrigerator, or a few months in the freezer.

Strawberry Lump Preserves

(1½ cups)

This method of making jam suits me just fine. You can add as much sugar as you wish and this recipe may be multiplied to any amount desired. It makes a bright red preserve and the full strawberry essence is captured in the lumps of strawberries. Strawberries are available for most of the summer, so I make the jam a little at a time.

About 4 cups (2 baskets) strawberries, washed, hulled, and sliced in half

½ cup sugar, approximately
½ cup fresh lemon juice

Choose a sunny, warm day to make this. Mash half the berries and put them in a sauté pan. Stir in the sugar and lemon juice and cook over medium-low heat for 1 or 2 minutes, stirring constantly. Add the rest of the halved strawberries. Turn the heat to medium and, still stirring constantly, bring the preserves to a boil. Spoon off the foam, let boil about 10 seconds more, and remove from the heat.

Pour the preserves into a large shallow dish so they are spread out in a thin layer. Cover the preserves with muslin or cheesecloth and put outdoors in the sunshine for at least 6 hours.

Spoon into jars and cover. Store in the refrigerator. If you want to keep these preserves longer than 10 days, put the jars in the freezer (remember to leave ½ inch of space in the jar).

Orange Marmalade

(three 8-ounce jars)

In some parts of England marmalade is called squish. Many commercial marmalades are so sweet that the orange flavor is lost, but you can make homemade marmalade to please yourself. The lemon in this recipe gives a nice tart edge to the marmalade.

3 large oranges	3 cups water
3 lemons	About 1½ cups sugar

Peel the oranges and two of the lemons, and cut the peel into very thin slices. Seed the oranges and cut up the pulp. Save the pulp of the two lemons for another use. Put the fruit and water in a pot. Bring to a boil and let simmer for 5 minutes. Remove from the heat and let stand overnight in a cool place.

Measure the fruit and liquid and, depending on your taste, add about ½ cup sugar for each cup fruit (you must add enough sugar to make the jam jell). Stir the sugar into the fruit and put the pot back on the stove over medium heat. Stirring often, let the jam cook about 30 minutes. Test for jell point by spooning a little jam onto a saucer and placing it in the refrigerator or freezer for a minute or two. If the jam jells it is ready to put into jars. I use the last lemon at this point. Peel the remaining lemon and slice the zest into very thin slices. Cut the pith away from the lemon and discard. Chop the lemon pulp into small pieces, remove any seeds, and add it and the zest to the jam.

Pour into three 8-ounce jars. If you seal the jars with paraffin, do so as follows. Leave ½ inch head space in the jar. Pour one thin layer of paraffin over the hot jam. Let this layer set until it is firm, and then pour on one more thin layer.

Orange Spread

(four servings)

A little stirring and cooking, and the result will be a warm, pleasing orange spread for your buttered toast.

1/4 cup water	1 to 4 tablespoons sugar, to taste
1 tablespoon cornstarch	Pinch of salt
1 cup orange pulp and juice	

Dissolve the water and cornstarch together in a small saucepan, add the orange, and stir until blended. Cook over medium heat, stirring constantly, for 1 minute; then add the sugar and salt. Continue cooking and stirring until the mixture has thickened and become translucent. Remove from the heat and serve on buttered toast. This will keep for several days in the refrigerator. Just reheat when you are ready to use again.

Beet Marmalade

(three cups)

This will be the biggest surprise your taste buds have had in a long time—Beet Marmalade is absolutely delicious. Try spreading this marmalade on Crisp Whole Wheat Buns (see page 18) along with a layer of yogurt or sour cream.

4 medium-large beets, cooked and peeled	1 large lemon
$1\frac{1}{2}$ cups sugar	2 tablespoons chopped fresh ginger

Put the beets in a food processor and process until coarsely chopped; or mash the beets by hand. Transfer the beets to a heavy-bottomed saucepan and stir in the sugar.

Put the lemon and ginger into the food processor and process until finely chopped; or chop them by hand. Add the lemon and ginger to the beet mixture and stir to blend. Cook over medium-low heat, stirring often, until the marmalade has thickened a little. This takes about 20 minutes—remember that the marmalade will get thicker considerably as it cools.

Remove from the heat and put up in sterilized jars if you are not going to use the marmalade for a month or more; otherwise it will keep well in the refrigerator.

Lemon Jelly

(about one cup)

It's surprising that citrus jellies are not made more often. Fresh citrus fruits are available all year round, jellies are very easy to make, and they are delicious.

½ cup freshly squeezed lemon juice	1⅓ cups sugar 2 ounces pectin (1 box)

In a 3- or 4-quart saucepan, mix together the lemon juice, sugar, and pectin and bring to a boil, stirring at first to smooth and blend the ingredients. Allow to boil *exactly* 2 minutes and remove from the heat.

Wet a strong paper towel or a fine-textured dishcloth with cold water, wring out, and place the paper or cloth in a strainer over a Pyrex 2-cup measure. Let the jelly slowly drip through. Cool and seal, or cool and refrigerate.

Orange Jelly   Use ½ cup orange juice plus ¼ cup lemon juice and the grated zest of 1 orange (this is strained out after imparting its flavor).

Lemonade Jelly with Orange Slices

(about 2½ cups jelly)

Clean, sparkling lemonade jellied with fresh orange pieces: refreshing as snowflakes in July. Eat this with plain yogurt or buttered toast.

¼ cup cold water
1 tablespoon unflavored gelatin
1½ cups boiling water
¾ cup sugar, or to taste
Pinch of salt
6 tablespoons freshly squeezed
    lemon juice

Grated zest of 1 lemon
6 large oranges, peeled, sectioned,
    and membranes removed
Optional: a few sprigs of fresh
    mint

Put the cold water in a bowl and sprinkle the gelatin over; stir and let stand for 5 minutes until the gelatin has dissolved.

Pour the boiling water over the gelatin mixture, stir, and add the sugar, salt, lemon juice, and lemon zest. Stir until the sugar has dissolved and the lemonade is clear. Pour into individual molds or one large one. Cover, then refrigerate for about 4 to 6 hours.

Unmold and arrange with the orange sections and a leaf or two of fresh mint.

Lemon Curd

(two cups)

Slightly sweet and tartly lemon, this is a sunshine yellow preserve that spreads deliciously over toast or on a Whole Wheat Sponge Roll (see page 248). It will keep for a few weeks in the refrigerator or you can put it up in sterile jars to keep it longer.

Grated zest from 2 large lemons	8 tablespoons (1 stick) butter
6 tablespoons freshly squeezed	1 cup sugar
lemon juice	4 eggs

Put the zest, lemon juice, butter, and sugar in the top of a double boiler, or in a metal bowl, over simmering water (the water must not boil). Stir occasionally until the butter melts and the sugar dissolves. In a bowl, beat the eggs until thoroughly blended. Stirring constantly, spoon a little of the hot lemon mixture into the eggs. Pour the egg mixture into the bowl or pan, still stirring constantly, and continue to cook over the simmering water until the curd is thick. Remove from the heat and store in the refrigerator until needed.

Spicy Orange Slices

(about sixteen large orange slices)

Spicy Orange Slices are soaked in a very hot, rather thick, shiny glaze that is mildly spiced with cloves and cinnamon. Put a slice or two in a bowl and pile raspberries or strawberries on top; or cut up a slice and put the pieces on a hot buttered biscuit or scone. These are very good with Pork Tenderloin with Biscuits and Gravy (see page 196).

3 oranges	1/4 cup water
2 cups sugar	10 whole cloves
1/2 cup vinegar	1 stick cinnamon

Cut each orange into 5 or 6 slices and discard the end pieces. Set aside.

Put the sugar, vinegar, water, cloves, and cinnamon in a sauté pan. Bring to a boil and boil about 3 minutes, or until the syrup thickens slightly.

Remove the pan from the heat. Put as many orange slices as the pan will hold in a single layer. Turn them over so each gets a thorough coating of glaze. Place the glazed slices in a bowl and continue to soak and coat all the remaining slices. Pour the remaining syrup over them. Cover and refrigerate, and use as needed. They will keep for 2 weeks in the refrigerator.

Lemon Pineapple Apple Relish

(five cups)

This relish is a pleasing merger of tastes. Serve it with ham, or spread it over toast and serve with a bowl of oatmeal.

2 cups coarsely chopped fresh
   pineapple
2 cups peeled, coarsely chopped
   apple
$\frac{1}{3}$ cup seeded and ground
   lemon pulp

$\frac{3}{4}$ cup sugar (depending on
   how sweet the pineapple and
   apples are)

Put the pineapple, apple, lemon, and sugar in a heavy-bottomed sauté pan. Turn the heat to medium-low and stir until the sugar dissolves and the juices run a little. Turn the heat to low and cook for about 30 minutes, stirring every now and then. Let the relish cool in the pan. Put in jars and seal if you are keeping it indefinitely, or put in covered containers and refrigerate until needed. This relish will keep for 10 days in the refrigerator.

Date Raisin Condiment

(2½ cups)

This Date Raisin Condiment makes a fine spread on toast or on a breakfast sandwich made with a rather tart cheese. It is also a good filling for stuffed dates for a breakfast fruit plate.

1 cup pitted and coarsely ground dates	1 cup coarsely chopped walnuts
½ cup ground raisins	1 tablespoon lemon juice
½ cup ground currants	3 tablespoons water
	2 tablespoons honey

Put the ingredients in a bowl and mix thoroughly. Keep in the refrigerator until needed; this will keep for several weeks.

Dried Apricot Orange Condiment

(1¼ cups)

This is to be eaten with gusto—on toast, stirred into a hot cereal, or over oatmeal pancakes. Measure the ingredients carefully, and taste critically to be sure the balance is just right.

½ cup orange juice	1 cup coarsely ground dried apricots
1 tablespoon lemon juice	
6 tablespoons sugar	⅓ cup ground orange rind

Put the orange juice, lemon juice, and sugar in a small, heavy-bottomed pan. Cook over medium heat until the sugar is dissolved. Stir in the apricots and orange rind and cook, continuing to stir, for several minutes, or until the mass gets thick. Let cool and store in a jar in the refrigerator. Seal if you are preserving for more than 10 days.

Papaya Pickle

(two cups)

This breakfast pickle can spruce up a plate of ham or hash. The papaya seeds give a peppery taste and a nice snap to the pickle.

1 cup water	2-inch stick cinnamon
1 cup sugar	2 bay leaves
½ cup cider vinegar	1 firm, ripe papaya, peeled,
¼ teaspoon freshly ground	seeded (reserve 2 tablespoons
pepper	seeds), and cut into bite-size
3 whole cloves	cubes

Put the water, sugar, vinegar, pepper, cloves, cinnamon stick, bay leaves, and papaya seeds in a saucepan and bring to a boil. Reduce the heat and simmer for 10 minutes. Add the papaya cubes and simmer for 30 minutes more.

Remove from the heat and let cool in the pan. Put into jars with lids and refrigerate or, if serving the same day, place in a bowl and serve at room temperature. Papaya Pickle will keep for 2 weeks in the refrigerator.

Spice Walnuts

($2\frac{1}{2}$ cups)

A small mound of Spice Walnuts, Breakfast Cheese (see page 286), figs, toast, and tea make a choice breakfast in bed. These crisp, sweet walnuts go well with many breakfast custards, or with ham and fruit.

$2\frac{1}{2}$ cups walnut halves
    (or large pieces)
1 cup sugar
$\frac{1}{2}$ cup water

1 teaspoon cinnamon
1 teaspoon salt
Optional: 1 tablespoon vanilla
    extract

Preheat the oven to 350°F.

Spread the walnuts in one layer on a baking sheet. Roast in the oven for 10 to 15 minutes (watch carefully—nuts scorch easily), until the nuts become a little toasted, or lightly browned.

Put the sugar, water, cinnamon, and salt in a heavy-bottomed saucepan. You will be cooking until the soft-ball (or spin-a-thread) stage (236°F). Let the syrup cook without stirring about 10 minutes. You will notice that the bubbles will become smaller and more compact as the syrup nears the soft-ball stage. Remove from the heat, stir in the vanilla, if using, and add the walnuts. Stir the mixture slowly and gently until it is creamy. Turn onto a buttered platter and separate the walnuts. Allow to cool and serve, or store in an airtight container.

Caramel Oatmeal Topping
(about three cups)

Sprinkle Caramel Oatmeal Topping over applesauce, cooked cereal, or baked bananas.

8 tablespoons (1 stick) butter	1/4 teaspoon salt
1 cup dark brown sugar	2 cups uncooked oatmeal
1 teaspoon vanilla extract	

Preheat the oven to 325°F. Mix the butter, brown sugar, vanilla, and salt in a small saucepan over low heat, stirring constantly until the sugar has dissolved.

Put the oatmeal in a bowl, pour the melted caramel sauce over, and toss the mixture until the oatmeal is coated with sauce. Spread the oatmeal in a thin layer on a baking sheet. Bake for 20 minutes, stirring the oatmeal once or twice. Remove from the oven and cool. Store in an airtight container.

MAPLE SYRUP

Real maple syrup is so much better than the maple-flavored pancake syrups that I strongly recommend you give it a try. It is graded according to color and strength: Grade A is divided into Light Amber, Medium Amber, and Dark Amber; and Grade B is the darkest. The lighter the syrup the more delicate and subtle the maple flavor. For some breakfast dishes, you may prefer the rich robust taste of Grade B. Real maple syrup is expensive, so here are two recipes to help get the most out of its incomparable flavor.

Maple Syrup Butter

(one cup)

You might not think that you could extend your maple syrup without diluting its flavor, but this recipe is not just economical, it actually enriches and rounds out the pure maple taste.

$\frac{1}{2}$ cup maple syrup
$\frac{1}{2}$ cup water

4 tablespoons ($\frac{1}{2}$ stick) unsalted butter

Put the syrup, water, and butter in a small saucepan and heat until the butter has melted. Stir to blend, and serve. Refrigerate any that is left over.

Whipped Maple Syrup

(about three cups)

This is a delectable topping for waffles, pancakes, muffins, fruits, or any dish that needs a pretty finish.

$\frac{1}{2}$ cup maple syrup
$\frac{1}{4}$ cup water
2 egg whites

1 teaspoon lemon juice
$\frac{1}{2}$ cup heavy cream, whipped

Mix together the maple syrup and water in a small, heavy-bottomed saucepan. Bring to a boil, turn the heat to medium, and let the syrup boil for about 5 minutes, or until it forms the soft-ball (or spin-a-thread) stage ($236°F$ on a candy thermometer). While the syrup is boiling, beat the egg whites with the lemon juice until the whites are stiff but still moist. When the syrup has reached the proper point, slowly beat the syrup into the egg whites. When the syrup is thoroughly mixed with the whites, fold in the whipped cream.

This mixture keeps well (although it does lose some of its air) for a few days. Stir it well before you use it to combine the liquid on the bottom with the lighter mixture on top.

Cinnamon Cream Syrup

(1⅓ cups)

Cinnamon Cream Syrup is a smooth and creamy topping with a mild cinnamon taste that goes well with Brown Rice Pancakes (see page 124) or Buckwheat Pancakes (see page 123). It is very rich, so a little bit goes a long way. Keep it in the refrigerator, and reheat as needed.

5 tablespoons butter	3 tablespoons sugar
1 cup heavy cream	1 teaspoon cinnamon

Melt the butter in a small saucepan and stir in the cream, sugar, and cinnamon. Whisking constantly, cook until the sugar has melted and the syrup is hot, about 1½ minutes.

English Custard

(two cups)

Don't be fooled by the word custard. English Custard is really a smooth sauce with the consistency of heavy cream — a pouring custard. This will give just the right finish to the stewed rhubarb on page 174, or any stewed fruit, and it is delicious with Lemon Pound Cake (see page 249) or Indian Loaf Cake (see page 252). Practice making this a few times and it will be in your permanent repertoire.

2 cups milk	1/8 teaspoon salt
1/2 cup sugar	2 teaspoons vanilla extract
4 egg yolks, lightly beaten with a fork	

Heat the milk in a heavy-bottomed saucepan to the simmer point (a film begins to form on top of the milk, bubbles appear around the edges of the pan, and steam starts to rise from the milk). Remove from the heat, add the sugar, and stir a few minutes to dissolve. Pour a little of the hot milk over the yolks, stirring briskly. Add the yolk mixture to the milk, return to the heat, add the salt, and cook over low heat, stirring constantly. After a few minutes pay close attention and keep stirring; when you feel a slight thickening of the custard, remove from the heat (it will be a thin sauce). Pour into a bowl through a sieve or strainer, add the vanilla, and stir a few seconds until the custard is cool. It will thicken somewhat as it cools. Serve either warm or chilled.

Salsa Verde

(about one cup)

Salsa Verde is as zingy and peppy as a mariachi band. This is the only recipe in this book that contains garlic and onions, which are not my idea of breakfast ingredients, but it is so particularly good with thin cornmeal pancakes and delicious spooned over scrambled eggs or an omelet that I couldn't leave it out.

3 large cloves garlic
2 tablespoons cilantro,
    approximately
1 small jalapeño pepper, seeded

$1/2$ medium onion
6 tomatillos
$1/2$ teaspoon salt

Finely chop by hand the garlic, cilantro, jalapeño pepper, onion, and tomatillos. Mix them together in a bowl with the salt. Or put all of the ingredients in a food processor and process until coarsely chopped. This sauce will keep in the refrigerator for 3 or 4 days.

Homemade Yogurt

(one quart)

This is Judith Jones's recipe for making yogurt. Homemade yogurt is easy to make and less expensive than store-bought. Yogurt all by itself is a quick and nourishing breakfast.

You can make flavored yogurt yourself that will taste better than the flavored yogurts you can buy in the market by adding fresh fruits and berries, or preserves, or grated lemon zest (for lemon yogurt).

1 quart milk
2 tablespoons fresh plain yogurt

Heat 1 quart milk to the boiling point for just 1 minute. Cool to 115°F. Gently stir in 2 tablespoons fresh plain yogurt (the starter) and pour into a crockery or glass bowl. Cover snugly with plastic wrap and set in a warm spot. An oven with just its pilot light on or its electric light burning is ideal. Or put it in a warm corner of the kitchen with a blanket draped over to protect it from drafts. The yogurt should be ready in about 5 to 8 hours—tilt the bowl to see if it holds together. It should then be chilled 3 hours to firm up even more. If the yogurt sets for too long a time or if you use too much starter, it will be watery. It will keep refrigerated for about a week.

Breakfast Cheese

(1½ cups)

This is exactly the cheese I've always wanted to make at home—firm enough to be spreadable and with a good, clean, wholesome taste. It is slightly sour and whips into a very smooth creaminess. You may double or triple this recipe with good results. Carlie Stillman shared this with me and she said it came from Jack Lirio—thank you both a lot.

1 quart milk
½ cup cultured buttermilk

Mix the milk and buttermilk together in a stainless-steel or glass bowl and choose a larger pot that will contain it. Cover the bowl with plastic wrap and let stand at room temperature at least one full day.

Fill the large pot with very hot tap water and place the bowl with the milk mixture inside. After 2 to 3 minutes, water will begin to appear around the edges of the mixture. Turn the heat on, start timing, and heat for 5 minutes, keeping the water just below a boil. A white, curdy mass will form. Remove the pot from the water bath, put it on a rack, and cool for 1 to 2 hours.

Ladle the contents of the pot into cheesecloth or a fine strainer set over a bowl. Drain for at least 2 hours. Put the cheese in a jar and refrigerate. It will keep for about 2 weeks refrigerated.

Breakfast Beverages

Tea
Coffee
Hot Chocolate
    Mexican Chocolate
Cuban Orange Juice
Cold or Hot Lemonade
Banana Milk
Garden Tomato Juice
Airy Eggnog
Malted Milk
Fruit Juice Food

Tea

Tea is a splendid breakfast beverage, and a little tea knowledge can give you a great cup of tea. Many people believe that tea goes better than coffee with most breakfast dishes. For breakfast, most tea drinkers prefer strong, hearty black teas that mix well with milk. There are English Breakfast and Irish Breakfast blends, and one called simply Breakfast Tea that is blended in Scotland. The classic breakfast tea is considered by many to be Keemun, a Chinese black tea that has a bouquet that reminds them of hot fresh toast. Green teas are good with rice porridge or with a bowl of farina and a coddled egg, but should not be drunk with milk. Lapsang Souchong, a black China tea with a strong smoky flavor, goes well with very savory breakfast foods, especially smoked meat and fish. The scented teas like Earl Grey (flavored with bergamot, giving it a citrus taste), jasmine tea, or Constant Comment (*strongly* flavored with spices and orange peel) can clash with anything other than the plainest breakfast foods.

When buying tea, try to get loose leaves, not tea bags: the tea will probably taste better. Store tea in a tea caddy or other airtight container, and keep it in a dark and dry place; tea shouldn't be kept in the refrigerator.

It is easy to make a good cup of tea. Use fresh, cold water, and bring it to a rolling boil. Have on hand a clean, warm teapot—earthenware, not metal—heated with hot tap water or just kept in a warm place. Add ½ to 1 teaspoon tea leaves to the pot for every 6-ounce cup. The keenest flavor is extracted when the water is at a full rolling boil, so the old rule "bring the pot to the kettle, not the kettle to the pot" makes sense. Pour the boiling water over the tea, stir once, cover, and steep for 3 to 5 minutes. Then pour out the tea into your teacups through a tea strainer, unless you don't mind a few tea leaves in the bottom of your cup. A tea ball can be a great convenience. The big, stainless-steel mesh kind is best (only half fill the tea ball): more water circulates through them and they don't lend any metallic taste to the tea.

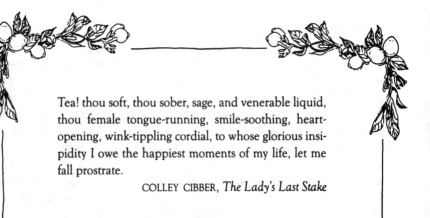

Tea! thou soft, thou sober, sage, and venerable liquid, thou female tongue-running, smile-soothing, heart-opening, wink-tippling cordial, to whose glorious insipidity I owe the happiest moments of my life, let me fall prostrate.

COLLEY CIBBER, *The Lady's Last Stake*

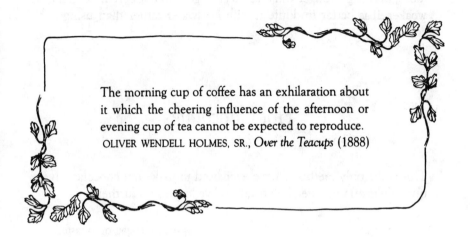

The morning cup of coffee has an exhilaration about it which the cheering influence of the afternoon or evening cup of tea cannot be expected to reproduce.
OLIVER WENDELL HOLMES, SR., *Over the Teacups* (1888)

Coffee

If you can afford the time, you can become a real coffee connoisseur, choosing your own beans and grinding, even roasting, them yourself. If you do, you will make a terrific cup of coffee. But you can also have a first-rate cup made from vacuum-packed canned coffee. For my electric drip machine, I usually use a blend of two brand-name coffees: a normal supermarket drip grind and an espresso-type dark roast. Coffee should be stored airtight in the refrigerator or freezer; you don't have to let it thaw out to use it.

There are a few things you should know to make a good cup of coffee. Don't let the coffee boil while it is being made, and don't let the coffee stay too long at a high temperature or try to reheat it: the coffee will taste harsh and bitter. I always pour my coffee as soon as it is made from the drip machine pot into a thermos jug: in it the coffee stays hot and fresh-tasting for hours. The general rule for regular strength coffee is to use 2 tablespoons coffee for each 8-ounce cup water. The cup markings on the side of your coffee maker will probably be for 6-ounce cups, or smaller, so adjust accordingly. To make very strong coffee, use more; brewing it longer will make it stronger but not better. To make it weaker, it is better to dilute it with hot water rather than using less coffee.

Hot Chocolate

(one cup)

This is the only method I have ever used to make hot chocolate. It is quite delicious and well balanced, so I've looked no further.

¼ cup water	2 teaspoons sugar, or to taste
1½ tablespoons cocoa	¾ cup milk

Put the water, cocoa, and sugar in a small saucepan over medium heat, and stir constantly until the mixture is smooth. Let it boil for a few seconds and slowly add the milk, stirring constantly. When the cocoa gets very hot, serve.

Mexican Chocolate   Add ⅛ teaspoon cinnamon to each cup, or put a 2-inch cinnamon stick in the saucepan when you are adding the milk.

ORANGE JUICE

A pitcher or a glass of fresh juice on the table is as nice as sunshine coming through the window. There is something very cheering about a glass of bright orange juice that has a sparkle to it—it just looks nice. Even if I don't drink it, I like to see orange juice on the breakfast table.

Cuban Orange Juice

(one glass)

One nice thing about this simple orange juice and milk drink is that if you add the optional egg, you won't detect any unpleasant raw eggy taste.

½ cup orange juice
½ cup milk
Optional: 1 egg

Put the orange juice, milk, and egg, if desired, in a blender. Blend until smooth and frothy, and serve cold.

Cold or Hot Lemonade

(one ten-ounce glass)

You might not think to have lemonade at your breakfast table; however, it is not only refreshing but a good way to get your vitamin C. Hot lemonade has always been considered a curative, and cold lemonade is just right for those hot summer mornings when your brow is dripping.

2 tablespoons freshly squeezed
   lemon juice
1½ to 2 tablespoons sugar syrup*

8 ounces water (soda water is
   sometimes refreshing)

*NOTE: To make sugar syrup, bring equal amounts sugar and water to a boil, stir, and remove from the heat. Cool before using.

For cold lemonade, put the lemon juice, sugar syrup, and water in a glass and stir. Add ice for the chill. For hot lemonade, add boiling water to the lemon juice and sugar syrup, stir, and serve.

Banana Milk

(one glass)

I drank Banana Milk all one spring when I had to hurry to class and didn't have time to linger in the kitchen. It is thick, fresh, and filling.

1 ripe banana, peeled
Pinch of nutmeg
¾ cup milk

Put the banana, nutmeg, and milk in a blender and whip until the mixture is smooth and light.

Garden Tomato Juice

(one twelve-ounce glass)

You will need a blender to make this, but you don't have to fuss with the tomatoes and peel and seed them. Bottled or canned tomato juice is as different from fresh tomato juice as Spam from ham. This is a frothy glass of garden tomato.

2 medium tomatoes
⅓ cup water
Salt and pepper to taste

Trim the stem away from the tomatoes and put them into a blender with the water. Blend for a minute, add salt and pepper to taste, and blend again until well mixed.

Airy Eggnog

(one eight-ounce cup)

This is a billow of air, an innocent eggnog without a drop of liquor.

1 egg, separated
About ⅛ teaspoon ground or
  freshly grated nutmeg

½ cup milk
About 1 tablespoon sugar syrup*

*NOTE: To make sugar syrup, bring equal amounts sugar and water to a boil, stir, and remove from the heat. Cool before using.

Put the egg yolk, nutmeg, and milk in a small bowl and beat until the mixture is pale and a little foamy (I use a hand-rotary beater). Add the sugar syrup and beat until blended.

Beat the egg white until stiff but moist: the peaks should be just holding upright. With a spoon, gently stir the beaten egg white into the yolk mixture until mixed. Taste and add a bit more nutmeg or sugar syrup if desired.

Malted Milk

(one eight-ounce glass)

Where has malt gone? I remember rich, thick chocolate malts that completely fulfilled any hungry cravings. I felt like purring after downing one of these cold, fluffy concoctions. These days when you order a malt, you get a mix of vanilla ice cream, chocolate syrup, and thin milk—so skimpy, and devoid of malt flavor. You can buy malt in the supermarket and make one perfect drink in the old style. One of these will probably tide you over until dinner, and the addition of ice cream makes it ideal.

Any of the following additions to your malt would be delicious: a scoop of vanilla or chocolate ice cream; a peeled, ripe banana; or a cup of washed, trimmed berries or peeled, pitted fruit.

$2\frac{1}{2}$ tablespoons malt
$\frac{2}{3}$ cup milk

Put the malt and the milk in a blender and whip until smooth and frothy.

Fruit Juice Food

(one eight-ounce glass)

Foods that are good for you often don't taste good, but I think you will find this to be quite refreshing and pleasing.

$\frac{1}{3}$ cup apple juice
$\frac{1}{3}$ cup skim (or whole) milk
2 teaspoons maple syrup
1 tablespoon wheat germ

3 tablespoons nonfat dry milk
2 tablespoons bran
2 ice cubes

Put all of the ingredients in a blender and blend until frothy. Drink cold.

Breakfast Menus

A SPECIAL BIRTHDAY

Grapefruit Juice
Cream Biscuits
Breakfast Steak
Rough and Ready Potatoes
The Coach House Bread and Butter Pudding

×

Baked Pineapple
Pork Tenderloin with Biscuits and Gravy
Madeira Poppy Seed Cake

EASTER BREAKFAST

Fresh Berries
Lemon Zephyrs
Fresh Ginger Cake

THANKSGIVING BREAKFAST

Ham
Pumpkin Mush
Ballymaloe Baked Breakfast Fruit

CHRISTMAS BREAKFAST

Fresh Fruit and Melon
Pulled Bread
Buttermilk Barley Biscuits
Kedgeree
Cranberry Raisin Pie

NEW YEAR'S

Brown Scones
Ham
Buttermilk Baked Eggs
Baked Stuffed Pears
Whole Wheat Sponge Roll

WINTER

Cranberry Poached Apples
Eggs Beatrice
Steamed Persimmon Pudding

×

Creamed Chipped Beef with Mushrooms
Boston Brown Bread Muffins
Baked Pineapple

×

Bannocks   Applesauce
Beet Marmalade   Soft Gingerbread
Scrambled Eggs with Ham   Tea

×

Orange Juice
Spice Walnuts
Breakfast Cheese
Dates and Figs
Toasted Raisin Cinnamon Wheat Bread

SPRING

Fresh Peaches and Berries
Custard-Filled Cornbread
Breakfast Sausage

✕

Fresh Grapefruit
Trout Fried with Oatmeal
Hash Browns

✕

Fresh Grapefruit Juice Ice
Sharlotka

✕

Fresh Orange with Marmalade
Cheese Bannocks

✕

Featherbed Eggs with Fresh Fruit and Cream Cheese
Raw Apple Muffins

✕

Melon
Calas
Hot Chocolate

SUMMER

Fresh Ripe Mango
Bridge Creek Fresh Ginger Muffins
Oatmeal Soufflé

×

Tea
Rhubarb with English Custard
Ginger Shortbread

×

Sliced Plums with Yogurt
Knothole Eggs
Bacon

×

Fresh Berries
Bridge Creek Heavenly Hots
Bacon

Inside-out Mango
Ginger Pancakes
Green Mango Fool

×

Melon
Crisp Whole Wheat Buns
Buttermilk Baked Eggs

×

Garden Tomato Juice
Creamed Mushroom Toast

×

Fresh Peaches
Brown Barley
Lemon Yogurt Muffins

FALL

Fresh Papaya with Seeds and Lime
Good Grits
Fried Eggs Sunny-Side-Up
Bacon
White Toast

×

Chinese Tea Eggs   Salt Cod Cakes
Rice Cereal   Shirred Lemon Eggs
Persimmons   Melba Toast

×

White Cornbread with Sage
Ham Loaf
Fried Apple Rings

×

Pink Grapefruit Apple Dish
Homemade Yogurt
Boston Brown Bread Muffins

×

Scotch Eggs
Melba Toast
Ballymaloe Baked Breakfast Fruit

×

Orange Juice
Goldenrod Eggs
Ruffled Ham

A SPECIAL DAY

Fresh Pineapple
Thin Yellow Cornmeal Pancakes
Salsa Verde
Mexican Chocolate

A DAY IN BED

Baked Banana
Milk Toast (Oven)

BREAKFAST IN BED

Ham and Farm Cheese Butter-Fried Sandwich
Baked Apple

×

Cuban Orange Juice
Pulled Bread
Figs with Breakfast Cheese

ANYTIME BREAKFAST

Pink Grapefruit Apple Dish
Butter-Basted Eggs
Oatmeal Biscuits

×

Fresh Grapefruit
Peerless Cornbread Muffins
Shirred Eggs with Bacon

A SPECIAL BREAKFAST

Fresh Lemon Juice Ice
Hard-Boiled Eggs
Smoked Salmon Toast

×

Baked Stuffed Pears
Sherry and Ginger Steamed Pudding

×

Fresh Orange and Cranberry Compote
Toasted Buttered Slices of Pound Cake

×

Malted Milk
Crumpets with Peach Rose Jam

A VERY, VERY SPECIAL BREAKFAST

Fresh Orange Juice Ice
Chocolate Walnut Butter Bread French Toast

Index

THE SUPPER BOOK

To Rover, who cleans his supper bowl every night

Acknowledgments

This book has had the benefit of many friends who have generously given wise advice and wonderful supper recipes. My deepest thanks to:

Michael Bauer   Bill Staggs
John Goyak   Fritz Streiff
Sharon Kramis   Susan Subtle
Loni Kuhn   Sherry Virbila
Mary Peacock

A special word of appreciation to Donnie Cameron for her great Rover drawings, and to Judith Jones, always a fine friend and editor.

Contents

Introduction

I love supper. The idea of supper always conjures up a simple, easy, flexible meal marked by the intimacy of family or friends. Or it is sometimes enjoyed blessedly alone. Sitting down to one dish, with bread, butter, and a dessert, can put the world back into a pleasant perspective.

If ever we needed supper back in favor, it is today. A one-dish meal can solve a lot of problems for almost everyone. It is a godsend for beginning cooks and for those who work away from home—which is just about everyone today.

The whole concept of supper is to use things that you have on hand, both standard shelf items and foods that keep well refrigerated, such as eggs, mayonnaise, cheese, carrots, celery, maybe a cabbage, some iceberg lettuce, apples, pears, and other fruits in season. Then you don't have to stop on the way home and buy the makings for a whole dinner. Many of my supper recipes, you'll find, are created with what's likely to be found in your own kitchen, if you've done some thinking ahead and replenished your stock when you shop.

In addition, a good number of the recipes are a meal in a casserole, and they often benefit from mellowing overnight in the refrigerator. Recently "fresh and fast" has become the cook's creed, but preparing a mixture of ingredients in one dish and letting it cook in the oven can produce great savory food with a depth and richness of flavor that "fresh and fast" doesn't achieve. Spanish *Riso*, Holey Moley Tamale Pie, and Applesauce Lamb Curry are all good examples of dishes that can be prepared ahead at some leisurely moment. They simply need reheating and they are ready, without any last-minute fuss, to go into action and provide a whole meal for whoever comes home hungry and impatient to eat.

In the past we have relegated soups and salads to first courses or side dishes, but why shouldn't they make ideal main dishes when the servings are ample? A flavorful, substantial soup like Chicken Custard in Broth, or a salad like Buffalo Chicken Wing Salad, or Posole Salad Soup, a dish that combines both salad and soup, makes a wonderful supper dish that is so much more inviting in the evening than the typical lamb chop, peas, and potato kind of dinner. And so much more interesting. I have drawn from many of the ethnic influences that are surfacing all around the country today to achieve bolder accents and a nice blending of flavors in these good earthy dishes with humble origins.

In a chapter I call "Fringe Dishes," I have offered some easy-to-prepare accompaniments to enliven simple fare, such as rice infused with jasmine (you just crush the contents of a tea bag into the cooking water) and store-bought rolls warmed and drizzled with garlic, parsley, and oil, which taste better than you can imagine. Also in this chapter are condiments that can be made in minutes on a rainy Sunday and preserved by refrigeration. A few pickles, a relish, a colorful salsa, or a crunchy slaw can transform a meal, and it's nice to be able to put a tempting bowl on the table to sharpen the flavors and textures of dishes for those who like bolder tastes.

Supper without something sweet wouldn't be complete for me. It may be as elementary as persimmons with maple syrup and cream, or a half a peach on a piece of sugared toast, or a soothing wine jelly, all of which you'll find in the dessert chapter. But if you don't have time to prepare anything, a plate of broken-up pieces of chocolate served with coffee can be a surprisingly good treat.

That offering of a little bit of chocolate instead of making a dessert reminds me of how much we miss if we think we have to serve a fancy dinner every time we invite someone over for a meal. Actually there are two schools of thought on this subject. One camp believes firmly that you do honor to guests, particularly if they've been invited in advance, by making something special and serving a full-course dinner with all the frills; just giving them potluck is somehow insulting, as though you couldn't bother to make the extra effort. The other camp—the one to which I belong—feels that sharing the family meal is a privilege, that there is something deeply satisfying about sitting down and partaking of just what would be ordinarily served in that home. In fact, it is often a relief to feel that the host hasn't spent hours in the kitchen and that the food, as long as there is enough of it, isn't something special. (I exclude, of course, holidays, birthdays, or a dinner for a visiting dignitary.) My argument is that during the last twenty or thirty years, with almost every adult working away from home, there has been a shortage of time, energy, and money too, for us to go all out to impress guests. But when you ask them to "come for supper," the expectation will be for a more scaled-down and intimate meal.

Supper is more a state of mind than a meal bound by rules. Above all, it shouldn't be prepared watching the clock and racing through all the cooking. Nothing destroys the pleasure and natural rhythm of kitchen work so quickly. The kitchen should be a soothing place, especially after a hectic day in the work world. Cooking supper for yourself and others can be a welcome change of thought and tempo. It can be one of the nicest times of the day.

Supper Salads

California Caesar Salad

Spinach Salad with Chutney Dressing

Green Rose Salad

Asparagus Salad

Potato Salad

Waldorf Salad

Avocado and Bacon Salad

Salmon Salad Niçoise

Tuscan Bean and Tuna Salad

Mustard Ring Salad

Buffalo Chicken Wing Salad

Beef Salad with Sour Pickles

Until not too long ago, Americans considered salads sissy food. Today salads are a symbol of health and nutrition, and salad bars are one of the biggest food businesses in this country. What is a salad? My definition is any greens, herbs, vegetables, or other foods, cooked or uncooked, that are served cold or at room temperature, with a dressing. Salads make ideal supper dishes, but they need a little heft to be satisfying. No matter how big a bowl of greens you serve, it won't suffice unless substantial fringe dishes are served, too.

Beware of the notion that salad can be made by tossing together a hodgepodge of ingredients in a bowl and then calling it a day. Turning out a splendid salad takes as much attention as braising fish. If greens are used, be ready to discard the coarse blemished leaves. Wash away all grit and dry the leaves thoroughly, because dressing won't adhere to water. Put the leaves in a plastic bag with a dampened paper towel and store in the refrigerator until chilled and ready to use. Carefully look over all your salad ingredients, and discard any cooked vegetables that are soggy or mushy. Cooked meats, chicken, fish, and shellfish must be carefully trimmed and fresh-tasting.

The dressing of salad is critical: how you make it and how you apply it. The most common dressing is vinaigrette, oil and acid blended, with a variety of other flavors often added. The acid is usually lemon or other citrus, or vinegar. The most popular oil used today is olive. Buying an olive oil you like is sometimes difficult. Money does not necessarily buy the best, and the labels of extra virgin, extra fine, and so on only confuse the issue. Use a robust olive oil for rustic, hearty salads and a fine, subtle olive oil for delicate salads. The only way you find an olive oil that pleases you is by tasting a variety of them. I don't know of any shortcuts to doing this.

A vinaigrette must be properly balanced. One of the most common errors is to use so much acid that the dressing tastes overwhelmingly sour and all the good qualities of the salad are lost. The old standard rule for making vinaigrettes was three parts oil to one part acid; this makes a far too acid mixture for most palates. You will notice that in some of my vinaigrettes, I have cut the dressing with a few spoonfuls of water, which makes it lighter and smoother. We are now back to my best basic rule for all cooking: taste as you make, and add only a little of whichever of the four basic taste-makers you are using. (They are sweet, sour, salty, or bitter.) Trust your own palate, and remember, to be a good cook you must be in control of the recipe you are making by critically tasting. This rule applies to everything you prepare.

A green salad should be dressed just before serving. Be careful to add only enough dressing to coat the leaves. Add a little at a time and toss gently until all leaves have a sheen. It is easy to overdo the dressing and end up with salad soup. Salads such as potato, chicken, fish, or other seafood should be dressed well before serving so the flavors can blend and mellow. Then taste and correct the salt and pepper just before serving, because this type of salad seems to become bland after a few hours of chilling. It is also important to add only enough creamy dressing to make a moist salad: it should be neither dry nor sodden.

I want you to try the Buffalo Chicken Wing Salad (see page 350); it is just the ticket for a supper picnic, with lots of fire, crunch, and flavor. The Waldorf Salad (see page 344) with applesauce dressing is better by far than the traditional version, and the Caesar Salad (see page 338) in the classic California style is easy to make and will get lots of good comments.

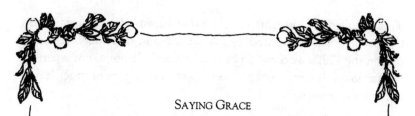

SAYING GRACE

Saying a prayer before supper is a custom common to all cultures and all religions that is probably as old as the human race. Gratitude is a basic human feeling and it is natural to have shared ways of asking for blessing, giving thanks, or remembering others. Many of us have heard a solemn grace said over a holiday turkey, but saying grace can also be as simple as saying "Enjoy your meal!"

I have been asking friends and acquaintances if they say grace and I have been glad to hear that many do (on special occasions, at any rate). Saying grace before supper can be a ritual of fellowship that reminds us that we're at the table for more than just the food.

California Caesar Salad

(four servings)

This is called a California Caesar Salad because it's a variation on the original salad invented by Caesar Cardini, a Tijuana restaurateur in the 1930s who had a ritzy Hollywood clientele. For a perfect Caesar salad, it's essential to use only the crisp, tender inner leaves of romaine lettuce.

4 slices homemade-style bread
3 tablespoons olive oil

2 heads romaine lettuce

Dressing
½ cup olive oil
3 cloves garlic
2 tablespoons lemon juice, or
   to taste
½ teaspoon salt

5 anchovy fillets, or to taste
   (start with just 3 anchovies
   and taste, adding more if
   desired)

1 ounce Parmesan cheese,
   freshly grated (⅓ cup)

To make croutons, preheat the oven to 250°F. Cut the slices of bread into cubes, first removing the crusts. Spread the bread cubes out on a baking sheet, and put in the oven for about 12 minutes, or until the bread is dried out. Heat the 3 tablespoons olive oil in a frying pan over medium heat, add the bread cubes, and fry them, turning frequently, until all sides are golden brown. Remove from the heat and reserve.

Separate the leaves from the heads of romaine lettuce, then wash and dry them. Discard the dark, coarse outer leaves and any that are wilted or blemished. The presentation of the salad is more attractive when the leaves are left whole, although it is more manageable to eat when they are cut into bite-size pieces—the choice is up to you.

Put the olive oil and garlic in a blender and blend until smooth and creamy. Add the lemon juice and the salt and mix. Pour the dressing into the bottom of a large salad bowl. Add the anchovy fillets to the bowl and mash them into the oil mixture until well blended. Put in the romaine leaves and toss until all the leaves are coated and shiny. Add the croutons and toss lightly to mix. Sprinkle the cheese over the salad just before serving.

Spinach Salad with Chutney Dressing

(four servings)

Crisp sweet apple slices, rich toasted pecans, big chewy raisins, and tender small-leafed spinach come together with a bold chutney dressing.

1 cup pecan halves	2 Red Delicious apples
2 bunches (about 1½ pounds) young, small-leaf spinach	½ cup muscat raisins
	½ cup chopped scallions
Chutney Dressing	
½ cup vegetable oil	1 teaspoon curry powder
4 tablespoons mango-ginger chutney (I prefer Sharwood Mango-ginger)	1 teaspoon dry mustard
	½ teaspoon salt
	2 tablespoons lemon juice

Preheat the oven to 300°F.

Spread the pecans out on a baking sheet and toast for about 12 minutes (watch carefully so they don't burn). Meanwhile, wash, stem, and dry the spinach. Then, leaving the apples unpeeled, core, halve, and cut them crosswise into thin slices.

Put the spinach, apples, pecans, raisins, and scallions in a large salad bowl and toss to mix.

Put the oil, chutney, curry powder, dry mustard, salt, and lemon juice in a bowl, and stir until well mixed. Add the dressing to the salad and toss gently to coat all the ingredients. Serve immediately.

Green Rose Salad

(four servings)

Crisp lettuce leaves in a roselike shape are filled with colorful vegetables and served in one large bowl with thick buttermilk or ranch dressing passed on the side. This idea came from Myrtle Allen, one of the owners of Ballymaloe, a lovely inn and cooking school in County Cork, Ireland.

Buttermilk Dressing

½ cup buttermilk

½ cup mayonnaise

2 teaspoons finely chopped garlic (or put through a garlic press)

½ teaspoon salt

½ pound fresh beets; or 1 cup canned sliced beets, plain or pickled

1 head iceberg lettuce

1 bunch watercress

2 tomatoes

1 cucumber

1 bunch scallions

4 hard-boiled eggs, shelled and quartered (see page 517)

¾ cup large pitted black olives

To make the buttermilk dressing, put the buttermilk, mayonnaise, garlic, and salt in a jar with a lid and shake until well blended. Refrigerate until needed.

If using fresh beets, cut off all but an inch of the beet tops; don't pare or remove the roots. Drop the beets into enough boiling water to cover them and cook them, uncovered, until they are tender, 30 minutes to an hour, depending on their size. Drain the beets, drop them in cold water to cool them, slip off their skins, and slice.

To prepare the lettuce, fill a large bowl with cold water, core the lettuce, and forcefully plunge it, cored end down, into the water. Shake free of excess water and wrap the head in several layers of towel. Refrigerate for at least 6 hours or overnight before using. (This process not only ensures ultimate crispness, it separates the leaves and makes them easier to peel away without tearing.) Carefully separate the lettuce leaves. Remove the tough stems from the watercress, then wash and dry. Cut the tomatoes into wedges. Peel, seed, and slice the cucumber. Slice the scallions.

Arrange the lettuce leaves like a rose in a large bowl, with the large leaves on the outside and the smaller ones in the center. Put sprigs of watercress, the tomato wedges, and the beet and cucumber slices and scallions between the leaves. Tuck the egg quarters and olives around the top. Pass the dressing at the table.

Asparagus Salad

(four servings)

It's a cheery sight to see the first bundles of asparagus in the super-markets. Asparagus is always a treat served simply with melted but-ter, salt, and pepper, but since most of us can't leave well enough alone, I am including one of my favorite vinaigrette dressings for chilled, lightly cooked asparagus. The sesame seed oil gives this dressing a toasted nutty flavor. Serve with Deviled Eggs (see page 516).

2 pounds fresh asparagus

Dressing
2 tablespoons white wine
    vinegar
1½ teaspoons Dijon mustard
¼ teaspoon salt
Pepper to taste
1 tablespoon finely chopped
    scallion

1 head butter lettuce

1 tablespoon finely chopped
    parsley
6 tablespoons vegetable oil
¼ to ½ teaspoon sesame seed
    oil

Wash the asparagus and cut or break off the tough colorless woody bottom of each stalk. If the asparagus spears are very large, peel a little of the coarse outer stalk at the butt end with a vegetable peeler. Plunge the spears into a large pot of boiling water and boil gently until they are just tender when pierced with a knife; begin testing after 5 minutes. When done, remove the spears and drain them. Put them on a plate, cover, and chill.

Separate enough lettuce leaves to make a bed for the asparagus. Wash and dry them, put in a plastic bag, and chill.

Mix together the vinegar, mustard, salt, pepper, scallion, and parsley in a bowl. Slowly add the vegetable oil and whisk until blended. Add the sesame seed oil, beginning with ¼ teaspoon, then taste. Just a faint nutty flavor should be present—add a little more if necessary but don't overdo. Cover and refrigerate.

When ready to serve, make a bed of butter lettuce leaves on a serving platter or on individual plates and arrange the asparagus spears on top. Spoon the vinaigrette over and serve cold.

Potato Salad

(four servings)

Potato salad makes a wonderful supper served with lots of whole hard-cooked eggs and a platter of lettuce and tomatoes. The secret to making this good potato salad is to toss the potatoes while they are still hot with the lemon juice and oil.

2 pounds red or white potatoes	3 stalks celery, diced
¼ cup olive oil	About 1¼ cups mayonnaise
¼ cup lemon juice	Salt and pepper to taste

Boil the potatoes until barely tender, about 15 minutes (potatoes continue to cook after they have been removed from the heat). Drain, and, as soon as they are cool enough to handle, peel and cut into ½-inch cubes.

While the potatoes are still hot, put them into a mixing bowl, sprinkle with the oil and lemon juice, and toss until the cubes are completely coated. Add the celery and mayonnaise. Season with salt and pepper and toss until well distributed. Serve chilled or at room temperature.

NOTE: This salad needs enough salt, pepper, and lemon juice to give good balance. Be generous enough with the mayonnaise so the salad is moist.

Waldorf Salad

(six servings)

Waldorf Salad harkens back to the tearoom, where it was served with tiny crustless white chicken sandwiches. This recipe is quite generous with walnuts and celery, and the addition of applesauce makes a superior dressing.

Dressing
½ cup mayonnaise
½ cup applesauce

3 tablespoons honey
1 tablespoon lemon juice

3 or 4 crisp, firm, green apples
   (pippins or Granny Smiths)
2 or 3 stalks celery
1½ cups walnuts, in large
   pieces

Salt to taste
Butter or iceberg lettuce
   leaves, washed and dried

In a small bowl, mix together the mayonnaise, applesauce, honey, and lemon.

Leave the apples unpeeled, core, and cut into bite-size chunks. Chop the celery into ½-inch chunks. Put the apples, celery, and walnuts in a large bowl and sprinkle lightly with salt. Pour the dressing over, mix well, and serve on a bed of lettuce leaves.

Avocado and Bacon Salad

(four servings)

Opposites do attract, and when salty, crunchy bacon meets soft, creamy avocado, they live happily ever after.

Dressing
1½ teaspoons lemon juice
¼ cup sour cream

½ cup mayonnaise

8 slices bacon (about ½ pound)
⅓ cup finely chopped scallions
2 avocados, peeled and cubed

1 head iceberg lettuce, cored, rinsed, wrapped, and chilled (see page 341), cut into bite-size pieces
Salt and pepper to taste

To make the dressing, mix together the lemon juice, sour cream, and mayonnaise in a small bowl. Stir until smooth, and set aside.

Dice the bacon, fry until crisp, and pat dry with paper towels. Toss together the bacon, scallions, avocado, and lettuce in a large bowl, and season with salt and pepper. Add enough dressing to coat all the ingredients and toss gently.

Salmon Salad Niçoise

(four servings)

If you can't afford a trip to the south of France, a Niçoise salad is the next best thing. This variation uses salmon instead of the classic tuna fish. Make it when you have some leftover cooked salmon.

Vinaigrette

$\frac{1}{4}$ cup white cider vinegar, or to taste

1 teaspoon salt, or to taste

$\frac{1}{2}$ teaspoon pepper

1 cup olive oil

2 tablespoons cold water*

10 small new potatoes

$\frac{1}{3}$ pound string beans (about $1\frac{1}{2}$ cups)

3 ripe but firm tomatoes

1 green bell pepper

1 onion

Crisp lettuce leaves

About 1 pound cooked salmon (see page 390), flaked (approximately 2 cups)

$\frac{1}{2}$ cup Niçoise olives if available; or other black olives

About $\frac{1}{4}$ cup anchovies, cut in half lengthwise

2 tablespoons capers

1 lemon, cut into wedges, for garnish

To make the vinaigrette, mix together the vinegar and salt in a small bowl and let stand a few minutes. Add the pepper and slowly stir or whisk in the olive oil. Taste for acidity and salt, and add more vinegar and/or salt if too bland. Stir in the water, mixing

*The water in this vinaigrette helps emulsify the oil and vinegar, and it also reduces the cloying oiliness.

briskly. Stir to blend before using, or store in a jar with a tight and shake well before using.

Put the potatoes in a saucepan, cover with cold water, bring to a boil, and gently boil until tender when pierced with a knife, about 15 minutes. Drain, peel while hot but cool enough to handle, and cut into bite-size pieces. Wash the beans, remove the ends and strings, and cut into 1-inch pieces. Drop them into a large pot of boiling water and boil gently for 5 to 10 minutes (taste one to see if they are done—they should still be slightly crunchy). Drain the beans and rinse them thoroughly in cold water to stop the cooking.

Cut the tomatoes into wedges. Remove the seeds and veins from the pepper and cut it into thin slices. Cut the onion into thin rings and put in a bowl with ice water and ice cubes to keep crisp.

This salad may be arranged on one large platter or presented on large individual salad plates. Arrange the lettuce leaves to make a bed for the other ingredients. Put a mound of the salmon in the center and arrange the potatoes, beans, tomatoes, and olives in mounds around it. Put the anchovy strips, pepper slices, and onion rings on top. Sprinkle the capers over all. Just before serving, pour the vinaigrette over all, and put the lemon wedges around the plate.

You can toss the salad, but the presentation isn't as enticing.

Tuscan Bean and Tuna Salad

(four servings)

The Italians are masters at using tuna in inventive ways. Vitello tonnato (veal with a creamy tuna sauce) is one example, and this recipe is another.

$1\frac{1}{2}$ cups dried cannellini beans
  (or any other white beans);
  or 6 cups canned beans
  (be sure to rinse them with water
  and drain them before using)
Salt and coarsely ground
  pepper to taste
2 tablespoons red wine vinegar

6 tablespoons olive oil
1 tablespoon chopped fresh
  basil
$\frac{1}{2}$ cup chopped Italian parsley;
  plus sprigs for garnish
1 large onion, finely chopped
1 pound cooked tuna, flaked;
  or canned tuna

If using dried beans, rinse, pick through (discard any shriveled beans or foreign matter), put in a pot, cover with water, and allow to soak overnight; or try the short method—cover the beans with water, bring to a boil, cook for 1 minute, and then cover the pot and let stand for 1 hour. Drain the water from the beans. Put the beans in a large heavy-bottomed pot. Add enough water to cover the beans. Add ¾ teaspoon salt (½ teaspoon salt for every cup of dried beans). Bring to a boil over medium heat. Reduce the heat to a simmer, cover, and simmer about 1 hour, or until the beans are tender. Make sure the beans are covered with water while they're cooking.

When the beans are tender, drain them (if using canned beans, drain). Allow the beans to cool, and put them in a large serving bowl. Season with salt and pepper. In a small bowl stir together the vinegar and olive oil. Pour over the beans, and toss until well mixed. Sprinkle the basil and Italian parsley over the beans and toss again. Add the onion and tuna and mix. Garnish with the sprigs of Italian parsley.

Mustard Ring Salad

(six servings)

It seems that aspic and gelatin salads have completely fallen out of fashion, but I don't know of another salad that's better at showing off the flavors of seafood. This one is bright yellow like a sunflower, and it has a snappy, sharp turmeric and mustard taste. You will want to make the ring early in the day or even the night before, because it must be chilled at least four hours before serving.

1 envelope unflavored gelatin	½ teaspoon salt
1¼ cups cold water	1 teaspoon turmeric
4 eggs, well beaten	1 cup heavy cream, whipped
½ cup white vinegar	1½ pounds raw unshelled
½ cup sugar	shrimp
1½ tablespoons dry mustard	

Soak the gelatin in ¼ cup cold water for 5 minutes. Put the beaten eggs, cup of water, and white vinegar in a heavy-bottomed saucepan or the top of a double boiler, and stir to blend. Add the gelatin, sugar, mustard, salt, and turmeric, and mix well. Heat the mixture over medium-low heat, stirring constantly, for about 5 minutes. Do not allow the mixture to boil. Remove from the heat and cool. Gently stir in the whipped cream. Pour into a 1½-quart ring mold and chill for 4 to 5 hours before serving.

Bring a large pot of salted water to a boil and add the raw shrimp. Turn the heat down so the water is boiling gently and cook the shrimp until they turn pink, about 1 to 3 minutes. Drain. When cool enough to handle, shell and devein the shrimp. Mound the shrimp in the middle of the mustard ring and serve.

Buffalo Chicken Wing Salad

(four servings)

Not buffalo as in the beast, but Buffalo as in western New York State, where spicy chicken wings with blue cheese dressing originated. Adding the cold crunch of celery and iceberg lettuce to the heat of the pepper and the bite of blue cheese makes an even greater combination of tastes and textures than Buffalo chicken wings alone. Individuals vary in their tolerance for heat, but this salad needs fire to succeed; those who want their Buffalo wings hotter yet can pass a bottle of Louisiana hot sauce at the table.

Blue Cheese Dressing

1 cup mayonnaise
2 tablespoons grated onion
1 teaspoon finely chopped garlic
1 tablespoon lemon juice

1 tablespoon white vinegar
Salt and pepper to taste
Optional: cayenne pepper
¼ cup crumbled blue cheese

⅓ cup flour
1 teaspoon salt, or to taste
2 teaspoons cayenne pepper,
    or to taste
1 to 1½ pounds chicken
    drumettes (12 to 16 chicken
    wings, second joints and wing
    tips removed)

3 tablespoons vegetable oil
1 head iceberg lettuce, cored,
    rinsed, wrapped, and chilled
    (see page 341), cut into bite-
    size pieces
4 to 5 stalks celery, cut into
    2- by ¼-inch strips

To make the dressing, mix together the mayonnaise, onion, garlic, lemon juice, and vinegar, and blend until smooth. Taste and correct the seasoning, adding salt, pepper, and optional cayenne as desired. Gently stir in the blue cheese.

Put the flour, salt, and cayenne in a bag and shake until mixed. Add the chicken to the bag and shake until all the pieces are well coated with the flour mixture.

Heat the oil in a large skillet, put in the chicken, and fry over a medium-high heat, turning the pieces occasionally, until all are cooked through, about 12 to 15 minutes. Remove from the heat and shake more cayenne and salt over the wings; don't be timid—this makes the dish lively. Set aside.

Put the lettuce and celery in a large salad bowl. Pour the dressing over and toss until the lettuce is evenly coated. Arrange the chicken pieces on top of the lettuce around the edges of the bowl. Serve at once.

"Avoid having too many courses. If the food is good, that is all the more reason to limit the number of dishes, so that each may be fully savored . . .

"Give as much care to simple dishes and the humbler foods as you do to elaborate dishes and ambitious menus. At the same time, do not neglect to take advantage of new developments in the growing, shipping, preserving, and cooking of food. Take time both to cherish the old and to investigate the new."

—from *The Fireside Cookbook*
by James Beard

Beef Salad with Sour Pickles

(six servings)

I would always prefer having leftover roast beef cold in a salad like this rather than eating it reheated.

3 hard-boiled eggs (see page 517)

3 cups thinly sliced, bite-size pieces cooked roast beef

4 medium potatoes, boiled, peeled, and sliced

1 bunch scallions, sliced

4 to 5 stalks celery, coarsely chopped

1½ cups large bite-size chunks of dill pickles

Dressing

1 tablespoon Dijon mustard

¾ cup olive oil

1 clove garlic, finely chopped and mashed with ¾ teaspoon salt

½ teaspoon freshly ground pepper

2 tablespoons red wine vinegar

2 tablespoons cold water*

¼ teaspoon Tabasco, or to taste

Optional: ¼ cup capers

Shell the hard-boiled eggs and separate the yolks from the whites. Set aside the yolks. Dice the whites and mix together in a large salad bowl with the beef, potatoes, scallions, celery, and pickles.

To make the dressing, in a small bowl mash the reserved egg yolks with a fork and stir in the mustard, olive oil, the garlic and salt, pepper, vinegar, water, and Tabasco. Taste the dressing and adjust the seasonings if necessary.

Pour the dressing over the beef salad and toss. Pass around the capers in a small bowl at the table, if you wish.

---

*The water in this dressing helps emulsify the oil and vinegar, and it also reduces the cloying oiliness.

Supper Soups

Ham and Bean Soup

Black Bean Soup

Navy Bean and Tomato Soup

Mustard Green Soup

Sharon's Lentil Salsa Soup

Celery Soup with Green and White Beans

Split Pea Soup

Borscht

Joyce McGillis's Creamy Corn Soup

Posole Salad Soup

Eggplant Soup

Leek and Potato Soup

Onion Soup

Tomato and Bread Soup

Chinese Hot and Sour Soup

Fish Chowder

Cioppino

Cream of Scallop Soup

Oyster Stew

Chicken Custard in Broth

Rich Chicken Noodle Soup

When I was very young the virtues of soup eluded me. I always wanted to start right in with the good solid dishes, and soup seemed superfluous. I lived a long time before I truly appreciated the soothing, satisfying qualities of a bowl of soup. But into every home cook's life there comes a moment when it's time to make soup.

When I was first married, my husband had several favorite dishes that his mother used to make, and one of them was a ham and bean soup. I tried to re-create the soup of his memory with one recipe after another. I added sage to ham and beans, I added thyme, I added everything but the kitchen sink. And each time he tasted my latest effort he would shake his head—nothing came close. This went on for almost two years. (To this day I don't know why I didn't contact my mother-in-law, Cecilia, right away. I guess I thought the next soup was going to be *it*.) When I finally asked for the recipe and Cecilia sent it to me, I was flabbergasted. It only took four plain and simple ingredients: beans, onions, ham, and water. It was a basic cooking lesson I have never forgotten: less can be more.

Soup runs the gamut from fancy clarified soups with expensive garnishes to peasant soups of bread and water. The soups in this chapter are not the light kind that tease the appetite; they are intended to fortify. They are solid and nourishing and meant to be the main event at suppertime. And they demonstrate all the virtues of soup: convenience, simplicity, frugality, and wholesomeness.

Soup making is often misunderstood. I used to be amazed that the students in my cooking classes thought that making soup was necessarily a long and arduous process of watching and stirring. You do not have to be an all-day babysitter to a simmering soup pot. Nor should soup be a catchall or a way of getting rid of tired vegetables. I'm leery of cooks who advise you to clear out the vegetable bins of your refrigerator and add the contents to the soup pot. Soup should be thought out and made with care. Once you've made it, it's a meal you can take out of the refrigerator and have ready in a hurry. And it's the one dish most easily extended for the unexpected guest.

Good soup depends on critical tasting and seasoning. Nothing is less appealing than a bland soup. Don't be timid about seasoning. It may surprise you to discover how much salt is needed to bring out the good flavor of a soup. The trick is to add carefully, and stir and taste after each addition. Always add only a little salt at the beginning, remembering that simmering causes evaporation and salt concentration; the final critical correction should take place just before serving.

If you have a neglected soup tureen that you inherited or got for a wedding present, get it down off the shelf where it's gathering dust and use it! There is nothing more welcoming than soup being ladled from a big steaming tureen at suppertime.

Ham and Bean Soup

(four servings)

Ham and Bean Soup holds a special place in my heart because it was one of my first and best lessons in cooking: making it fancy won't make it better.

1 pound (about 2 cups) Great Northern beans, soaked overnight and drained (see page 348)	2 onions, chopped 2 cups cut-up ham or smoked pork butt Salt and pepper to taste

Put the beans, onions, and ham pieces in a large pot. Pour in enough cold water to cover the beans by 1½ inches. Bring the mixture to a boil over medium heat. Reduce the heat to a simmer, removing any scum that rises to the surface. Simmer about 2 hours, or until the beans are tender. Add water, if needed.

Season with salt and pepper. Skim off any fat that rises to the top and serve.

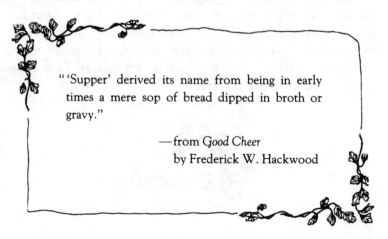

" 'Supper' derived its name from being in early times a mere sop of bread dipped in broth or gravy."

—from *Good Cheer*
by Frederick W. Hackwood

Black Bean Soup

(six servings)

Black beans have a rich flavor and their dramatic color looks striking with white rice or sour cream, purple onion, lemon slices, chopped chiles, and hard-boiled egg. In the Caribbean, black beans are served with white rice in a dish called Moors and Christians.

1 pound (about 2 cups) dried black beans, soaked overnight (see page 348)	1 large green bell pepper, peeled, seeded, and chopped
About 2½ teaspoons salt	6 cloves garlic, chopped
½ cup olive oil	1¼ teaspoons dried oregano
1 large onion, chopped	¼ teaspoon cayenne pepper
	½ teaspoon black pepper

Drain the beans, and put them in a large pot. Add enough water to cover the beans by 1½ inches and 1 teaspoon salt and cook over medium heat for 45 minutes.

Heat the olive oil in a large heavy-bottomed skillet, add the onion, green pepper, and garlic, and sauté until tender, about 2 or 3 minutes. Add the vegetables to the beans and then add the oregano, cayenne, and black pepper, and the remaining 1½ teaspoons salt.

Simmer for 1 hour. Add more water, if necessary. Taste for seasoning, and add more salt if needed.

Navy Bean and Tomato Soup

(four servings)

One more of those lessons in cooking that teaches you how a meager list of ingredients doesn't necessarily result in a meager-tasting soup. All it takes here is a sure hand with seasoning, but with the salt pork, watch your addition of salt.

½ pound (about 1 cup) dried white navy beans, soaked overnight (see page 348)
28-ounce can whole tomatoes
2 onions, chopped
½ pound salt pork, cut into small pieces

2 cloves garlic, finely chopped
1 teaspoon dried thyme
Salt and pepper to taste
About 4 cups water

Drain the water from the beans and put them in a large heavy-bottomed pot. Stir in the tomatoes, onions, salt pork, garlic, thyme, and salt and pepper and add the water, making sure it covers the contents of the pot. Simmer for 3½ hours, or until the beans are tender. Adjust the seasonings and serve.

Mustard Green Soup

(four servings)

I wish people would get braver about using mustard greens. They are in almost every supermarket now. I remember driving around with my Italian mother and grandmother many years ago and stopping by yellow fields to gather wild mustard greens, which were then cooked with garlic and dressed with olive oil and vinegar. Navy beans have an unobtrusive flavor that blends well with the bite of bitter greens. Serve with wheat rolls and a mild cheese like fontina.

2 pounds turnips, peeled and diced

4 tablespoons olive oil

About 3 cloves garlic, finely chopped

1 large leek (or 1 large onion), chopped

2 cups cooked navy beans (see page 348)

½ pound mustard greens (or any bitter greens), washed and coarsely chopped

6 cups chicken broth (see page 377)

Salt and pepper to taste

In a pot of boiling water, cook the turnips for about 5 minutes. Drain and reserve.

Heat the olive oil in a soup kettle or pot. Add the garlic and leek and cook over medium-low heat, stirring often, until the garlic and leek are softened but not browned. Stir in the turnip, beans, greens, and broth. Add salt and pepper to taste, and simmer for about 15 minutes. Serve hot.

Sharon's Lentil Salsa Soup

(four to six servings)

I never knew that lentils were used in Mexican cooking until I tried this recipe. The peppy salsa adds flavor to the earthy lentils. (By the way, some people seem to think you need to presoak lentils before you cook them. You don't.)

1 tablespoon olive oil	1¼ cups lentils
3 cloves garlic, finely chopped	2 cups Red Salsa (see page
2 carrots, peeled and sliced	494)
1 onion, chopped	1½ teaspoons salt
6 cups water	

Put the olive oil in a soup pot (I use a 6-quart pot) and spread it so it films the bottom. Set over medium heat and stir in the garlic, carrots, and onion. Cook, stirring constantly, until the vegetables are softened, but not brown. Add the water, lentils, Red Salsa, and salt. Cover, let the soup come to a boil, then reduce the heat so that it bubbles without boiling too hard. Occasionally stir and check that the water isn't boiling away, adding a little water if the soup gets too thick. Simmer for about 45 minutes, or until the lentils are tender. Serve hot.

SUPPER ALONE

Sometimes eating supper alone feels private, quiet, and blessedly liberating. You may eat anything you want; you needn't be conventional. I like a baked potato with olive oil and coarse salt and pepper followed by vanilla ice cream, which proves to me that money doesn't buy a good meal. One night not long ago I had freshly baked cookies and milk, and found that uplifting.

If my spirit is less than cheerful, it helps me to fix something restorative when eating alone. Split Pea Soup (see page 364) is easy to make—it takes only a few minutes to get started and is ready in 1 to 1½ hours. Kitchen preparations, the busyness of chopping, stirring, and watching a bubbling pot, can help dispel any gloom, at least for me.

I like to fix supper on a tray and carry it back to the desk in my bedroom. I have a fireplace there and I can sit and eat while listening to music or watching the news on TV. Eating in bed will always seem like the height of luxury to me, but spilling one's soup on the bed destroys the mood, so only food that doesn't slosh is recommended.

Celery Soup with Green and White Beans

(six servings)

Celery has a delicate flavor and is a faint presence in many soups, but here it gets to stand up on its own. The beans add texture, color, and body.

About 8 stalks celery, coarsely chopped	1½ cups cooked Great Northern beans (see page 348)
1 large onion, diced	10 ounces (2 cups) frozen lima beans
4 cups chicken broth (see page 377)	Salt and pepper to taste

Put the celery and onion in a large pot, add 3 cups of the chicken broth, and bring to a boil. Reduce the heat and simmer for 15 minutes, or until the vegetables are tender.

Drain and reserve the liquid from the vegetables. Put the vegetables in a food processor or blender, adding a little of the hot liquid, and process until puréed. Put the puréed vegetables back in the pot with the hot liquid and the rest of the chicken stock. Add the beans and simmer for 10 minutes, or until the beans are heated through. Salt and pepper to taste, being careful not to add too much pepper—a little goes a long way.

Split Pea Soup

(four servings)

Many old-fashioned pea soups were stodgy. Today's split pea soups are a brighter color and have a far fresher flavor. These days you don't have to presoak the peas, so you can count on an hour to an hour and a half to put Split Pea Soup on your table. Serve with dark rye bread and melon.

1 pound (2 cups) split green peas	3 stalks celery with leaves,
1½ pounds ham hocks, or a	chopped
leftover ham bone with a little	8 cups water
meat attached	Salt and pepper to taste
2 medium onions, chopped	

Put the split peas, ham hocks, onions, and celery in a soup pot, add the water, and bring to a boil. Reduce the heat to medium, and lightly salt and pepper. Cook, stirring occasionally, for 1 to 1½ hours. The soup is done when the peas are soft. Taste, add more salt, if needed, and a generous amount of pepper. Remove the bones and any skin from the ham hocks, and shred the meat if the chunks are too large.

If a smooth soup is desired, remove the meat and purée the soup. I don't bother, and rather like the slight texture that the peas have when they are whole.

Borscht

(six servings)

This borscht is so chunky and thick that it's almost not a soup at all. If you want it more soupy, just add two to three more cups of broth. Borscht has a nice taste of beet sweetness and lemon sourness.

4 medium potatoes, peeled
1 large onion
2 carrots
4 to 5 stalks celery
2 tablespoons chopped fresh
   parsley
6 cups beef broth
2 pounds fresh beets, peeled
   and finely chopped

$1\frac{1}{2}$ tablespoons lemon juice
2 tablespoons fresh chopped
   dill; plus a little more for
   garnish, if desired
2 tablespoons sugar
Salt to taste
Optional: $\frac{1}{2}$ cup sour cream,
   for garnish

Finely chop the potatoes, onion, carrots, and celery, either by hand or in a food processor. Put the vegetables, parsley, and beef broth in an 8-quart heavy-bottomed pot. Bring to a boil over medium heat. Reduce the heat and simmer for 30 minutes. Add the beets, and simmer for another 30 minutes. Remove from the heat and add the lemon juice, dill, sugar, and salt. If you like, serve garnished with a little more chopped dill, and pass around the sour cream in a small bowl.

Joyce McGillis's
Creamy Corn Soup

(four servings)

It takes only three ingredients to make creamy corn soup. Serve with a grilled cheese and tomato sandwich or, if you're lazy, with Rye Crackers (see page 475).

6 cups corn kernels—fresh (about 9 ears), frozen, or canned and drained	4½ cups milk ½ teaspoon salt, or to taste

If you are using fresh corn, first cut the kernels from the cob with a sharp knife. Put the corn, 3 cups of the milk, and salt in a heavy-bottomed saucepan and bring to a boil. Reduce the heat and simmer for 20 minutes.

Pour the milk and corn mixture into a food processor and process until the corn is puréed. Add the remaining 1½ cups milk and process until well blended. Correct salt if necessary. Return to the saucepan and gently reheat, stirring frequently.

Posole Salad Soup

(six servings)

It may seem weird putting your salad in the middle of your soup. It isn't. The salad looks great and stays crunchy in the middle of the soup, adding a sparkling contrast in texture. Posole is the Spanish name for hominy soup.

4 cups chicken broth (see page 377)	3 cups canned yellow or white hominy,† drained
2 teaspoons ground cumin	1 cup coarsely chopped cilantro
2 cups canned stewed tomatoes, broken up	2 cups coarsely chopped iceberg lettuce
6 tablespoons masa harina* in 1 cup cold water, blended until smooth	1 avocado, peeled, pitted, and cut into 1-inch dice
Salt and pepper to taste	

In a large saucepan, stir together the broth, cumin, tomatoes, masa harina mixture, salt and pepper, and hominy. Bring to a boil, reduce the heat, and simmer for 5 minutes, stirring occasionally. Toss together the cilantro and lettuce in a bowl. Add the avocado to the soup just before serving. Serve the soup, and pass around the lettuce and cilantro at the table, letting everyone put some on top of their soup.

*Masa harina is corn treated with lime water and ground into a flour. With the addition of water it makes the dough used for tamales and tortillas. Quaker Oats makes masa harina that is widely available in supermarkets.

†Hominy is dried corn that has had its hull and germ removed with lye or soda.

Eggplant Soup

(four servings)

There's no middle ground on the issue of eggplants: either you're an eggplant lover or an eggplant loather. This recipe will satisfy eggplant lovers, because it's thick, creamy, and all eggplant. Serve with Garlic Rolls (see page 479) and a tomato salad.

2 eggplants, about 1 pound each	Salt and pepper to taste
Olive oil	4 cups chicken broth (see page 377)

Preheat the oven to 375°F.

Remove the stems from the eggplants and cut them into ½-inch lengthwise slices. Brush both sides of the slices with olive oil, salt and pepper them, and place on baking sheets in a single layer. Bake for 20 to 25 minutes, until lightly golden and completely tender when pierced with a fork. Using a spoon, remove the pulp from the skin.

Put the pulp and 2 cups of the broth into a food processor and process until smooth. (If you don't have a food processor, pass the pulp through a food mill.) Pour into a saucepan, stir in the remaining broth, and gently heat until hot. Taste for salt and pepper. Add more broth for a thinner soup.

Leek and Potato Soup

(four servings)

Whenever I see leek and potato soup on a restaurant menu or in a cookbook, I've come to expect a purée rich with heavy cream. *This* soup is neither puréed nor enriched, so it has more character and a homey texture. Bread, fruit, and Almond Diamond cookies (see page 540) complete the supper.

1½ tablespoons butter
3 leeks, washed thoroughly
   and thinly sliced
2 stalks celery, thinly sliced
1½ cups water

3 medium potatoes, peeled
   and diced
2¾ cups milk
Salt and pepper to taste

Melt the butter in a large heavy-bottomed pot. Put in the leeks and celery and cook over moderate heat for 10 minutes, stirring often to prevent sticking. Stir in 1 cup of the water, cover, and cook for 10 more minutes. Add the potatoes and the remaining ½ cup of water, stir, cover, and cook over low heat for 10 more minutes. Stir in the milk, cover, and cook 10 minutes, or until the potatoes are tender. Add salt and pepper to taste, and serve.

Onion Soup

(four servings)

For economy, this is the next best thing to stone soup. It takes just two pounds of onions to feed four people. But there is one thing you cannot skimp on when you're making onion soup, and that's the time it takes to caramelize the onions. You have to cook them slowly for about an hour until they've turned a rich golden brown. That's where all the flavor comes from.

2 tablespoons vegetable oil	4 slices completely dried
7 large onions, thinly sliced	French-style bread
Salt to taste	2 ounces Monterey Jack
6 cups water	cheese, grated ($2/3$ cup)

Put the oil in a large heavy-bottomed skillet. Add the onions, lightly salt, and cook patiently over medium-low heat for 1 hour, stirring every 5 to 10 minutes.

After 1 hour, when the onions have caramelized and turned a rich golden brown, add the water, cover, and simmer for 30 minutes. Put a slice of the bread in each bowl, sprinkle about 2 tablespoons of cheese over each bread slice, and ladle the onion soup over the bread. Serve hot.

Tomato and Bread Soup

(four servings)

How can anything as humble and insignificant as stale bread be transformed into something so absolutely good as this soup?

⅔ cup olive oil
4 cloves garlic, crushed
2 large onions, finely chopped
6 medium tomatoes, peeled, seeded, and chopped
4 cups chicken broth (see page 377)

½ loaf French bread, sliced and broken into pieces
3 ounces Parmesan cheese, freshly grated (1 cup)

Heat the oil in a large heavy-bottomed saucepan over medium heat. Stir in the garlic and onions and cook until soft, about 1 to 2 minutes. Add the tomatoes and simmer for 10 minutes—watch carefully and stir often. Pour in the broth, stir to blend, and bring to a boil. While the soup is boiling, add the bread pieces, and continue to cook over medium heat for 2 more minutes. Cover and let stand for 1 hour, then reheat and serve. (This may be served without reheating, but the flavors are stronger when the soup is allowed to stand.) Pass around a bowl of the grated Parmesan cheese at the table.

Chinese Hot and Sour Soup

(eight cups or four servings)

Here is a light and spicy recipe everyone will ask for after they've tasted it. Serve with warm flour tortillas spread with plum sauce (available in Chinese markets or in the international sections of supermarkets) and sprinkled with scallions, and have The Best Rice Pudding (see page 547) for dessert.

6 cups chicken broth (see page 377)
$\frac{1}{4}$ pound fresh mushrooms, wiped clean and sliced ($1\frac{1}{2}$ cups)
$\frac{1}{4}$ pound fresh raw spinach, washed ($1\frac{1}{2}$ cups)
3 tablespoons light soy sauce
3 tablespoons cider vinegar
$\frac{3}{4}$ teaspoon black pepper
$2\frac{1}{4}$ tablespoons sesame seed oil
$\frac{1}{2}$ teaspoon hot pepper oil or Tabasco sauce (taste the soup carefully before adding the full amount)

$\frac{3}{4}$ pound tofu (soybean cake, found in the produce section of most supermarkets), cut into small dice
3 tablespoons cornstarch, dissolved in 5 tablespoons water
1 egg, beaten
3 tablespoons finely chopped cilantro
2 scallions, finely chopped

Put the chicken broth, mushrooms, and spinach in a soup pot. Simmer for 4 minutes.

Mix the soy sauce, vinegar, pepper, sesame seed oil, and the hot pepper oil or Tabasco together in a small bowl. Stir until well blended and then add to the broth. Taste and correct the seasonings.

Add the tofu and the cornstarch, stirring constantly until the soup thickens. Pour the beaten egg into the simmering broth, and continue to stir until the egg forms ribbons. Add the cilantro and scallions and serve at once.

Fish Chowder

(four servings)

I have tasted New England chowders and Manhattan chowders, and New England chowder wins my vote. A whole small new potato in the middle of the bowl is a friendly touch.

4 new potatoes, peeled and
   left whole (potatoes must be
   hot when served)
1½ pounds firm-fleshed
   white fish fillets
¼ cup diced salt pork
1 onion, chopped
3 medium potatoes, peeled
   and thinly sliced (about
   ⅛ inch thick)

4 cups milk
Salt and pepper to taste
1 tablespoon fresh thyme
   plus 1 tablespoon dried
   thyme; or 1½ tablespoons
   dried thyme
½ cup chopped parsley

Put the 4 new potatoes in a medium-size pot and boil in salted water for about 20 minutes, then cover to keep warm and set aside. While the potatoes are cooking, cut the fish into chunks, put it in another pot with 2 cups water, and simmer for 3 or 4 minutes over medium heat. Remove from the heat and set aside.

In a large soup pot cook the salt pork until it is golden brown; with a slotted spoon scoop up the browned pork, drain on paper towels, and set aside; discard all but 2 tablespoons of the pork fat left in the pot. Add the onion and cook until softened, about 2 to 3 minutes. Drain the fish cooking liquid into the pot, reserving the fish; add the 3 sliced potatoes, and more water, if needed, to cover. Boil until the potatoes are cooked, about 10 minutes. Add the fish, milk, salt and pepper, and the thyme. Just heat thoroughly, don't boil.

Put one of the whole, cooked potatoes in the center of each soup bowl, ladle in the soup, and sprinkle around a few of the fried pork bits. Scatter the parsley over all, and serve.

Cioppino

(six servings)

There are about as many versions of cioppino, the Italian fish stew, as there are cooks who make it. You can be creative here and use whatever fish or shellfish you like. There are no rigid rules, but have a good loaf of Italian sourdough bread with this.

¼ cup olive oil	1 teaspoon dried oregano
3 cloves garlic, minced	1 teaspoon sugar
2 pounds fresh white fish fillets, cut into large chunks	2 bay leaves
	Salt and pepper to taste
1 cup dry white wine	1 cup chopped parsley
About 8 Italian plum tomatoes (1 pound), finely chopped	

Heat the oil in a large sauté pan over medium heat. Add the garlic and cook about 1 minute, until just softened, but not brown. Add ½ cup of the fish, then the wine, tomatoes, oregano, sugar, bay leaves, and salt and pepper. Bring to a simmer, cover, and cook for 5 minutes. Add the remaining fish and cook, covered, for about 5 minutes more. Sprinkle with the parsley and serve.

Cream of Scallop Soup

(four servings)

What's best about this soup is the flavors of fresh dill and briny scallops. Serve with Lemon Crackers (see page 476) and a big bowl of chopped seeded cucumbers mixed with scallions.

5 tablespoons butter	2 pounds scallops, cut into
2 tablespoons finely chopped	$\frac{1}{4}$-inch pieces (4 cups)
onion	1$\frac{1}{2}$ tablespoons chopped
5 tablespoons flour	fresh dill; or 1 teaspoon
4 cups milk	dried dill
$\frac{1}{2}$ bay leaf	Salt and pepper to taste

Melt the butter in a soup pot over medium heat. Add the onion and cook for about 5 minutes, until it is soft and translucent. Stir in the flour and cook over low heat for 2 minutes. Stir in the milk, bay leaf, and 1 cup of the scallops, and simmer for 5 minutes.

Remove the bay leaf. Add the remaining scallops, 1 tablespoon of the fresh dill or all of the dried, and salt and pepper. Heat for 1 minute and serve. Sprinkle the rest of the fresh dill over the soup just before serving.

Oyster Stew

(four servings)

Everyone is crazy about oysters on the half shell these days, but hardly anyone remembers that oyster stew can be even better.

3 cups milk
2 cups heavy cream
$2\frac{1}{2}$ cups shucked fresh oysters
with their liquor

Salt and pepper to taste
3 tablespoons butter

Heat the milk and cream in a pan, but do not boil. Add the oysters and their liquor and simmer just until the edges of the oysters curl a little, about 1 minute. Season with salt and pepper, and add the butter. Heat until the butter melts, and serve very hot.

Chicken Custard in Broth

(four servings)

Young children will love this. They can break up the custard into pieces and let it float about in the broth to look like small boats and shore birds.

1 cup chopped cooked chicken
meat (approximately 1 whole
chicken breast)
$6\frac{1}{3}$ cups chicken broth (recipe
follows)

4 eggs
$1\frac{1}{2}$ ounces Parmesan cheese,
freshly grated ($\frac{1}{2}$ cup)
Salt and pepper to taste

Preheat the oven to 350°F.

Butter 4 ramekin dishes, each about ½ cup in size (I use Pyrex). Put the chicken, ⅓ cup of the chicken broth, eggs, Parmesan cheese, and salt and pepper in a food processor or blender and process until smooth. Pour the mixture into the prepared ramekins and place them in a shallow baking dish or pan filled with enough boiling water to come up the sides of the ramekins by 1 inch.

Place the water bath in the oven and bake for 12 to 15 minutes, checking the custard after 10 minutes; when it is just firm around the edges and trembly in the center it is done. Be careful not to overcook. Meanwhile, heat the rest of the chicken broth. Remove the custards from the oven and invert each dish in a soup bowl. Surround the custards with hot chicken broth and serve.

Rich Chicken Noodle Soup

(six servings)

This chicken soup is the real thing. You make your own rich broth, strain it, and then turn it into a supper dish with egg noodles and chicken pieces. Serve it with dinner rolls, and have strawberry ice cream for dessert.

Chicken Broth

2½ pounds chicken backs, wings, necks

9 cups cold water

1 onion, cut in half

2 carrots, cut in thirds

3 stalks celery, with leaves, cut in half

1 bay leaf

1 teaspoon dried thyme, crumbled

Salt and pepper to taste

4 ounces flat dried egg noodles

½ chicken breast, skinned, boned, and cut into tiny pieces

1½ tablespoons finely chopped parsley

Put the chicken backs, wings, necks, the water, onion, carrots, celery, bay leaf, and thyme in a soup pot and bring to a boil. Reduce to a simmer and cook for 1 hour. Remove from the heat and strain the broth through two layers of paper towel into a bowl or large measuring cup. You will have approximately 6½ cups.

Add enough water to the broth to make 8 cups. Return the liquid to the soup pot, turn the heat to medium, and add salt and pepper and the egg noodles. Cook, simmering, for 10 minutes. Add the chicken breast pieces and simmer 5 minutes more. Remove from the heat, add the parsley, and cool. Refrigerate until needed. Reheat and serve hot.

Fish and Shellfish

Fillet of Sole with Fresh Bread Crumbs

Halibut Baked on Vegetables

Sweet Walnuts and Prawns

Laguna Beach Shrimp Curry

Baltimore Crab Cakes

Salmon with Cucumber and Caper Sauce

Scandinavian Salmon Sandwich

Tarragon Fish on Toast

Fish Tacos

Oyster Buns

Scallops with Corn and Cilantro

During the early 1940s, the war years, I was in Laguna Beach, California, learning to cook. My husband was in the Marine Corps, stationed nearby, and we had rented a tiny house close to the ocean. During the five years we lived there, every friend we knew from our school days arrived to visit (and often to stay). I loved those years—cooking and eating with cheery, hungry friends.

Among my great memories of that time are grunion hunts, which were wildly suspenseful and always exciting. Grunions are small silvery fish about five inches long that belong to the smelt family. They spawn during the summer on the beach above high tide, by the light of the full moon. Grunion runs are accurately predicted by the Fish and Game Department, but no one knows on which stretch of beach they will choose to spawn; it could be Santa Monica or San Juan Capistrano.

On the appointed night we would congregate on the main beach in Laguna at about ten o'clock, along with lots of other grunion enthusiasts. Groups of us spread out along the beach, sitting around fires, while the full moon made a path across the water. We would watch and wait while we talked about the last grunion run.

The popular alcoholic beverages in those days were Southern Comfort and beer, and they were in ample supply at all grunion runs. If we were lucky, and in the right spot, the magic moment would arrive around midnight and someone would yell, "Here they come!" The sight of those shining, silvery fish wiggling on the sand was most unbelievable. We would grab pails and head into the surf, facing the beach knee-deep in water, so we could catch the grunions as they were swept past us, back into the tides. They would be on the beach for only seconds, but for several hours wave after wave would bring in more.

Gazing down the beach when the grunions were running heavily, it looked as though bits of stars were strewn on the sand. We had to use our hands to catch the fish—it is illegal to use nets. It was almost dawn when we carried our buckets home. We would fix the grunions simply, frying them quickly in sizzling bacon fat, and serve them with scrambled eggs and buttered toast.

More than any other food you cook, fish has to be fresh. If it's not it loses all its better qualities. I've been spoiled by those early Laguna days of eating fish and shellfish as fresh as those grunions. When you shop for fish, be sure it has a clean, briny smell. I know I've annoyed supermarket clerks by returning fish fillets after I've opened the plastic wrap, but let's face it, if it smells fishy, it isn't fresh.

Fillet of Sole with Fresh Bread Crumbs

(four servings)

Pan-frying fish with bread crumbs is as good a way as any I know of fixing fish. Serve with the tiny creamy pasta called orzo (see Orzo with Fresh Dill, (page 516). The orzo will be even better with fish if it has some grated lemon zest added to it.

1½ pounds fillets of sole, or other white fish	3 tablespoons butter
½ cup flour	⅓ cup dried coarse bread crumbs
Salt and pepper to taste	2 lemons, quartered
2 tablespoons olive oil	

If the fish fillets are very thin, make one fat fillet from two fillets by stacking one on top of the other. This keeps the moisture in and prevents overcooking. Lightly dust the layered fish fillets with flour. Salt and pepper the fish to taste.

In a large frying pan, heat the olive oil and 1 tablespoon of the butter over medium-high heat. Add the floured fish and cook quickly, turning the fillets over after about 2 minutes. Continue cooking until the fish flakes easily and looks opaque at its thickest point. While the fish is cooking, melt the remaining 2 tablespoons butter in a small skillet and toss the bread crumbs in the butter until golden. Serve the fish on a platter or on individual plates, topped with the buttered bread crumbs and surrounded by the lemon quarters.

Halibut Baked on Vegetables

(three or four servings)

A good, straightforward way to cook halibut with a few winter vegetables. Serve with Buttermilk Cornbread (see page 485).

2½ tablespoons butter, melted	1 pound fillet of halibut or
About ¼ head cabbage, finely	other white fish (about
chopped (3 cups)	4 fillets)
3 stalks celery, chopped	Salt and pepper to taste
2 carrots, grated	1½ tablespoons lemon juice

Preheat the oven to 450°F.

Pour the melted butter into a 9-inch square baking dish. Layer the cabbage, celery, and carrots in the baking dish. Put the fish fillets on top of the vegetables in a single layer. Sprinkle with salt and pepper to taste and drizzle with the lemon juice. Cover the dish and bake for about 15 to 20 minutes (the time will vary depending upon the thickness of the fish fillets). The fish is done when the fillets have turned opaque at their thickest part. Serve directly from the dish.

Sweet Walnuts and Prawns

(four servings)

I love this dish. The slightly sweet walnuts and the peppy horseradish seem meant for each other. Serve Maple Persimmons (see page 560) for dessert.

Steamed Rice

2⅔ cups water	1⅓ cups long-grain white
1 teaspoon salt	rice (makes 4 cups cooked)
1 cup water	3 tablespoons cream-style
1 cup sugar	horseradish
1½ cups walnuts, in large	1 pound shrimp (about 20
pieces	large shrimp), cooked,
¾ cup mayonnaise	shelled, and deveined (see
2 tablespoons light corn syrup	page 349)

Using a deep heavy-bottomed pot, bring the 2⅔ cups water and salt to a boil. Add the rice slowly so the boiling doesn't stop. Cover and simmer for 20 minutes without stirring or removing the cover. Then check: the rice should be just soft and the water absorbed.

While the rice is simmering, preheat the oven to 350°F. Put the 1 cup water and sugar in a heavy-bottomed saucepan and bring to a boil. Add the walnuts and simmer for about 4 minutes. Drain and spread the walnuts in a single layer on a baking sheet. Put in the oven and roast for about 5 or 6 minutes. Watch carefully so the walnuts don't brown—you just want to dry them out. Remove from the oven and set aside.

Mix the mayonnaise, corn syrup, and horseradish together in a large bowl, stir until smooth and well blended, and set aside. Bring a pot of water to a boil, drop the shrimp in, and let simmer for about 30 seconds, just long enough to heat the shrimp through. Drain the shrimp and quickly stir them into the horseradish sauce, coating them on all sides. Fluff up the rice with a fork. Serve the shrimp with the sweet walnuts on top and the rice on the side. This dish is good served warm or at room temperature.

FLAVOR

The hardest thing to learn in cooking is how to give a dish the right tone of flavor. Flavoring a dish requires critical tasting and your full attention.

Even though recipes give specified amounts of herbs, spices, or aromatics, you can't depend on these ingredients being uniformly fresh. The flavors of ingredients kept in jars can vary from lots of "oomph" to almost no taste at all. One essential rule: Always taste each ingredient before adding it to your preparation, so you know how strong or weak it is, and if it still retains its good quality.

I use garlic, citrus, and ginger quite often to flavor food. If you chop these ingredients with salt or sugar the flavors are magically diffused throughout the dish. The salt and sugar crystals act like little missionaries, spreading the flavors.

To infuse garlic flavor: Put as many peeled garlic cloves as needed on a chopping board. Sprinkle coarse salt or regular table salt over the cloves (proportion the amount of salt used to the size of the recipe you're making). Chop the garlic cloves finely, or run them through a mini-processor until the garlic juice blends with the salt crystals. Add this mixture to your recipe and proceed. (The small jars of garlic salt, onion salt, and celery salt that you see in the markets are made using this general principle.)

Generally I use citrus zest and ginger in sweet dishes, so I mix these flavors with sugar. I put a portion of sugar and the ginger or citrus in the food processor or chop by hand. The flavors will be captured in the sugar crystals and then melted into the dish.

Laguna Beach Shrimp Curry

(six servings)

When I started making Laguna Beach Shrimp Curry, back in the 1940s, I first used Campbell's Cream of Tomato soup for the sauce. Later, a neighbor taught me how to make coconut-milk sauce, which seems more mellow with the shrimp. And it is nice to have the toasted coconut for a condiment. In those days around beach towns, shrimp was considered an economy food; they were as cheap as squid is today.

1 cup water	1½ tablespoons curry powder
1 cup milk	½ teaspoon salt, or to taste
1 cup grated unsweetened	2 teaspoons lemon juice
coconut	2 pounds shrimp, cooked,
5 tablespoons butter	shelled, and deveined
1 medium onion, chopped	(see page 349)
¼ cup flour	6 cups steamed long-grain
2 cups chicken broth	white rice (see page 385)
(see page 377), warmed	

Heat the water and milk in a saucepan until it begins to bubble. Add the coconut, stirring to mix, cover the pan, and remove from the heat. Let the mixture stand for 1 hour.

After an hour, drain and squeeze excess milk from the coconut, reserving both the coconut and the milk mixture. Toast the coconut by spreading it on a cookie sheet and broiling for about 5 minutes. Watch constantly so the coconut doesn't burn.

Melt the butter in a 10-inch frying pan, add the onion, and cook over medium heat until the onion is tender, about 5 minutes. Add the flour and stir until smooth. Slowly add the chicken broth, curry powder, and salt, and cook over medium-low heat until thick, stirring constantly. Slowly add about ⅓ cup of the coconut-milk mixture and the lemon juice. Add more of the milk if a thinner sauce is desired. Add the shrimp, heat through, and serve over the rice. Top with the toasted coconut.

Baltimore Crab Cakes

(makes eight 3-inch-wide ¾-inch-thick crab cakes)

If you love crab cakes, American history, and miles of green grass horse country, head for Maryland. I did and I found the best crab cakes at Faidley's, a food stall in the Lexington Market in Baltimore, the oldest market in the United States. Incredible crab cakes—moist, creamy, and full of the taste of crab. A large sign on the wall says that Faidley's makes them with backfin crab, mayonnaise, Dijon mustard, and saltine crackers. I experimented with these four ingredients until I came up with this example of Faidley's winning crab cakes. Serve the cakes with Coleslaw (see page 517), bread and butter, and ice-cold beer.

1 cup mayonnaise
1 tablespoon plus 1 teaspoon
  Dijon mustard
2 cups saltine cracker crumbs
About ⅔ pound crab meat (2 cups)

2 tablespoons vegetable oil
Lemon wedges
Tabasco sauce

Put the mayonnaise and Dijon mustard in a mixing bowl and stir until well blended. Add 1 cup of the cracker crumbs and all the crab meat and mix well.

Put a large piece of waxed paper on the counter and spread the remaining 1 cup of cracker crumbs on top. Divide the crab mixture into 8 equal portions and pat each into a ball. Gently flatten each ball into a round cake about 3 inches in diameter. Lightly coat the top and bottom of each cake with cracker crumbs.

Heat a large skillet over medium heat and film the bottom with the oil. Place the cakes in the skillet and fry over medium heat for a minute or so on each side, until just golden. Serve hot with lemon wedges and Tabasco sauce on the side.

Salmon with Cucumber and Caper Sauce

(three or four servings)

Cucumber and capers give salmon a crisp texture and sharp acid taste that bring out the best in this rich fish. Salmon is more full-bodied than most fish and calls for a peppy accent. Cook an extra pound of salmon and use what is left over to make Salmon Salad Niçoise (see page 346).

About 2 pounds of salmon
   steaks (allowing 1 pound of
   leftover salmon for Salmon
   Salad Niçoise)

Cucumber and Caper Sauce

1 cucumber, peeled and seeded	1 tablespoon capers, drained
3 tablespoons butter	2 tablespoons finely chopped
Salt to taste	parsley
3 tablespoons water	

Rinse the salmon under cold running water. Lay the salmon on a rack that fits in a pot with a lid. Cover the salmon with salted water. Put on the lid and simmer for about 10 minutes, or until the meat loses its deep pink color.

While the salmon is cooking, make the sauce.* Dice the cucumber into small pieces. Melt the butter over low heat, add the cucumber, and salt lightly. Cook for about 2 minutes, stirring constantly. Add the water and the capers and stir to blend. Taste and add more salt if needed. Stir in the parsley and cook, stirring for a second or two. Remove the salmon from the pot and serve with the sauce.

*Or you can make the sauce earlier in the day and refrigerate it. Heat before serving with the salmon.

Scandinavian Salmon Sandwich

(two open-face sandwiches)

For a Scandinavian-style supper, serve this open-face sandwich on a board with a cold glass of beer and Chilled Marmalade Grapefruit (see page 559) for dessert.

2 tablespoons whipped cream cheese	Salt and pepper to taste
2 tablespoons mayonnaise	A few drops of lemon juice
A little milk to thin cream cheese	$\frac{1}{2}$ cup cooked flaked salmon (see preceding recipe)
1 teaspoon chopped fresh dill, plus a few sprigs for garnish	2 slices light rye bread

Put the cream cheese and mayonnaise in a bowl and beat until smooth. Add a little milk if the mixture is too thick and stiff to spread easily. Add the dill, salt and pepper, and lemon juice, and stir until mixed well. Add the salmon and mix well.

Spread the salmon mixture over each slice of rye bread, and garnish with fresh dill.

Tarragon Fish on Toast

(four servings)

This is a snap to make and therefore a good recipe for busy people. Serve with a bowl of chopped seeded cucumber and red onion with vinaigrette.

1 tablespoon salt	4 thick slices white bread
½ cup milk	Soft butter
1½ to 2 pounds white fish fillets, about ½ to ¾ inch thick, cut into serving pieces	1 teaspoon chopped fresh tarragon; or ½ teaspoon dried tarragon
1 cup dry bread crumbs	
3 to 4 tablespoons butter, melted	

Preheat the oven to 500°F.

Butter or grease a baking pan that is large enough to hold the fish in a single layer. Stir the salt into the milk until the salt has dissolved. Dip the fish fillets into the milk, then coat both sides of each fillet with the bread crumbs. Place in the prepared baking pan in a single layer and pour the melted butter over the fish. Bake about 10 to 12 minutes, or until the fish is opaque and flakes easily with a fork.

Meanwhile, prepare the toast: spread the slices of bread with soft butter, sprinkle the tarragon on top, and put in the oven on a baking sheet 5 minutes before the fish is done. When the fish and toast are ready, remove the fillets from the baking pan with a spatula and arrange equal amounts on top of the toast. Pour any pan juices over and serve.

Fish Tacos

(eight tacos, or four servings)

When Americans think of tacos, they almost never think of fish; but corn tortillas with fish, seasoned with cumin, lime juice, and cilantro, are typical Mexican tacos. Just about any kind of fish or shellfish is good this way.

⅔ cup sliced scallions
6 medium tomatoes, diced
1 cup loosely packed chopped
   cilantro
Salt to taste
½ teaspoon ground cumin
1 pound white fish fillets
   (sole, halibut, snapper, cod,
   and so on)

2 tablespoons lime or lemon
   juice
4 tablespoons corn oil
8 tortillas (corn, flour, or
   whole wheat)

Toss the scallions, tomatoes, and cilantro in a bowl and add salt to taste. Set aside.

Sprinkle salt and the cumin evenly over one side of the fish fillets, and drizzle the lime juice over the fillets. Heat a large skillet over medium heat, film the bottom with 2 tablespoons of the corn oil, add the fish, and cook until the fish is done, only a minute or two, depending on the thickness of the fillets.

In another large skillet, heat the remaining 2 tablespoons of corn oil and quickly fry the tortillas, one at a time, over medium-high heat for a few seconds on each side. Drain on paper towels. Place a piece of fish on each tortilla, top with some of the tomato mixture, and serve at once.

Oyster Buns

(two to four servings)

Be prepared to make twice as many of these as you think people might eat. They'll ask for more.

4 round buns, about 3½ inches in diameter, cut in half (see Hamburger Buns, page 474)	⅓ cup cornmeal
	⅓ cup flour
	Pinch of cayenne pepper
⅓ cup Tartar Sauce (see page 492)	12 fresh oysters, shucked
	4 tablespoons (½ stick) butter
1 cup shredded iceberg lettuce	4 lemon wedges

Scoop out a small chunk of bread from the center of each bun half to allow room for the oysters. Spread each half evenly with Tartar Sauce and put some of the shredded lettuce on the bottom half of each bun.

In a dish or pie tin, mix together the cornmeal, flour, and cayenne. Pat the oysters dry, and roll each one in the breading mixture, coating it evenly. Put the butter in a frying pan over high heat. Quickly fry the oysters in the hot butter until golden on each side—this will take no more than 15 seconds on each side. Put the oysters on paper towels and pat to remove oil. Place 3 oysters on the lettuce and put the other half of the bun on top. Do not slice. Serve immediately.

Scallops with Corn and Cilantro

(four servings)

This is an unusual combination that captures some of the mysterious Mexican flavors that most of us love. The corn, cilantro, and scallops complement one another, and the masa harina contributes an earthy taste. Serve with warm tortillas and cold beer.

4 tablespoons ($\frac{1}{2}$ stick) butter	Salt to taste
$2\frac{1}{2}$ cups corn kernels (if fresh is available, you will need 3 or 4 large ears)	1 teaspoon (or more) hot pepper sauce
1 pound bay scallops	1 tablespoon lime juice
$1\frac{1}{2}$ cups milk	1 cup whole cilantro leaves
4 tablespoons masa harina (see Note, page 367)	(if not available, substitute $\frac{1}{3}$ cup finely chopped scallions)

Melt the butter in a sauté pan. Stir in the corn and scallops and cook for about 3 minutes, continuing to stir constantly. Remove from the heat and set aside.

Put the milk in a small bowl and add the masa harina. Stir briskly until the mixture is smooth. Put the sauté pan with the scallops over low heat and pour the milk mixture in, stirring constantly until the sauce thickens. Taste and add salt as necessary and the hot pepper sauce. Remove from the heat and just before serving stir in the lime juice, then sprinkle the cilantro leaves over the top. Serve with warm tortillas.

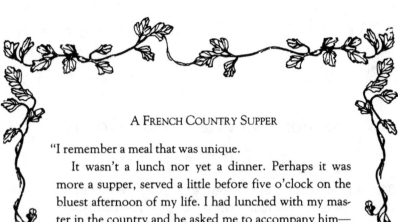

A French Country Supper

"I remember a meal that was unique.

It wasn't a lunch nor yet a dinner. Perhaps it was more a supper, served a little before five o'clock on the bluest afternoon of my life. I had lunched with my master in the country and he asked me to accompany him—for I practically never left him—to visit two old friends of his family, who lived in a little house in a big garden. An ancient servant opened the door and showed us into the drawing-room. Holland covers were on the furniture, an Empire clock had stopped on the mantelpiece, and through a high open door, I saw long shelves full of drying plums and apples.

The masters of this old abode came in arm-in-arm. They were a sweet old couple.

He was dressed in a frock-coat and grey trousers, she in a silk dress of the colour of dead leaves and of an antiquated cut. Only a big straw hat trimmed with a bunch of Mahon violets was lacking to make it a model of the fashion of 1830.

They faced us, rosy and fresh as the apples they preserved in the next room; they welcomed us, and immediately invited us to supper, for so they called the meal of which they partook at about half-past four in the afternoon.

What a pleasant little dolls' dinner party!"

—from *Clarisse, or The Old Cook*

Chicken

Chicken Under a Brick

Roast Chicken with Smothered Potatoes

Chicken with Fresh Herbs and Potatoes

Chicken Sauté with Vinegar

Chicken Provençale

Mahogany Chicken Legs with Fresh Ginger

Smothered Chicken with Mushrooms

Hen Braised with Onions

Sara Tyson Rorer's Spanish Rice with Chicken

Lone Star Chicken

Chicken Succotash

Minced Chicken in Lettuce Leaves

Chicken Mock Hollandaise

I remember when I was first married I decided to buy a whole chicken and roast it. I dimly remembered that you were supposed to wash poultry, so I got a big bowl of sudsy water and gave the chicken a bath. I scrubbed the bird, rinsed, and dried it, and after it was roasted, I thought it was outstandingly good. However, when I told my neighbor that I had given my chicken a bath with Tide soap, she was appalled. It is not necessary to bathe your chicken, especially now that chickens are bathed for you on the production line.

Chicken used to be a very special and a rather expensive dish reserved for Sunday dinner. Today chickens are cheap and found everywhere, and of all the meats, chicken is probably the most popular.

Every now and then, someone starting a household who doesn't know much about cooking will ask me what she ought to cook for supper. I almost always reply, "Get a chicken and roast it." And if the cook is a real beginner, I add, "Be sure to take out the bag of giblets from the cavity." When I roast a chicken, I just rub it all over with oil, salt, and pepper, put it in a 400°F. oven, and then let it roast undisturbed, in a baking dish or a pan, for about forty-five to fifty-five minutes.

This chapter includes some exceptional chicken recipes in which chicken gets cut up and sautéed, smothered and braised, and flattened and fried. For example, there are two quick chicken sautés that are miles apart in flavor: Chicken Sauté with Vinegar (see page 405) is a smooth-tasting classic of subtlety (tarragon, tomato, wine vinegar . . .); Mahogany Chicken Legs with Fresh Ginger (see page 407) is a more bold-tasting dish (soy sauce and lots of fresh ginger). Here, too, is a rustic Italian way of frying chicken (Chicken Under a Brick) that results in a very crisp, juicy bird. Unlike chickens, any recipe in this chapter will fly.

Chicken Under a Brick

(four servings)

Weighting down a chicken while it fries is a wonderful Italian method that gives dramatic results. Your chicken will be very crisp on the outside and very juicy on the inside, and will taste of garlic, thyme, and olive oil. Serve with Garlic Rolls (see page 479), tomatoes, and Brown Sugar Custard (see page 557).

One 2½-pound frying chicken
3 tablespoons olive oil
3 cloves garlic, chopped
1 teaspoon dried thyme, crumbled

Optional: red pepper flakes
3 tablespoons peanut oil

Split the chicken down the back and remove the backbone. Flip the chicken over and remove its rib cage with a small sharp knife. Flatten the chicken with the heels of your hands. Mix together the olive oil, garlic, thyme, and optional red pepper flakes, and rub the mixture all over the chicken with your hands.

Heat the peanut oil in a 10- to 12-inch skillet over medium-high heat. Put the chicken in the skillet, skin side down. Rub any leftover olive oil mixture on the exposed side. Cover the chicken with foil, tucking the foil down around the chicken. Weight down with another, slightly smaller heavy skillet that has additional weights in it, such as bricks, a heavy rock, or another heavy pan. Press down firmly. Cook for 15 minutes, checking to make sure the chicken isn't browning too fast, lower the heat to medium, and cook 10 minutes more. Turn the chicken over, cover and weight down again, and cook for a final 10 minutes.

Roast Chicken with Smothered Potatoes

(four servings)

The reason the potatoes are called smothered here is because they are roasted under the flattened chicken, where they absorb all its juices. Try this with Tiny Herb Salads (see page 520) made with parsley and marjoram.

3 tablespoons olive oil
One 3-pound frying
　chicken
Salt and pepper to taste
3 medium red onions, cut
　into quarters
8 new potatoes, cut in half

1 tablespoon chopped fresh
　rosemary; or 2 teaspoons
　dried rosemary; plus fresh
　rosemary branches for
　garnish
2 large cloves garlic, finely
　chopped

Preheat the oven to 425°F.

Film a 9 × 13-inch baking dish with 1 tablespoon of the olive oil.

Using a sharp knife or poultry shears, split the chicken down the back along the edge of the backbone. Then cut along the other side of the backbone and remove it. Remove the pads of fat from around the breast and the cavity.

Salt and pepper the red onions and the potatoes. Put the potatoes in the middle of the baking dish and sprinkle the rosemary and garlic over them. Flatten the chicken out over the potatoes, and surround with the onions. Drizzle and spread the remaining 2 tablespoons of olive oil over the chicken and then salt and pepper generously.

Put the chicken in the oven and roast for 45 to 50 minutes, or until the skin of the chicken is nicely browned. Pour off all the liquid and garnish with fresh rosemary branches. Serve hot or cold.

ROUSSEAU'S PARADOX

Jean-Jacques Rousseau observed that civilized man has become more and more separated from the world of home and family, orchards and farms, and all our deep, human links with life. He believed that sophistication, modernization, and urban life tend to corrupt the ideal integrity of the rural, simple, and traditional. "In every city dweller there is a displaced yearning for the rustic farm and land, the taste of the homegrown, all the natural foods. The paradox is that we do want authentic country flavors and integrity, but we do not seek the discomforts of the simple life, so we rediscover regionalism vicariously amid modern convenience and luxury." It is somehow both alarming and consoling to know that Rousseau wrote these words over two hundred years ago.

I think the best cure for this separation is home cooking. Looking for and buying raw ingredients, handling and preparing them in your familiar kitchen, and then eating at your own kitchen table will daily restore a feeling of connection with the natural world.

Chicken with Fresh Herbs and Potatoes

(four servings)

This is a rustic Italian dish from Irma Goodrich Mazza. She became a fine cook and cookbook author after she fell in love with a handsome Italian who taught her to cook with onions, garlic, olive oil, and herbs. This was long ago, when the average young American woman used only a hint of seasoning in her cooking.

One 3-pound frying chicken, cut into serving pieces
3 large russet potatoes, peeled and cut into 2-inch cubes
Salt and pepper to taste
3 tablespoons olive oil
3 tablespoons finely chopped parsley (Italian flat-leaf, if tender)

$1\frac{1}{2}$ teaspoons finely chopped fresh rosemary
2 cloves garlic, finely chopped

NOTE: Don't chop the herbs and garlic in a food processor—chop them by hand so they don't get soggy and wet.

Spread the chicken pieces and potatoes out on a piece of waxed paper and lightly salt and pepper on all sides.

Heat the olive oil in a large sauté pan. Add the chicken and potatoes and cook over medium heat until golden brown on all sides, moving and turning the pieces frequently. This will take about 10 minutes. Cover and lower the heat and cook 10 minutes more, or until the chicken is done. Remove the chicken and potatoes from the heat and put in a large serving bowl. Sprinkle the fresh herbs and garlic over the chicken and potatoes and toss until evenly distributed. Serve hot.

Chicken Sauté with Vinegar

(three or four servings)

Ideally, suppers should be made from things already in your kitchen and in this recipe everything but the chicken is probably on your shelf. Try making it the first time with red wine vinegar and the next using a less acidic vinegar such as rice vinegar: the dish will be much softer in flavor. Serve with plain buttered noodles, nicely peppered.

One 2½-pound frying chicken, cut into 8 serving pieces
Salt and pepper to taste
4 tablespoons (½ stick) butter
½ cup red wine vinegar
¼ cup water
1 teaspoon minced garlic

1 tablespoon tomato paste
½ teaspoon crumbled dried tarragon, or 1 teaspoon finely chopped fresh tarragon
1 tablespoon minced parsley

Sprinkle the chicken with salt and pepper. Heat 2 tablespoons of the butter in a large skillet and put the chicken pieces in, skin side down. Brown on one side, turn over, and brown on the other. This takes about 8 minutes. Pour in half of the wine vinegar and all of the water, and cover. Turn the heat to low and cook about 10 to 15 minutes more. Check for doneness after 10 minutes—don't overcook. The chicken is done when the juices run clear when the flesh is pierced with a sharp knife.

Transfer the chicken to a platter and cover to keep warm. Add the garlic to the skillet and cook over medium heat for 1 minute. Add the remaining ¼ cup vinegar and boil quickly to reduce slightly, about 1 minute. Add the tomato paste, and the remaining

2 tablespoons of butter. Cook a few seconds, pour the sauce over the chicken, and sprinkle with the tarragon and parsley. Serve right away.

Chicken Provençale

(four servings)

A favorite recipe in James Beard's cooking classes during the 1970s was this rich, full-flavored blend of garlic, mayonnaise, and chicken, tempered and balanced with vinegar and lemon juice. (Don't worry—a whole head of garlic isn't too much; it mellows to just the right intensity during the slow simmering.) The dish is a meal in itself and needs only good peasant bread to round it out.

4 tablespoons olive oil
1 head of garlic, cloves separated and peeled
3 slices white bread, crusts removed
¼ cup red wine vinegar
Salt and pepper to taste
½ cup whole almonds
1 bay leaf, stem and vein removed, crumbled

3 whole chicken breasts, cut in half (making 6 halves)
1 cup chicken broth (see page 377)
½ cup mayonnaise
3 tablespoons fresh lemon juice

Heat 2 tablespoons of the olive oil in a large skillet over medium-high heat. Add the garlic and stir for about 1 minute, then remove and reserve. Soak the bread in the vinegar and season with salt and pepper. Lightly brown the bread on both sides in the skillet for 2 to 3 minutes, then remove and reserve. In a blender or food processor, put the garlic, bread, almonds, and crumbled bay leaf and process until you have a paste.

To the same large skillet add the remaining 2 tablespoons of olive oil and brown the chicken pieces on both sides; this takes about 8 minutes. Mix the garlic paste with the chicken broth, add it to the pan with the chicken breast side up, cover, and simmer about 20 minutes, or until the chicken is done.

Remove the chicken to a serving dish and cover to keep warm, leaving the sauce in the pan. Skim off and remove any excess fat with a spoon. Mix the mayonnaise and lemon juice together and gradually add to the pan, stirring it into the sauce. Pour the finished sauce over the chicken and serve.

Mahogany Chicken Legs with Fresh Ginger

(four servings)

Now you don't have to go to your favorite Chinese restaurant to enjoy the distinctive Asian tastes of this hard-to-flub recipe. I like this sauce best with dark meat, but you may use breasts or a whole cut-up chicken.

4 tablespoons peanut oil
8 chicken thighs and legs
$\frac{1}{3}$ cup peeled and sliced ($\frac{1}{4}$ inch thick) fresh ginger
$\frac{1}{3}$ cup soy sauce
$\frac{1}{3}$ cup sherry

$\frac{1}{3}$ cup sugar
$\frac{1}{2}$ cup sliced scallions
$\frac{1}{2}$ cup whole cilantro leaves
4 cups steamed long-grain white rice (see page 385)

Put the peanut oil in a deep skillet over medium-high heat. When the oil is hot, add the chicken pieces, skin side down, and the ginger slices. Brown the chicken for 10 minutes, then turn over and brown for 5 more minutes. (It is important to use a deep skillet because the chicken tends to spatter while browning.) Reduce the heat if necessary to keep the chicken and ginger from burning. If the ginger slices brown too quickly, remove them to a paper towel and put them back in the skillet when you add the soy mixture.

Mix together the soy sauce, sherry, and sugar. Pour the soy mixture over the chicken, cover, and cook for about 2 minutes. Transfer to a serving dish and garnish with the scallions and cilantro leaves. Serve immediately with the rice.

Smothered Chicken with Mushrooms

(four servings)

The old-fashioned version of this recipe added heavy cream at the end, but the dish doesn't need the extra calories: all the flavors are captured in the simple white sauce that binds together the delicate chicken flavor and the earthy mushrooms.

One 3-pound frying chicken, cut into serving pieces	4 tablespoons flour
Salt and pepper to taste	2 cups chicken broth (see page 377)
4 tablespoons olive or vegetable oil	1 pound fresh mushrooms, wiped clean and sliced
2 medium onions, chopped	¼ cup chopped parsley

Preheat the oven to 400°F.

Season the chicken pieces with salt and pepper. In a large heavy-bottomed skillet, heat the oil over high heat and brown the chicken pieces for 6 to 8 minutes, turning when necessary. Adjust the heat so that the chicken browns quickly, but does not burn. Transfer the chicken to a shallow casserole large enough to hold it in one layer.

Put the onions in the skillet and cook, stirring frequently, for about 5 minutes, or until they are soft and light colored. Stir in the flour and mix it well with a spoon. Pour in the chicken broth and, stirring constantly, let it come to a boil. Reduce the heat and let it simmer for 2 to 3 minutes. Pour the sauce over the chicken in the casserole, cover tightly, and bake in the oven for about 20 minutes.

Scatter the mushrooms over the chicken, re-cover, and bake for another 10 minutes, or until the chicken is tender. Sprinkle the parsley over the top and serve.

Hen Braised with Onions

(four servings)

Because this recipe is so easy, a child who is old enough to use a knife can enjoy making it. If there's any left over the next day, add some chicken broth and make the remains into a soup.

6 large yellow onions, sliced about ⅛ inch thick
1½ tablespoons ground ginger
2 teaspoons salt
1½ teaspoons pepper
3 pounds chicken pieces: legs, thighs, breasts

1 cup water
Optional: 8 small red potatoes, unpeeled and cut in half
Chopped parsley, for garnish

Put half the onion slices in the bottom of a Dutch oven, or in any heavy-bottomed pot with a lid. Mix together the ginger and salt and pepper, and spread out over a piece of waxed paper. Roll each piece of chicken in the seasoning mixture so that all sides are covered. Place the chicken pieces over the layer of onion slices and cover the chicken with the remaining onion slices.

Pour the water over all, and cover the pot with its lid. Braise over medium-low heat for 2 hours. If you're using potatoes, put them on top of the onions the last 30 minutes of cooking. Serve in bowls and sprinkle the top of each serving with chopped parsley.

Sara Tyson Rorer's Spanish Rice with Chicken

(four servings)

I adapted this recipe for Spanish rice from the one in *Mrs. Rorer's New Cookbook*, published in 1902. Sara Tyson was highly respected for her tasty dishes, and when I tasted her Spanish rice recipe, she didn't disappoint me. As she wrote at the end of the recipe, "If this dish is properly cooked and highly seasoned, this is a very delicious dish." True.

2½ cups water	1 teaspoon red pepper flakes
1½ cups tomatoes, broken up, with juice	2 large onions, chopped
	Salt and pepper to taste
3½ pounds chicken pieces: thighs, legs, breasts	1 cup chopped parsley
	1 cup long-grain white rice

Put the water, tomatoes with juice, chicken pieces, red pepper, onions, and salt and pepper in a heavy-bottomed pot with a lid. Bring to a boil and immediately reduce the heat to a simmer. Let simmer for 20 minutes, and turn the chicken pieces over. Add more tomato juice or water if too much liquid is evaporating and the chicken is drying out.

Add the parsley and rice, being sure there is a full 2 cups of liquid, and stir until mixed well with the other ingredients. Cover and simmer about 15 more minutes, checking once or twice to make sure the liquid hasn't all been absorbed by the rice: add more boiling water if it has. Taste and correct salt and pepper, and serve hot.

Lone Star Chicken

(four servings)

Don't be fooled by this ordinary-looking recipe: it's an outstanding dish, big and special, like the Lone Star State. Serve hot or cold. The recipe yields extra sauce (freeze it if not used within three days) that you can use later on other dishes, such as pasta.

$18\frac{3}{4}$-ounce can solid-pack tomatoes	$1\frac{1}{2}$ teaspoons dried oregano, crumbled
1 large onion, chopped	2 tablespoons wine vinegar
4 cloves garlic, minced	Salt and pepper to taste
2 bay leaves	One $2\frac{1}{2}$- to 3-pound chicken,
2 teaspoons ground cumin	cut into 8 pieces

Put the tomatoes and juice in a large casserole and break the tomatoes into bits. Add the onion, garlic, bay leaves, cumin, oregano, and vinegar, and stir to blend. Add salt and pepper. Simmer the sauce on top of the stove, stirring occasionally, for 30 minutes.

Preheat the oven to 350°F.

Add the chicken parts, pushing them down into the sauce. Cover the casserole and bake for about 1 hour.

Chicken Succotash

(six servings)

This old Southern recipe comes from Virginia, where it was first made over a hundred years ago. What is left of the old recipe is the corn and lima beans (the original meat used was squirrel). Serve with warm Buttermilk Cornbread (see page 485) and honey; have Wine Jelly (see page 555) for dessert; and you'll have a Southern-style supper.

4 to 5 pounds chicken pieces	3 potatoes, peeled and diced
2 teaspoons salt	1 cup corn kernels (fresh,
2 medium fresh tomatoes,	frozen, or canned and
chopped; or 1 cup canned	drained)
tomatoes	1 teaspoon sugar
2 onions, thinly sliced	$\frac{1}{8}$ to $\frac{1}{4}$ teaspoon cayenne
1 cup frozen green lima beans	pepper

Put the chicken pieces in a large pot with the salt and water to cover. Bring to a boil and simmer for 40 minutes.

Preheat the oven to 350°F. Remove the chicken from the pot, reserving the broth. Take the meat from the bones, and set aside. Put the tomatoes, onions, lima beans, potatoes, corn, sugar, and cayenne pepper in a large casserole. Add the reserved broth, cover, and bake for 30 minutes.

Stir the chicken meat into the casserole and bake for another 10 to 15 minutes, uncovered. Taste and add more salt and cayenne pepper, if necessary. Serve hot.

Minced Chicken in Lettuce Leaves

(four servings)

Minced squab is a recipe from Mandarin China that is equally good made with chicken. Because iceberg lettuce is sturdy it makes the perfect wrapping for the warm filling. Serve with a big cup of Chinese Hot and Sour Soup (see page 372).

3 tablespoons vegetable oil
About 1 pound chicken
   breast, finely chopped
   (1⅓ cups)
1 small green bell pepper,
   seeded and finely chopped
1 teaspoon sugar
1 teaspoon salt

Pepper to taste
2½ tablespoons peeled and
   finely chopped fresh ginger
1½ tablespoons soy sauce
3 tablespoons water
1 tablespoon lemon juice
½ cup finely chopped walnuts

Sauce
½ cup rice vinegar
½ tablespoon soy sauce

1 teaspoon sesame seed oil
Hot sauce to taste

8 whole iceberg lettuce leaves,
   trimmed and chilled

To prepare the filling, heat the oil in a medium skillet, and add the chicken, bell pepper, sugar, salt, and pepper. Stir constantly over medium-high heat until the bell pepper turns a deeper green, about 2 to 3 minutes. Add the ginger, soy sauce, water, lemon juice, and walnuts, mix well, and cook a few seconds more. Remove the filling from the heat and put into a bowl.

To prepare the sauce, stir together the vinegar, soy sauce, sesame seed oil, and hot sauce until well mixed.

To assemble, put 3 or 4 tablespoons of filling on a lettuce leaf, spoon a little sauce over, and roll up the leaf. Serve hot or cold.

Chicken Mock Hollandaise

(four servings)

Mock hollandaise is hollandaise sauce made with chicken broth instead of melted butter. Serve this dish with asparagus and Popovers (see page 345).

4 tablespoons ($\frac{1}{2}$ stick) butter
2 tablespoons minced onion
6 tablespoons cornstarch
3 cups chicken broth (page 377)
1 or 2 stalks celery, chopped ($\frac{3}{4}$ cup)

Grated rind from 1 lemon
$1\frac{1}{2}$ tablespoons lemon juice
3 cups diced cooked chicken
8 ounces dried egg noodles
2 egg yolks, lightly beaten
Salt
Pinch of cayenne pepper

Bring a large pot of water to the boil. Meanwhile, melt the butter in a medium-size heavy-bottomed saucepan and add the onion. Cook over medium heat, stirring, until soft. Stir in the cornstarch and cook over medium-low heat until smooth and blended. Slowly add the chicken broth, celery, lemon rind, lemon juice, and chicken. Cook, stirring, for 3 to 4 minutes. Remove from the heat, cover, and set aside.

Cook the noodles in the boiling water for about 8 minutes. While they are cooking, put the yolks into a small bowl and beat in $\frac{1}{4}$ cup of the hot sauce. Add the yolk-sauce mixture to the rest of the sauce in the saucepan. Cook for 1 minute more, and add salt and cayenne to taste. Drain the noodles and serve with the chicken and sauce on top.

Meat

Beef
Speed Steaks
Theater Steak
Beef Stroganoff
Tri-Tip Pot Roast
Stuffed Cabbage Rolls
The Perfect California Hamburger
Holey Moley Tamale Pie
American Meatloaf

Lamb
Ireland's Irish Stew
Shepherd's Pie
Applesauce Lamb Curry

Pork
Black Pepper Ribs
Pork Tenderloin with Jalapeño Sauce
Pork with Sage and Brown Rice

We Americans are just not the meat-and-potatoes people we once were. Chicken, fish, vegetables, grains, and beans have moved ahead in popularity, and meat no longer has the number-one status. Without consciously thinking about it, I find that I eat less meat too, and I don't know why. Maybe it's because meat doesn't taste as flavorful as it used to. Today's meat comes from pigs and cattle that are slimmer, trimmer critters than they used to be. They've been engineered to grow up faster and leaner, and they tasted better to me when they were a little less streamlined.

Still, my all-time favorite supper is a hamburger. It is a perfect composition of meat and condiments and, ideally, a little salad, packaged between two halves of a bun. I think of hamburgers as being the classic regional food of Southern California, where I grew up. (Actually, they originated around 1850 aboard a German-American ship, but they were vastly different then— tough, dried chunks of meat cooked with a little onion.) Please note the small tribute I've written to the hamburger along with the recipe for the all-time best hamburger (see page 425).

There are also those moments when nothing is better than steak and onions. I've found a trick that I use when it is time for a steak. I buy a T-bone steak at my supermarket and ask the butcher to cut it horizontally in half lengthwise (so it is half as thick). I freeze each half separately. When it's time to fry the steak I don't thaw it. I put it in a very hot skillet, salt and pepper generously, and fry on one side only for two to three minutes. (I add a sliced onion to the skillet for the last minute or two.) Frying it frozen keeps the inside meat pink and juicy. (See Speed Steaks; recipe follows.)

Some of the recipes in this chapter make use of cooked meat. So if you do a roast of lamb, for instance, on the weekend, plan to have some left to make Shepherd's Pie (see page 430) or Applesauce Lamb Curry (see page 431).

Speed Steaks

(four servings)

Now you can halve your steak and eat it, too. It can be difficult to cook a thin steak so that it is rare on the inside and seared on the outside. The secret is to fry it while it is still frozen.

2 tablespoons vegetable
  shortening
2 T-bone steaks (approximately
  1 pound each), each cut in half
  horizontally, lengthwise, so it is
  half as thick, all 4 halves wrapped
  and frozen separately (do not
  thaw the steaks)

Salt and pepper to taste
1 large onion, thinly sliced in
  rings

Heat a large skillet over high heat until very hot. Add the shortening and swirl it around to film the bottom of the skillet. Generously salt and pepper the steaks. Put them into the skillet and fry on one side only for 1 minute. Add the sliced onion and cook quickly for 1 to 2 minutes more. Turn the steaks over and count to 5. Remove the steaks; the centers should still be pink. Serve with the onion rings on top.

Theater Steak

(four servings)

A perfect small meal all in one dish. The texture of the bread is very important: it needs to be sturdy enough to hold up to the mushroom and steak juices.

5 tablespoons butter	Salt and pepper
2 large onions, cut into thin rings	4 thick slices white bread (homemade is perfect)
½ pound fresh mushrooms, wiped clean and sliced	2 bunches watercress, washed, dried, and stems removed
Two 8-ounce fillets of beef steak (about 1 to 1¼ inches thick), cut in half lengthwise	

Melt the butter in a large skillet. When hot, add the onions and mushrooms, and cook for about 2 minutes, stirring constantly, just until they are soft. Remove the vegetables to a warm plate. Turn the heat up to medium-high and fry the steak quickly. Salt and pepper each side, and fry until the desired doneness is achieved. (After cooking 2 minutes on each side, cut into the steak with the tip of a knife. If it looks rosy and you like your steak rare, remove from the pan, remembering that the steak will continue cooking. If you want your steak medium, cook another minute or two.)

Remove the steak from the skillet and keep warm with the vegetables. Quickly put the bread into the skillet and fry, turning it over once, so it sops up all the pan juices.

To assemble, put a slice of bread on each plate, and spoon over a quarter of the onions and mushrooms onto each slice. Pile some watercress on top, then top with the steak. Gently press down on the steak with a spatula so some of the warm juices drip down. Serve at once.

Beef Stroganoff

(six servings)

Named for a nineteenth-century Russian count, beef Stroganoff was popular in this country during the 1960s and 1970s, but our fickle, trendy eating habits have left it languishing. Aristocratic credentials aside, it is just plain delicious. It makes a good dinner for harried cooks, because once the beef and onions have been sliced, the dish can be ready to serve in twenty or thirty minutes. Customarily served with white rice, it is much better with narrow, quarter-inch-wide noodles. Even simpler, spoon the Stroganoff over toast. Serve a watercress salad on the side.

2 pounds fillet or tri-tip (triangle tip) of beef, cut into $\frac{1}{2} \times 2$-inch strips	3 large onions, chopped
	1 pound fresh mushrooms, wiped clean and sliced
Salt and pepper to taste	2 cups beef broth
2 tablespoons vegetable oil	2 cups sour cream

Sprinkle the meat with salt and pepper. Heat the oil in a large heavy-bottomed sauté pan, add the meat, and cook for just 1 minute over medium-high heat. Add the onions and cook over low heat, stirring often, for 4 to 5 minutes. Stir in the mushrooms, then the beef broth, and reduce the heat to a simmer. Simmer for 15 to 20 minutes, stirring often, until the meat is tender. Taste and add more salt if needed.

Stir the sour cream briskly, then add to the beef mixture. Mix well, and allow the Stroganoff to thoroughly heat through. Serve at once.

Tri-Tip Pot Roast

(four to six servings)

The tri-tip (or triangle tip) is a small cut of beef from the bottom sirloin that is tender enough not to need long cooking. You end up with the same rich pot roast flavors that take two to three hours to produce with other cuts. Don't forget a jar of hot mustard on the side.

3 tablespoons vegetable oil
One 2½-pound tri-tip beef
  roast
Salt and pepper to taste
2 cloves garlic, chopped
1 cup water

2 onions, halved
5 carrots, peeled and cut
  into 2-inch lengths
4 medium potatoes, peeled
  and cut into quarters

Heat the oil in a heavy Dutch oven (with a lid), add the meat, salt and pepper liberally, and brown on all sides over medium-high heat. Add the garlic, water, and onions, reduce the heat, cover, and simmer for about 20 minutes.

Add the carrots and potatoes, re-cover, and cook for another 20 to 30 minutes. Serve on a large platter with the vegetables all round.

Stuffed Cabbage Rolls

(four servings)

On a chilly night, there can't be a nicer supper than cabbage rolls with a little sour cream, warm Applesauce (see page 509), and homemade Rye Crackers (see page 475). Since it is simple to make twice as much, double the recipe and freeze the extra cabbage rolls for another night.

1 large head savoy cabbage	1 teaspoon allspice
3 tablespoons butter	Salt and pepper to taste
1 medium onion, chopped	¼ cup brown sugar
2 cloves garlic, finely chopped	1½ cups steamed long-grain
2 cups tomato sauce, homemade	white rice (see page 385)
or canned	1 pound ground beef
¼ cup water	

Grease a 9 × 13-inch baking dish. Preheat the oven to 350°F.

Bring a large pot of salted water to a boil. Remove and discard the core from the cabbage and put the cabbage into the boiling water, cover, and let gently boil for 4 or 5 minutes. Drain well and set aside.

Melt the butter in a large saucepan, add the onion and garlic, and stir over medium heat, cooking only until the onion and garlic are soft, not browned. Add the tomato sauce, water, allspice, and salt and pepper to taste. Lower the heat, and let the sauce simmer for about 15 minutes. Taste and correct the seasoning. The sauce should be thickened, but not so thick that it "plops" when poured from a spoon.

Remove about 15 of the tougher outer leaves from the cabbage and set aside to be used for wrapping the rolls. Chop the remaining cabbage coarsely and spread over the bottom of the greased baking dish. Sprinkle the brown sugar over the chopped cabbage, and lightly salt and pepper.

Put three quarters of the sauce into a mixing bowl with the rice and beef and mix well. Divide the filling into approximately 12 parts and roll each portion in a cabbage leaf. Place each roll on the chopped cabbage, seam-side down. Spoon a little of the remaining sauce on top of each roll. Cover the top with the remaining coarser outer leaves. Bake for 1 hour, and serve.

"Supper, after all, is our most social meal and, of all the day's contacts (apart, at least, from acts of love), perhaps the most needingly personal one."

—from *Simple Cooking*
by John Thorne

The Perfect California Hamburger

(one hamburger)

1 sturdy, fresh, tender hamburger
   bun
3 to 4 tablespoons mayonnaise
4 tablespoons finely chopped
   onion
Vegetable oil or shortening

$\frac{1}{4}$ to $\frac{1}{3}$ pound fresh ground
   beef with $\frac{1}{3}$ part fat
Salt and pepper to taste
$\frac{1}{3}$ cup shaved (chiffonade)
   clean, crisp iceberg lettuce
2 to 3 tablespoons sweet relish

Only if you must:
2 tablespoons ball-park
   mustard (no Dijon)
2 tablespoons ketchup

Cheese (only mild Cheddar,
   please)

Slice the hamburger bun in half. Stir the mayonnaise and onion together and spread on one half of the bun. Heat a skillet and film the bottom with a little shortening or oil. Lightly form the meat into a patty and put it into the hot skillet. Salt and pepper the top very liberally. Fry for 2 or 3 minutes (don't press down with a spatula because this will dry the meat). Turn the hamburger over and salt and pepper it again. Fry until cooked to your liking. Put the hamburger patty on the onion mayonnaise, and spread the other half of the bun with relish and whatever additional condiments you may be using. Spread the lettuce over, add a slice of cheese, if you must, and put the bun together.

THE PERFECT HAMBURGER

My hamburger credentials come from the home of the one and only authentic hamburger, which was developed in Glendale, California, in August of 1936. The originator of this perfect hamburger is Bob Wian, the man who turned one rickety hamburger stand into a chain of 1,136 Bob's Big Boy restaurants across the country.

In order to make this hamburger you must have the following ingredients. You cannot allow yourself any creative license.

1. One sturdy, fresh, tender bun. It must have good, sound construction to keep the hamburger intact. See my recipe on page 474.

2. Lots of mayonnaise. (A dry hamburger is not acceptable.)

3. If onion is desired, it must be chopped and stirred into the mayonnaise so it doesn't slide around and become unevenly distributed.

4. Freshly ground beef. It must come from a cut that has enough fat (at least one third) to make a moist patty. Form the patty very gently so that the meat just holds together. (When ground meat is pressed firmly the hamburger becomes dry and rather tough.) The patty must be salted well before cooking.

5. Clean, crisp, fresh iceberg lettuce, thinly shredded so that it can be evenly distributed.

6. A liberal spread of relish. (Bob made his own.)

7. If you must have cheese on this hamburger, only mild Cheddar, please.

I guarantee that if you make this hamburger once, you will never fall back into making or eating those gourmet beef sandwiches called hamburgers.

Holey Moley Tamale Pie

(six servings)

I always wanted to open a tamale shop called Holey Moley Tamales and serve this dish as the specialty of the house. It is one of the rare examples of a lot of ingredients making a better pie. Double the recipe, make two pies, and freeze one. Serve with tropical fruit such as pineapple, mango, or papaya, with a little coconut sprinkled on top.

4 cups water
$1\frac{1}{2}$ cups yellow cornmeal
2 cups cold water
3 teaspoons salt
$\frac{1}{4}$ to $\frac{1}{2}$ cup butter or lard
$\frac{1}{2}$ pound bulk sausage
2 tablespoons chili powder
$\frac{3}{4}$ teaspoon ground cumin
1 clove garlic, minced
2 medium onions, finely chopped
1 small green bell pepper, seeded and chopped
2 stalks celery, finely chopped
$1\frac{1}{2}$ pounds ground beef

3 cups canned Italian plum tomatoes; or 4 cups peeled and seeded fresh tomatoes ($1\frac{1}{2}$ pounds)
2 cups corn kernels 6 ears), frozen, or canned and drained
4 ounces canned mild green chile peppers, diced
Optional: 1 teaspoon minced jalapeño chile peppers
1 cup pitted ripe olives
6 ounces medium or sharp Cheddar cheese, grated (2 cups)

Bring the 4 cups of water to a boil in a 3-quart kettle. Meanwhile, stir the cornmeal into the 2 cups of cold water (this helps prevent lumping), and then stir this into the boiling water. Continue to stir while the water returns to a boil. Turn the heat to low, stir in $1\frac{1}{2}$

teaspoons of the salt and butter, cover, and simmer 30 to 40 minutes, stirring often. This will become very thick.

Meanwhile, in a kettle or large frying pan, mash the sausage and cook over medium heat until it begins to lose color. Add the chili powder and cumin, stir, and cook about 5 minutes. Add the garlic, onions, green pepper, celery, and remaining salt. Stir and cook until the vegetables are soft, about 3 to 5 minutes. Crumble the beef into the pan and mash and cook until the raw color disappears. Add the tomatoes, corn, green chile peppers, and the jalapeño peppers, if using, and let the mixture simmer for 15 to 20 minutes.

Preheat the oven to 350°F.

Grease or oil a large baking pan that is at least $10 \times 14 \times 2$ inches. Spread two thirds of the cornmeal mixture on the bottom and sides of the pan. Spoon in the filling and distribute the olives evenly over. Spoon the remaining cornmeal over the top and sprinkle with the cheese. Bake for about 1 hour. If you make an extra tamale pie, freeze it unbaked.

American Meatloaf

(six servings)

I've been looking for the perfect meatloaf for years. Too many meatloaves are carelessly put together with too many unassimilated ingredients. This meatloaf is the all-time winner in my house. It is cooked freeform rather than in a loaf pan so that it browns on all sides. Ketchup and Worcestershire sauce are in every American larder, and it seems to me that they belong in an American meatloaf. Instead of serving with mashed potatoes, bake a few potatoes, carrots, and onions in the pan with the meatloaf.

2 tablespoons butter
1 large onion, finely chopped
2 to 3 medium carrots, finely
   chopped
2 to 3 celery stalks, finely
   chopped
1 pound ground beef (chuck or
   round)
2 boneless pork chops (about
   $\frac{1}{2}$ pound), ground
3 cloves garlic, minced or put
   through a garlic press
$1\frac{1}{4}$ cups fresh bread crumbs

Salt, at least 1 teaspoon, or to
   taste
Pepper to taste
$\frac{3}{4}$ teaspoon nutmeg
$\frac{1}{8}$ teaspoon cayenne pepper
$1\frac{1}{2}$ teaspoons Worcestershire
   sauce
$\frac{1}{4}$ cup tomato ketchup
$\frac{2}{3}$ cup water
Optional: potatoes, carrots,
   and onions to bake with the
   meatloaf

Preheat the oven to 350°F.

Melt the butter in a large skillet. Add the onion, carrots, and celery, and over medium-low heat cook until softened, stirring often, about 5 to 6 minutes.

In a large bowl, put the beef and pork, sautéed vegetables, garlic, bread crumbs, salt, pepper, nutmeg, cayenne, Worcestershire sauce, tomato ketchup, and water. Mix thoroughly with your hands. Gently pat the meatloaf into an oval-shaped mound in an 11 × 7-inch baking dish. (If pressed together too firmly, the meatloaf won't remain moist and tender.) Bake for 45 to 50 minutes. Feel free to surround your meatloaf with small whole onions and/or carrots and small new potatoes.

Ireland's Irish Stew

(six servings)

You will love this Irish stew even if you are Italian. It has the taste of the land—natural and inviting. Irish Soda Bread (see page 486) belongs with this stew.

2 pounds lamb for stewing,
   some fat removed, cut in large-
   bite size pieces
Salt and pepper to taste (be
   generous)
4 large onions, thickly sliced
8 medium potatoes, peeled and
   thickly sliced

2 tablespoons chopped fresh
   thyme; or 1 tablespoon
   crumbled dried thyme
2 cups water
3 tablespoons finely chopped
   parsley

Preheat the oven to 325°F.

Spread the lamb pieces on a sheet of waxed paper and salt and pepper liberally. Do the same with the onions and potatoes. Put the potatoes, onions, and lamb in layers in a large heavy casserole, sprinkling the thyme over each layer, and starting and ending with potatoes. Add the water slowly, without disturbing the layers, cover the casserole, put in the oven, and bake for 2 hours. Sprinkle with parsley and serve in bowls.

Shepherd's Pie

(four servings)

The mashed potato crust on Shepherd's Pie makes it unlike any other dish I know. You may not remember it from your childhood, but it's never too late to introduce it and enjoy it. It is such a tasty way to use leftover lamb.

4 medium potatoes	2 large cloves garlic, peeled
Salt and freshly ground	1 medium onion, quartered
black pepper to taste	1 teaspoon crumbled dried
8 tablespoons (1 stick) butter	rosemary
3 cups chopped cooked lamb	2 tablespoons flour
(any leftover lamb will do)	¾ cup beef broth

Peel the potatoes and cut them into quarters. Put them in a pan and just cover them with cold water. Bring to a boil and boil gently for 15 to 20 minutes, or until tender when pierced with a fork. Drain well. Add salt, pepper and four tablespoons of the butter, and mash by hand until the lumps disappear, or put through a ricer. Set aside.

While the potatoes are boiling, preheat the oven to 325°F. Mix together the lamb, garlic, onion, and rosemary. Put through a meat grinder twice or chop until fine in a food processor.

Melt the remaining 4 tablespoons of butter in a large skillet and stir in the flour. Cook for a few minutes over medium heat until smooth and blended. Slowly add the beef broth. Cook, stirring constantly, until the gravy is thickened. Cook at least 5 minutes to get rid of the raw flour taste. Remove from heat, add the lamb mixture, and stir to blend. Add salt and pepper to taste.

Spread the lamb mixture evenly into a 1½-quart casserole or

deep pie dish. Spread the mashed potatoes evenly on top to the edge of the casserole. Make a crisscross design with a fork. Bake for 45 to 50 minutes, or until the meat is bubbling hot and the potatoes are browned.

Applesauce Lamb Curry

(four servings)

I never saw a lamb curry with fresh applesauce in it before this one. The mild hint of apple sweetness blends nicely with the spiciness of the curry.

4 tablespoons ($\frac{1}{2}$ stick) butter
2 tablespoons curry powder
$2\frac{1}{2}$ teaspoons ground ginger
$\frac{1}{2}$ teaspoon salt
$\frac{1}{2}$ teaspoon allspice
$\frac{1}{2}$ teaspoon mace
$\frac{1}{4}$ cup flour
$1\frac{1}{2}$ cups canned chicken broth

$\frac{1}{2}$ cup heavy cream
$1\frac{1}{2}$ cups Applesauce (see page 509)
2 cups sliced cooked lamb (for example, leftover roast leg of lamb), at room temperature
4 cups steamed long-grain white rice (see page 385)

In a medium-size saucepan, melt the butter. Add the curry powder, ginger, salt, allspice, mace, and flour and stir until smooth and well blended. Slowly stir in the chicken broth and cream, and cook over medium heat, stirring constantly, until thickened. Add the applesauce and cook for 2 minutes more. Serve on a platter, making a mound of hot rice and adding sliced lamb on top, with the sauce poured over.

Black Pepper Ribs

(four servings)

This recipe came from James Beard, who dearly loved ribs cooked this way, as did all of us in his cooking classes. Many of us had never had spareribs without barbecue sauce. Ribs roasted this way are crisp around the edges and have a fine pork flavor. I am partial to a little Rhubarb-Onion Relish (see page 506) on the side.

3 pounds pork spareribs   Salt and pepper to taste

Preheat the oven to 400°F.

Put the spareribs in a baking pan large enough to accommodate them in a single layer. *Generously* salt and pepper both sides and bake for 30 minutes on each side—1 hour in all. Serve right away.

Pork Tenderloin with Jalapeño Sauce

(four servings)

This shocking-pink sauce with its bright, peppy flavor turns ordinary roast pork into a flavor fiesta. Serve with Buttermilk Cornbread (see page 485) and black-eyed peas.

Salt and freshly ground   6 tablespoons jalapeño jelly
   black pepper to taste $\frac{1}{3}$ cup sour cream
2 pounds pork tenderloins*

*The tenderloin is the tender cylindrical muscle, about 2½ inches in diameter and about 7 inches long, from the inside of the pork loin.

Preheat the oven to 425°F.

Line a small roasting pan with heavy aluminum foil. Generously salt and pepper the tenderloins. Melt 3 tablespoons of the jelly in a small pan over low heat and brush over the top of each tenderloin.

Put the tenderloins in the roasting pan about 1½ inches apart, and roast until a meat thermometer registers 160°F, about 15 minutes (don't overcook; pork tends to become dry). While the pork is roasting, stir the remaining jelly into the sour cream.

When the pork is almost done, heat the jelly–sour cream sauce in a small pan over very low heat, until *just* warm. Remove the pork from the oven, slice the tenderloins on the diagonal into ½-inch medallions, and serve with the warmed sauce.

Pork with Sage and Brown Rice

(four servings)

It's surprising how good sage and brown rice are together. Add pork and you have a more substantial supper dish. Fried Apple Rings (see page 510) are a nice addition, and you might serve Wirtabel's Melon Chutney (see page 508) or Pike's Perfect Pickles (see page 500) alongside.

½ cup flour	1 large onion, chopped
½ teaspoon salt	1 cup brown rice
⅛ teaspoon pepper	2 teaspoons crumbled dried
1 pound boneless pork (loin	sage leaves
or shoulder), cut into bite-	3 cups water
size pieces	Optional: 1 cup raisins
4 tablespoons vegetable	
shortening	

Stir together the flour, salt, and pepper in a mixing bowl. Add the pork and toss to lightly coat the pieces. Shake free of any excess flour mixture. Heat 2 tablespoons of the shortening in a large skillet over medium-high heat. Add the onion and cook about 5 minutes, or until it is soft and golden brown. Add the pork and continue cooking and stirring until all the pieces are browned, adding more shortening if needed to prevent sticking.

Remove the onion and pork from the skillet and set aside on a plate. Add the remaining 2 tablespoons of shortening to the skillet, and melt over medium heat. Add the brown rice. Cook the rice until it is golden brown, about 7 minutes, stirring frequently. Put the onion and meat back into the skillet along with the sage, water, and the optional raisins. Bring to a boil, cover, reduce the heat to a simmer, and cook for 45 minutes or until the rice is tender and the water is almost gone. Taste and add more sage if too faintly flavored. Be sure to stir the rice occasionally so it doesn't stick to the bottom of the pan. Taste for salt and pepper and correct seasonings. Serve hot.

Mostly Vegetables

Southern Green Beans

Red Beans and White Rice

Boston Baked Beans

Bean Stew with Raw Onions

Green Peppers and Cheese

Filled Green Peppers

Baked Green Peppers with
    Anchovies, Rice, and Dill

New Red Potatoes with
    Rosemary

Idaho Sunrise

Eggs, Tomatoes, and Potatoes
    with *Gremolata*

Eggplant Filled with Roasted
    Vegetables

Winter Vegetable Cobbler

Vegetable Porridge

Mark Peel's Barley Risotto

Humble Rice

Creamy Rice

Spanish *Riso*

Marietta's Spaghetti

Iceberg Lettuce and Noodles

Pasta Shells, Mushrooms, and
    Brown Butter

Macaroni and Cheese

Curried Macaroni

Custard Sandwich

Frieda and Elinor's Onion Pie

Papusas

Green Chile Pie

Potato and Pepper Frittata

Tomato Rarebit

Linda Sue's Tomato Stew

Bread and Bacon Pancake

Fifty years ago, if my mother had put a plate of vegetables with no meat in front of my father for dinner, he would have thought she was demented or that we had suffered some financial disaster he didn't know about. Actually, my husband would have thought the same thing a few dozen years back. Those were the meat and potato years: bacon for breakfast, cold meat for lunch, and a roast for dinner.

When I was growing up in a small foothill town in Southern California, it seemed as if there were only about five or six fresh vegetables in our grocery store: carrots, string beans, cabbage, lettuce, and corn, and maybe one or two others. Vegetables certainly played second fiddle in my mother's cooking. I know we had string beans because I can remember stringing them. And I know we had carrots, but always raw, because my mother had read in some government pamphlet that they were better for us that way. My Irish father considered corn-on-the-cob to be cattle fodder, so our table never saw an ear of corn. He said almost every other vegetable was rabbit food.

Times have changed. The produce departments in supermarkets are huge, and we have a vast variety of vegetables. Cooks from around the world have introduced us to tomatillos, gingerroot, chile peppers, bok choy, and cilantro, to name a few plant foods new to most of us, and our cooking is far more interesting because of them.

All the recipes in this chapter are main supper dishes, and all of them are vegetable dishes except for a few pasta and rice recipes. Many of them have been collected over the years from friends and strangers eager to share a favorite vegetable dish. Green Chile Pie (see page 465) came from a county fair winner long ago. Linda Sue's Tomato Stew (see page 468) came from a photographer who doesn't cook except once in a while when she's homesick for this dish from her childhood. And Frieda and Elinor's Onion Pie (see page 463) came from the Swiss Alps by way of an Idaho housewife.

Southern Green Beans

(four servings)

For the last few years most of us have been following the recommended way of cooking green beans until *just* tender, because we believed that long cooking destroyed flavor and vitamins. But Southern Green Beans with potatoes and a hint of bacon have a fullness of flavor and depth of character that crunchy beans don't have. Serve with warm cornbread.

3 or 4 slices smoky-style bacon, diced	Salt and pepper to taste
	1 cup water
1 pound green snap beans, washed, ends trimmed, and cut into 1-inch lengths	2 scallions, sliced
	2 medium potatoes, peeled and diced

Heat a Dutch oven or heavy-bottomed pot with a lid. Add the bacon, and cook over medium-low heat until lightly brown, about

5 minutes. Add the green beans, salt and pepper, and water. Cover and cook for about 10 minutes over medium-low heat. Add the scallions and potatoes, stir to mix, cover, and cook for 30 minutes more. Check once or twice to make sure the liquid hasn't all evaporated. Serve hot.

FARMERS' MARKET

A visit to the farmers' market can be as inspiring and as uplifting as a trip to Yosemite. If you've never eaten fruit that has been tree ripened, or cooked vegetables at their peak of maturity, you can't imagine what you've been missing. Going to the farmers' market, walking from stand to stand, and talking to friendly people is a very pleasant experience.

Supermarkets, with their vast array of foods, are fascinating and indispensable, but a farmers' market, with fewer foods to buy, all of them fresh and sold by their growers, is so much more personal. There's an appreciation at my supper table when the dishes have been made from the produce of farmers I know.

Often you'll find people exchanging recipes at the market and that can be rewarding. I usually return home each week with some cooking tip or a fresh herb to cook a new way with a favorite vegetable. Some of the recipes I collected at the farmers' market are Wirtabel's Melon Chutney (see page 508), Green Peppers and Cheese (see page 443), and New Red Potatoes with Rosemary (see page 446).

Red Beans and White Rice

(six servings)

Beans and rice are oddly delicious together. You may approach this Creole dish with low expectations, but once you've tried it, you'll see why it's a beloved staple in the South. The nutritionists keep telling us to put more legumes and grains in our diets, and I can't think of a better way to do that than serving red beans alongside white rice.

2 cups (about 1 pound) dried red beans, soaked overnight (see page 348)	1 bay leaf
	2 teaspoons Tabasco sauce
	1 pound salt pork, diced
1 carrot, peeled and diced	Salt and pepper to taste
1 large onion, chopped	2 cups steamed long-grain
¼ cup chopped celery with leaves	white rice (see page 385)

Drain and rinse the beans, return them to the pot, and add the carrot, onion, celery, bay leaf, Tabasco sauce, and salt pork. Add enough water to cover, bring to a boil, reduce the heat, and simmer for about 2 hours, or until the beans are tender. Some of the beans should be mushy. Add more water if necessary, or mash some beans to thicken. Salt and pepper to taste, being careful not to oversalt. Serve the beans in the same bowl with the rice, side by side.

Boston Baked Beans

(four servings)

I don't think Bostonians bake their beans overnight in the ashes of their fireplaces anymore, but Boston baked beans still need to be long cooked to have that rich, mellow flavor that only long, slow cooking creates. Once you have quickly assembled the dish and put the beans in the oven, they don't need you, except to check up hourly to see if more liquid is needed. This dish can be made on a Sunday and reheated. Serve with Piccalilli (see page 507) and Coleslaw (see page 517).

2 cups Great Northern beans, or small dried white beans, soaked overnight (see page 348)	3 tablespoons molasses
	¼ pound salt pork, cut into ½-inch cubes, leaving the bottom attached to the rind
2 teaspoons dry mustard	
3 tablespoons dark brown sugar	

Preheat the oven to 325°F.

Drain the beans, cover with fresh water, and cook until tender, about 1 hour. Drain, reserving the liquid. Stir together the mustard, brown sugar, molasses, and 2 cups of the reserved liquid. Put the salt pork in a 2-quart bean pot or casserole, add the beans, and then add the molasses mixture. Stir to blend. Cover and bake for 5 to 6 hours. They are done when soft. Check every hour or so to make sure the beans don't dry out. Add more of the reserved liquid, or water, as needed to keep the beans moist. Taste and correct seasonings. Serve hot.

Bean Stew with Raw Onions

(four servings)

Adding fresh raw onions to this dish just before you serve it boosts the taste and texture. Make this bean stew and taste it before and after you add the chopped raw onion: you will be surprised by the difference.

1¼ cups dried red or pinto beans, soaked overnight (see page 348)	1 cup chopped parsley
	⅓ cup yellow cornmeal
	⅛ to ¼ medium head cabbage, chopped (2 cups)
6 slices bacon	1½ teaspoons ground sage
8 cups water	1½ teaspoons salt
1 large onion, chopped (1 cup)	2 medium onions, chopped (1½ cups)
3 stalks celery, chopped	

Drain the beans. Put aside 1 slice of bacon and dice the rest. In a large (5-quart) soup pot, put the beans, diced bacon, and water. Bring to a boil and cook over low heat for 30 minutes.

In a frying pan, cook the remaining bacon slice until crisp. Remove from the pan, crumble, and set aside. Add the 1 cup chopped onion, celery, and parsley to the bacon drippings. Sauté the vegetables over medium heat until soft, about 5 minutes.

Add the cornmeal to the beans and bacon in the soup pot, and stir to mix. Add the sautéed vegetables, cabbage, sage, and salt, and stir. Cover and cook for 30 more minutes. Just before serving, stir in the 1½ cups chopped onions or sprinkle the onions on top of individual servings with the crumbled bacon. Serve hot.

Green Peppers and Cheese

(four servings)

One Saturday at the farmers' market I was buying some Anaheim chiles and the woman next to me asked me if I had ever made Peppers and Cheese. "It's so simple," she said. "Do try it!" I did, and she was right.

2 tablespoons olive oil
8 Anaheim or California chile
  peppers,* split, seeded, and
  deveined
6 ounces Monterey Jack,
  fontina, or Gouda cheese,
  sliced

1 large onion, finely chopped
2 tablespoons corn oil
8 tortillas (corn, flour, or
  whole wheat)
Fresh cilantro

Heat the olive oil in a frying pan. Put in the peppers, open and skin sides down, and flatten them with a spatula as they cook. Cook over medium heat for about 5 minutes, or until the skins are blistered and browned. Put 1 slice of cheese and 2 tablespoons of onion in each pepper. Fold the pepper over the cheese and cook over low heat 1 minute, then remove from the heat. Warm the tortillas by putting two at a time in a steamer over boiling water. Leave only for a few seconds. Remove and keep warm in a covered dish. Put a filled pepper and a few sprigs of cilantro into each warm tortilla and fold the tortilla in half. Serve hot.

*Anaheim peppers are about 6 inches long, light green, and about 1½ inches in diameter. They are one of the milder peppers. The hottest and least flavorful parts, the seeds and veins, are almost always removed before cooking.

Filled Green Peppers

(four servings)

In the summertime, all the ingredients for this dish will be at the farmers' market. The quality of the tomatoes is important, and for a short time in the summer they will be perfect: sweet, acidic, firm, juicy, and bright red. This is a very practical dish: the filled bell pepper halves are easy to pick up and eat cold on a picnic, yet they are just as good served hot on a plate. Serve a sharp, creamy cheese, green onions, and whole wheat bagels on the side.

4 green bell peppers, halved
    lengthwise, seeded, and
    deveined
2 tablespoons olive oil
3 cloves garlic, finely chopped
1 large onion, chopped
2 medium tomatoes, peeled
    and chopped

1 small eggplant, chopped
1 tablespoon chopped fresh
    oregano; or 1½ teaspoons
    dried crumbled oregano
Salt to taste
Generous amount of pepper
Fresh basil leaves, for garnish

Preheat the oven to 350°F. Film a 9 × 13-inch Pyrex baking dish with olive oil.

Put the peppers into a pot of salted, boiling water; place a plate in the pot on top of the peppers to keep them under the water; and parboil for 4 minutes. Remove and set aside.

Film a sauté pan with the olive oil and heat. Add the garlic and onion and cook over medium heat for a minute or two, just to soften. Add the tomatoes, eggplant, oregano, salt, and pepper. Stir to mix and blend thoroughly. Taste for salt and correct if necessary. Cover the pan and cook over medium-low heat for 10 minutes, stirring once or twice. Uncover and cook another 3 minutes, stirring often. Remove from heat.

Put the pepper halves in the prepared baking dish. Using a slotted spoon, fill the halves with the tomato/eggplant mixture. Bake for 20 minutes. Remove and serve hot or cold, with whole, fresh basil leaves on top.

Baked Green Peppers with Anchovies, Rice, and Dill

(four servings)

Unless you know you love anchovies, this dish may not be for you. The pepper halves are filled with the brazen flavors of olives, garlic, lemon, dill, and salty fish.

4 green bell peppers, cut in half lengthwise, stemmed, seeded, and deveined
2-ounce can anchovy fillets, packed in oil
2 tablespoons finely chopped onion
3 cloves garlic, minced
1½ tablespoons chopped fresh dill

2 tablespoons chopped parsley
3 cups steamed long-grain white rice (see page 385)
2 tablespoons lemon juice
3 tablespoons olive oil
Pepper to taste
12 whole black olives

Preheat the oven to 350°F.

Bring a large pot of water to a boil. Put the pepper halves in the boiling water; place a plate in the pot on top of the peppers to keep them under water; and blanch them for about 4 minutes, or until they are just cooked and slightly soft. Remove the peppers from the water and set aside.

Drain the anchovies and put the anchovy oil in a skillet over medium heat. Add the onion and garlic and cook until soft, but not browned. Add the dill and parsley and stir until blended. Remove from the heat. In a bowl, mix together the onion mixture, rice, lemon juice, olive oil, pepper, black olives, and half the anchovy fillets (or more if you wish). Fill the pepper halves with the mixture and place them in an oiled baking dish. Cover and heat in the oven for about 20 minutes, or until heated through. Serve warm.

New Red Potatoes with Rosemary

(four to six servings)

I first had tiny red new potatoes fixed this way at a cocktail party and watched platter after platter disappear. Everyone loved them. This is also a dandy dish for supper with scrambled eggs, cottage cheese, or cold chicken.

4 pounds tiny red new potatoes
(approximately 60), about 1½
inches in diameter, unpeeled
¼ cup olive oil
3 teaspoons kosher salt

4 tablespoons fresh rosemary
leaves; or 2 tablespoons
crumbled dried rosemary
leaves; plus some rosemary
branches, for garnish

Preheat the oven to 350°F.

Put the potatoes in a large bowl and toss with the olive oil, salt, and rosemary leaves. Put the potatoes in a roasting pan, and put them in the oven for about 30 minutes, until just done in the center when pierced with a fork. Serve on a platter, surrounded by rosemary branches.

Idaho Sunrise

(one serving)

This is simply a baked potato with a bright yellow egg sitting on top of it, but when you mash the egg into the buttered potato it's like the sun coming up over the mountains.

1 medium baking potato (Idaho or russet Burbank), about ½ pound
1 tablespoon butter plus 1 teaspoon melted butter

Salt and pepper to taste
2 tablespoons milk
1 egg

Preheat the oven to 450°F.

Scrub the potato and then dry it. Pierce with a fork, put in the oven, and bake for about 40 to 50 minutes, or until it feels soft when pierced with a small knife.

Remove from the oven, and, using a potholder to hold the hot potato, slice a piece off the potato lengthwise, large enough so you can scoop out the insides. Put the scooped-out potato in a small bowl, add the 1 tablespoon butter, salt and pepper, and milk, and mash with a fork, mixing well.

Refill the potato shell. Put the filled potato on a pie plate or baking sheet. Break the egg and drop it on top of the potato, spoon the teaspoon of melted butter over the egg, salt and pepper it, and put in the oven. Bake for about 8 to 10 minutes, or until the egg is set but the yolk is still soft enough to make a nice sauce for the potato. Serve hot.

Eggs, Tomatoes, and Potatoes with Gremolata

(four servings)

The combination of lemon zest, parsley, and garlic is called *gremolata* in Italy. Have some chunks of bread on the side to dunk in the extra *gremolata*. Drink a glass of strong iced espresso for dessert with Plain Jane Sugar Cookies (see page 539).

1½ pounds small new red potatoes, about 1½ inches in diameter, unpeeled	2½ tablespoons finely chopped parsley
8 eggs	4 teaspoons finely chopped garlic
½ cup olive oil	4 medium tomatoes, each cut into 6 wedges
2½ teaspoons finely chopped lemon zest	1 teaspoon kosher salt

Put the potatoes and eggs in a large pot of salted water. Bring to a boil and cook about 12 minutes, or until the potatoes are tender when pierced with a knife.

While the potatoes and eggs are cooking, mix the olive oil, lemon zest, parsley, and garlic together. Drain the potatoes and eggs and let cool slightly. Shell and quarter the eggs.

While they are still warm, put the potatoes and eggs and the tomatoes in a large bowl, and add the salt. Add a little more than half the *gremolata* and toss to coat the potatoes, eggs, and tomatoes thoroughly. Put the remaining *gremolata* in a small bowl to pass at the table.

Eggplant Filled with Roasted Vegetables

(four servings)

All the ingredients in this recipe come together like a good jigsaw puzzle. Every part fits and everything gets used: the roasted eggplant pulp makes the relish and the relish completes the dish.

1 large long eggplant (or 2 small ones)
1 pound zucchini, chopped into ½-inch chunks
1 pound yellow crookneck or pattypan squash, chopped into ½-inch chunks
2 onions, chopped
Salt and pepper to taste

2 teaspoons crumbled dried marjoram
6 tablespoons olive oil
3 cloves garlic, finely chopped, or put through a garlic press
1 cup finely minced parsley
2 medium tomatoes, finely chopped
½ teaspoon cayenne pepper

Preheat the oven to 350°F.

Slice the eggplant lengthwise and place on a baking sheet, cut side down. On another large baking sheet, spread the zucchini, squash, and onions. Salt and pepper liberally, and sprinkle the marjoram and 3 tablespoons of the olive oil over the mixture. Using your hands, toss and mix on the baking sheet, spreading the vegetables evenly over the sheet. Put the eggplant and vegetables into the oven and set the timer for 30 minutes. Check eggplant for doneness by piercing the center with a fork; it should be tender. Remove the eggplant, but continue to cook the remaining vegetables for 15 to 20 minutes more, or until slightly brown on top. Remove from the oven and set aside.

While the vegetables finish baking, make the relish. Spoon out the pulp from the eggplant, leaving ¼ inch of pulp attached to the skin. Process the pulp in a food processor or finely chop it by hand. Put the eggplant pulp in a mixing bowl and add the garlic, parsley, tomatoes, salt, cayenne pepper, and the remaining 3 tablespoons of olive oil. Mix well, taste, and add salt and more cayenne if needed. Cut the eggplant shells in half so there are 4 sections. Divide the roasted vegetables into four portions and fill each shell. Put about ½ cup of relish beside each portion of filled eggplant. Serve hot or cold.

Winter Vegetable Cobbler

(six servings)

People get excited when they hear the name Winter Vegetable Cobbler, and nobody yet has been disappointed after making it.

1 turnip, peeled and cut into bite-size wedges
1 potato (russet or baking), peeled and diced
1 celery root, peeled and diced (about 1½ cups)
1 onion, coarsely chopped
3 carrots, peeled and sliced

½ cup chopped parsley
1 cup chicken broth (see page 377)
1 tablespoon cornstarch
1 teaspoon salt
Freshly ground pepper to taste
4 tablespoons (½ stick) butter

Cobbler Dough
1¾ cups flour
1 tablespoon baking powder
½ teaspoon salt

6 tablespoons (¾ stick) butter, chilled and cut into pieces
¾ cup heavy cream

Preheat the oven to 325°F.

Put the turnip, potato, celery root, onion, carrots, and parsley in a 2-inch-deep, 3-quart ovenproof baking dish (I use an approximately $13 \times 9 \times 2$-inch Pyrex baking dish). You should have about 6 cups of vegetables. In a small mixing bowl, blend the chicken broth with the cornstarch. Pour over the vegetables and mix well. Add the salt and pepper and mix to blend. Dot the top of the vegetables with the butter.

Mix the flour, baking powder, and salt in a large mixing bowl and stir with a fork to blend. Put the pieces of chilled butter into the flour mixture and rub quickly with your fingertips until the mixture resembles coarse crumbs. Using a fork, slowly stir in the cream, until roughly mixed. Gather the dough into a shaggy mass and knead 5 or 6 times. Roll out the dough on a lightly floured board until it is the size of the top of the baking dish. The dough should be about ¼ inch thick.

Place the dough on top of the vegetables. Bake for 55 to 65 minutes, until the vegetables are cooked through and the crust is browned. Test vegetables for doneness with a knife tip or skewer. Remove from the oven and serve hot.

Vegetable Porridge

(four servings)

I love the word porridge, but lots of people don't. To me, the word sounds wholesome and comforting. Here it stands for a flavorful dish of oats, barley, and vegetables. Even though everyone doesn't love the name, everyone loves the dish.

2 tablespoons butter	1 cup pearl barley
1 large yellow onion, chopped	Salt and pepper to taste
3 carrots, peeled, halved, and sliced	2 zucchini, sliced ¼ inch thick
3 stalks celery, sliced	1 cup firmly packed fresh spinach, washed
8 cups chicken broth (see page 377)	½ cup rolled oats

Melt the butter in a 5-quart heavy-bottomed soup pot, and add the onion, carrots, and celery. Cook over medium heat, stirring often, for 5 minutes. Add the chicken broth, barley, and salt and pepper. Simmer for 1½ hours, or until the barley is tender, stirring every so often so the barley does not stick to the bottom of the pot.

Add the zucchini, spinach, and oats. Simmer for another 10 minutes. Taste and correct the seasonings. Serve hot.

Mark Peel's Barley Risotto

(four servings)

Mark Peel, the chef of Campanile Restaurant in Los Angeles, made up this dish, which is greater than the sum of its parts. This is a speedy risottolike dish. Intermingled, the earthy flavors of mushrooms, barley, and rice taste unexpectedly new and different.

½ cup barley
½ cup short-grain rice
3 tablespoons butter
½ pound mushrooms, wiped
  clean and sliced (3 cups)

½ cup chicken broth (see
  page 377)
Salt to taste

In a large (at least 2-quart) pot, bring 6 cups of salted water to a boil. Add the barley and rice and let simmer for 25 minutes, or until tender. Drain any water that remains after the barley and rice are cooked.

Melt the butter in a large skillet. Add the mushrooms and slowly cook over low heat for about 7 to 10 minutes. Mix in the cooked barley and rice and the chicken broth. Salt to taste and serve.

"In our family, we have always found that eating together aids family solidarity. When we face serious problems, we have a way of saying, 'Well, let's have supper first.' We find that tensions ease and difficulties can be handled after we have gathered around the table and had a good meal."

—from *My Own Cook Book*
by Gladys Tabor

Humble Rice

(four servings)

Humble Rice is a thin layer of rice and vegetables that turns golden and crisp on top when baked. If you like crunchy rice, then this is your kind of recipe.

3 tablespoons olive oil
2 cups steamed long-grain
   white rice (see page 385)
2 medium tomatoes, cut into
   bite-size pieces

2 small zucchini, cut into bite
   size pieces
1 cup whole pitted black
   olives
Salt and pepper to taste

Preheat the oven to 350°F.

Spread 1½ tablespoons of the olive oil in the bottom of an 11 × 17-inch baking dish. Toss the rice, tomatoes, zucchini, and olives together and spread in a thin layer in the baking dish. Drizzle the remaining 1½ tablespoons of olive oil over the top. Add salt and pepper. Bake for 30 to 40 minutes.

Creamy Rice

(four servings)

You have to try Creamy Rice at least once. It's thick and thin at the same time, and it can be eaten both in winter and in summer. It's the all-purpose dish! Try it with a small dish of buttered green peas or a piece of braised fish. Put a little Creamy Rice aside, add some sugar and a few raisins, and there's your dessert.

4 cups water
1 teaspoon salt
½ cup long-grain white rice
2 tablespoons butter
3 tablespoons flour
4 cups milk

2 teaspoons lemon juice
½ teaspoon grated or ground nutmeg
1½ teaspoons grated lemon zest

Put the water and ½ teaspoon of the salt in a 5- or 6-quart pot. Bring the water to a boil and slowly pour in the rice; shake the pot to level the rice, and reduce heat to a simmer. Cook the rice (be sure the water is bubbling) for 15 minutes, stirring often. After 15 minutes, the rice should be soft and there should be some liquid left in the pot. Remove from the heat and set aside.

Put the butter and flour in a 5- or 6-quart pot. Stir to blend, and cook over medium heat, stirring constantly, for 2 or 3 minutes. Continue stirring, slowly add the milk, and cook for 3 or 4 minutes—the sauce will thicken slightly. Add the rice with its liquid, the lemon juice, nutmeg, and remaining ½ teaspoon salt. Stir to blend, taste for seasoning, and correct if needed. Cook, stirring often, for about 5 minutes. The sauce will thicken more after the addition of the rice and water. Stir in the lemon zest just before serving and serve hot.

Spanish Riso

(five servings)

Riso is the name given to the tiny cut of pasta that resembles grains of rice (*riso* means rice in Italian). There are several kinds of pasta of similar size and shape, including orzo (barley in Italian) and *seme di melone* (melon seeds); you can use them interchangeably.

1½ cups *riso* pasta
6 tablespoons olive oil
8 medium tomatoes, chopped
  (about 4 cups)
2 green bell peppers, seeded,
  deveined, and chopped into
  small dice (about 1½ cups)

½ cup chopped scallions
4 cloves garlic, finely chopped
Salt and pepper to taste
4 tablespoons chopped fresh
  basil
½ teaspoon Tabasco sauce

Bring a large pot of salted water to a boil. Add the *riso*, stir, and boil until the pasta is tender, about 10 minutes. Drain and set aside.

While the *riso* is cooking, put 3 tablespoons of the olive oil in a large sauté pan over medium heat. Add the tomatoes, bell peppers, scallions, and garlic. Cook the tomato mixture about 10 minutes, stirring often. Remove from the heat and stir in the cooked *riso*. Use a whisk to stir if the *riso* is in clumps. When the *riso* is separated, add salt and pepper, and stir in the fresh basil, Tabasco sauce, and the remaining 3 tablespoons of olive oil. Reheat if necessary and serve hot. This will keep several days in the refrigerator.

Marietta's Spaghetti

(four servings)

Marietta is the Italian daughter-in-law of my very old friend Comfort Scott, and this is her suppertime claim to fame. Tomato sauce made in this utterly simple way is quite delicious, and it has an appealing mixture of textures and flavors.

12 Roma or plum tomatoes (1¾ pounds), cut in half lengthwise
Salt and pepper to taste
3 cloves garlic, finely chopped
½ cup chopped parsley

½ cup olive oil
1 pound dried spaghetti
2 tablespoons butter, melted
½ cup fresh basil, torn into small pieces

Preheat the oven to 350°F.

Put the tomatoes, cut side up, in a 9 × 13-inch baking dish. Salt and pepper them lightly.

Mix together the garlic, ⅓ cup of the parsley, and 2 tablespoons of the olive oil in a small bowl. Pat the garlic mixture on the tomatoes and drizzle 2 more tablespoons of the olive oil over all. Bake, uncovered, for about 45 to 55 minutes, or until the tomatoes are mushy.

About 20 minutes before the tomatoes are done, put a large pot of salted water on for the spaghetti. When the water is boiling, add the spaghetti, stir, and after about 12 minutes, start testing every minute or so until the spaghetti is tender, but firm. Drain.

Mix together the remaining parsley and olive oil, the butter, and the basil in a large bowl. Add the tomatoes and spaghetti. Toss to mix well, and serve.

Iceberg Lettuce and Noodles

(six servings)

This is an exciting dish. It is the kind of recipe I like: a few plain ingredients; a little measuring, cooking, stirring, and tossing—briefly, in one pot; and a wholesome, unusual dish is brought forth. (It is *not* a cold pasta salad. One of the best things about this dish is the contrast between the cold crisp lettuce and the soft hot noodles.)

5 cups chopped iceberg lettuce (in large bite-size pieces)	4 medium zucchini, chopped into bite-size pieces (3 cups)
2 or 3 medium tomatoes, chopped, at room temperature	Optional: 2 cloves garlic, minced
Salt and pepper to taste	6 tablespoons olive oil
8 ounces dried egg noodles, ⅛ to ¼ inch wide	1½ ounces Parmesan cheese, freshly grated (½ cup)

Bring 4 quarts of water to a boil. Meanwhile, put the lettuce and tomatoes in the bottom of a 4- or 5-quart serving or mixing bowl, and lightly salt and pepper. Set aside.

Put the noodles into the boiling water and cook for about 5 minutes. Add the zucchini and cook until the noodles and the zucchini are tender, about 3 more minutes. Drain and heap on top of the lettuce mixture. If using the optional garlic, add it now, salt and pepper the noodles, and pour the olive oil on top. With your hands, quickly and lightly toss and mix. Sprinkle the cheese over and serve, or fill individual bowls and sprinkle the cheese evenly over each serving. Do the last mixing quickly and serve at once.

Pasta Shells, Mushrooms, and Brown Butter

(three or four servings)

This is a winter supper dish. The pasta shells are rich and filling, suffused with the flavors of beef broth, mushrooms, and nutlike browned butter. Crisp, toasted bread crumbs finish the dish perfectly.

½ pound large pasta shells
1 cup beef broth
½ pound fresh mushrooms,
 wiped clean and sliced
 (4 cups)

1 cup white bread crumbs
4 tablespoons (½ stick) butter
Salt and freshly ground
 pepper to taste

Bring a large pot of salted water to a boil. Stir in the pasta shells and cook 20 to 25 minutes, stirring occasionally, so they don't stick to the bottom of the pot. They should be tender, not undercooked.

Meanwhile, heat ½ cup of the beef broth in a large sauté pan. Add the mushrooms and cook over low heat, stirring constantly, until they darken a little and soften, about 3 to 5 minutes. Remove them to a large serving bowl and set aside.

Preheat the oven to 350°F.

Spread the bread crumbs on a cookie sheet and toast them, checking them often because they can burn in a minute or two. Stir so they get evenly toasted. When they are golden, remove and set aside; turn off the oven.

Place the mushrooms with their broth and the remaining ½ cup beef broth in a bowl. Add the cooked, drained pasta shells to the bowl. Place the bowl in the still-warm oven.

Heat the butter in a small saucepan over medium-high heat. It will foam up, subside, then quickly begin to brown. Watch carefully and as soon as it is nut brown, remove from the heat. Stir the browned butter into the pasta, tossing to coat all the shells. Taste and add salt and pepper as needed. Sprinkle the crumbs over the top and serve.

Macaroni and Cheese

(three servings)

A good macaroni and cheese dish should be moist and creamy, with a little bit of chewiness, and a noticeable cheese taste. You get it all with this dish. The recipe can easily be doubled.

1 cup dried elbow macaroni	2 tablespoons flour
Optional: 1 cup buttered bread crumbs to sprinkle over the top	1½ cups milk
	Salt to taste
2 tablespoons butter	3 ounces sharp Cheddar cheese, grated (about 1 cup)

Bring a pot of salted water to a boil and add the macaroni, stirring once or twice while cooking. Cook about 7 minutes, or until just tender, and drain, leaving a little water in the bottom of the pot. Toss the macaroni in the pot and loosely cover until the cheese sauce is made.

Preheat the oven to 350°F. Butter a 1-quart casserole. If using the optional bread crumbs, make them now: lightly brown the bread crumbs in a skillet with butter over medium-high heat; 1 tablespoon of butter is enough for 1 cup of crumbs.

Melt the 2 tablespoons butter in a sauté pan, add the flour, and stir constantly, cooking the *roux* (flour and butter) for about 2 minutes. Slowly add the milk, stirring constantly, add salt to taste, and continue to cook over medium heat, stirring until the sauce is thickened. Remove from the heat and stir in the grated cheese until it has melted and is smoothly blended. Pour the sauce over the macaroni and toss and mix well. Put the pasta and sauce into the casserole, sprinkle the bread crumbs over the top, if desired, and bake for about 30 minutes, or until lightly golden on top. Don't overbake or the macaroni will dry out.

Curried Macaroni

(six servings)

A pleasing dish that looks Indian to me, with its dramatic colors of orange curry and bright green cilantro. Accompany this with dark bread and a mild, white cheese, and Wirtabel's Melon Chutney (see page 508).

2 cups dried elbow macaroni	4 teaspoons curry powder
2 tablespoons butter	Salt and pepper to taste
2 tablespoons flour	½ cup cilantro leaves
2 cups milk	

In a large pot, bring 6 quarts of salted water to a boil. Add the macaroni and cook until it is just barely soft, about 10 minutes. Drain the macaroni and put it in a bowl.

Melt the butter in a medium-size saucepan over medium heat. Add the flour, stirring constantly until thoroughly blended. Slowly add the milk and continue to stir while the sauce cooks. Stir until it is thickened, about 2 or 3 minutes. Add the curry powder and salt and pepper to taste. Pour the sauce over the macaroni and mix together. Stir in the cilantro leaves and serve.

Custard Sandwich

(four servings)

This dish can't fail as long as it sits at least six hours before you bake it. Prepare it the night before or in the morning. It will puff and turn golden brown on top while baking. It is a rich custard, delicate but filling. Serve with small plates of salad and Pineapple Blizzard (see page 557) for dessert.

6 slices bread, buttered
Salt and pepper to taste
4½ ounces sharp Cheddar,
   Gouda, Provolone, Monterey
   Jack, or any other melting
   cheese, grated (1½ cups)

1½ cups milk
6 eggs, slightly beaten

Arrange the slices of bread in a single layer in a shallow, buttered baking dish. Sprinkle lightly with salt and pepper. Sprinkle the grated cheese evenly over the bread. Put the milk and eggs in a bowl, and stir until blended. Pour the milk mixture over the bread and cheese. Cover and refrigerate at least 6 hours, or overnight.

As the dish will be chilled when you are ready to bake it, start it in a cold oven, then immediately turn the heat on to 350°F. Bake for about 1 hour, or until the bread custard is puffy and lightly golden.

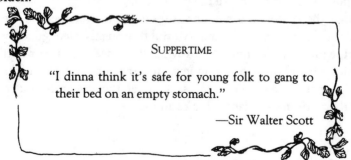

SUPPERTIME

"I dinna think it's safe for young folk to gang to their bed on an empty stomach."

—Sir Walter Scott

Frieda and Elinor's Onion Pie

(eight to ten servings)

If you are ever entertaining a concert artist after a recital, this is your recipe! Elinor got it from a Swiss friend, Frieda, and served it at late-night suppers for community concert guests who played in her Idaho town. This pie is just an onion quiche by another name, transformed by the flavor of tiny caraway seeds.

4 tablespoons (½ stick) butter
8 medium onions, thinly sliced
  and lightly salted
3 eggs
½ cup flour
1 teaspoon salt
½ teaspoon freshly ground
  pepper

1 teaspoon caraway seeds
2 cups half-and-half (half milk
  and half cream)
10-inch pie shell, prebaked 10
  minutes

Preheat the oven to 350°F.

Melt the butter in a large skillet, add the onions, and cook over medium heat for about 15 minutes, or until quite brown. In a large bowl, lightly beat the eggs, then add the flour, salt, pepper, caraway seeds, and half-and-half, and mix well. Mix in the onions, and pour the mixture into the pie shell. Bake for 35 to 45 minutes, or until the pie is just set. Serve warm or cold.

Papusas

(six papusas)

In El Salvador, vendors everywhere sell a street food called *papusas*. They look like slightly thick tortillas, about three inches in diameter. Hidden inside is a filling—either of cheese, as in this recipe, or spicy meat. They are always served with a finely chopped, vinegary coleslaw with fiery pepper and sometimes cilantro (see L.A. Slaw, page 518).

2 cups masa harina (see Note, page 367)
1½ cups warm water
1 tablespoon ground cumin, made from lightly toasted cumin seeds (*comino* in Spanish)

Salt and pepper to taste
6 ounces Ranchero cheese, or mild melting cheese such as Monterey Jack, grated (2 cups)
½ cup chopped cilantro

In a mixing bowl, mix together the masa harina, water, cumin, and ½ teaspoon salt and stir into a manageable dough. The dough should be soft but not sticky; add more flour if needed. If dough is dry and hard to form, add more water. To make 3-inch round *papusas*, put about ½ cup of the dough in your hand for each *papusa*. Roll into a ball and flatten in your hand. Put ⅓ cup cheese, 1 teaspoon cilantro, and salt and pepper to taste in the center. Work the edges up over the filling and again form a ball, completely enclosing the filling. This takes only a few seconds. Flatten each ball to about ¼ inch or less and cook the *papusas* on a hot, lightly oiled griddle for about 3 minutes per side, or until both sides are lightly browned. Serve warm.

Green Chile Pie

(one 9-inch pie)

This is a recipe that makes one of the best all-around supper dishes I can think of. Instead of a pastry crust, the chilis form the shell holding the filling. It is fast to make, and it fits anywhere, anytime.

6 or 7 California or Anaheim chile peppers (see Note and roasting instructions, page 443), peeled, split, and seeded; or about 10 ounces canned roasted whole green chile peppers
3½ ounces fontina or any mild soft white cheese, grated (1¼ cups)

4 eggs
2 cups light cream (or 1½ cups milk)
½ teaspoon salt
Pepper to taste
¼ cup whole cilantro leaves, stems removed

Preheat the oven to 425°F.

Butter the bottom of a 9-inch pie pan. Line the buttered pie pan with the split chiles, insides up, so that they cover the bottom and sides of the pan. Sprinkle the cheese evenly over the chiles.

Break the eggs into a bowl and lightly beat with a whisk until they are broken and blended. Add the cream and the salt and pepper. Mix well. Pour the custard over the cheese.

Bake for 15 minutes at 425°F, then lower the heat to 325°F. Bake for 20 to 30 minutes more, or until the custard seems set. If the center trembles a bit, remove from the oven (the custard continues to cook a little). Don't overcook: a knife inserted halfway from the center should come out clean when the pie is done. Put lots of cilantro on top. Serve hot or cold with warm tortillas (see page 443).

Potato and Pepper Frittata

(four servings)

I'm not crazy about frittatas because they often taste too much like overcooked cold eggs. This one is different. All its flavors come together somehow without that excessive eggy taste. And it looks pretty, with bright green strips of pepper embedded in its crisp golden top.

4 tablespoons olive oil
1 medium potato, peeled, quartered, and sliced ¼ inch thick
1 green bell pepper, seeded, deveined, and sliced in strips
1 medium onion, halved and sliced
1 clove garlic, finely chopped
6 eggs
Salt and pepper to taste

In a 10- to 12-inch skillet, put 2 tablespoons of the olive oil. Add the potato and cook over medium heat until it is tender and browned, about 10 to 15 minutes. Remove to a plate and set aside.

Put the remaining olive oil in the skillet over medium heat, add the pepper and onion and cook until soft, about 10 minutes. Stir in the potato and garlic. Put the eggs in a bowl and beat lightly, just until yolks and whites are blended. Add salt and pepper and pour over the vegetable mixture. Reduce the heat to low, cover the skillet, and cook for 8 to 10 minutes, or until the top looks set. Check the frittata after about 7 minutes—overcooking will make the eggs too dry. Cut the frittata into wedges and serve right away with the golden bottom side up.

Tomato Rarebit

(four servings)

Tomato Rarebit is a simple, old-fashioned one-pan supper dish. Serve with some extra toast and Tiny Herb Salads (see page 520).

2 medium tomatoes, finely chopped	2 eggs, slightly beaten
¼ teaspoon baking soda	1 teaspoon dry mustard
2 tablespoons butter	¼ to ½ teaspoon cayenne
2 tablespoons flour	pepper
1 cup milk, heated	Salt to taste
5 ounces Cheddar cheese, grated (1½ cups)	8 slices toast

Mix together the chopped tomatoes and the baking soda and set aside. Melt the butter in a saucepan, stir in the flour, and cook for about 2 to 3 minutes, stirring constantly. Slowly pour in the heated milk and stir until the mixture is smooth and thick.

Add the tomatoes, cheese, eggs, mustard, cayenne pepper, and salt. Cook over very low heat, stirring until the cheese melts and the mixture is smooth and well blended. Serve hot over the toast.

HAVING SUPPER OUT

"I went into the Parker House one night about midnight, and I saw four doctors there eating lobster salad, and deviled crab, and washing it down with champagne, and I made up my mind that the doctors needn't talk to me any more about what was wholesome. I was going for what was *good*. And there ain't anything better for supper than Welsh rabbit in *this* world."

—William Dean Howells, 1882

Linda Sue's Tomato Stew

(four servings)

My friend Linda Sue told me that when she was growing up her Aunt Fanny Scott would make her this tomato stew whenever Linda Sue was feeling blue.

3 slices smoky-style bacon, diced
1 red onion, chopped
4 cups stewed tomatoes; or about 8 fresh tomatoes, chopped
1 teaspoon sugar

Salt and pepper to taste
½ teaspoon Tabasco sauce, or to taste
4 or 5 biscuits, broken into large pieces; or 4 slices bread, torn into large pieces

Heat a Dutch oven, or other heavy-bottomed pot, and add the bacon and onion. Cook over medium-low heat, stirring often, until the onion is soft and the bacon is slightly browned. Add the tomatoes, sugar, salt and pepper, and Tabasco. Cook for 10 minutes, stirring often. Add the broken biscuits and cook 2 or 3 minutes more. Serve hot, but this is good served cold, too.

Bread and Bacon Pancake

(one thin 10-inch pancake, or four servings)

This makes a crunchy pancake with a robust smoky taste. It would be good with strong-flavored green vegetables such as spinach with garlic, mustard greens, or curly endive or chicory in garlic vinaigrette.

6 slices white bread, cut into ½-inch cubes (6 cups in all)
4 teaspoons cider vinegar
1 cup water

4 slices smoky-style bacon, cut into small dice
Salt and pepper to taste

Put the bread cubes in a bowl. Mix the vinegar with the water and sprinkle evenly over the bread cubes. Gently toss to mix well. Let the cubes stand a couple of hours.

Put the diced bacon in a 10-inch skillet. Cook a minute or two over medium-low heat, stirring often (you should have about ¼ cup fat; if not, add 1 tablespoon or so of vegetable oil). Sprinkle the bread cubes on top of the bacon. Using a spatula, press the bread cubes down, and salt and pepper liberally. Turn the heat to simmer and let the pancake slowly brown and crisp on the bottom. After 10 to 15 minutes, gently lift the edge of the pancake with the spatula to see that it is not cooking too rapidly and burning.

When the pancake is a deep golden color, cut down the center and turn over each half. Continue to cook until the other side is crisp and golden. Remove to a platter, cut to make 4 wedges, and serve hot.

EXPATRIATE SUPPERS

"When in 1908 I went to live with Gertrude Stein at the rue de Fleurus she said we would have American food for Sunday-evening supper, she had had enough of French and Italian cooking . . . So I commenced to cook the simple dishes I had eaten in the homes of the San Joaquin Valley in California—fricasseed chicken, corn bread, apple and lemon pie . . . "

—from *The Alice B. Toklas Cookbook*

Supper Breads

Hamburger Buns

Rye Crackers

Lemon Crackers

Lil's Ice-Water Crackers

Garlic Rolls

Popovers

Crusty Popovers

Sharp Cheddar Biscuits

Brown Bread Muffins

Buttermilk Cornbread

Irish Soda Bread

Date-Nut Bread

Gingerbread or Gingercake

You may be a born-to-bake person who has never given it a try. Anyone can bake good things at home. Baking is a different experience from cooking. Stir a few mundane ingredients together, pop the batter or dough into the oven, and as if by sleight of hand, what went into the oven is transformed into something golden, lofty, and usually delicious.

To be confident when you begin baking, you need to have good recipes. Recipes vary a lot, and some produce better results than others. The best way to get a good baking book is to ask a friend who bakes a lot, or the local food editor on your newspaper, or someone in town who runs a cooking school. Also buy an inexpensive oven thermometer and double-check the temperature of your oven. Always use a kitchen timer when baking: it is very easy to become distracted at home and let baking things burn.

The recipes in this chapter are mostly for breads you can't buy in stores, including some things one doesn't generally think of as breads. For example, there are great Popovers, an almost forgotten supper treat (see page 480); homemade Rye Crackers (see page 475); and Gingerbread with a split personality—it can be a bread with roasted spareribs, or a cake (see page 488). And there are recipes to transform the bread you *do* buy in stores: the amazing Lil's Ice-

Water Crackers (see page 478) and magic Garlic Rolls (see page 479)—the danger with these is that people will devour them and forget to eat anything else!

Hamburger Buns

(makes sixteen 3½-inch buns)

This recipe makes the world's best hamburger buns—they stay together so fillings aren't falling all over the place, and yet they are moist and tender. Wrapped carefully, these freeze well. Use them within two months.

1½ cups warm water	3 tablespoons sugar
⅔ cup instant nonfat dry milk	2 packages dry yeast
⅓ cup lard or vegetable shortening	1 egg
1½ teaspoons salt	About 5½ cups all-purpose flour

Put the water, dry milk, lard, salt, and sugar in a mixing bowl and stir to blend. Sprinkle the yeast over the mixture, stir, then let stand to dissolve for a couple of minutes. Add the egg and 2 cups of the flour. Beat vigorously until thoroughly blended and smooth. Add enough of the remaining flour to make a manageable dough. Turn out onto a lightly floured surface and knead for a minute. Let rest for 10 minutes.

Add enough additional flour so that the dough is not sticky, and resume kneading until smooth and elastic. Place the dough in a large greased bowl, cover, and let rise until it is double in bulk.

Grease some baking sheets. Punch the dough down and divide in half, then cut each half into 8 equal pieces. Roll each piece between your palms into a smooth ball and place about 3 inches apart on the baking sheets. Pressing down with the palm of your hand, flatten each ball into a circle about 3 inches in diameter. Cover lightly and let rise for about 45 minutes, or until double in bulk.

Preheat the oven to 425°F.

Bake the buns for 20 to 25 minutes, or until lightly browned. Remove from the baking sheets and cool on racks.

Rye Crackers

(about forty 2½-inch squares)

Homemade rye crackers are so much better than the store-bought variety. They're coarser and crunchier, with a hardy, rustic taste. Nothing could be simpler to make, and, stored in an airtight container, they keep almost indefinitely.

1½ cups all-purpose flour	⅔ cup milk, plus a bit more
½ cup rye flour	if needed
½ teaspoon salt	2 teaspoons kosher salt
2 tablespoons cold butter	

Preheat the oven to 425°F.

Put the flours and salt in a large mixing bowl and stir to blend with a fork. Cut the butter into small bits and add to the flour mixture. Use your fingertips or a pastry blender to rub or cut the butter into the flour. The mixture should look like coarse meal. Slowly add the milk, stirring with a fork, until the dough forms a rough ball and pulls away from the side of the bowl. If the dough seems dry, add a few drops more milk; it should be soft and pliable, not wet and sticky.

Divide the dough in half and shape each piece into a rough

square with your hands. Lightly dust a board with flour and roll out the first piece into about a 14-inch square—the thickness should be less than ½ inch. Trim the edges so they are neat. Roll the dough up on the rolling pin and unroll onto an ungreased baking sheet. Use a sharp knife to score the dough into 2½-inch squares, cutting almost through so the finished crackers will break apart in neat squares. With a fork, prick each square in 3 places. Sprinkle 1 teaspoon of the kosher salt evenly over the dough. Bake for 5 or 6 minutes, or until the edges are nicely browned. Slide off the baking sheet and cool. Break apart.

Meanwhile, roll out the remaining rough square of dough, following the directions above, and bake. Store the crackers in an airtight container.

Lemon Crackers

(seventy-two 2-inch square crackers)

Before I'd ever seen—let alone tasted—a lemon cracker, I felt the need for one. These go well with many things: salads, vegetable soups, and fish dishes such as Fillet of Sole with Fresh Bread Crumbs (see page 383) or Cioppino (see page 374).

2 cups all-purpose flour	4 tablespoons (½ stick)
1½ tablespoons sugar	butter
½ teaspoon salt	⅔ cup milk, plus a few
3 tablespoons finely grated	drops more if needed
lemon peel	1 tablespoon kosher salt

Preheat the oven to 325°F.

In a large mixing bowl, mix together the flour, sugar, salt, and 1½ tablespoons of the lemon peel. With a pastry blender, cut in the butter until the mixture resembles fine crumbs. With a fork, mix the milk into the flour mixture until a ball of dough is formed. If there are a few dry crumbs, add a little more milk, a few drops at a time, until all of the dough is moistened.

Divide the dough in half. On a lightly floured board, form half of the dough into a 4-inch square. Roll into a 12-inch square, making sure to flour the board and rolling pin as needed to prevent sticking. The finished dough should be very thin, no more than $\frac{1}{8}$ inch thick. Transfer the dough to an ungreased cookie sheet by placing the sheet alongside the dough, then gently lifting the dough onto the sheet. With a knife, score the dough into 2-inch squares, then with a fork prick each dough square in 3 places, poking all the way through to the cookie sheet. Mix together the kosher salt and remaining lemon peel. Sprinkle half of this lemon salt over the square and press lightly into the dough. Bake for 15 minutes, or until an even golden brown. Remove from the oven and turn the cracker over. Return to the oven and bake for an additional 5 to 6 minutes, or until lightly golden brown on the second side. When the cracker is done, remove from the oven and gently break into pieces along the scored lines.

Repeat the procedure with the remaining dough. Cool the crackers completely and store in an airtight container.

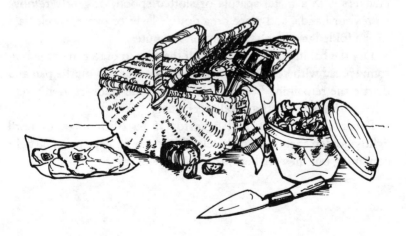

Lil's Ice-Water Crackers

(two dozen crackers)

This unlikely recipe was given to me a long time ago in Los Angeles. It turns ordinary saltines into crunchy, buttery crackers. They are worth the little trouble they take and eating one invites you to eat a hundred. Try Lil's Ice-Water Crackers with Chicken Custard in Broth (see page 376) or Joyce McGillis's Creamy Corn Soup (see page 366).

24 plain saltine crackers	½ cup (1 stick) butter, melted
4 cups ice water	Optional: 1 teaspoon salt

Preheat the oven to 475°F.

Lay the crackers in a single layer in a 10 × 15 × ¾-inch baking pan. (A pan this size will hold 35 crackers, but use only 24 because they swell and expand when soaked in ice water.) Pour the ice water over them and let stand for about 5 minutes. Carefully remove the crackers with a metal spatula or slotted spoon, or gently remove with your hands, and place on a double layer of paper towels (laid over a folded tea towel) to drain for 5 minutes.

Dry the baking pan and pour half the melted butter over the bottom; spread with your fingers. Arrange the crackers on the pan and drizzle the remaining butter over them. If the crackers aren't very salty, sprinkle the optional salt over them.

Put in the hot oven and bake for 15 to 20 minutes, or until lightly golden. Serve immediately. They can be kept in an airtight container, but they are best just out of the oven.

Garlic Rolls

(eight rolls)

These garlic rolls are a thrill. When you read this recipe you'll think "garlic bread," and feel like you know what Garlic Rolls are all about. You don't. This is a whole different kind of experience. You can even justify your indulgence in these since you'll skip using butter entirely. The Italians take credit for this invention, and so do the Ukrainians.

½ teaspoon kosher salt	¼ cup vegetable oil
1 tablespoon water	8 heated soft, white dinner
1 teaspoon finely chopped garlic	rolls, American homemade-type, like Parker House or
2 teaspoons finely chopped parsley	cloverleaf

In a small bowl, stir the salt into the water and let stand for 5 minutes until the salt is dissolved; then stir again. Add the garlic, parsley, and oil and mix well. Put the heated rolls close together in a shallow dish and drizzle the flavored oil evenly over them. Serve immediately.

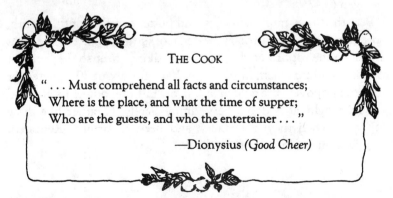

THE COOK

" . . . Must comprehend all facts and circumstances;
Where is the place, and what the time of supper;
Who are the guests, and who the entertainer . . . "

—Dionysius (*Good Cheer*)

Popovers

(about seven popovers)

The glory of popovers is their incredible size, crusty outsides, and creamy, tender, and almost hollow insides just waiting for butter and a spoonful of strawberry jam. But I had about given up on making them over the last few years because they kept turning out to be sullen little muffins, pop-unders. I had forgotten that popovers rise highest when they get a forceful amount of heat quickly, and I had been using muffin tins instead of separate containers like ovenproof Pyrex glass baking cups, which work perfectly. I had a thrill when I opened the oven door and my popovers were once again giant golden balloons. Popovers are meant to go with chicken, roasts, salads, and soups; they don't belong with spaghetti, curries, or chili. For perfect popovers, see the popover principles at the end of the recipe.

1½ cups all-purpose flour	3 eggs
1½ cups milk	3 tablespoons butter, melted
1 teaspoon salt	

Grease Pyrex glass ¾-cup-size cups (I use butter or Pam). Preheat the oven to 425°F.

Beat the flour, milk, salt, eggs, and butter together until smooth. I use a blender, but a rotary beater works fine, too. Fill the cups almost to the top. Place the cups on a baking sheet so they are not touching and put them in the oven. Bake for about 30 minutes, or until the popovers are golden and light. Lift one out of its cup and if it feels light, it is done. Serve immediately. (I rather like these popovers when they have fallen and been rewarmed. Reheated, they get some of their puffiness back.)

POPOVER PRINCIPLES

1. Individual baking cups, such as Pyrex, work the best.

2. Fill the cups almost to the top with batter.

3. Always bake popovers in the bottom third of the oven.

4. Spear the popovers with a very sharp knife to release the steam from inside right after they are taken out of the oven.

5. Serve them immediately from the oven as popovers do fall slowly as they cool.

Crusty Popovers

(twelve popovers)

A little sleight of hand in the kitchen: remarkable that this cream puff dough gives results so similar to popover batter. However, these Crusty Popovers are guaranteed to hold their shape and not collapse. They can do double duty, either as popovers with savory foods or as cream puff shells for dessert fillings. Be sure they bake long enough; their hollow centers won't be creamy like the insides of popovers. Serve immediately.

1 cup water
½ cup (1 stick) butter
1 cup all-purpose flour

1 teaspoon salt
5 eggs

Preheat the oven to 400°F.

In a medium-size saucepan, bring the water and butter to a boil over medium-high heat. When the butter is melted and the mixture is boiling, add the flour all at once and briskly stir until the mixture forms a ball and pulls away from the side of the pan. Cook, stirring, about 2 to 3 minutes. Remove the pan from the heat and let cool for about 5 minutes, stirring occasionally. The temperature should be 140°F. Add the eggs, one at a time, briskly beating until each egg is completely blended into the dough. Grease twelve ¾-cup Pyrex dishes and place a mound of the dough the size of a golf ball in each dish. Place the dishes on a cookie sheet and bake for 35 minutes, or until the popovers are deep golden and sound hollow when tapped. Remove from the cups and serve immediately, unless you are filling them to serve as dessert.

Sharp Cheddar Biscuits

(sixteen biscuits)

Little savory cheese biscuits flecked with Cheddar, fresh and warm from the oven, are just what you need with some of the cold supper salads in this book like Green Rose Salad (see page 340), and Waldorf Salad (see page 344). Certainly they are the right biscuit with Mustard Green Soup (see page 360).

2 cups all-purpose flour
½ teaspoon salt
4 teaspoons baking powder
1 tablespoon sugar
3 ounces sharp Cheddar
   cheese, grated (1 cup)

½ cup vegetable shortening,
   chilled
⅔ cup milk

Preheat the oven to 425°F.

In a mixing bowl, mix together the flour, salt, baking powder, sugar, and cheese. Using a pastry blender or two knives, cut the vegetable shortening into the flour mixture until it resembles coarse meal. Add the milk all at once and stir with a fork until the dry ingredients are moistened.

Turn the dough out on a lightly floured board and knead 10 times. Pat the dough until it is $\frac{1}{2}$ inch thick and cut into rounds, using a 2-inch cutter. Pat the scraps into a square and recut. Arrange the rounds on an ungreased cookie sheet so that the edges of the rounds touch. Bake 15 to 20 minutes, or until the tops are lightly browned. Serve immediately.

Brown Bread Muffins

(eighteen muffins)

The combination of cornmeal, two kinds of flour, and raisins makes brown bread muffins moist, flavorful, and nutritious. They are accommodating to lots of different foods—the New England tradition is to eat them with Boston Baked Beans (see page 441)—or try them with Ham and Bean Soup (see page 357) or Tri-Tip Pot Roast (see page 421). For an early spring supper, serve Asparagus Salad (see page 342) and soft white cheese with them.

1 cup all-purpose flour	¾ cup dark molasses
1 cup whole wheat flour	4 tablespoons cider vinegar
1 cup yellow cornmeal	1¼ cups milk
1½ teaspoons baking soda	2 tablespoons butter, melted
1½ teaspoons salt	1 cup raisins

Preheat the oven to 400°F. Grease 18 muffin tins.

Put the all-purpose flour, whole wheat flour, yellow cornmeal, baking soda, and salt in a large mixing bowl. Stir the dry ingredients with a fork to mix and blend well. Add the molasses,vinegar, milk, and butter, and stir briskly to blend. Stir in the raisins. Fill the muffin tins three-quarters full with the batter.

Bake for about 12 minutes, or until a straw inserted into the center of a muffin comes out clean. Remove from the oven and serve warm. These freeze well.

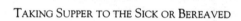

TAKING SUPPER TO THE SICK OR BEREAVED

The old custom of taking homemade food to a sick friend or a bereaved family is almost forgotten today. Sympathy or get-well cards, flowers, and house plants have replaced chicken noodle soup. Cards and flowers are consoling, but food is the best gift of all. When there has been a death in the family the last thing anyone cares to think about is food, but when friends and relatives arrive to pay their respects, being able to offer some cold sliced ham and a salad or a plate of cookies and a cup of coffee or tea gives one the feeling that life can go on as usual.

The most appropriate food to take to a bereaved family is good, plain food that keeps well and requires little fuss to serve. I think it is hard to beat a baked ham, the makings of a salad, a loaf of homemade bread, some Applesauce (see page 509), and Parker Brownies (see page 541).

When visiting a sick friend, my old standbys are Rich Chicken Noodle Soup (see page 377) and Baked Vanilla Custard (see page 553). Chicken noodle soup has well-known curative powers, and plain custards almost always seem nourishing and digestible, even to someone who is very ill.

Buttermilk Cornbread

(six servings)

There are many types of cornbread. This one is fine textured and slightly buttermilk sour, with a very thin layer of custard formed by the milk poured over it just before it's baked.

2 tablespoons butter	1 teaspoon baking soda
$\frac{1}{2}$ cup all-purpose flour	2 eggs
$1\frac{1}{4}$ cups yellow cornmeal	2 cups buttermilk
1 teaspoon salt	$1\frac{1}{2}$ cups milk

Preheat the oven to 350°F.

Put the butter in a $8 \times 8 \times 2$-inch square baking dish. Put the dish in the oven and let the butter melt. Remove the dish from the oven and tilt the dish so the butter coats the sides and bottom.

Sift the flour, cornmeal, salt, and baking soda into a mixing bowl. Beat the eggs until they have a little foam on top, and add to the dry ingredients. Add the buttermilk and 1 cup of the milk, and stir briskly until well blended.

Pour the batter into the baking dish and, without stirring, pour the remaining $\frac{1}{2}$ cup of milk in the center of the batter. This will create a thin white layer of custard. Bake for about 40 to 50 minutes, or until a straw comes out clean when inserted in the center. Serve warm.

Irish Soda Bread

(one 9-inch round loaf)

With Irish Soda Bread you don't have to wait around for risings and proofings—you just stir it up and put it in the oven. When it comes out it looks as if it just arrived from the Irish countryside: rustic and homey, brown whole wheat flecked with creamy-colored oats. In theory you should wait for it to cool before you slice it, but I always weaken and slice it while it's warm, even though it crumbles.

2½ cups milk
2 tablespoons white vinegar
4 cups whole wheat flour
1 cup all-purpose white flour

½ cup rolled oats
1 teaspoon baking soda
2 teaspoons salt

Preheat the oven to 375°F.

Put the milk in a small bowl. Stir in the vinegar and mix to make the milk sour; set aside. In a large mixing bowl, mix together the whole wheat flour, white flour, oats, baking soda, and salt. Add the soured milk to the flour mixture and stir until all the dry ingredients are moistened. Place the dough on a floured board and lightly knead about 10 times, until the dough is smooth.

Form the dough into a 9-inch round loaf, place it on a cookie sheet, and with a sharp knife, mark the top of the loaf with an X, cutting into the dough about ⅛ inch deep. Bake for 50 to 60 minutes, or until the bread is brown and sounds hollow when tapped. Cool and serve.

Date-Nut Bread

(one 8½ × 4½ × 3-inch loaf)

This is the best-tasting of all the date-nut breads, and I've made a lot of them. It has good texture, it's more moist, it's more flavorful, and the balance of sweetness is just right. Date-nut bread used to be the most popular of the sweet breads, or tea breads. Sliced very thin and spread with cream cheese or sweet butter, it was served in all the tearooms. The recipe came to me from Mary Jo Thompson, who used to own and run a little country inn in Fiddletown, California.

1 cup coarsely chopped pitted dates	1 cup granulated sugar
1½ teaspoons baking soda	1½ cups all-purpose flour
3 tablespoons butter	½ teaspoon salt
¾ cup boiling water	1 teaspoon vanilla
2 eggs	1 cup coarsely chopped walnuts

Lightly mix together the dates and the baking soda, and add the butter. Mix in the boiling water, and let stand for 20 minutes.

Preheat the oven to 325°F. Butter the loaf pan.

In another bowl, beat the eggs lightly with a fork, and add the sugar, flour, salt, and vanilla, and mix well. Add the walnuts and then the date mixture and stir until just blended. Pour into the buttered loaf pan and bake for 40 to 50 minutes; the bread is done when a toothpick comes out clean. Be careful not to overbake. Let cool and spread thin slices with cream cheese.

Gingerbread or Gingercake

(six servings)

Years ago gingerbread was often served as bread with supper, and I wish this old custom could be revived. Ham and Bean Soup (see page 357) and gingerbread make a great combination, and you've missed something if you've never had Black Pepper Ribs (see page 432)with gingerbread hot from the oven. For a light supper, serve warm gingerbread with Applesauce (see page 509) and sharp Cheddar cheese, as the English do; for a lively one, try gingerbread with curried dishes such as kedgeree or Laguna Beach Shrimp Curry (see page 388). With four more tablespoons of sugar added, the flavors are more dessertlike, and the gingerbread becomes Gingercake.

½ cup (1 stick) butter, room temperature	½ teaspoon salt
	1 teaspoon baking soda
¾ cup sugar	1 tablespoon ground ginger
1 egg	1 teaspoon cinnamon
½ cup molasses	½ teaspoon ground cloves
2 cups all-purpose flour	1 cup boiling water

Preheat the oven to 350°F. Butter and lightly flour a 7 × 11-inch baking dish.

Put the butter and sugar in a mixing bowl and beat until creamy and blended. Add the egg and molasses and mix well. Add the flour, salt, baking soda, ginger, cinnamon, and cloves, and beat until well blended. Stir in the boiling water and quickly pour into the baking dish. Bake for 35 to 40 minutes, or until a toothpick comes out clean when inserted in the center of the cake, or the sides of the cake shrink a little around the edge of the baking dish. Serve warm.

Fringe Dishes

Sauces, Salsas, and Spreads

Tartar Sauce

Green Sauce

Red Salsa

Apple Butter

Swiss Cheese Spread

Beet Marmalade

Port Wine Jelly

Pickles and Relishes

Pike's Perfect Pickles

Pickled Peppers

Chow Chow

Real Relish

Corn Relish

Fire and Ice Relish

Rhubarb-Onion Relish

Piccalilli

Wirtabel's Melon Chutney

Side Dishes, Slaws, and Small Salads

Applesauce

Fried Apple Rings

Baby Peas and Iceberg Lettuce

Blanche's Cabbage with Bacon

Carrots with Fresh Mint

Cornmeal-Fried Tomatillos

Jasmine Rice

Orzo with Fresh Dill

Deviled Eggs

Coleslaw

L.A. Slaw

Turnip Slaw

Tiny Herb Salads

Crouton Salad

Cucumber Salad

Lettuce in Cream

Wedge of Iceberg with Thick
    Creamy Dressing

Mustard Celery Salad

Relish Salad

Grapefruit, Black Olive, and Mint
    Salad

Persimmon-Pear Salad

Fringe dishes are exciting. Sometimes they are thought to be superfluous, but they are very important. They are the small dishes that surround the main supper dish—condiments, relishes, pickles, preserves, small salads, sauces, and salsas. They are hospitable gifts from the cook which you may choose to eat or ignore. Fringe dishes give you a chance to balance the flavors and texture of your food to suit your taste. Small but mighty, they prove how a little can do a lot: they do what the right jewelry does for an understated dress. Good examples of this would be a spoonful of Beet Marmalade (see page 498) and with Beef Salad with Sour Pickles (see page 352), or the Piccalilli (see page 507) with the American Meatloaf (see page 428). The Jasmine Rice (see page 515) and the Tiny Herb Salads (see page 520) are so brimming with flavor they will bowl you over.

I lament the loss of homemade condiments from the American table. Americans a hundred years ago understood that the niceties of a well-set table included lots more than salt and pepper to entice the appetite. Their tablecloths were almost hidden by small dishes filled with condiments and relishes, and their cellars were generously stacked with quarts of pickles, chow chow, and chutney.

We don't need cellars full of preserves, but a few jars made up in advance and kept on hand in your refrigerator will do wonders for your table. These recipes are for small amounts that are easy to prepare and that keep well when refrigerated.

Tartar Sauce

(one and one-half cups)

Tartar sauce is a lively sauce for fish, presumably named after the marauding nomads of Central Asia—perhaps because it, too, makes a rapid conquest. Tartar sauce is one of those things that people buy out of habit without stopping to think that they can make it in a jiff at home. It is a must on Oyster Buns (see page 394).

1 cup mayonnaise
2 tablespoons finely chopped
  scallions
½ cup finely chopped dill
  pickles

1½ teaspoons chopped capers
½ teaspoon cayenne pepper

In a bowl, put the mayonnaise, scallions, dill pickles, capers, and cayenne and stir until well mixed. Store in the refrigerator in a covered container.

Green Sauce

(about one cup)

This green sauce has a fine sparkle to it that makes it a great all-purpose sauce. Spoon some over cottage cheese, or over new potatoes, or serve it with cold meats. Thinned down with a little more oil, it can be used as a vinaigrette on salads.

½ cup olive oil
2 tablespoons water
1½ tablespoons cider vinegar
½ teaspoon kosher salt
Pepper to taste
1 teaspoon Dijon mustard

2 teaspoons cream-style horseradish
2 large cloves garlic
⅓ cup chopped parsley
2 scallions, including tender greens, chopped

Put the olive oil, water, vinegar, salt, and pepper in a food processor and process until well blended. Add the mustard, horseradish, garlic, parsley, and scallions and blend well. Store in an airtight jar in the refrigerator until needed.

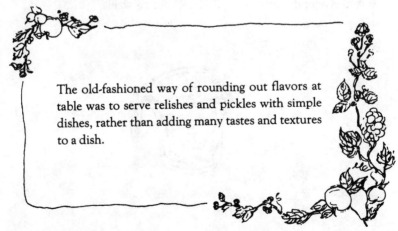

The old-fashioned way of rounding out flavors at table was to serve relishes and pickles with simple dishes, rather than adding many tastes and textures to a dish.

Red Salsa

(three cups)

Salsas have almost become a kitchen staple over the last several years. This is a moderately hot salsa that has a fresh, balanced flavor. You control the heat of this salsa by the amount of hot sauce or Tabasco you use. The Anaheim pepper is mild. Red Salsa is like a good relish: it can give sparkle to pastas, eggs, or soups (see Sharon's Lentil Salsa Soup, page 361).

6 medium very ripe tomatoes
1 Anaheim pepper (see Note, page 443), seeded and deveined
1 large onion
1½ cups loosely packed cilantro leaves

3 large cloves garlic, finely chopped
5 tablespoons lemon juice
1½ to 2 teaspoons hot sauce, such as Tabasco
1 teaspoon salt

Coarsely chop the tomatoes, pepper, onion, and cilantro in a food processor or by hand. Stir in the garlic, lemon juice, hot sauce, and salt. Refrigerate until needed. This keeps a week.

A VISION OF PLENTY

I have a favorite book, *The Country Kitchen*, by Della Lutes, published in 1935, that describes unforgettably the fringe dishes on her family's table at Christmastime in rural Michigan in the late 1800s: "A tumbler of wild grape jelly quivered upturned upon a small glass plate—wild grape because of the muskier tang. Pickled watermelon rind—translucent pink shading to opaque green—drenched in a luscious syrup of citron and lemon flavor reposed on a small dish shaped of two graceful hands . . . of alabaster white." The meal was simple by today's standards, but, she writes: "I have a vision of plenty, appetizingly prepared."

Apple Butter

(six cups)

Apple butter captures the essence of apple—it becomes thick, deeply flavored, and dark from its long, gentle cooking. It is wonderful spread on warm rolls or toast. Use the spices only if your apples are bland.

4 pounds apples, washed, cored, and cut into eighths	$\frac{1}{2}$ to $\frac{2}{3}$ cup sugar, to taste
$1\frac{1}{2}$ cups apple cider; or water; or a mixture of both	Optional: 2 teaspoons cinnamon, 1 teaspoon ground cloves, and $\frac{1}{2}$ teaspoon allspice
2 tablespoons lemon juice	

Put the apples, liquid, and lemon juice in a large enamel or stainless-steel pot. Bring to a boil, reduce the heat to simmer, and cook until the apples are tender and soft. Remove from the heat and purée until smooth, using either a food mill or a food processor. If your apples are flavorful, use no spice, or very little. If they have the blahs, add the cinnamon, clove, and allspice. Add the sugar and spice at this point and stir to mix well.

Return the puréed apples to the pot and cook over very low heat, stirring often, until the mixture is reduced to about half its volume; this will take about $1\frac{1}{2}$ hours. Test for doneness by placing a spoonful of apple butter on a plate: when it cools there should be no moisture around the rim of the fruit.

To preserve less than a month, spoon into clean jars, cover, and refrigerate when cool. For longer preserving, fill sterilized jars with the hot apple butter, leaving $\frac{1}{4}$-inch headspace, put on the lids and tighten, and process in a boiling-water canner for 10 minutes.

Swiss Cheese Spread

(two and one-half cups)

Never have I served this without someone saying, "I love it, what's in it? Will you give me the recipe?" Then they are astonished at how simple it is. This recipe makes a pint plus. That is a lot, but it has so many uses: spread it on toast and run under the broiler; or stir a spoonful into your soup—it is quite nice with clear chicken broth.

½ cup mayonnaise
6 ounces Swiss cheese, thinly
  grated (2 cups)

2 tablespoons finely chopped
  parsley

Mix the mayonnaise thoroughly with the Swiss cheese, using enough mayonnaise to make it spreadable. Put in a bowl just large enough to hold it, cover with plastic wrap, and refrigerate. When ready to serve, turn out onto a platter and mold into a mound, using your hands. Sprinkle with the parsley and place crackers around the edge.

Beet Marmalade

(about two cups)

Even those who normally resist beets will like this—their natural sweetness blends perfectly with the flavor of ginger. Serve with Tarragon Fish on Toast (see page 392), Laguna Beach Shrimp Curry (see page 388), or Tri-Tip Pot Roast (see page 421).

4 medium-large beets, cooked and peeled (see page 341)	1 large lemon
1½ cups sugar	2 tablespoons chopped fresh ginger

Put the beets in a food processor and process until coarsely chopped, or mash the beets by hand. Transfer the beets to a heavy-bottomed saucepan and stir in the sugar.

Cut, seed, and quarter the lemon. Put the pieces and the ginger into the food processor and process until finely chopped, or chop by hand. Add the lemon and ginger to the beet mixture and stir to blend. Cook over medium-low heat, stirring often, until the marmalade has thickened a little. This takes about 2 minutes—remember that the marmalade will get even thicker as it cools.

Put the hot marmalade into clean jars, cover, and refrigerate when cool. This will keep for a month. For longer preserving, fill sterilized jars with the hot mixture, leaving ¼-inch headspace. Put on the lids and tighten, and process in a boiling-water canner for 15 minutes.

Port Wine Jelly

(four and one-half cups)

There is something old and complex, musty and mysterious, about the flavors of port wine combined with rosemary that makes chicken or turkey taste better.

2 cups port wine
3 cups sugar
3 tablespoons lemon juice
2 teaspoons chopped fresh
   rosemary; or 1½ teaspoons
   dried rosemary

½ teaspoon salt
6 ounces liquid pectin

Put the wine, sugar, lemon juice, rosemary, and salt in a saucepan and bring to a boil, stirring until the sugar dissolves. Simmer for 2 minutes, then remove from the heat. Immediately stir in the pectin and strain the jelly into a large measuring cup that will make it easy to pour into four 1-cup jelly glasses. There will be an extra ½ cup left over: put it in a ramekin and use it that evening for supper. I put a sprig of fresh rosemary on top of the jelly when it has set. Cover with a lid and store in the refrigerator. Keeps well for a month.

Pike's Perfect Pickles

(eight cups)

Pike's Perfect Pickles have been a favorite of my old friends, the Edward Pike family, for thirty years. They are like the ideal glass of lemonade, with just enough acid and flavor and just enough sugar.

16 pickling cucumbers, about 4 to 5 inches, washed and thinly sliced

2 medium onions, thinly sliced

1 green bell pepper, seeded, deveined, and sliced into thin strips,

1 sweet red pepper, seeded deveined, and sliced into thin strips

Salt to taste

4 cups sugar

1½ teaspoons ground turmeric

½ teaspoon ground cloves

1 teaspoon celery seed

1 tablespoon mustard seed

1 quart cider vinegar

Put the sliced cucumbers, onions, and green and red pepper strips in a kettle. Sprinkle lightly with salt and toss so the salt is distributed. Cover the mixture with ice cubes and set aside, covered, for 3 hours.

Drain thoroughly. Stir together in a bowl the sugar, turmeric, cloves, celery seed, mustard seed, and vinegar and mix well. Pour over the cucumber mixture in the kettle. Bring just to a boil, stirring, and immediately remove from the heat.

Spoon the pickles into clean jars, pour the liquid over, and let cool. Cover and refrigerate. These are ready to eat at once. If long preservation is desired, fill sterilized jars with the hot pickles and liquid, leaving a ½-inch headspace at the top of each jar. Put on the lids and tighten, and process in a boiling-water bath for 10 minutes. Remove the jars from the kettle and cool.

Pickled Peppers

(two cups)

Pickled Peppers are a little tart and a little tangy with a roasted pepper taste. They are great with a Swiss cheese sandwich—or just about any other mild cheese. You can use any color pepper for this, as long as it's sweet and not fiery.

½ cup olive oil
2 pounds green bell pepper, or
   any sweet pepper, seeds and
   membranes removed and cut
   into quarters

½ cup dry sherry
2 tablespoons vinegar
Salt to taste
½ teaspoon lemon juice

Put the olive oil in a large skillet, lay the peppers in, skin side down, and cook slowly over medium-low heat until brown, about 10 minutes. Add the sherry, vinegar, and salt, cover, and cook 10 minutes more. Remove from the heat and let cool. Drain and reserve the peppers, putting only the olive oil mixture in a bowl, and add the lemon juice. Cut the peppers into ¼-inch strips and stir them into the olive oil mixture. Keep in the refrigerator until ready to use.

Chow Chow

(seven cups)

Chow chow was originally a Chinese sweetmeat made of orange peel, ginger, and other spices preserved in a thick syrup. Today chow chow is defined as any mixed vegetable pickle flavored with mustard or mustard seed. Chow chow has a flamboyant flavor that lights up roast chicken and lamb.

4 cups cauliflower flowerets ($\frac{1}{3}$ to $\frac{1}{2}$ head cauliflower)	1 large onion, chopped
2 cups coarsely chopped cabbage ($\frac{1}{8}$ to $\frac{1}{4}$ head cabbage)	3 teaspoons salt
	$\frac{1}{3}$ cup flour
	1 tablespoon dry mustard
1 cup cut-up cucumber (sliced $\frac{1}{4}$ inch thick, and cut into quarters)	1 teaspoon ground turmeric
	$1\frac{1}{2}$ cups sugar
	3 cups white vinegar
1 sweet red pepper, coarsely chopped	

Bring a large pot of salted water to a boil. Blanch the cauliflower, cabbage, cucumber, red pepper, and onion: Put the vegetables in a strainer, one kind at a time, and lower into the boiling water. Leave for about 5 seconds, remove, and drain. Put the vegetables into a large bowl.

Mix together the salt, flour, mustard, turmeric, sugar, and 1 cup of the vinegar in a small pan, and stir briskly until blended. Cook over low heat for a few minutes, stirring constantly, then add the remaining 2 cups of vinegar, and continue to cook until smooth and thick. Remove from the heat.

Fill clean jars with the vegetables and spoon the mustard mixture over them to cover. Put lids on the jars and refrigerate. Use within a month.

Real Relish

(four cups)

A relish that has withstood the test of time, from a recipe that's been around since at least the 1920s. It's a benchmark for basic relish. It's sweet and spicy, and the best relish for beef.

1 pound tomatoes, chopped	1 cup cider vinegar
1 medium onion, chopped	1 cup sugar
2 stalks celery, chopped	2 teaspoons mustard seed
1 green bell pepper, chopped	1 tablespoon pickling spice
Salt to taste, plus 1 teaspoon	

Put the tomatoes, onion, celery, and green pepper in a large bowl, lightly salt, and toss and mix until blended.

Put the vinegar, sugar, mustard seed, pickling spice, and the teaspoon salt in a saucepan and bring to a boil. Reduce the heat and let the pickling brine simmer for 2 or 3 minutes. Remove from the heat and strain the hot brine over the vegetable mixture. Stir, then put the relish into clean jars. Cover and refrigerate until needed.

Corn Relish

(six cups)

This relish is as corny as Kansas in August. Open a jar when you're serving Roast Chicken with Smothered Potatoes (see page 401), or use it when you're eating a mild dish that needs sprucing up.

4 cups corn kernels, fresh (about 6 ears) or frozen	2 teaspoons dry mustard
1½ green bell peppers, chopped	2 teaspoons ground turmeric
5 to 6 stalks of celery, chopped	2 teaspoons celery seed
2 medium onions, chopped	2½ cups white vinegar
1 cup sugar	¼ cup water

If you're using fresh corn, cut the kernels from the cob with a sharp knife. Mix together the corn kernels, bell peppers, celery, onions, sugar, mustard, turmeric, celery seed, vinegar, and water in a large pot and bring to a boil. Reduce the heat to simmer, and cook 15 minutes.

Put the hot corn relish into clean jars, cover, and when cool refrigerate. Will keep for a month. For longer preserving, fill sterilized jars with the hot mixture, leaving ½-inch headspace. Put on the lids and tighten, and process in a boiling-water canner for 10 minutes.

Fire and Ice Relish

(about five cups)

This relish was all the rage during the 1940s. Little dishes of Fire and Ice Relish kept dainty lunches company in tearooms all over California.

3 cups cherry tomatoes	$1\frac{1}{2}$ teaspoons mustard seed
1 large green bell pepper	4 teaspoons sugar
1 large red onion	$\frac{1}{8}$ teaspoon cayenne pepper
$\frac{1}{4}$ cup cider vinegar	$\frac{1}{2}$ teaspoon black pepper
$\frac{1}{2}$ teaspoon salt	$\frac{1}{4}$ cup water
$1\frac{1}{2}$ teaspoons celery seed	

Cut the cherry tomatoes in half, or, if they are large, into quarters, and put in a bowl. Seed and coarsely chop the bell pepper and add to the tomatoes. Finely chop the onion and add to the tomatoes.

Mix together the cider vinegar, salt, celery seed, mustard seed, sugar, cayenne pepper, black pepper, and water in a small saucepan and bring to a boil. Boil for 1 minute. Remove from the heat and immediately pour over the prepared vegetables. Cool, then cover and refrigerate at least 3 hours before serving. This is a fresh relish and will keep no more than a day or two.

Rhubarb-Onion Relish

(six cups)

Serve this relish cold, rather than at room temperature. It makes an agreeable contrast to a hot meat dish like Black Pepper Ribs (see page 432).

2 cups chopped rhubarb	2 cups light brown sugar
4 medium white onions, chopped (2 cups)	$\frac{1}{2}$ teaspoon ground cloves
1 cup vinegar	$\frac{1}{2}$ teaspoon allspice
1½ teaspoons salt	$\frac{1}{2}$ teaspoon cinnamon

Mix together the rhubarb, onions, vinegar, salt, brown sugar, cloves, allspice, and cinnamon in a large heavy-bottomed pot, bring to a boil, and simmer for 45 minutes, until the relish is quite thick.

Put the relish into clean jars, cover, and when cool refrigerate. For longer preserving, fill sterilized jars with the hot mixture, leaving ¼-inch headspace. Put on the lids and tighten, and process in a boiling-water canner for 15 minutes.

Piccalilli

(seven cups)

I have no idea how this East Indian relish got to New England, where it was traditionally served with Boston Baked Beans (see page 441), but the tradition is worth upholding.

1½ pounds firm unripe tomatoes, coarsely chopped (4 cups)
4 to 5 stalks celery, chopped
1 green bell pepper, chopped
1 sweet red pepper, chopped
2 cups chopped cauliflower (⅛ head cauliflower)
2 large yellow onions, chopped

5 cups cider vinegar
3 cups sugar
3 teaspoons celery seed
1½ tablespoons mustard seed
¾ teaspoon cinnamon
¾ teaspoon allspice
2 teaspoons salt, or to taste

Put the tomatoes, celery, peppers, cauliflower, and onions in a large kettle, add 2 cups of the vinegar, bring to a boil, and simmer for 1 minute. Drain well. In another pot, put the remaining 3 cups vinegar and the sugar, celery seed, mustard seed, cinnamon, allspice, and salt, bring to a boil, and simmer for 10 minutes.

Spoon the vegetables into jars, and pour the marinade over; cover and when cool refrigerate. For longer preserving, fill sterilized jars with the hot mixture, leaving ¼-inch headspace. Put on the lids and tighten, and process in a boiling-water canner for 15 minutes.

Wirtabel's Melon Chutney

(eight cups)

This is the chutney my friend Wirtabel's family made every year with the melons on their farm that didn't ripen properly. It is excellent, and it beats mango chutney by a mile, as well as being far less expensive to make.

12 cups fruit, peeled, seeded, and diced. Use about 6 cups melon, cantaloupe or honeydew (either ripe or unripe), cut into 1-inch cubes; the remaining fruit may be pear, apple, or peach
2 cups raisins (1 cup golden raisins and 1 cup dark raisins, mixed)

1 cup peeled chopped fresh ginger
4½ cups sugar
3 cups white vinegar
1 teaspoon whole allspice
½ teaspoon whole cloves
2 cinnamon sticks, each 2 inches long

Mix together the fruit, raisins, ginger, sugar, and vinegar in a large Dutch oven or kettle. Tie the allspice, cloves, and cinnamon sticks in a piece of cheesecloth. Use a hammer to smash the spices in the cheesecloth a couple of times to release more flavor during cooking. Add to the kettle.

Bring the mixture to a boil, stirring occasionally. Reduce heat to simmer, and cook for about 2 hours, or until thickened and darker. Taste occasionally to check on the need for more spices or sugar or salt. When thick and darker, remove from the heat and discard the spice bag.

Put the hot chutney into clean jars, cover, and when cool refrigerate; will keep for up to a month. For longer preserving, fill sterilized jars with the hot mixture, leaving ¼-inch headspace. Put on the lids and tighten, and process in a boiling-water canner for 15 minutes.

Applesauce

(four servings)

The best applesauce you ever tasted can be made from the new crop of Gravenstein apples that appear in the market in late August or early September; but don't hesitate to try other varieties as well. (I don't recommend Delicious apples because they are very sweet.) Warm applesauce makes a grand dessert with vanilla ice cream, heavy cream, or a dusting of cinnamon.

8 apples, peeled, cored, and cut into eighths (use Gravensteins, if possible)	Sugar to taste
	2 tablespoons lemon juice
	1 tablespoon finely chopped
½ cup water	lemon zest

Put the apples and water into a heavy-bottomed pan; cook over low heat, stirring occasionally, until the apples begin to get tender. Add a little sugar—be sparing until the apples mash easily. (Most Gravensteins are so sweet they need very little sugar.) Add the lemon juice and cook until the applesauce is soft enough to be mashed with a fork.

Remove from the heat, add the lemon zest, and mash with the tines of a fork, leaving some coarse texture. Serve warm or cold.

Fried Apple Rings

(two servings)

Rings of apple sautéed gently in a little butter are the garnish you need for just about any ham or pork dish. You can make a lot of Apple Rings and keep them in the refrigerator for a day or two. Spread them out on a baking sheet and reheat them in the oven just before serving.

4 tablespoons (½ stick) butter
1 medium-large firm apple, cored and sliced into six or seven ¼- to ½-inch rings

3 tablespoons sugar
1 teaspoon cinnamon

Melt the butter in a large skillet over medium heat, then place the apple rings in a single layer in the skillet. Mix together the sugar and cinnamon, and sprinkle over the apple rings. Cook for 2 minutes, then turn the apple rings over and reduce the heat to very low. Cover the skillet and cook for 2 or 3 more minutes. Test for doneness. Some of the rings will be tender—stack those on top of the ones that need another minute. Add more rings as needed to the skillet without using more butter, but continue to sprinkle on the sugar/cinnamon coating. Serve warm.

Baby Peas and Iceberg Lettuce

(four to six servings)

Iceberg lettuce lifts the garden pea to new heights. Because of the lettuce, you're able to cook the peas in less water, and they don't lose their delicate flavor.

4 pounds unshelled petite green peas (about 4 cups shelled)
6 tablespoons (¾ stick) butter
1 small head iceberg lettuce, cored, rinsed, wrapped, and chilled (see page 341), cut into julienne strips

Salt and pepper to taste
1 teaspoon sugar
½ cup water

Shell the peas. Heat the butter in a saucepan, add the peas and lettuce, salt and pepper, sugar, and water; stir to mix well. Bring to a boil and quickly reduce heat to a simmer. Cover and simmer for about 5 minutes, or until the peas are tender—the timing depends on the age of the peas. Serve hot.

Blanche's Cabbage with Bacon

(four servings)

Cabbage blanched for just twelve seconds turns a lovely celery-green color. This is *the* dish to have with sausage and rye bread. A small head of cabbage torn into bite-size pieces looks like a huge amount, but it wilts and cooks down to serve four ordinary appetites.

1 medium head cabbage, 2 to 2½ pounds (about 16 cups prepared)	4 tablespoons bacon fat (from cooking bacon)
¼ pound bacon, diced	4 tablespoons cider vinegar
½ teaspoon sugar	Salt to taste

Core the cabbage and carefully separate the leaves. Remove the thick center vein from each leaf and tear the leaves into large bite-size pieces.

Bring a large pot of water to a boil. In a small skillet, slowly cook the diced bacon until it is golden brown. Remove the bacon and drain on a paper towel. Save 4 tablespoons of bacon fat, mix it together with the sugar, and set aside. Plunge the cabbage into the boiling water and blanch for 12 seconds. Immediately drain the cabbage and toss in a bowl with the bacon, the sugar mixture, and the vinegar. Add salt and serve.

Carrots with Fresh Mint

(four servings)

Carrots with Fresh Mint is like having supper in the garden. There is a real difference between eating a whole mint leaf and little snippets of one. Leave them whole and bring the garden right to your plate.

1 pound carrots (about 5 medium), peeled and sliced $\frac{1}{4}$ inch thick 2 cups water Salt to taste	3 tablespoons butter 2 teaspoons brown sugar $\frac{1}{3}$ cup whole fresh mint leaves, small if possible

Put the carrots, water, and salt in a saucepan and bring to a boil. Turn the heat to low and cook for about 5 minutes, or until the carrots are just tender. Remove from the heat and drain.

Melt the butter and sugar over low heat in a skillet. Add the carrots, stirring and tossing for about 1 minute to coat with the butter mixture. Put the carrots in a serving dish and toss with the fresh mint leaves. Serve.

Cornmeal-Fried Tomatillos

(about thirty slices)

A tomatillo looks exactly like a shiny miniature green tomato hidden by an ugly husk. You find these tangy-tasting fruits in the supermarket the year round. As a fringe dish, tomatillos have the same complementary effect lemon does on black beans or fish and chicken dishes.

15 medium or large tomatillos	2 tablespoons vegetable oil
¾ cup yellow cornmeal	Salt and pepper to taste

Remove the husks from the tomatillos, cut off the tops and bottoms, and slice ½ inch thick. Spread the cornmeal on a large piece of waxed paper and coat both sides of the tomatillo slices with the cornmeal.

Put the oil in a 12-inch skillet and heat until quite hot. *Quickly* place the tomatillo slices in a single layer in the skillet. As soon as all of the slices are in the pan, lightly salt and pepper, and begin turning them over. Cook just a few seconds, and remove from the heat. The tomatillos must not cook longer than a few seconds or they will become mushy. Serve right away.

Jasmine Rice

(six servings)

I love the delicate fragrance of jasmine, but I never tasted it in food until I finally figured out how to put it there. I tried different methods until I succeeded with this. You'll find that this rice is perfectly tuned to white fish and seafood. The jasmine tea leaves must be fragrant when you smell them or they won't impart anything to the rice, so check yours before you make this.

2 teaspoons jasmine tea leaves
3½ cups water
1½ teaspoons salt
1½ cups long-grain white rice

If you are using teabags, cut them open and measure out 2 teaspoons of tea. Put the tea leaves in a small processor and process until they are tiny flecks, or use a mortar and pestle.

Put the water and salt in a saucepan and bring to a boil. Add the tea, and slowly add the rice. Shake the pan to level the rice and turn the heat down to simmer. Cover the pan and allow to cook for 15 minutes, or until the rice is tender. Remove from the heat, mix with a fork to fluff, and serve hot.

Orzo with Fresh Dill

(four servings)

Orzo is one of the kinds of pasta that look like rice. It was James Beard's favorite pasta to serve with lamb, and it's a favorite of mine with fish. You can have just plain orzo for supper, too, mixed with grated cheese, or salsa.

1 cup orzo pasta	2 tablespoons butter
⅓ cup chopped fresh dill	Salt to taste

Bring 4 quarts of salted water to a boil in a large pot. Add the orzo and cook for about 8 minutes, or until tender, stirring occasionally. Drain the orzo and put in a bowl. Add 2 tablespoons of the dill and the butter, and stir until the butter is melted. Salt to taste and serve hot. Pass around the rest of the dill to sprinkle over each serving.

Deviled Eggs

(four eggs)

I'm always happy when I see deviled eggs served. They please most people and add substance and heartiness to a supper of salad or soup that might not otherwise be filling enough.

4 eggs	1 teaspoon ball-park mustard
4 tablespoons mayonnaise	Black pepper to taste

Pierce the large end of each egg with an egg piercer or a needle; this will release the pressure that often cracks the shell. Put the eggs in a pan and fill it with water. Bring to a boil, and simmer for 15 minutes.

Remove from the heat and place the eggs in cold water immediately. (An overcooked egg yolk develops a harmless dark ring that isn't as appetizing as the bright yellow yolk.) Shell the eggs, cut in half lengthwise, and gently remove the yolks.

Put the yolks in a small bowl, mash with a fork, and stir in the mayonnaise, mustard, and pepper. Fill the hard-boiled egg whites with the mixture and serve.

Coleslaw

(six servings)

All-American coleslaw in a plain and simple version that's the best one I've found.

$\frac{1}{3}$ head green savoy cabbage, finely shredded (5 cups)

2 to 3 stalks celery, finely chopped

Salt and pepper to taste

Coleslaw Dressing
$\frac{1}{2}$ cup mayonnaise

$\frac{1}{4}$ teaspoon salt

$\frac{1}{2}$ teaspoon sugar

1 tablespoon cider vinegar

Put the cabbage and celery in a bowl and salt and pepper to taste.

Blend together the mayonnaise, salt, sugar, and vinegar until smooth. Pour over the cabbage and celery, mix well, and refrigerate until needed.

L.A. Slaw

(six servings)

There are lots of Salvadoran restaurants in Los Angeles that serve *papusas* (see page 464), slightly plump little tortillas filled with spicy meat or cheese. This is the peppy slaw that goes along with them.

¾ cup white vinegar
6 tablespoons vegetable oil
4 cloves garlic, finely chopped
   and mixed with ⅓ cup ice
   water
½ teaspoon Tabasco sauce, or
   to taste

1½ tablespoons chili powder
1½ teaspoons salt, or to taste
1 head green savoy cabbage,
   chopped into small pieces

Put the vinegar, oil, garlic in ice water, Tabasco, chili powder, and salt in a large mixing bowl. Mix very well. Add the cabbage and toss and stir until it is well coated with the dressing. Cover and chill and use as needed. This keeps well.

Turnip Slaw

(six servings)

The turnip is a neglected root, a vegetable that is never discussed, and rarely seen in public. Here it gets its proper due in a recipe that sets off the little bite in its flavor and the little crunch of its texture. Use it wherever you would use coleslaw.

½ cup mayonnaise
3 tablespoons sour cream
2 teaspoons tarragon vinegar
1 teaspoon prepared mustard
1 teaspoon sugar
Dash of salt

¼ teaspoon celery seed
¼ teaspoon pepper
1 teaspoon chopped fresh dill;
   or ½ teaspoon dried dill
1 pound white turnip, peeled
   and shredded (4 cups)

In a large bowl, stir together the mayonnaise, sour cream, tarragon vinegar, mustard, sugar, salt, celery seed, pepper, dill, and turnip. Mix well and refrigerate until needed.

Tiny Herb Salads

(six to eight servings)

Here is an exciting and novel idea that's become fashionable in some Parisian restaurants: tiny portions of intensely flavored salads made from one or more fresh herbs and served alongside main courses as a fresh condiment. This is an extremely simple way for you to get to know herbs: which herbs go together, which herbs go with what. Your palate should be your guide: getting a working knowledge of herbs and their qualities in this way is better than a shelf full of cookbooks.

Vinaigrette
4 tablespoons olive oil
2 teaspoons wine vinegar
2 tablespoons cold water

½ teaspoon salt
1 teaspoon Dijon mustard

Salad
1 cup herb leaves and/or flowers,
   stems removed, leaves left whole
   (one or more of the following:
   thyme, sage, parsley, tarragon,
   marjoram, oregano, savory,
   chervil, basil, cilantro, dill . . .)

2 cups chopped iceberg lettuce
2 tablespoons finely chopped
   green onions or scallions

Put all of the vinaigrette ingredients in a jar and shake vigorously until thoroughly blended. Set the dressing aside while preparing the salad.

Select the herb or herbs you want to enhance your supper. Toss the lettuce, onions, and herbs in a bowl. Pour the vinaigrette over the salad, toss, and serve about ½ cup salad per person.

Crouton Salad

(four servings)

This is for people who feel there are never enough croutons in their salad. Instead of a green salad with only three croutons per serving, here, finally, is a crouton salad with just a few greens. The important thing to know is that a Crouton Salad could take the place of rice or potatoes or a dinner roll with your supper. And of course you can change the greens to suit the main supper dish; in place of parsley and celery, try baby spinach leaves, for example.

½ cup olive oil
2 cloves garlic, put through a
  garlic press
Salt to taste
4 cups dried bread cubes,
  1 to 2 inches square

2 cups loosely packed Italian
  flat-leaf parsley sprigs
½ cup finely chopped scallions
2 tablespoons red wine vinegar
Optional: 1 cup celery leaves

Heat the oil and garlic in a large skillet over medium heat for 1 minute. Liberally salt the bread cubes, then add them to the skillet and heat for another minute or two, stirring and turning them over until they are lightly browned. Remove from the heat, add the parsley, scallions, vinegar, and optional celery leaves. Toss and serve immediately.

Cucumber Salad

(four servings)

Whenever something sweet and sour and fresh is called for, Cucumber Salad is usually it. The light and puckery dressing for this little salad is the simplest form of a pickle solution. Serve on a leaf of butter lettuce as the side salad with a fish dish or with something as basic as crackers and cheese.

¾ cup water
1½ teaspoons salt
⅓ cup sugar
1½ tablespoons white vinegar

2 medium cucumbers, peeled, seeded, and sliced
A few leaves of butter lettuce

Mix together the water, salt, sugar, and vinegar in a bowl. Add the cucumbers and stir. Put in the refrigerator until ready to serve. Remove the cucumbers from the dressing and serve on the leaves of butter lettuce.

Lettuce in Cream

(four servings)

This dish is just right the way it is. You shouldn't touch it with salt and pepper. And don't be dismayed by the cream—just remember that there is a lot of lettuce. Lettuce in Cream goes well with a plainly cooked rich fish, like salmon.

1 medium head iceberg lettuce, cored, rinsed, wrapped, and chilled (see page 341)	¼ cup sugar ¼ cup white vinegar ¾ cup light cream

Cut the lettuce into large pieces. Put the sugar, vinegar, and cream in a large mixing bowl and stir to blend well.

Ten minutes before serving, put the lettuce in the bowl and toss to coat the leaves. Serve on individual salad plates.

Wedge of Iceberg with Thick Creamy Dressing

(four servings)

Iceberg lettuce would smile if it could. It is a perfect creation, round and crisp and sturdy, despite its delicate flavor, and unlike some of the frail field lettuces that wilt, swoon, and have the vapors readily. My dog, Rover, loves it, especially dunked in meat drippings. He wouldn't touch arugula with a ten-foot pole. When made properly, this salad is as great as Caesar salad.

½ cup sour cream
½ cup mayonnaise
2 scallions, finely chopped
2 to 3 tablespoons lemon
    juice
½ cup crumbled Roquefort or
    other blue cheese

Pepper to taste
1 head iceberg lettuce, cored,
    rinsed, wrapped, and chilled
    (see page 341)

Put the sour cream, mayonnaise, scallions, and lemon juice in a bowl and stir until well blended. If too thick, add a little vegetable oil. Stir in the crumbled cheese, and pepper to taste. Refrigerate at least 4 hours before serving.

Cut the lettuce into 4 thick wedges and spoon about 6 tablespoons of dressing over each wedge.

Mustard Celery Salad

(four servings)

This dish that falls somewhere between a salad and a relish is a good way to round out a simple main course, such as fish.

6 to 7 stalks celery, cut into
   small dice (3 cups)
1 cup finely chopped (loosely
   packed) parsley
½ cup mayonnaise

1 tablespoon prepared mus-
   tard (French's or ball-park)
Pepper to taste
Butter lettuce leaves

Put the celery and parsley in a large bowl and toss. Stir the mayonnaise and mustard together until smooth, taste, and add more of either to balance the taste. Stir and toss into the celery mixture and add pepper to taste. Chill until needed. Serve on butter lettuce.

PUCCINI SPURNS THE SAVOY

" . . . [Chef] Francois Latry asked him to be allowed to prepare a rich Tuscan-style dish and name it after him. Puccini declined the honour on the grounds that it would give people a false impression of his eating habits, and his letters, indeed, testify to the simplicity of his tastes in this respect. For example, on 30 April 1880 he revealed to his younger brother: 'I worked till three o'clock this morning . . . Then I had a bunch of onions for supper.' Sometimes he would chop an onion very finely and enjoy it mixed with a can of tuna fish and its oil."

—from *Good Cheer*
by Frederick W. Hackwood

Relish Salad

(four servings)

Crunchy Relish Salad is a sweet-and-sour side dish that sharpens up the flavor of whatever gets served with it. It can be made in advance, even the day before.

$\frac{1}{2}$ teaspoon salt	$\frac{1}{8}$ head savoy cabbage,
3 tablespoons brown sugar	chopped (2 cups)
$\frac{1}{2}$ teaspoon dry mustard	$\frac{1}{2}$ green bell pepper, chopped
$\frac{1}{3}$ cup cider vinegar	2 to 3 stalks celery, chopped

Put the salt, brown sugar, dry mustard, and cider vinegar in a bowl and stir until blended. Add the cabbage, bell pepper, and celery and stir until all is well mixed. Serve chilled.

Grapefruit, Black Olive, and Mint Salad

(four servings)

I couldn't imagine how grapefruit, olives, and mint could commingle until I tried it. It turned out to be a striking sight, with a taste to match.

1 large grapefruit, peeled and	2 tablespoons olive oil
sectioned	1 teaspoon lemon juice
1 cup pitted black olives	$\frac{1}{4}$ teaspoon salt, or to taste
1 cup whole fresh mint leaves	

To extract whole grapefruit sections, first put the fruit on a cutting board. Hold it firmly with one hand and with the other pare off the skin with a sharp knife. Cut away the white layer of pith beneath the skin as you pare. Remove the sections, cutting them away from the membrane, first on one side of a section, then the other. Cut off any white bits that remain and remove seeds, so that you have perfect whole segments of fruit.

Put the grapefruit segments, olives, and mint leaves in a bowl. Add the olive oil, lemon juice, and salt, and mix well.

Persimmon-Pear Salad

(six servings)

Pears and persimmons are kindred winter fruits that belong together in a salad like this one. The sliced fruit looks like flower petals tossed among the lettuces.

⅓ cup olive oil
2 tablespoons rice vinegar
1½ teaspoons Dijon mustard
½ teaspoon salt
2 tablespoons water
1 tablespoon sugar
2 Fuyu persimmons, peeled
   and sliced

2 pears (Bosc, if possible),
   peeled, cored, and sliced
4 cups mixed bitter green
   lettuces (such as curly
   endive, escarole, and
   chicory), washed and
   dried

Put the olive oil, vinegar, mustard, salt, water, and sugar in a large bowl and blend until well mixed. Then add the persimmons, pears, and lettuce and toss until well coated.

Welsh Rabbit

" . . . at the beach the same dish was very pleasant for supper when the air was brisk or the fog swept in from the sea. It was often made in a chafing dish and sometimes over a low wood fire in a heavy casserole or saucepan. With it went quantities of hot, hot toast, well buttered and crisp, and enormous amounts of beer. Knowing that some delicate appetites were not equal to so heavy a dish for late supper, Mother and Let always provided an alternate dish of chicken with a light cream sauce and mushrooms, flavored with a good deal of sherry . . . As a conclusion to this supper a light fruit dessert . . . "

—from *Delights and Prejudices*
by James Beard

Desserts

Beginner's Coconut Pie
Joyce's Paper Lemon Cookies
Black and White Chocolate
   Cookies
Crisp Ginger Cookies
Lemon Teasers
Oatmeal Raisin Cookies
Fresh Orange Cookies
Plain Jane Sugar Cookies
Almond Diamonds
Parker Brownies
Joyce's Almond Cakes
Sharon's Orange Scone Berry
   Cakes
Orange Sour Cream Cake
Chocolate Brownie Cake
Pineapple Upside-Down
   Cake
The Best Rice Pudding
Creamy *Riso* Pudding
Spanish Cream
Apple-Walnut Pudding

Bread Pudding
Chocolate Pudding
Baked Vanilla Custard
Brown Sugar Custard
Apples in Custard
Wine Jelly
Pralines
Pineapple Blizzard
Grapefruit Ice
Chilled Marmalade Grapefruit
Sautéed Pears
Maple Persimmons
Grapes with Sour Cream and
   Brown Sugar
Berry Sandwiches
Peach on Sugared Toast
Baked Plums and Apricots with
   Almonds
Baked Bananas with Berries or
   Mango
Rhubarb and Kumquat
   Compote

For me a meal is never quite finished without dessert. I have always loved sweets. Baking cookies and cakes is still an adventure for me. A little flour, salt, sugar, eggs, and butter; some brisk stirring; into the oven—and there is an amazing transformation into golden cookies and lofty cakes. One puts in so little for such great returns.

When I was growing up in La Crescenta, California, we always had the same dessert every night during the summer. Long summer evenings, after breathlessly hot days, meant sitting in the porch swing and eating ice cream. It seemed like everyone in our small foothill town retired to their front porch after supper to watch the stars come out and catch any little breeze that rippled by. Around eight o'clock, couples and families would begin to stroll down to Mr. Watson's drugstore to buy a quart of ice cream. He had chocolate, vanilla, strawberry, tutti frutti, and spumoni. I never knew anyone who bought tutti frutti or spumoni. My memory of Mr. Watson's ice cream is that it was perfect, and we never became tired of the same dessert every night. It was as good in August as it was in June.

There are no recipes for ice cream in this book because you can buy very good ice cream everywhere, but it is seldom that you can buy anything nearly as good as the Almond Diamond cookies (see page 540), the Parker Brownies (see page 541), the Fresh Orange Cookies (see page 538), or the Pineapple Upside-Down Cake (see page 546) in the pages that follow.

Beginner's Coconut Pie

(one 9- or 10-inch pie)

This is a mouth-watering, creamy custard baked in a pie plate *sans* crust, with golden crisp coconut on top. Slice in wedges, as you would any pie, and serve with a spoonful of unsweetened whipped cream.

2 cups milk	1¼ cups sugar
½ cup all-purpose flour	1½ teaspoons vanilla
1 teaspoon baking powder	1 cup grated sweetened
¼ teaspoon salt	coconut
4 eggs	

Preheat the oven to 350°F. Butter a 9- or 10-inch pie pan.

Put the milk, flour, baking powder, salt, eggs, sugar, and vanilla into a blender or food processor. Blend for 3 minutes. Add the coconut and blend for 2 or 3 seconds more. Pour the mixture into the pie pan. Bake for 30 to 35 minutes, or until the edges are set and the center trembles a trifle. Remove from the oven and let cool, or serve warm. If cooling and serving later, refrigerate, and warm a bit before serving.

Joyce's Paper Lemon Cookies

(about fifty cookies)

My friend Joyce McGillis is a fine home cook and she created these cookies—they're crisp and paper-thin, with an intense lemon flavor.

¾ cup (1½ sticks) unsalted butter, softened
1¼ cups sugar
1 teaspoon vanilla
2 tablespoons grated lemon rind
¼ cup freshly squeezed lemon juice

1½ cups all-purpose flour
1½ teaspoons baking powder
½ teaspoon baking soda
½ teaspoon salt
Optional: raw sugar for sprinkling on top

In a bowl, cream the butter and sugar together (an electric mixer is almost a must for the recipe). Add the vanilla, lemon rind, and lemon juice and continue to beat until smooth. Mix or sift together into another bowl the flour, baking powder, baking soda, and salt. Add to the butter and sugar mixture and blend well. Turn the dough out onto waxed paper or plastic wrap and form it into 2 logs about 1 to 1½ inches in diameter and about a foot long. Refrigerate for at least 2 hours, or wrap tightly and freeze until ready to use.

Preheat the oven to 350°F. Don't grease the cookie sheets.

Cut the logs into about ⅛-inch slices (less than ¼ inch) with a sharp knife, and place cookies about 3 inches apart on the cookie sheets. Sprinkle with raw sugar, if desired. Cut only enough cookies to fill the cookie sheets, then return the uncut dough to the refrigerator to keep chilled. (I put only 6 to 8 cookies on a sheet at a time to keep them from spreading together when baking.) Bake for

7 to 8 minutes, or until the cookies are lightly golden. Watch carefully during the last 1 to 2 minutes of cooking. Remove from the oven and let cool slightly on the cookie sheets before removing to racks to finish cooling.

Black and White Chocolate Cookies

(about two and one-half to three dozen cookies)

These little chocolate domes, crackled on top, are crisp outside and slightly chewy inside. These are nice, rich cookies after a supper salad.

3 ounces (3 squares) unsweetened chocolate	2 eggs
1 cup granulated sugar	1 cup all-purpose flour
6 tablespoons (¾ stick) butter, room temperature	1¼ teaspoons baking powder
2 teaspoons vanilla	¼ teaspoon salt
	⅓ cup confectioners' sugar, sifted

Put the chocolate in a pan over barely simmering water until it has melted. Remove from the heat.

Put the sugar, butter, chocolate, and vanilla in a mixing bowl and stir to blend. Add the eggs and mix briskly until well blended. Add the flour, baking powder, and salt and stir until well mixed. Cover and refrigerate at least 3 hours or overnight.

Preheat the oven to 350°F. Don't grease the cookie sheets.

Sift the confectioners' sugar onto a large piece of waxed paper. Shape the cookie dough into rounded teaspoon-size balls and roll them in the confectioners' sugar. Place about 2 inches apart on cookie sheets. Bake for about 10 to 12 minutes, or until the top of the cookies feels almost firm to the touch. Remove from the oven and let cool for about 10 minutes before removing from the cookie sheets. Cool on racks.

Crisp Ginger Cookies

(about three and one-half dozen 2-inch cookies)

Paper-thin Crisp Ginger Cookies go especially well with papaya, mango, pineapple, or banana.

½ cup (1 stick) butter, softened
1 cup sugar
1 tablespoon ground ginger
½ teaspoon salt

½ cup milk
2 cups all-purpose flour
Optional: 1 cup coarsely
    chopped candied ginger

Preheat the oven to 350°F. Grease two cookie sheets.

Cream the butter and sugar together in a mixing bowl. Add the ground ginger, salt, and milk to the butter mixture and mix well. Slowly add the flour and blend well.

On the 2 greased cookie sheets spread the dough very thin, using a spatula or your hands. It helps to wet your fingers in cold water so the dough doesn't stick to your hands. If desired, scatter the chopped candied ginger over the dough; gently roll or pat the ginger into the dough. Bake for 20 to 25 minutes, or until lightly browned. While still hot, cut the cookies into 2-inch squares and remove from the pans. The cookies will be very thin and crisp.

Lemon Teasers

(sixteen 2-inch squares)

Butter crust covered with sharp lemon custard and dusted with confectioners' sugar, this cookie is a version of an old recipe from the era when every Junior League cookbook had lemon bars with names like "Melting Moments" and "Love Notes."

1 cup flour	¾ cup granulated sugar
⅓ cup confectioners' sugar; plus a little more to dust the top of the cookies	½ teaspoon salt
	¼ cup freshly squeezed lemon juice
½ cup (1 stick) butter, chilled and cut into bits	2 tablespoons flour
2 eggs	½ teaspoon baking powder

Preheat the oven to 350°F. Butter an 8 × 8 × 2-inch baking pan.

Put the 1 cup flour and ⅓ cup confectioners' sugar in a bowl and, using a fork, stir to mix well. Add the bits of butter and, using your fingers, rub the butter and flour together until the mixture resembles coarse bread crumbs. Pat the mixture into the bottom of the baking pan. Bake for about 10 to 15 minutes, or until it is light golden. Remove from the oven.

Put the eggs into a mixing bowl and beat until they are thick and pale. Add the sugar, salt, and lemon juice and beat until well blended. Add the 2 tablespoons flour and the baking powder and beat until thoroughly mixed.

Pour the mixture over the partially baked crust and bake for about 15 minutes, or until the custard is light golden. Remove from the oven and dust the top with confectioners' sugar. Cool and cut into 16 squares.

Oatmeal Raisin Cookies

(about four dozen 2-inch round cookies)

These are homey, coarse cookies with oatmeal and raisins. They are satisfying between meals, and they go with puddings at suppertime, too.

1 cup sugar	1 teaspoon baking soda
½ cup (1 stick) butter, softened	1 teaspoon salt
⅓ cup honey	2 cups rolled oats
2 eggs	1 cup raisins
1¾ cups all-purpose flour	

Preheat the oven to 350°F. Grease the cookie sheets.

Mix the sugar, butter, and honey in a large bowl, beating until the mixture is creamy and smooth. Add the eggs and beat well. Stir in the flour, baking soda, and salt. Mix well. Add the oats and raisins and stir until well mixed.

Drop tablespoonfuls of the dough 2 inches apart on the cookie sheets. Flatten each mound of dough with your fingertips. If the dough sticks, occasionally dip your fingers in a bowl of cold water to prevent sticking. Bake for about 8 to 10 minutes, or until the cookies are light brown. Remove from the oven and cool about 5 minutes on the cookie sheets. Remove the cookies to finish cooling on a rack, and store in an airtight container. These cookies freeze well: Put in plastic bags, close with a twist tie, and freeze until needed.

Fresh Orange Cookies

(about three dozen 2-inch round cookies)

Here is a sugar cookie that doesn't have to be refrigerated, rolled out, cut out, re-refrigerated, and rerolled. It is awfully good when something sweet is needed.

1 cup (2 sticks) butter, softened
1 cup sugar
1 medium unpeeled orange, cut into pieces, seeds removed
½ lemon, cut into pieces, seeds removed

2 cups all-purpose flour
½ teaspoon baking soda
½ teaspoon salt

Icing

3 tablespoons butter, softened
2 cups confectioners' sugar, sifted

2 tablespoons finely chopped or ground orange and lemon (from above)
2 tablespoons orange juice

Preheat the oven to 350°F. Do not butter the cookie sheets.

Put the butter and sugar into a mixing bowl and beat until smooth and creamy. Finely chop the orange and lemon (or grind in the food processor). Put the ground or chopped orange and lemon into a strainer and press to extract excess juice. (Don't worry if you don't remove all the moisture.) There should be approximately 1 cup of ground or chopped orange and lemon. Add ½ cup, firmly packed, of the orange and lemon to the butter mixture and mix well. Reserve 2 tablespoons of the remaining orange and lemon for the icing and freeze the rest for some other use. Add the flour, baking soda, and salt and beat until well blended.

Drop the dough by tablespoons onto the cookie sheets, leaving 2 inches between. Flatten the dough with your fingers. If the dough is sticky, dip your fingers into cold water before pressing. Bake for 10 to 12 minutes, or until the cookies are golden. Remove to racks.

While the cookies are baking, make the icing. Cream together the butter and confectioners' sugar. Add the ground orange and lemon and the orange juice and beat until smooth. Spread on the top of the cookies while they are still warm.

Plain Jane Sugar Cookies

(about fifty 2½-inch round cookies)

A no-frills, all-purpose cookie, Plain Janes take just ten minutes to make and ten minutes to bake. You can eat them with fruit, or just by themselves, and they're good with chocolate ice cream.

½ cup butter (1 stick), room temperature
1 cup sugar
1 egg, lightly beaten

2 teaspoons vanilla
1½ cups all-purpose flour
1½ teaspoons baking powder
½ teaspoon salt

Preheat the oven to 350°F. Grease the cookie sheets.

Cream the butter in a mixing bowl. Add the sugar and beat until blended and smooth. Stir in the egg and vanilla and mix well. Add the flour, baking powder, and salt, and stir until well mixed.

Drop well-rounded teaspoons of dough onto the cookie sheets about 2½ inches apart. Use the bottom of a glass or small cup to flatten the mounds of dough; begin by putting the bottom of the glass in dough to make it sticky and then dip the glass in sugar before pressing down each cookie. Repeat when stickiness disappears. Bake for 10 to 12 minutes, or until the edges of the cookies are light golden. Remove from the cookie sheets and cool on racks.

Almond Diamonds

(about thirty-two cookies)

Almond Diamonds are just a little fancier and more delicate than your everyday cookie. These diamonds aren't forever, though. They get eaten up fast, especially with fruit compotes, ice cream, or custards.

$\frac{1}{2}$ cup (1 stick) butter, room temperature
$\frac{3}{4}$ cup sugar
1 egg, separated
1 teaspoon vanilla

1 cup sifted all-purpose flour
$\frac{1}{4}$ teaspoon salt
$\frac{1}{2}$ cup coarsely chopped sliced almonds
$\frac{1}{2}$ teaspoon cinnamon

Preheat the oven to 400°F. Grease a 17 × 12 × 1-inch jelly-roll pan.

Cream together the butter and $\frac{1}{2}$ cup of the sugar until very light. Beat in the egg yolk and vanilla, then gradually stir in the flour and salt. With a spatula dipped in cold water, spread the dough evenly and thinly over the bottom of the jelly-roll pan. (The dough is somewhat stiff, so dot spoonfuls of it all over the pan, then spread with the spatula.)

Beat the egg white until it is just stiff, then brush it all over the top of the dough. Mix together the almonds, cinnamon, and the remaining $\frac{1}{4}$ cup sugar. Sprinkle this mixture on top of the egg white. Bake for 8 to 10 minutes. The cookies are done when the edges are golden and shrinking away from the sides of the pan. Remove from the oven and immediately cut diagonally into diamond shapes, with each side of the diamonds measuring about $2\frac{1}{2}$ inches. Cool and store in an airtight container.

Parker Brownies

(sixteen brownies)

I renamed these brownies after a young man who was crazy about them. He told me that when he was in Spain studying flamenco guitar, he imagined that if he had to, he could make a living making and selling these brownies.

2 ounces (2 squares) unsweetened chocolate
¼ cup (½ stick) butter
1 cup sugar
1 egg
⅛ teaspoon salt

½ cup all-purpose flour
½ cup chopped walnuts
1 teaspoon vanilla
Optional: confectioners'
  sugar for dusting

Preheat the oven to 300°F. Butter an 8-inch square baking pan. Line the bottom of the pan with waxed paper, then butter and flour the paper.

In a saucepan over very low heat, melt the chocolate with the butter, stirring to blend. Remove from the heat and stir in the sugar, egg, salt, flour, walnuts, and vanilla. Spread in the prepared pan and bake for about 30 minutes. Remove from the oven and cool for about 5 minutes, then turn out onto a rack and peel the waxed paper from the bottom. Transfer to a cutting board and cut into squares. Dust brownies with confectioners' sugar, if desired.

Joyce's Almond Cakes

(eight cakes)

These are small muffin-size dessert cakes that are tailored to go with fruits, especially berries.

½ cup (1 stick) butter, room
  temperature
¾ cup sugar
2 eggs, well beaten
1⅓ cups cake flour
2 teaspoons baking powder

¼ teaspoon salt
⅓ cup milk
1¼ cups coarsely chopped
  blanched almonds
Confectioners' sugar for
  dusting the tops of the cakes

Preheat the oven to 375°F. Butter 8 muffin tins well.

Cream the butter and sugar together until light and creamy. Add the eggs, beating thoroughly. Stir in the flour, baking powder, and salt; beat, then add the milk. Mix well and stir in the almonds.

Spoon the batter into the muffin tins, filling each two-thirds full. Bake for about 12 to 14 minutes, or until the center is dry when a straw is inserted. Dust the tops with confectioners' sugar. Serve warm.

"Who goes to bed supperless tosses all night."

—Italian proverb

Sharon's Orange Scone Berry Cakes

(fourteen cakes)

Sharon Kramis has never given me a recipe I didn't like. These little cakes are meant to be served as a supper dessert with a bowl of berries, but it's okay if you don't have the berries. They make an absolutely exemplary dessert by themselves, with just a cup of good coffee.

2 cups all-purpose flour less
  2 tablespoons
1 tablespoon baking powder
1 teaspoon salt
2 tablespoons plus ½ cup sugar
⅓ cup (⅔ stick) butter, chilled
1 egg, beaten

½ cup heavy cream
2 tablespoons butter, melted
2 tablespoons grated orange
  zest
Optional: fresh berries or
  berry preserves

Preheat the oven to 400°F.

In a bowl, stir together the flour, baking powder, salt, and the 2 tablespoons sugar. Using a pastry blender or two knives, cut the chilled butter into the flour mixture. Mix together the egg and cream in another bowl and add to the dry ingredients; stir until just blended.

Turn out onto a floured board and knead for 1 minute. Shape the dough into a rectangle that is 8 inches wide, 14 inches long, and ¼ inch thick. Brush on the melted butter, then sprinkle with the ½ cup sugar and orange zest. Roll up jelly-roll fashion from the longer, 14-inch side, and cut into 1-inch slices.

Arrange the slices, cut side down, on an ungreased baking sheet and bake for 10 to 12 minutes, or until lightly browned. Serve with butter and fresh berries or berry preserves.

Orange Sour Cream Cake

(one 8½ × 4½ × 3-inch loaf cake)

This recipe was a gift from Marlene Sorosky, a fine baker who used to have a Cake of the Month Club. (James Beard once told me that her cakes were the best he ever ate.) This one blooms with orange flavor, it's simple to make, and it keeps well.

½ cup (1 stick) butter, room temperature

¾ cup sugar

2 large eggs, separated (may also be added whole)

¼ teaspoon salt

1 teaspoon orange extract

1 teaspoon grated orange zest

1 cup all-purpose flour

½ teaspoon baking powder

½ teaspoon baking soda

½ cup plus 2 tablespoons sour cream

½ cup finely chopped walnuts

Preheat oven to 325°F. Grease and lightly flour a loaf pan.

Beat the butter and ½ cup of the sugar in a large mixing bowl until light, about 2 minutes. Add the yolks and beat well. (If using whole eggs, add them here and use all ¾ cup of the sugar.) Add orange extract and zest, and blend. Stir together the flour, baking powder, and baking soda in another bowl. Add alternately with the sour cream and beat until well mixed. Mix in the walnuts. Beat the egg whites and slowly add the remaining ¼ cup sugar to them; beat until the whites hold stiff peaks. Gently fold the whites into the batter, then spoon into the loaf pan.

Bake for about 40 to 50 minutes, or until a straw comes out clean when inserted in the center. Don't overbake! Cool on a rack.

Chocolate Brownie Cake

(four servings)

It's hard to believe that just six tablespoons of cocoa can make a chocolate cake so rich, dark, and moist. This cake will stay fresh longer than most. Serve it warm.

¼ cup (½ stick) butter, softened	⅓ cup plus 1 tablespoon
½ cup plus ⅓ cup brown sugar	cocoa powder
2 eggs	2 tablespoons water
1 teaspoon vanilla	⅓ cup hot water
¾ cup all-purpose flour	Confectioners' sugar for
¼ teaspoon salt	dusting the top of the cake
½ teaspoon baking soda	Heavy cream, softly whipped

Preheat the oven to 350°F. Grease an 8-inch square baking pan.

Cream together the butter and the ½ cup of brown sugar in a mixing bowl. Add the eggs and vanilla and mix until blended. In a small bowl, mix together the flour, salt, baking soda, and the ⅓ cup cocoa. Add the flour mixture to the butter mixture and blend. Stir in the 2 tablespoons water. Pour the batter into the baking pan. Mix together the remaining ⅓ cup brown sugar, 1 tablespoon cocoa, and the ⅓ cup hot water. Pour the hot water mixture over the batter.

Place the pan in a slightly larger ovenproof dish. Add 1 inch of boiling water to the larger dish and put into the oven. Bake for 20 to 25 minutes, or until a skewer comes out clean. Dust with confectioners' sugar. Serve with lightly whipped cream.

Pineapple Upside-Down Cake

(six to eight servings)

Pineapple Upside-Down Cake was my very favorite dessert as a child. I first remember my mother making it around 1928 for special occasions. She always lacked confidence in the kitchen, especially when baking, but this cake turned out perfect every time. It is a simple cake for a beginning baker.

¼ cup (½ stick) butter	1 teaspoon vanilla
¾ cup packed dark brown sugar	2 eggs
7 canned pineapple rings	1⅔ cups all-purpose flour
7 maraschino cherries	2 teaspoons baking powder
⅓ cup shortening	¼ teaspoon salt
⅔ cup granulated sugar	⅔ cup milk
	Whipped cream

Preheat the oven to 350°F.

Melt the butter over medium heat in a 9-inch cast-iron or other ovenproof skillet. Add the brown sugar and continue to cook, stirring constantly, until the sugar melts and is very thick and bubbly.

Arrange the pineapple rings in a single layer in the pan, pressing them down into the hot syrup. Place a cherry in the center of each ring. Set aside.

Cream the shortening in a large mixing bowl. Add the granulated sugar gradually, beating well. Add the vanilla and the eggs, and continue to beat until the mixture is well blended and light. Stir together the flour, baking powder, and salt in another bowl. Add to the creamed mixture along with the milk, beating about 30 seconds, until the batter is smooth. Spread evenly over the pineapple rings.

Bake for 35 to 40 minutes, or until a skewer comes out clean when inserted in the center of the cake, and thick, syrupy juices are bubbling around the edges. Remove from the oven and let cool for 5 minutes. Place a serving plate face down over skillet, turn both upside down, and remove the skillet. Serve warm with whipped cream.

The Best Rice Pudding

(six servings)

This is certainly the best rice pudding for today, because it short-cuts the old-fashioned method of cooking rice for hours and hours in large quantities of milk. Use short-grain rice because it's starchier than long-grain rice, and it makes a creamier pudding.

1 cup water	2 teaspoons vanilla
½ cup short-grain white rice	½ cup plus 2 tablespoons
½ teaspoon salt	sugar
2 cups milk	2 eggs
½ cup golden raisins	¼ teaspoon cinnamon
1 cup heavy cream	Optional: heavy cream

Preheat the oven to 350°F. Butter an 8-inch square baking dish.

Bring the water to a boil in a 2-quart saucepan. Add the rice and salt. Cover and cook over low heat for 10 minutes. Add the milk and the raisins, cover, and cook over low heat for 10 to 15 minutes more, or until the rice is tender.

In a small bowl, blend the cream, vanilla, sugar, and eggs. Add to the rice. Pour into the baking dish, and sprinkle with the cinnamon. Place in a slightly larger ovenproof dish. Add 1 inch of boiling water to the larger dish and place in the oven. Bake for 30 to 45 minutes. Serve at room temperature with heavy cream if desired.

Creamy Riso Pudding

(four to six servings)

This is the creamiest rice pudding you've ever eaten, because it's made with *riso* (or orzo), the pasta that impersonates rice. It's better than the real thing.

½ cup *riso* (or orzo) pasta (this makes 2 cups cooked)	2 egg yolks
	1½ teaspoons vanilla
2 cups milk	½ cup golden raisins
½ cup sugar	Nutmeg to sprinkle lightly on
½ teaspoon salt	top of baked pudding
1 egg	Heavy cream

Preheat the oven to 350°F. Butter an 8-inch square baking dish.

Bring a pot of salted water to a boil. Stir in the *riso* and cook, stirring occasionally, for 10 minutes, or until the pasta is tender. Drain and set aside.

Put the milk and 6 tablespoons of the sugar into a pan and bring to a simmer. Add the salt, stir, and remove from the heat. Lightly blend together the whole egg and egg yolks, and pour a little of the blended eggs over the hot milk, stirring constantly. Add the remaining eggs and stir briskly. Return the pan to the heat and cook a minute or two, stirring constantly. Remove from the heat and whisk the cooked *riso* into the milk mixture. Add the vanilla and raisins, and whisk until any little clumps of *riso* are separated.

Pour into the buttered baking dish and bake for about 30 to 35 minutes, or until just set. Remove from the oven and sprinkle the top with nutmeg and the remaining 2 tablespoons of sugar. Serve warm with cream.

Spanish Cream

(four servings)

Spanish cream was among the recipes in the first *Fannie Farmer Cookbook*, written in 1896. Many early American cookbooks include Spanish cream, Spanish rice, and Spanish omelet as daring and exotic additions to their collections of mild Anglo-Saxon recipes. Spanish Cream (the Spanish touch is the addition of sherry wine) is a lovely, light chilled dessert.

1 envelope unflavored gelatin	2 eggs, separated, yolks lightly
¼ cup cold water	beaten with a fork
2 cups milk	4 tablespoons dry sherry
½ cup sugar	½ cup heavy cream
¼ teaspoon salt	

Sprinkle the gelatin over the cold water, stir, and let soften for 5 minutes.

Put the milk and sugar in a heavy-bottomed saucepan and heat until a tiny ring of bubbles forms around the edge of the pan. Remove from the heat, stir in the salt, and slowly pour the hot milk mixture over the egg yolks, stirring constantly. Pour back into the saucepan, add the softened gelatin, and cook over low heat, stirring until the custard thickens. This custard will not thicken very much, so remove from the heat as soon as you notice a slight change in texture. Stir in the sherry. Pour the mixture into a bowl to cool, and then refrigerate. Check after 1 hour.

As soon as the mixture becomes thick and syrupy, beat the heavy cream until soft peaks form and gently stir it into the custard. Cover the bowl with plastic wrap and chill at least 4 hours or longer before serving.

Apple-Walnut Pudding

(six servings)

This recipe originally called for dates, but in recent years we seem to have lost our taste for them. I think we have forgotten how splendid they are. Use apples or pears, but try dates sometime too.

1 cup all-purpose flour
1 cup sugar
2 teaspoons baking powder
½ teaspoon salt
½ cup milk

2½ cups diced apples or pears
  (cored and with skin on); or
  1 cup pitted and chopped
  dates
1 cup chopped walnuts

Topping
2 cups boiling water
1 cup light brown sugar

1 tablespoon butter

Whipped cream

Preheat the oven to 350°F. Butter a 10 × 10 × 2-inch baking pan.

Put the flour, sugar, baking powder, and salt in a mixing bowl. Stir and mix well with a fork. Add the milk and briskly mix until smooth. Stir in the fruit and nuts. Spread the batter in the baking dish.

Put the water, brown sugar, and butter in a saucepan and bring to a boil, then pour the topping evenly over the batter. Bake, uncovered, for about 1 hour, or until the top is golden and bubbling. Serve with whipped cream.

Bread Pudding

(six servings)

This was a great pacifier for generations of boarding school pupils, since it would sometimes be the only decent dish on the menu. It is important to take it out of the oven while it is still trembling so it will be tender and soft rather than firm and dry. Serve with a little cream.

3 eggs	½ cup raisins
½ cup sugar	6 slices good home-style white
⅛ teaspoon salt	bread, crusts removed, but-
2½ cups milk	tered on one side
1½ teaspoons vanilla	

Preheat the oven to 350°F.

In a mixing bowl, stir together the eggs, sugar, and salt. Put the milk in a saucepan and heat over medium-high heat until the milk is scalded or tiny bubbles form around the edge of the pan. Remove the milk from the heat and slowly add the egg mixture, stirring constantly. Stir in the vanilla and raisins.

Place the bread, buttered sides up, in a 9-inch square baking dish. Pour the milk mixture over the bread. Put boiling water in a pan larger than the 9-inch baking dish and place in the oven. Put the baking dish in the larger pan, making sure the boiling water comes halfway up the side of the baking dish. Bake about 20 to 30 minutes, or until the custard is set. Serve warm.

Chocolate Pudding

(four servings)

This is the chocolate pudding of my childhood. As simple as a smile, it is creamy and smooth with a subdued chocolate flavor. It uses only two tablespoons of cocoa which give a light, delicate chocolate taste. Pour a tablespoon of heavy cream over each serving.

2 cups milk	2 tablespoons cocoa powder
3 tablespoons cornstarch	1 teaspoon vanilla
4 tablespoons sugar	Optional: 4 tablespoons heavy
¼ teaspoon salt	cream

Put 1½ cups of the milk in a heavy-bottomed saucepan and scald (this is the point of heat that is just short of boiling: there is steam rising from the milk and a ring of tiny bubbles around the edge). This is not critical; it is just that the milk should be very hot.

While the milk is heating, put the cornstarch, sugar, salt, and cocoa in a bowl. Stir with a spoon to mix, then add the remaining ½ cup cold milk, stirring until well blended. When the milk is hot, stir it into the cornstarch mixture and mix until well blended. Pour the mixture back into the saucepan and stir constantly until the pudding begins to boil. Boil *only 1 minute*, stirring briskly all the while. Remove from the heat and pour into a bowl. When cool add the vanilla. Cover and refrigerate until needed. Serve with a spoonful of heavy cream over each serving, if you wish.

Baked Vanilla Custard

(eight servings)

Baked custards are simple to make and always silkier, smoother, and more delicate than stirred custards.

2 egg yolks	3 cups very hot milk
3 eggs	1 tablespoon vanilla
½ cup sugar	Nutmeg
Salt to taste	

Preheat the oven to 325°F. Butter an 8-inch square baking dish or 8 ramekins. Set a shallow pan large enough to hold the baking dish or ramekins in the oven, and fill it with 1 inch of hot water.

Mix the yolks and eggs together until just blended. Stir in the sugar and salt and slowly add the hot milk, stirring constantly. Add the vanilla. Strain into the baking dish or ramekins and sprinkle with some nutmeg.

Put the dish or ramekins in the shallow pan and bake for about 45 minutes; the custard is set when a knife inserted in the center comes out clean. Be careful not to overbake; I remove custard from the oven when the very center still trembles a tiny bit.

Brown Sugar Custard

(six servings)

Brown Sugar Custard is rich and creamy. Serve it in small portions.

6 egg yolks   2 cups heavy cream
½ cup brown sugar

Preheat the oven to 350°F. Butter a 9-inch pie plate.

Put the egg yolks, brown sugar, and cream in a bowl and beat until smooth. Pour into the buttered pie plate and bake for 20 minutes, or until the center is set. Cool and serve portions in individual dessert dishes.

Apples in Custard

(four servings)

The amazing thing about this recipe is that the apples get perfectly baked in just the same length of time it takes for the custard to set.

4 medium cooking apples,   8 tablespoons sugar; plus 1 to
  cored and peeled (Rome Beauty   2 tablespoons for sprinkling
  apples are best)

Custard
½ cup sugar   Salt to taste
2 cups milk   Optional: cream and maple
3 eggs   syrup
2½ tablespoons flour

Preheat the oven to 350°F.

Place the peeled and cored apples in a square baking dish. Put 2 tablespoons of sugar in the center of each apple. Make the custard by mixing the $\frac{1}{2}$ cup sugar, the milk, eggs, flour, and salt together. Pour over the apples and bake for 45 minutes, or until the custard is set.

At the end of the baking time, sprinkle the 1 to 2 tablespoons of sugar over the apples and custard, place under the broiler, and broil until lightly brown. Serve in individual bowls. You may put a small amount of cream and maple syrup over the top for additional flavor.

Wine Jelly

(eight servings)

This fine, no-fat dessert deserves the popularity it had a hundred years ago. It seems to me you need a little something that is slightly sweet to put a period at the close of supper, and wine jelly can do it.

2 envelopes unflavored gelatin	3 to 4 tablespoons freshly squeezed lemon juice
$\frac{1}{2}$ cup cold water	1 cup good sherry or Madeira wine
$1\frac{2}{3}$ cups hot water	
1 cup sugar	

In a small bowl, sprinkle the gelatin over the $\frac{1}{2}$ cup cold water. Stir and let stand for 5 minutes.

Put the hot water and sugar in a saucepan and bring to a boil. Stir until the sugar dissolves. Remove from the heat and add the gelatin mixture; stir until it has dissolved. Add the lemon juice and wine, then taste, and add a little more lemon juice if it seems blah. Pour into individual dessert glasses or one pretty glass dish. Refrigerate until firm, about 2 hours.

Pralines

(thirty 2-inch round pralines)

Because candymaking at home has all but disappeared along with butter churning and preserving, no one thinks of making pralines anymore. These slightly grainy brown sugar pecan candies are so good, I wish I could get everyone to try these just once.

$2\frac{1}{3}$ cups *light* brown sugar
1 cup heavy cream
$\frac{1}{4}$ teaspoon salt

2 cups coarsely chopped
pecans or walnuts

Put the sugar, cream, and salt in a 3-quart or larger heavy-bottomed saucepan. Turn the heat to medium, stirring the syrup until the sugar has dissolved. It will now take 15 to 20 minutes to finish cooking. Let the syrup come to a boil, without stirring. The mixture will boil up, becoming foamy with large bubbles, but it will soon settle down and the bubbles will become smaller and the foam will subside. Cook until the mixture reaches 238°F on a candy thermometer, or until it reaches the soft-ball stage. Start testing after 10 to 12 minutes. I prefer the soft-ball test because it is easy and it doesn't require a thermometer This is how it works: have a small cup of cold water near the cooking syrup, spoon out about $\frac{1}{2}$ teaspoon of syrup, and drop it into the cold water. Gently roll the syrup between your fingers and if it holds together in a soft ball, it is ready to remove from the heat.

Have a long piece of waxed paper spread on the counter.

Remove the syrup from the heat and stir in the pecans; then stir briskly, for about 1 minute, but as soon as the syrup begins to look like it's getting firm, drop it onto the waxed paper. Drop the syrup by rounded tablespoonfuls onto the paper. Allow to cool completely, then remove from the paper and store in an airtight container between pieces of waxed paper. Or freeze.

Pineapple Blizzard

(four servings)

Abby Mandel, an exceptional cook and cookbook author, first made this dessert for me. I call it a "blizzard" because it is icy and it drifts up the sides of the food processor like wind-blown snow. It is creamy without cream and it keeps its soft frozen texture in the freezer.

4 cups fresh pineapple, cut into approximately 1-inch cubes
½ cup to ¾ cup sugar, depending on the sweetness of the pineapple

2 egg whites

Spread the pineapple cubes on a jelly-roll pan and put in the freezer for 8 hours. The cubes must be rock hard.

Put the cubes in the food processor and process until drifts of iced fruit are on the sides of the container (ignore the racket these little rocks make). This takes about 1 minute. Stop and scrape down the sides with a spatula, add some of the sugar, about ½ cup, and then add the egg whites. Process, stopping to scrape down the sides once or twice, until the mass begins to flow easily in the processor container. Process for 2 or 3 minutes, taste, and add more sugar if needed. Continue to process another 2 minutes, or as long as it takes for the mixture to become pale, light, and smooth. You will have the most creamy, fluffy pineapple dessert, and it will be difficult to believe that it only has sugar and egg white in it.

Cover well, and put into the freezer. This keeps for a week or two, but is at its best the first 3 or 4 days after making.

Grapefruit Ice

(four servings)

A glass of grapefruit juice is bracing at breakfast; turned into ice chips, it is my favorite fruit ice. With a few Plain Jane Sugar Cookies (see page 209) it makes a nice finish to almost any supper, but particularly one of Baltimore Crab Cakes (see page 389).

¾ to 1 cup sugar (depending on the tartness of the grapefruit juice)

½ cup water
3 cups grapefruit juice, freshly squeezed

Mix together the sugar and water in a saucepan and boil until the sugar is dissolved, about 1 minute. Cool, and stir in the grapefruit juice. Pour into ice cube trays (the smallest cubed trays are ideal because you can turn out a small dish of cubes for each serving). Or pour the juice mixture into a bowl. Cover and freeze. Remember to soften the ice a trifle so you can serve it easily if you are not freezing it in the tiny cubed ice trays. Serve in small glasses or bowls.

Chilled Marmalade Grapefruit

(four servings)

This is a short recipe that will win a long ovation. Icy cold, a little sour, and a little sweet, it goes with any plain cookie.

2 cups fresh grapefruit sec- ¾ cup orange marmalade
tions (see page 527)

Put the grapefruit in a bowl and stir in the marmalade. Chill until very cold.

Sautéed Pears

(four servings)

The interesting thing about pears is that they are never ever robust—not even when they are raw and crunchy. Sautéed, they are at their delicate best, and are a welcome dessert after a rich dish such as Beef Stroganoff (see page 420). Serve warm with a little cream poured on top. These are also good with a sprinkle of finely chopped crystallized ginger.

4 tablespoons (½ stick) butter ½ cup water
4 firm, ripe pears, peeled, 2 tablespoons dark brown
halved, and cored sugar

Melt the butter in a large skillet that has a lid, or in a sauté pan. Slice each pear half into quarters, add the slices to the pan, and slowly stir and turn for 1 minute. Add the water and stir in the brown sugar. Turn the heat to very low, cover, and let simmer for about 3 or 4 minutes. Check for doneness after 2 minutes, so the pears don't become too soft. They are done as soon as they are easily pierced with a fork. Remove from heat and serve warm.

Maple Persimmons

(one serving)

This Fuyu persimmon dessert is so good that you must try it once. Fuyu persimmons are the apple-shaped ones that can be eaten while still firm. (The acorn-shaped Hachiya persimmons must be very soft to be edible.) Maple syrup with cream and persimmons is a dessert to rave about.

1 Fuyu persimmon   2 tablespoons maple syrup
2 tablespoons heavy cream

Peel the persimmon and remove the core and seeds (sometimes only the seeds need to be removed). Cut into bite-size pieces and put in a dessert dish. Pour the heavy cream and maple syrup over the top. Serve chilled.

Grapes with Sour Cream and Brown Sugar

(four servings)

Brown sugar and sour cream melt together to make a light caramel sauce that turns an ordinary bunch of Thompson grapes into a fine dessert.

4 cups Thompson seedless grapes, stemmed and washed
½ cup sour cream

6 tablespoons light brown sugar

Chill the grapes thoroughly in the refrigerator. Divide them among 4 dessert bowls, spread 2 tablespoons sour cream over each serving, and chill again. Thirty minutes before serving, sprinkle 1½ tablespoons brown sugar over each bowl of grapes, then return to the refrigerator. Of course, this can all be done in one bowl to be passed around the table.

Berry Sandwiches

(four servings)

When summer berries are sold all over the place, one of the simplest ways to serve them is to make berry sandwiches. It is essential to have a good fresh loaf of white bread.

4 cups berries (strawberries, blackberries, raspberries, any combination; strawberries hulled and sliced, other berries cleaned)

Sugar to taste (about 1 cup)
8 thin slices fresh white bread, crusts removed
1 cup heavy cream, sweetened lightly, whipped

Just before serving, spread the berries over 4 slices of bread. Put the other 4 slices of bread over the berries, and neatly spread the top and sides of the sandwiches with whipped cream. Garnish tops with a little swirl of berry juice. Slice each sandwich diagonally and place two halves on each serving plate.

Peach on Sugared Toast

(six servings)

Are you wondering why this is even a recipe? Because you may never have thought of it, and because it is actually better than some desserts that take a lot of fuss.

6 slices dense white bread,
   crusts removed
½ cup butter (1 stick), cut
   into 6 equal pieces

6 tablespoons sugar
3 large ripe peaches, halved
   and pitted
¾ cup heavy cream

Preheat the oven to 350°F. Butter a 9 × 13-inch baking dish.

Place the slices of bread in the baking dish. Spread each slice with a piece of the butter. Sprinkle 2 teaspoons of sugar over each slice of bread. Place a peach half, cut side down, on each slice and sprinkle 1 teaspoon of sugar over each peach half. Put the peaches in the oven and bake for 15 minutes. Remove, spoon 2 tablespoons of cream over each peach, and serve warm.

Baked Plums and Apricots with Almonds

(six servings)

This French country dessert was served to me in Paris by Claudia Roden, the cosmopolitan food historian and cookbook author. Put it in the oven just before you sit down at the table, and it will come to the table bubbling hot for dessert. Serve with heavy cream or vanilla ice cream.

8 large apricots, halved and pitted (about 2 pounds)
6 large plums, halved and pitted (about 1 pound)
$2/3$ cup sugar plus 6 table-spoons

$2/3$ cup water
$1\frac{1}{4}$ cups whole unblanched almonds

Preheat the oven to 325°F.

Put the apricots and plums in a large sauté pan. Stir the $2/3$ cup sugar into the water, and pour into the pan. Cover and simmer over low heat for 5 to 7 minutes, or until the fruit is tender when pierced with a fork. Don't overcook. Set aside.

In a food processor, process the almonds and the remaining 6 tablespoons sugar until the mixture is very fine, but not a paste. Spread the mixture evenly in a 10-inch round baking dish. Arrange the fruit, cut side down, over the almond mixture. Pour $2/3$ cup of the fruit juices remaining in the sauté pan over the fruit and almonds, and bake for 1 hour.

After baking, you may want to taste the fruit for sweetness. If necessary, while the dessert is still hot, sprinkle more sugar on top. Serve warm.

Baked Bananas with Berries or Mango

(four servings)

There are people who have bunches of bananas in their kitchens and who think they don't have anything for dessert, but a few of those bananas plus a little coconut or some berries make a better dessert than you can imagine.

1 tablespoon butter
4 firm ripe bananas, peeled
2 tablespoons lemon juice
4 tablespoons sugar
½ cup grated sweetened
   coconut

2 cups stemmed blueberries
   or diced mango, sweetened
   to taste

Preheat the oven to 375°F. Butter a baking dish approximately 8 inches square.

Put the bananas in the baking dish and evenly drizzle the lemon juice over them. Sprinkle 1 tablespoon sugar over each banana, and then sprinkle 2 tablespoons coconut over each. Bake the bananas for 10 to 15 minutes, or until they are hot throughout. Remove from the oven and place on serving dishes, arranging ½ cup berries or diced mango over each serving. Serve while the bananas are hot.

Rhubarb and Kumquat Compote

(four servings)

This is unusual and wonderful—I found myself serving this repeat-edly and no one got tired of it. Serve it with Almond Diamonds (see page 540) for a light supper dessert.

2 cups rhubarb, cut into
½-inch pieces
1 cup thinly sliced, seeded
kumquats

¾ to 1 cup sugar
¼ cup water

Mix together the rhubarb, kumquats, ¾ cup sugar, and water in a saucepan. Cook over medium heat for about 5 minutes, or until the fruit is soft. Taste and add more sugar if necessary. Serve chilled, warm, or at room temperature.

Supper Readings

When my son and daughter were about ten and twelve, I decided it would be a good idea to have the whole family read aloud at the table after supper. Actually, I first tried to persuade the children that memorizing poetry could be fun. The Victorians taught their children to memorize sentimental verses and recite these "memory gems" on special occasions. This sounded like a good exercise for young minds, but the children didn't cooperate and we didn't end up with any gems here. Next I proposed spending fifteen to twenty minutes each evening reading aloud at the table. At first there was more grumbling than reading, but somehow we managed to stick to the regime and even came to look forward to it. We read some classics, such as works of Mark Twain; and we read humor and nonsense by James Thurber and Ogden Nash. We read everything from Dr. Schweitzer to Dr. Seuss. Supper readings didn't make the children more obedient, helpful, or cheerful, but I'm glad we did it. We stayed together a little longer at the supper table, and I remember those times with pleasure.

Seasonal Supper Menus

SPRING

Asparagus Salad

Deviled Eggs

Lil's Ice-Water Crackers

Rhubarb and Kumquat Compote

Sweet Walnuts and Prawns

Jasmine Rice

Pineapple Blizzards

Salmon with Cucumber and Caper Sauce

Orzo with Fresh Dill

Sharon's Orange Scone Berry Cakes

SUMMER

Theater Steak

Fire and Ice Relish

Spanish Cream

Buffalo Chicken Wing Salad

Joyce's Almond Cakes with Berries

Eggs, Tomatoes, and Potatoes with *Gremolata*

Garlic Rolls

Grapes with Sour Cream and Brown Sugar

FALL

Posole Salad Soup

Sharp Cheddar Biscuits

Baked Plums and Apricots with Almonds

Southern Green Beans

Crouton Salad

Maple Persimmons

Chinese Hot and Sour Soup

Lil's Ice-Water Crackers

Baked Bananas with Berries

WINTER

Winter Vegetable Cobbler

Warm Applesauce and Crisp Ginger Cookies

Mustard Green Soup

Buttermilk Cornbread

Wine Jelly

Papusas

L.A. Slaw

Chocolate Pudding

Index